Twentieth Century Design

Oxford History of Art

Jonathan M. Woodham has been involved with the development of design history as an area of academic study in Britain for many years. He is Professor in the History of Design at the University of Brighton, a leading centre for study and research in the field, where he is also Director of the Design History Research Centre. His publications include *Twentieth-Century Ornament: Decoration from 1900 to* *1990*, and he currently serves on the editorial boards of the *Journal of Design History* (OUP) and *Design Issues* (MIT). He is also chair of the Design History Society. He has been invited to contribute lectures and seminar presentations at home and abroad, including France, Italy, the United States, Russia, and Poland. He lives in Brighton with his wife and two sons.

Oxford History of Art

Twentieth Century Design

Jonathan M. Woodham

Oxford NewYork

OXFORD UNIVERSITY PRESS

1997

Oxford University Press, Great Clarendon Street, Oxford OX2 6DP

Oxford New York

Athens Auckland Bangkok Bogota Bombay
Buenos Aires Calcutta Cape Town Dar es Salaam
Delhi Florence Hong Kong Istanbul Karachi
Kuala Lumpur Madras Madrid Melbourne
Mexico City Nairobi Paris Singapore
Taipei Tokyo Toronto
and associated companies in Berlin Ibadan

Oxford is a trade mark of Oxford University Press

First published 1997 by Oxford University Press

British Library Cataloguing in Publication Data
Data available

Library of Congress Cataloging in Publication Data
Data available

0-19-284204-8 Pbk
0-19-284247-1 Hb

10 9 8 7 6 5 4 3 2 1

Picture Research by Elisabeth Agate
Designed by Esterson Lackersteen
Printed in Hong Kong
on acid-free paper by
C&C Offset Printing Co., Ltd.

Contents

	Introduction	7
Chapter 1	Towards the Twentieth Century	11
Chapter 2	Design and Modernism	29
Chapter 3	Commerce, Consumerism, and Design	65
Chapter 4	Design and National Identity	87
Chapter 5	The Second World War: Reconstruction and Affluence	111
Chapter 6	Multinational Corporations and Global Products	141
Chapter 7	Design Promotion, Profession, and Management	165
Chapter 8	Pop to Post-Modernism: Changing Values	183
Chapter 9	Nostalgia, Heritage, and Design	205
Chapter 10	Design and Social Responsibility	221
	Notes	240
	List of Illustrations	252
	Bibliographic Essay	258
	Timeline	274
	Index	282
	Oxford History of Art Series	288

Introduction

The writing of a comprehensive single volume on the history of twentieth-century design is a daunting prospect, not simply in terms of the
seemingly limitless range of products and associated meanings from
which such a text might be fashioned but also in terms of the considerable geographical scope which might be encompassed. Changing
centres of gravity of design activity, different and evolving national
perspectives, imperial trading mechanisms and their legacy, the
operation of multinational corporations and the creation of global
products all have a potential bearing on the ways in which design may
be historically evaluated. Furthermore, during its comparatively brief
life as an area of academic study, the history of design has regularly
provided a forum for vigorous debates about appropriate methods and
approaches.[1] Its focus has shifted quite dramatically from the cultural
high ground, where individual designers, style, and aesthetic significance were dominant considerations, onto the texture of everyday life
in which far greater emphasis is placed on the role and behaviour of the
consumer and user.

The values that were embraced by Nikolaus Pevsner's seminal text,
Pioneers of Modern Design: From William Morris to Walter Gropius, first
published in 1936,[2] now have a very dated feel, although it is a text
which has undergone a number of key revisions and many reprints. As
the publicity for the 1977 edition of the text proclaimed,

Sir Nikolaus Pevsner tells the exciting story of how the efforts of a relatively
small group of men lifted our visual concepts away from stale Victorian
Historicism and infused them once more with honesty, fitness of purpose and
contemporary expression. He shows how the foundation of the best that sur-
rounds us today was laid then by men who thought and taught as well as
designed.[3]

Since the first publication of *Pioneers* more than sixty years ago the
central focus of the history of design as a field of academic study has
moved away from such explicit emphasis on the artistic creativity of
celebrated individuals towards an evaluation of the wider social, economic, political, and technological climate in which design has been
made and used. Texts such as Siegfried Giedion's *Mechanisation Takes*

Detail of 81

Command: A Contribution to Anonymous History,[4] first published in 1948, and Herwin Schaefer's *The Roots of Modern Design: The Functional Tradition in the 19th Century*[5] of 1970, were among those which posited alternatives to the Pevsnerian canon in their exploration of the social and cultural impact of anonymous, vernacular design. In the 1980s Adrian Forty published *Objects of Desire: Design and Society 1750–1980*,[6] further undermining the traditional acceptance of the dominance of the designer in many design-historical studies. Published at a time when contemporary designers were widely celebrated in the media, his book was generally criticized in the design press since his underlying thesis was that a historical understanding of an object's significance and value resided in a wide range of influences and ideas, a complex social and cultural mix in which the designer was seen as a relatively minor consideration—if, indeed, he or she could be identified at all. The stress conventionally laid on celebrated individuals came under attack from anthropologists as well as design historians. Arguing that an understanding of design in industrialized society involved an analysis of modern consumption, the anthropologist Daniel Miller concurred with Forty's demythologizing of the 'designer as creator of mass culture' in his 1987 book *Material Culture and Mass Consumption*.[7]

As the Pevsnerian prioritization of concepts such as 'the best' gave way to the consideration of the realities of mass-consumption and the meaning of objects in everyday life, design history had also begun to reconsider the implications of gender in its construction. Just as feminist art historians such as Anthea Callen and Griselda Pollock had questioned the criteria implicit in art-historical practice in the late 1970s and 1980s,[8] so several writers concerned with the history of design have turned their attention to the typecasting of women as producers in particular fields of design such as the crafts or textiles.[9] The significance of the often complex relationship between women, design, and the history of design is one which now informs an increasing number of studies in the field[10] and provides the impetus for a reconsideration of many facets of design-historical interpretations in the twentieth century.

There are several barriers to overcoming the many inherent difficulties in arriving at an understanding of the wider issues affecting design and its consumption in daily life, past and present. Not the least of these, as many aspects of this publication indicate, is the question of the ways in which potential historical sources have survived, whether in the archival repositories of individual designers and leading companies, the self-published and inevitably partial accounts of organizations, institutions, and related personnel, or, indeed, artifacts which have been selected for display in a museum or exhibition context. Such evidence, as will be suggested in instances such as the Bauhaus in

Germany, the Council of Industrial Design in Britain, and the construction of corporate identity in the 1950s, has tended to dominate historical perceptions, taking little account of the broader patterns of consumption, taste, and socio-cultural significance. Whilst a single volume dealing with major issues of twentieth-century design, its significance and study, cannot present a fully articulated interpretation of design in everyday life, it is hoped that a number of the inherent complexities will have been signalled; also that the text will serve both to inform the reader about major considerations and to set a possible agenda for future investigations.

By addressing a range of themes such as 'national identity', 'heritage and nostalgia', and 'Postmodernism' I seek to reveal the limitations of studying design in overly neat decades or movements. Particular objects or designs change their meanings when used or viewed in different periods and places: William Morris textiles and wallpapers in the late nineteenth-century upper-middle-class English home or their Arthur Sanderson's reprinted counterparts in 1980s Manhattan apartments in the United States; the baseball cap as worn by American sporting heroes in the 1920s or by Eastern European teenagers in the 1990s; porcelain tableware for the Imperial Hotel, Tokyo, designed by Frank Lloyd Wright in the early 1920s or its Tiffany & Co, New York, reissue of 1980. Contrastingly, there are many other designs which have been in production throughout the period and continue to sell steadily, free from the vagaries of style and fashion that have outwardly characterized the periods in which they have been purchased.

This volume is centred on the Western industrialized world, with an emphasis on the more affluent nations of Europe, the United States, Scandinavia, and the Far East. Its prime focus relates to design and industrialized culture within that world, although a number of complex issues have had to be omitted for reasons of space, as well as a lack of developed and published research in the field. These include the ways in which design may be seen to have been mediated by notions of multiculturalism and regionalism within nation states, the implications of peristroika and the demolition of the Berlin Wall for design and patterns of consumption in Eastern Europe, or even the cultural impact of the package holiday and global travel for the everyday consumer. It is to be hoped that the absence of these and similar considerations will stimulate further publications that will complement and critically enhance this investigative foray into the broader picture of twentieth-century design.

Towards the Twentieth Century

During the nineteenth century manufacturers' relentless exploitation of new techniques and materials increasingly made accessible to middle-class consumers a wide range of objects with rich and elaborate decorative detailing in an encyclopaedic variety of historicizing styles. Superficially exuding a resonance of education and taste, such products had previously been the preserve of a cultural élite who often purchased furniture, furnishings, and domestic equipment which embodied the skills and virtuosity of individual craftsmen. This new class of widely available mass-produced goods was made possible through such processes as electroplating, stamping and moulding, and the exploration of materials such as gutta-percha, papier-mâché, or cast-iron which possessed rich possibilities for the imitation of more expensive and individually-produced artefacts and the lavish fabrication of decorative detailing.

Such designs were heavily criticized by many nineteenth-century critics, particularly in Britain by John Ruskin, William Morris, and Arts and Crafts followers, who not only viewed them as 'dishonest' through their 'inappropriate' use of materials and modes of construction, but also deplored what they felt were the dehumanizing consequences of industrialization for those involved in their manufacture. However, although such opinions, writings, and design practice aroused considerable interest amongst progressive designers and critics of the industrialization process in Europe and the United States in the later nineteenth century, their actual impact upon the majority of manufacturers involved in the mass-production of consumer goods was extremely limited.

By the closing years of the nineteenth century the significance of the various shifts in industrial power that had been taking place in Europe and North America for some time became increasingly apparent. Britain, once characterized as 'the workshop of the world', found her capacity for industrial innovation challenged not only by the United States, but also by a number of other countries including Germany. The latter, following her unification in 1871, had developed new steel, chemical, and electrical industries alongside the establishment of technical high schools which offered a positive educational programme for engineers, manufacturers, and industrial managers. British concern about her own comparative trading position had been acknowledged in governmental circles since the early 1830s when Sir Robert Peel had attributed the decline in her exports to poor standards of design in British manufacture, a *cri de cœur* which has been voiced at times of significant economic crisis over the succeeding 160 years.[1] The superior industrial strategy of Germany and the United States was clearly identified in a Royal Commission of 1886, and by the turn of the century economic and industrial comparisons with these two countries were being made frequently in British journals and other publications. Furthermore, the twin concepts of Taylorism and Fordism developed in the United States in the early years of the twentieth century became highly influential throughout the industrialized world, and were important facets of her dominance in economic mass-production in the interwar years. Taylorism was a system which sought to achieve industrial efficiency on the factory floor. Devised by Frederick Winslow Taylor in the late nineteenth century through a series of 'time and motion' studies which broke down workplace activities into their most efficient constituent parts, it was documented in his *Principles of Scientific Management* of 1911. It was applied subsequently to several areas of human activity with consequent implications for design, such as in the planning of efficient, labour-saving kitchens and domestic equipment. Fordism related to Henry Ford's introduction of the moving assembly line for the Model T Ford automobile in 1913. Dramatically cutting down the time for car chassis production, it had obvious wider economic implications for standardized mass-production (and thus patterns of consumption) throughout the industrialized world.

By the early 1900s many of the key inventions which were to become fundamental to life in the new century were becoming increasingly available to the everyday consumer: electric lighting and domestic appliances; homogenizing communications media such as the telephone, the gramophone, and the cinema; and the automobile which also played a key role in bringing together rural and urban communities. Before long the radio and the aeroplane further transformed people's lives in terms of dissolving national and regional barriers.

Few progressive design theorists and practitioners managed to exert a significant impact in such areas prior to the First World War. However, there was a growing recognition of the importance of reconciling design thinking with the realities of mass-production technology if such an outlook was to have a significant bearing on everyday life. Amongst avant-garde design groups of the early twentieth century the Italian Futurists, founded by Filippo Tommaso Marinetti in 1909, were perhaps the most unequivocal in their embrace of the possibilities afforded by technological innovation and perceptions of the dynamism

1 Giacomo Balla

Futurist clothing from the *Manifesto Futurista*, 1914

The dynamic spirit of Italian Futurism embraced many spheres of design activity including furniture, interior design, and clothing, all of which Balla explored extensively. In his 1914 *Manifesto on Menswear* (later retitled *Antineutral Clothing*) he argued for Futurist clothing which could be dynamic, aggressive, amazing, violent, phosphorescent, and decorated with electric light bulbs; also for designs with adaptors, 'having pneumatic devices that can be used on the spur of the moment; thus everyone can alter his dress according to the needs of his spirit'.

IL VESTITO ANTINEUTRALE

Manifesto futurista

Glorifichiamo la guerra,
sola igiene del mondo.
MARINETTI.
(1° *Manifesto del Futurismo* - 20 *Febbraio 1909*)

Viva Asinari di Bernezzo!
MARINETTI.
(1° *Serata futurista* - *Teatro Lirico, Milano, Febbraio 1910*)

L'umanità si vestì sempre di **quiete**, di **paura**, di **cautela** o d'**indecisione**, portò sempre il lutto, o il piviale, o il mantello. Il corpo dell'uomo fu sempre diminuito da sfumature e da tinte **neutre**, avvilito dal nero, soffocato da cinture, imprigionato da panneggiamenti.

Fino ad oggi gli uomini usarono abiti di colori e forme statiche, cioè drappeggiati, solenni, gravi, incomodi e sacerdotali. Erano espressioni di timidezza, di malinconia e di **schiavitù**, negazione della vita muscolare, che soffocava in un passatismo anti-igienico di stoffe troppo pesanti e di mezze tinte tediose, effeminate o decadenti. Tonalità e ritmi di **pace desolante**, funeraria e deprimente.

OGGI vogliamo abolire:

1. — Tutte le tinte **neutre**, « carine », sbiadite, *fantasia*, semioscure & umilianti.
2. — Tutte le tinte e le foggie pedanti, professorali e teutoniche. I disegni a righe, a quadretti, a **puntini diplomatici.**
3. — I vestiti da lutto, nemmeno adatti per i becchini. Le morti eroiche non devono essere compiante, ma ricordate con vestiti rossi.
4. — L'equilibrio **mediocrista**, il cosidetto buon gusto e la cosidetta armonia di tinte e di forme, che frenano gli entusiasmi e rallentano il passo.
5. — La simmetria nel taglio, le linee **statiche,** che stancano, deprimono, contristano, legano i muscoli; l'uniformità di goffi risvolti e tutte le cincischiature. I bottoni inutili. I colletti e i polsini inamidati.

Noi futuristi vogliamo liberare la nostra razza da ogni **neutralità**, dall'indecisione paurosa e quietista, dal pessimismo negatore e dall'inerzia

Vestito bianco - rosso - verde
portato dal parolibero futurista Cangiullo, nelle dimostrazioni dei Futuristi contro i professori tedescofili e neutralisti dell'Università di Roma (11-12 Dicembre 1914).

of modern city life. Although highly nationalistic, the Futurists firmly rejected the splendours of Italy's cultural past in favour of new advances in science and technology, embracing wholeheartedly the concept of change as an intrinsic aspect of their activities and ideology. Industrialization had made itself felt in Italy much later and more dramatically than in other European countries such as Germany, France, or Britain, where it had been evolving over a far longer period and it was not until after Italy's unification in 1861, when Rome became her capital a decade later, that the life and environment of the Italian city was radically altered. The most dramatic changes took place in the industrial north, which was the birthplace not only of Futurism but of many other avant-garde groupings far later in the century, of which the best known were perhaps Studio Alchymia and Memphis: the first power station was constructed in Milan in 1883, and the first automobile factory opened in Turin in 1895. The racing car in particular was an important symbol of modernity for the Futurists, symbolizing speed and danger on the one hand, and, given the emergence of automobile racing at the turn of the century, a symbol of national pride and international competitiveness on the other. Although originally focused on literature and the fine arts, Futurist activity centred upon many other facets of contemporary life, including fashion [1], furniture, typography, interior design, architecture, cinema, photography, music, and the theatre. None the less, despite the apparent centrality of Futurism to twentieth-century life and undoubted influence on other avant-garde developments elsewhere in Europe prior to 1914, its significance for design was ultimately more symbolic than material.

The problematic legacy of the Arts and Crafts Movement

A number of design histories have laid particular emphasis on the impact of the Arts and Crafts Movement on progressive design thinking in the early years of the twentieth century.[2] In the years before the First World War the concerns of many of these theorists and practitioners were centred on a desire to bring about higher standards of design and aesthetic awareness, firmly allied to the economics of mass-production. However, their nineteenth-century predecessors, such as William Morris, had generally identified the mass-production process itself with the dehumanized working conditions prevalent in the majority of manufacturing industries. Their problem was how to marry, on a scale sufficient to provide affordable well-designed goods for the majority, the economics of mass-production to their requisite sense of the importance of job satisfaction and the 'joy of making' for the factory worker. They also relied upon the assumption that mass-consumers actually wanted to surround themselves with products which respected concepts such as 'truth to materials' and 'honesty of construction' and rejected the stylistic encyclopaedism which was the hallmark of most contemporary mass-produced goods. The realization that the overwhelming majority did not led design reformers and organizations throughout most of the twentieth century to lay the blame variously at the door of manufacturers, retailers, buyers, or the general public and, as corrective measures, to promote educational reforms in the visual arts, to mount didactic design exhibitions, to commission reports, to publish dedicated periodicals, and to utilize radio and television as media for 'elevating' public taste. Despite concerted moves in a number of countries, particularly Germany, to instil a greater awareness of the economic potential of design in the national and international marketplace, the resultant visible impact was largely restricted to the output of specific design workshops, particular displays at national and international exhibitions, and the more abstract realms of ideological debate rather than in the output of the vast majority of factories producing consumer goods.

Retailing before 1914

By 1900 advertising agencies in the United States such as J. Walter Thompson, founded in New York in 1864, and N. W. Ayer & Son, founded in Philadelphia in 1869, had done much to help stimulate consumer demand and create desires, and their influence was reflected in the increasing sophistication of marketing techniques in Europe. Changes in retailing practice effected similar changes through the growth of department stores in the second half of the nineteenth century: the Magasin au Bon Marché and Le Printemps in Paris, R. H. Macy in New York, and Marshall Field in Chicago, were early leaders in the field.[3] Such stores brought together under one roof the whole gamut of industrially produced goods and soon became socially acceptable venues for unaccompanied women to meet as well as shop without damaging their reputations. By the early years of the twentieth century department stores, centrally-heated and electrically-lit, were a feature of cities across the industrialized world: the new buildings for the Tietz department store (1898) in Berlin, À l'Innovation (1901) in Brussels, the Magazzino Contratti (1903) in Milan, La Samaritaine (1905) in Paris, and Harrods (1901/5) and Selfridges (1908) in London all typified this new breed. The department store shopper was generally offered a wide range of products which, although also subject to the particular nuances of contemporary ephemeral styling, embraced a considerable range and diversity of historic styles in their decoration. Such stores were generally the province of the more well-to-do sectors of society, and their history has been more fully addressed than that of retailing establishments geared to the needs of working people, partly on account of the fact that their buildings and interiors were often commissioned from well-known architects and designers and that their wares have often been considered subsequently by design historians, collectors, and museums as aesthetically more significant and thus more worthy of research and preservation.[4] However, more recently there has been a far greater interest in the wider historical significance of shopping, both in behavioural terms and its importance and meaning across a wider social spectrum.[5]

An important insight into patterns of taste in late nineteenth- and early twentieth-century everyday life is revealed in mail-order shopping catalogues, an innovation which commenced in the United States with Montgomery Ward Mail Order in 1872. The mail-order catalogue soon grew from its origins as a single sheet to a comprehensive illustrated book which provided the full range of domestic goods, furniture and furnishings, clothing, and equipment, giving rural com-

Cover of Sears Roebuck
Catalogue, *Consumers Guide*,
no. 108, 1899

This richly illustrated cover
demonstrates the workings of
this major mail order company.
Behind the upwardly stretched
arm of the female figure of
Abundance, holding an order
addressed to Sears Roebuck,
is the city of Chicago, seen with
smoking factory chimneys and
railway lines running from it for
transporting the finished
goods. Abundance, the
symbolic persona of Sears
Roebuck, is holding a
cornucopia from which a rich
variety of products—including
clothing, a piano and tools—
pour forth to serve the needs
of small agricultural
communities such as that
depicted in the bottom right.

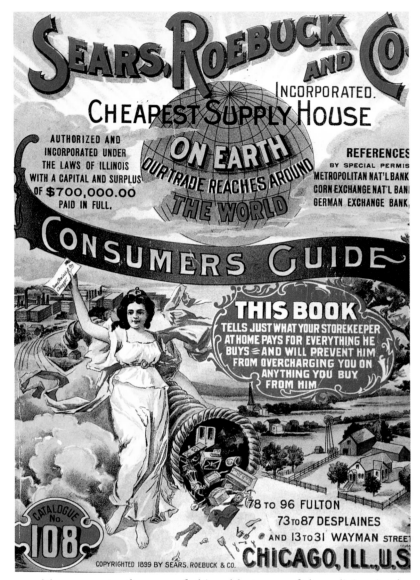

munities access to the more fashionable tastes of those living in the
major American cities. R. W. Sears produced his first mail-order catalogue in 1891, soon joining with Roebuck to form Sears Roebuck [2]. In
catering for the everyday needs of rural communities Sears Roebuck
and Montgomery Ward provided a potent challenge to the often
expensive general stores which were at the centre of such communities.
Often the largest book in the house other than the Bible, the mail-
order catalogue, or 'wish book' as it was often known, has been seen as
a guidebook to American living, one which also had a particular value
to immigrants as a means of achieving social conformity. Significantly,
both Montgomery Ward and Sears Roebuck were based in Chicago,

the centre of the American railway network. The tremendous growth of the railways, together with the modernization of the American postal system, ensured the overwhelming success of mail order and, by the outbreak of the First World War, consumers could purchase from catalogues almost anything from a complete house to a knife and fork, from a barn to the smallest item of agricultural equipment [3].

Mail order also developed on the other side of the Atlantic, thus providing the design historian with insights into wider patterns of consumption in Europe. In Germany, for example, the mail-order company of August Stukenbrok grew from its origins as a bicycle manufactury in 1890 to a powerful mail-order company which by 1914 was issuing more than a million catalogues per year.[6] Such catalogues, whether American or European, revealed a considerable predilection

3

Parlour Suites from the Sears Roebuck Catalogue, 1897

This page shows the rich variety of historicizing styles that purchasers across the United States were able to order for home delivery. The upholstering of the Turkish Parlor Suite (above) is 'in the latest design and patterns of imported goods' whilst the wooden-framed suite (centre), 'finished in imitation mahogany, a most desirable and attractive finish', has 'decorations in the way of hand carving [that] are decidedly unique and attractive'. The sheer range of styles and convenience of mail order purchase was very attractive to many consumers outside the larger cities.

for highly decorated products, particularly in the sphere of domestic furniture and furnishings. Cups and saucers, cutlery, glassware, door furniture, sewing machines, and countless other accoutrements of everyday living could be purchased in a plethora of styles drawn from a wide range of historic, cultural, and geographic roots. It was this widespread desire on the part of consumers for ephemeral styling or historicizing ornamentation and surface decoration that attracted the scorn of the design reformers of the early twentieth century. The latter sought increasingly to establish a design vocabulary and syntax which was compatible with the realities of modern mass-production technology, exploring the possibilities of new materials and forms which were infused with what they saw as the 'true spirit' of the twentieth century. However, such a radical shift away from the prevalent climate of historicism and the ephemerality of fashionable styling towards a set of attitudes which were receptive towards ideas about standardization and the establishment of product types was not without its own ideological problems even within more progressive circles, as will be discussed below.

The arts and crafts, design and industry: debates in Germany before 1914

Hermann Muthesius was one of the most important figures in design debates in Germany before 1914, providing a link between the Arts and Crafts Movement in Britain and the quest for a modern industrial design culture in Germany. Having been appointed as architectural attaché to the German Embassy in London in 1896, he came into contact with a number of leading British designers such as Charles Rennie Mackintosh and Walter Crane and wrote frequently about British architectural and design practice in reports, periodicals, and books, the best-known of which was the three-volume *Das Englische Haus* (*The English House*) of 1904/5. After returning to Germany in 1903 he was appointed to the Prussian Ministry of Trade and Commerce, and was charged with particular responsibility for art and design education. To forge stronger links between art and industry, he sought to reform education in the applied arts by placing a greater emphasis on workshop training. In order to facilitate such changes he influenced a number of key appointments: in 1903 Peter Behrens was made Director of the Düsseldorf School of Applied Arts, and Hans Poelzig Director of the Royal School of Arts and Crafts at Breslau; and in 1907 Bruno Paul was appointed to the Berlin School of Applied Arts. Muthesius' own appointment to the first Chair of the Applied Arts at Berlin Commercial University in 1907 caused a considerable furore. In his inaugural lecture entitled 'Die Bedeutung des Kunstgewerbes' ('The Significance of Applied Arts') he attacked German manufacturers for producing cheap and shoddy imitations of luxury goods, products which he felt were exploiting the public's appetite for conspicuous consumption and stylistic fads rather than developing a set of values which respected materials and stood for quality. Muthesius sought to set a fresh agenda for modern design in German industry, which he saw as essential for economic success in the international marketplace. He argued that German goods ought to be recognized for their own positive characteristics of modernity, quality, and aesthetic excellence rather than as the poor, showy imitations of foreign goods which generally predominated. As a result Muthesius came under vociferous attack from many quarters, perhaps the most strident opposition coming from the Fachverband für die Wirtschaftlichen Interesse Kunstgewerbes (Trade Association for the Economic Interests of the Applied Arts), which had been founded in 1892 to promote the commercial interests of manufacturers in the applied arts. By 1907 the Fachverband, despite the comparatively recent date of its establishment, had become closely identified with traditional, conservative values in the applied arts and found its influence increasingly undermined by progressive thinking in the Werkstätten (Workshop) movement. The latter, through the bringing together of craft skills and artistic creativity in design production, sought to offer a fresh, well-designed alternative to the general mundaneity of everyday products. In fact a number of these workshops began to operate on a significant commercial scale, the most notable early examples being the Dresdener Werkstätten für Handwerkskunst (the Dresden Workshop for the Arts and Crafts) and the Munich-based Vereinigte Werkstätten für Kunst im Handwerk (the United Workshops for Art in Crafts), both of which were founded in 1898. By the early years of the new century the scope of their activity, which included ceramics, furniture, fitments, textiles, and other fields of design, embraced simple forms, a sense of practicality, and an appropriate use of materials closely allied to an understanding of the realities of production processes. By about 1902 Jugendstil (the German variant of Art Nouveau), which in the closing years of the nineteenth century had seemed to offer avant-garde artists and designers a vibrant alternative to the historicism of the artistic establishment, was superseded by a desire to explore an aesthetic which, through its appropriateness for machine production, could provide quality goods at a competitive price—at least for an educated middle-class clientele.

The Third German Applied Arts Exhibition, which was mounted in Dresden in 1906, marked a significant change in German design reform. In contrast with the two previous exhibitions, where manufacturers and organizations had been able to buy space and thus retain control over what was displayed, a selection committee was established in order to ensure that only artists and designers with modernizing tendencies were shown. In seeking to demonstrate that high standards

4 Hermann Haas

Stoneware tableware, tea and coffee service and children's playset for Villeroy & Boch, shown at the Deutscher Werkbund Exhibition at Cologne, 1914

The Villeroy & Boch company was closely associated with progressive tendencies in early twentieth-century applied arts in Germany, showing at major exhibitions at home and abroad. The form and decoration of these pieces, though simple and unpretentious, reveal that there was in fact a considerable plurality of styles shown at the 1914 exhibition which has often been simplistically represented as an important landmark in the development of a twentieth-century functional aesthetic.

in design were potentially important dimensions of German social, cultural, and economic reform, the 1906 exhibition provided the impetus for the foundation of the Deutscher Werkbund (DWB) in Munich in October 1907.

Championed by the liberal-democratic politician Friedrich Naumann and Karl Schmidt, founder of the Dresdener Werkstätten für Handwerkskunst, the DWB sought to bring together artists and industrialists to improve the quality and design of German consumer products as part of the wider impetus to social, cultural, and economic reform. There were already in existence a number of organizations which also sought to bring about such reforms in Germany but the DWB had a more sharply defined membership, one which was restricted to those directly involved with furthering its aims.[7] Boasting 45 branches of local Werkbund groups, by 1914 its membership stood at 1,870, which ensured its significance and influence as a campaigning organization. As well as organizing symposia and mounting exhibitions, the DWB produced a wide range of propagandist pamphlets and other publications. The most significant of these were its Yearbooks which commenced publication in 1912, achieving sales of 20,000 by 1914.

Despite its prominence in accounts of German design of before the

First World War, the DWB was not an unqualified success: its impact upon the German consumer goods industry was limited, except in fields such as electrical appliances where the range of precedents was restricted. There was also considerable internal debate about the relative importance of standardization for modern German design, which came to a head in 1914 when two of the DWB's leading figures, Henry Van de Velde and Hermann Muthesius, clashed on ideological grounds. These had been simmering below the surface almost since the organization's founding in 1907. Muthesius, who even at the time of the 1906 Dresden Exhibition had been wary of the restrictions which a commitment to artistic individuality would impose upon German industry, argued that significant economic success linked to quality in manufacture could only be achieved through the adoption of forms which were compatible with mass-production. Van de Velde, on the other hand, felt that artistic creativity and freedom of expression was being strait-jacketed by economic, industrial, and political interests and that aesthetic quality in manufacture could only be brought about through artistic patronage. Such radically differing viewpoints were not new in DWB circles and had much to do with attempts by Van de Velde and his sympathizers to reassert the importance of the artist at the core of Werkbund policy. They sought to engineer a change in

5 Fritz Hellmut Ehmcke

Deutscher Werkbund cigar box, 1914

The striking clarity of this packaging and typographic design reflects the more progressive strand of the Werkbund outlook just before the First World War. It may be seen as a two-dimensional counterpart to Walter Gropius's Model Factory and Administration Buildings at the 1914 Cologne Exhibition which have tended to dominate accounts of early modernism in twentieth-century design. Ehmcke also designed a number of publications and posters for the Werkbund at this time and, in 1918, the organization also published his *Amtliche Graphik*, a strong critique of graphic design commissioned by the State.

As seen in the stoneware in
4, this room setting of goods
produced by leading Hamburg
manufacturers reveals the
considerable stylistic diversity
at the 1914 exhibition even in
progressive circles, including
furniture by J. D. Heyman,
decorative glass for a staircase
at the Hamburg School of Art
& Design, and hand-printed
wallpaper designed by C. O.
Czeschka, and the *Anchor*
pattern linoleum designed by
Bruno Paul.

leadership, although ultimately the membership as a whole preferred to ensure that the wider goals of the Werkbund would not be jeopardized by a fundamental rift in ideology at this stage of the organization's evolution.

A key event in the history of the DWB prior to the First World War was the mounting of a major exhibition in Cologne in 1914 which sought to put forward in material form the organization's achievements and outlook. In almost a hundred buildings, there was on show a tremendous range of both crafts-based and industrially produced design [**4**, **5**]. Although the appearance of many of the products and buildings endorsed a predominantly functional aesthetic [**6**], there was none the less quite a profusion of styles and approaches on show: something of the neo-Baroque was evident in Paul Ludwig Troost's dining-room in the Bremen-Oldenburg House, reminiscences of Jugendstil in Van de Velde's Theatre and furniture, Neoclassicism in Behrens's furniture for the German Embassy in Leningrad, and Expressionism in Bruno Taut's Glass Pavilion, all of which contrasted strongly with the clean, functional, modern lines of Walter Gropius's Administration Building and Model Factory. None the less, it is the latter that have often been heavily emphasized by design historians in order to illustrate the positive achievements of the Cologne Exhibition and its significance in the genesis of modernism.

Peter Behrens and the Allgemeine Elektrizitäts Gesellschaft (AEG)

There were some notable instances where a progressive design outlook was adopted in German industry, most significantly in relation to the newly established electricity industry for which consumer products were not unduly tied to traditional formats. Manufacturers Siemens and AEG were the leaders in the field, being involved in all aspects of electricity from the construction of power stations to the manufacture of lightbulbs. Continuing in the company's enlightened policy in the employment of a number of leading architects and designers, Peter Behrens was appointed as design adviser to the AEG company in June 1907 and soon imposed a strong visual coherence for the company. This commenced with graphics, but further evolved through AEG buildings, appliances, shops, workers' housing, and other elements, which resulted in a strikingly modern corporate identity. This emphasis on a coherent aesthetic which was manifest in all aspects of the company's work was an important ingredient in market penetration at home and abroad [**7**]. Behrens's earliest product design work for the company was centred on the design of arc lamps, which were given clean efficient lines, an approach which he carried through into other product ranges such as electric kettles [**8**], fans, clocks, and domestic heaters. Because of the scale of its manufacturing base and the fact that the majority of the AEG's products were being developed for new markets which were not dominated by design precedents, the company was able to impose its aesthetic outlook upon consumers in ways that older craft-based industries were unable: their products had strong roots in traditional forms and decoration, being largely responsive to consumers' anticipated expectations and aspirations.

Progressive design tendencies elsewhere in Europe

The German avant-garde was not alone in being influenced by the ideals of British Arts and Crafts writers and practitioners, many of whose work and beliefs were transmitted by the periodical *The Studio*, which was founded in 1893 and soon enjoyed an international readership. In Austria, for example, the Wiener Werkstätte (Vienna Workshops) was founded in 1903 by Josef Hofmann and Koloman Moser who much admired the simplicity of form inherent in the work of the British designers C. R. Ashbee (and his Guild of Handicraft) and Charles Rennie Mackintosh. The roots of the Wiener Werkstätte lay also in the late nineteenth-century Secessionist movement which was formed in opposition to the conservative values of the art establishment and which also extended its interests to the applied arts. Through participation in exhibitions and articles in periodicals featuring the applied arts the Werkstätte soon attracted international attention in progressive design circles, establishing a reputation for work in the textile, wallpaper, ceramic, jewellery, and furniture fields.

7 Peter Behrens
AEG Showroom, Berlin, *c.*1912
Behrens's appointment as artistic adviser to the AEG company in June 1907 marked a new direction in corporate policy, reflecting the company's desire to bring together art and industry in a modern industrial context. Much in line with the ideals of the Deutscher Werkbund, founded four months later, the adopted aesthetic embraced qualities which were attuned to progressive design thinking of the time: simplicity, efficiency, modernity, and advances in contemporary technology.

ELEKTRISCHE TEE- UND WASSERKESSEL
NACH ENTWÜRFEN VON PROF. PETER BEHRENS

Messing glatt, matt achteckige Form				Kupfer flockig gehämmert achteckige Form				Messing vernickelt, glatt achteckige Form			
Pl. Nr	Inhalt ca. l	Gewicht ca. kg	Preis Mk.	Pl. Nr	Inhalt ca. l	Gewicht ca. kg	Preis Mk.	Pl. Nr	Inhalt ca. l	Gewicht ca. kg	Preis Mk.
3588	0,75	1,75	20,—	3589	0,75	0,75	22,—	3587	0,75	0,75	19,—
3598	1,25	1,0	22,—	3599	1,25	1,0	24,—	3597	1,25	1,0	22,—
3608	1,75	1,1	24,—	3690	1,75	1,1	26,—	3607	1,75	1,1	23,—

ALLGEMEINE ELEKTRICITÄTS-GESELLSCHAFT
ABT. HEIZAPPARATE

However, although over 100 craftsmen were employed within two years of its founding alongside an increasing emphasis on retailing outlets, its impact in terms of volume production and consumption by other than the wealthier sectors of society remained insignificant: industrialization in Austria was less developed than in Germany, France, and Britain, and the Werkstätte remained largely committed to the ethos of the artist-craftsman. The rectilinearity and simplicity of many of the designs in the earliest phase of the Wiener Werkstätte (which superficially appear to echo early twentieth-century German concerns for standardized forms and product types) were more significant for a symbolic, rather than actual, compatibility with the economic possibilities of modern industrial production.

In Britain the legacy of the Arts and Crafts endured for many years. Indeed, a respect for materials, concern for appropriate modes of construction, and a high premium on craftsmanship, can be discerned in much British design over the next half century or more, as in the furniture designs of Gordon Russell Ltd. in the 1930s or clothing, textile, and furniture designs produced under the Utility Scheme in the 1940s. However, in the early 1900s the difficulties of reconciling the ideals of producing well-designed goods at an affordable price with the economic realities of mass-production set the agenda for many years.

By the time of the Deutscher Werkbund's Cologne Exhibition of 1914 a number of British designers had begun to take note of the concerted attempts of Muthesius and others to bring about a closer relationship between design and industry. Harry Peach of the Dryad furniture company, the silversmith Harold Stabler, and the furniture designer and retailer Ambrose Heal were among those who visited the Cologne Exhibition, forming positive opinions about what had been achieved in Germany. Following the outbreak of war and the cessation

9 Edward Johnston

Signage for London Underground Electric Railways, post 1916

Johnston's *Railway* typography, commissioned by the highly influential design manager Frank Pick, marked a clear commitment to clean, easily read, and modern letterforms. After 1918 Johnston also redesigned the bar-and-circle motif which is now widely recognized as a key element in London Underground's corporate identity. Johnston worked for the company until 1933, the year in which Henry C. Beck's now classic underground map (a version of which is seen on the right of the illustration) was first printed.

of German imports into Britain the Board of Trade organized a series of exhibitions of previously imported cheap German goods as potential exemplars for British industry to adopt. However, Peach, Heal, and others felt strongly that such exhibitions gave a false idea of the significant achievements made by certain sectors of German industry and sent a memorandum to that effect to the Permanent Secretary of the Board of Trade, Sir Hubert Llewellyn Smith, in January 1915. Their concerns resulted in the formation of the Design and Industries Association (DIA) in May of that year, a campaigning body of manufacturers, distributors, and designers which sought to instil in the general public 'a more intelligent demand . . . for what is best and soundest in design'[8] and to echo their belief that the 'machine enters to a greater or lesser extent into the making of all our products to-day'.[9] Despite such well-intentioned words, and the commitment of a small number of sympathetic educationalists, manufacturers, retailers, businessmen, and designers [**9**], the DIA's discernible impact upon the core of British manufacturing industry remained slight, a phenomenon which was also to be shared with post-First World War state-funded bodies such as the British Institute of Industrial Art, established in 1920,[10] and the Council for Art and Industry, set up in 1933.

Despite a number of initiatives such as the foundation of the Société de l'Art pour Tous in the early twentieth century there were no equivalents in France before the First World War to the Deutscher Werkbund in Germany or the DIA in Britain. However, the Société sought to promote a design aesthetic of simplicity, practicality, and everyday relevance, inspired by the outlook of British Arts and Crafts designers and theorists, publishing its own magazine. Despite a thriving membership of over 2,000 in the early 1900s, its impact as an effective campaigning body was slight. Ultimately little more successful was the Union Centrale des Arts Décoratifs which had been founded in the middle of the nineteenth century[11], seeking to forge links between industry and the arts under the slogan 'Beauty in Utility'. The Union was concerned to stimulate the production of better designed, high quality, affordable everyday products but, by the early 1900s, came under attack for its lack of commercial realism in the face of public taste, patterns of retailing, and the economics of mass-production. However, as in Britain, following the Deutscher Werkbund Cologne Exhibition of 1914 and the outbreak of the First World War, there were concerted attempts to reorganize French industry in order to compete more effectively with German industry after the war. In the years immediately preceding the war German imports had increasingly pervaded many aspects of daily life in France, and so in 1916 the state established the Comité Central Consultatif Technique des Arts Appliqués which looked to the Werkbund as a model for bringing about better standards of design in manufacturing industry. However, its founding remained more significant as a symbolic act of intent rather than the implementation of an effective programme of reform.

The more progressive tendencies in French design of this period were generally the province of the wealthier sectors of society, inclining towards the fine arts and high fashion where individual artistic expression flourished. Typifying such an outlook was the Société des Artistes Decorateurs, which was founded in 1901 to promote the decorative, industrial, and applied arts in France through the organization of exhibitions at home and abroad, together with the development of French design education. From 1907 the Société mounted annual exhibitions as a means of bringing new design ideas to the attention of the public, echoing the opportunities afforded by the annual shows of the Salon d'Automne (founded in 1903), which from 1906 had included a section devoted to the decorative arts. None the less, the inclinations of such groups leant towards the tastes of the more affluent sectors of the market where there was a strong emphasis on craftsmanship and quality, blended with a strong awareness of the heritage of the past. It was partly for this reason that a chill wind blew through the ranks of French designers in response to an exhibition of progressive German design by the Munich-based Vereinigte Werkstätten für Kunst im Handwerk at the Paris Salon d'Automne in 1910. Admired by a number of French critics for its simplicity, lack of ornamentation, and sense of co-ordination of furniture, furnishings, and room-settings, the French design world saw its compatibility with the ideology of mass-production as a threat to its belief in the freedom of artistic creativity untainted by the economics of the mass-market.

Design and Modernism

Modernism and the history of design

For several decades following the publication in 1936 of Nikolaus Pevsner's seminal text, *Pioneers of the Modern Movement*,[1] accounts of the history of twentieth-century design were dominated by investigations into the Modern Movement and its antecedents in the design reform movement of the nineteenth century.[2] The reasons for this are historically and ideologically complex, and may be seen to derive from the widespread ready availability for historical analysis of the considerable legacy of the modernists' output. This has survived in terms both of design production and the written word, as evidenced in the collections of many leading museums, art libraries, and archives throughout the Western industrialized world. The long-standing ideological dominance of modernism has also been underpinned by moral and political connotations, given that many of its most vociferous opponents were closely associated with repressive regimes, such as those in National Socialist Germany and Stalinist Russia. The modernists saw themselves as the creators of a 'machine age' aesthetic truly redolent of the twentieth century which, freed from the shackles of historicism, explored new forms and materials that were felt to be symbolically, if not actually, compatible with the mass-production capacity of a progressive industrial culture[3] [**10, 11**]. An additional consideration which has coloured more recent design-historical debates centred on modernism is the fact that much analysis has been predicated upon the theory and practice of celebrated individuals, with an emphasis on the celebration of aesthetic excellence. With the comparatively recent emergence of an interest in social anthropology and studies in material culture a significant number of scholars have sought to address the issues raised by wider patterns of design consumption and use.[4] Others have sought to reconsider modernism from a feminist perspective, raising important issues of professional and educational opportunity in the stereotyping of women within particular historical moments.[5]

Modernism: museums, archives, and libraries of art and design

The design legacy of many theorists and practitioners of modernism has been extensively preserved in museums and, through the very act of

Cover for *RED* magazine,
Czechoslovakia, 1928

RED was the journal of the
Devetsil Group of avant-garde
artists, designers, architects,
and writers, founded in Prague
in 1920. Published by the
Odeon Press and edited by
the influential Karol Teige, it
was an important vehicle for
modernist ideas. The strong
horizontal and vertical bars,
stencil-like lettering of the
title, and the geometric
block of type ally this image
stylistically to progressive
developments in German and
Russian Constructivist design.

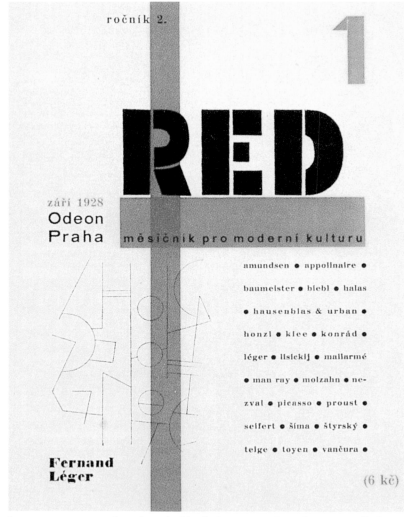

its exposure on pedestals or behind glass cases, has also generally been viewed for its aesthetic qualities, divorced from any real sense of its original everyday context and function. Such galleries and museums have been powerful conditioning agents in the establishment of cultural hierarchies. Perhaps the most celebrated example is the Museum of Modern Art (MOMA) in New York. Established in 1929, it was for many decades closely associated with the promotion of a 'Bauhaus aesthetic'.[6] Its first specifically design-oriented show was the 1934 'Machine Art' Exhibition [**12**], organized by Philip Johnson, with an emphasis on clean, geometric, and classical forms, symbolically and materially attuned to new materials and modern mass-production technology. Later in the decade, shows devoted to the work of Alvar Aalto and the Bauhaus further consolidated MOMA's position as a propagandist for the modern aesthetic, an association which was later bolstered by Edgar Kaufmann's 'Good Design' exhibitions of the 1950s. Such an outlook became closely linked to the cultural imprint of the multinational corporation and what may be seen as the globalization of a very particular kind of modernist design culture. This became evident in many exhibitions and museum displays across the world, a theme which will be discussed in more detail in Chapter 6. Although self-evident, it is important to remember that such collections have been formed in the light of particular beliefs as to what was culturally significant at specific historical moments and that the high premium placed on aesthetic content necessarily distinguishes their exhibits from what was generally consumed, used, and experienced by the majority.

The modernist creed has also been reinforced by the constant production of avant-garde manifestos, magazines, and books in the early

11 Qian Jun-tao

Ahead of the Times, published by Ahead of the Times Magazine Association, Shanghai, January 1931

During the 1920s and 1930s a significant number of Chinese designers, particularly those in the metropolitan centre of Shanghai, drew on influences from Europe and the United States, sustained by a widespread interest in western lifestyles. An increased commitment to the simplification of typographic form, blended with an interest in the functionalist symbolism of the arrangement of geometric elements on the page, echoed the exploration of abstract forms by western avant-garde designers. Qian Jun-tao was a leading figure in this progressive movement.

12

Installation view of the *Machine Art* exhibition, MOMA, New York, 1934

Held between 5 March and 29 April 1934, this exhibition was curated by the arch-modernist Philip Johnson. Adopting a similar standpoint to that explored by Herbert Read in Britain in his book *Art and Industry*, published in the same year, Johnson interpreted the functional forms and materials of aircraft propellers, industrial insulators, and ball-bearings in purely aesthetic terms. Such emphasis on the clarity of abstract form set MOMA apart from the commercially widespread application of streamlined forms to all kinds of objects.

twentieth century, many of which have been specifically oriented towards an international readership. Furthermore, organizations committed to the promotion of modern design, such as the Deutscher Werkbund (DWB), the Swedish Society of Industrial Design (Svenska Slöjdföreningen) or the rather less effective Design and Industries Association (DIA) in Britain, all left a legacy of exhibitions, related catalogues, periodicals, and other publications which have occupied the shelves of major art and design libraries ever since being committed to print. A number of art, architectural, and design educational institutions have also left their mark through similar outputs. Perhaps the most celebrated self-propagandist body in this respect has been the Bauhaus, formed in Weimar, Germany, in 1919 under the directorship of Walter Gropius, moving to Dessau in 1925 and thence to Berlin in 1932, where it was finally closed by the Nazis in the following year. Fourteen *Bauhausbücher* (Bauhaus Books) were published between 1925 and 1930, explaining Bauhaus aims, objectives and practice to an international readership. It also published a journal, *Bauhaus*, which appeared in fifteen issues at intervals between 1926 and 1931. Furthermore, the Bauhaus Archive was founded in Darmstadt in 1960 (moving to Berlin in 1971), another stimulus for research into the history and ideology of the institution, a process which subsequently continued through the mounting of exhibitions such as *Fifty Years Bauhaus* which travelled in Europe and North and South America between 1968 and 1971. Similar developments concerning Bauhaus heritage were taking place in East Germany, with the mounting of a major exhibition in 1967 which led to the formation of a Bauhaus archive in Dessau.[7] Until comparatively recently the ready availability of such resources for historians has tended to overshadow research into the wider patterns of design manufacture and consumption in Germany in the 1920s and 1930s.[8]

Modernism: moral and political dimensions

The moral dimension of modernism originated in the nineteenth-century design reform movement. It reflected a growing belief in early twentieth-century avant-garde design circles that products which both disguised their modes of construction through ornamental embellishment and were out of tune with the 'spirit of the age' (or *Zeitgeist*) were exemplars of 'bad' design. Adolf Loos, an important theorist of the early twentieth century who had been characterized by Pevsner as a 'Pioneer' of modernism, went so far as to claim in his celebrated text *Ornament und Verbrechen* (Ornament and Crime) of 1908:

the modern ornamentalist is either a cultural laggard or a pathological case. He himself is forced to disown his work after three years. His productions are unbearable to cultured persons now, and will become so to others in a little while.[9]

Writing almost two decades later the architect-designer Le Corbusier, a central figure in the modernist debate, further clarified the moral implications of such an outlook in L'Art décoratif d'aujourd'hui (*The Decorative Art of Today*) of 1925 in which he declared forthrightly:

Trash is always abundantly decorated; the luxury object is well-made, neat and clean, pure and healthy, and its bareness reveals the quality of its manufacture. It is to industry that we owe the reversal in this state of affairs: a cast-iron stove overflowing with decoration costs less than a plain one; amidst the surging leaf patterns flaws in the casting cannot be seen.[10]

For Corbusier the adjectives 'neat', 'clean', and 'pure' were linked with healthiness; there was also an implicit charge of deceit in his account of ornamentation as a disguise for flaws in manufacture, a rather more measured view than Loos's inference that the ornamentalist was not only criminal but somehow mentally unstable. However, bound up in the writings of both is a sense of cultural élitism: Loos's claim that the ornamental designer's 'productions are unbearable to cultured persons now, and will become so to others in a little while', presages Corbusier's assertion, also from *The Decorative Art of Today*, that 'the more cultivated a people becomes, the more decoration disappears'. Indeed, in a turn of phrase which many today would find distasteful, Corbusier went on to deplore the fact that 'decorative objects flood the shelves of the Department Stores; they sell cheaply to shop-girls'.

The modernists' spiritual affinity for abstract forms and new materials was also wedded to a democratic ideal whereby the majority would be able to enjoy an improved quality of life in a hygienic, healthy, and modern environment. This social utopian commitment was potently expressed in the housing and design programmes implemented by progressive municipalities in Holland and Germany and, with considerable variation in intensity, realization, and influence, in a wide range of other countries including France, Italy, the USSR, Czechoslovakia, Hungary, Poland, Sweden, Denmark, Britain, the United States, and Japan. At its heart modernism was committed to a social and cultural agenda which was not constrained by national boundaries; indeed, the internationalizing outlook which characterized many of its publications and products received tangible recognition at the Museum of Modern Art (MOMA) in New York in 1932 when the art historian Henry Russell Hitchcock and architect Philip Johnson mounted an exhibition entitled 'Modern Architecture—International Exhibition'. The term 'International Style' was adopted both in the accompanying publication and in Russell and Hitchcock's book of the same year *The International Style: Architecture since 1922*.[11]

With heightened political tensions spreading across Europe in the later 1920s, further exacerbated by the economic consequences of the 1929 Wall Street crash, there was a strong reawakening of nationalism and a growing antipathy to what was often portrayed as the 'cultural Bolshevism' of the internationalizing modernist outlook. In the face of international economic crisis there was a widespread reassertion of national values and traditions, together with a rejection of the modernist agenda of abstract forms, new materials, and modern technology; the modernist antipathy to historical references in design, architecture, and the visual arts, found itself under increasing attack from the National Socialist Party under Adolf Hitler in Germany and the dictates of Socialist Realism under Josef Stalin in the USSR. As will be indicated later, the position in Fascist Italy under Mussolini was rather more ambivalent although still a battle of ideologies, whilst in the calmer political climate of Scandinavia and Holland modernism found considerable room for expression and development. In many other countries the modernist aesthetic was most fully represented in the pages of the architectural and design press, exhibitions, related reviews and caricature and was generally oriented more to the tastes of a sophisticated élite than to effecting any significant change in the demands of the mass-market.

Modernist design: a working definition

The Modern Movement is generally seen to have developed in two main phases: the first originated in the theories and practice of the design reformers of the late nineteenth century, gathering impetus in the years before the outbreak of war in 1914 and coming to fruition in the early 1920s; the second phase, known as the International Style, can be seen to have run from the later 1920s through to the 1960s. In the 1950s it became a powerful form of expression for the architecture and interiors of multinational corporations, but by the 1960s was associated by many critics, theorists, and practitioners with a sense of social alienation and cultural remoteness in a fast-changing, pluralist, and multicultural society dominated by the mass media. Such Postmodernist critiques were considerably bolstered by popular associations of modernism with social and economic problems in mass-housing and urban planning, and a style of aesthetic anonymity.

Although modernism has perhaps been most visible in terms of its architectural legacy it none the less generated widespread experimentation and production in many fields of design including appliances, ceramics, glassware, furniture and fittings, carpets, textiles, typography, posters, and wallpaper. Its appearance was generally characterized by clean, geometric forms, the use of modern materials such as chromium-plated steel and glass, and plain surfaces articulated by the abstract manipulation of light and shade. The use of colour was often restrained, with an emphasis on white, off-white, grey, and black. When decoration was applied its appearance generally conformed to the abstract aesthetic which had been forged by the artistic avant-garde in the years leading up to the First World War, but had found fuller expression in the work of the Constructivists in Eastern Europe, those associated with De Stijl, and others in the early 1920s. All such characteristics of modernism were felt to be unambiguous affirmations of twentieth-century life, symbolically attuned to the possibilities of modern materials and manufacturing processes. However, although this drive to adopt a creative vocabulary imbued with the new 'functionalism' of the twentieth century looked to the creation of standardized forms and types in furniture and equipment, such 'functionalism' was often far more symbolic than material. The adage so often associated with modernism, 'form follows function' can be seen as the culmination of the acrimonious 'Standardization Debate' which took place between Henry van de Velde and Hermann Muthesius at the Deutscher Werkbund congress of 1914, when Muthesius' commitment to *Typisierung* (standardization), based on economic as well as aesthetic grounds, was opposed by those who felt that this restricted the creativity of the individual designer.[12]

Modern movement design: the First World War and its aftermath

The massive disruption engendered by the First World War ensured that German efforts to establish an emphatically twentieth-century aesthetic, typified by the more progressive factions of the Deutscher Werkbund and evident in the work of Pieter Behrens at the AEG,

13

Tea and Coffee Service from
the *Deutsches Warenbuch*,
1915

Selected by a group of experts
drawn from the Werkbund, the
Warenbuch was intended to
bring about a more
widespread acceptance
of well-designed German
products as well as to educate
the consumer in matters
of domestic taste. Consisting
of 248 pages of German
household goods in current
production, it also listed
prices and suppliers, rather
as *Das Frankfurter Register*
was to do later in the following
decade (see **24**).

were substantially disrupted. None the less, the war also bolstered German initiatives to break free of foreign cultural influences as well as providing the impetus to establish a system of standards for industry. This was realized in 1917 when the Normenausschuss der Deutschen Industrie (Standards Commission of German Industry) was founded, an important body which continued to play a key role after the war. Nor was design propaganda entirely forgotten: in 1915 the Deutscher Werkbund and the Dürerbund[13] jointly published the *Deutsches Warenbuch* [**13**], a handbook of well-designed German products, together with prices and retail outlets. Originally planned in 1913, its effect was somewhat diminished by the war although it was favourably received by a wide range of organizations and individuals.

Progressive design initiatives were taken up elsewhere during the war years, especially in Holland which remained neutral. The most important fulcrum for debate was the De Stijl group, which was founded by Theo van Doesburg in 1917, together with a magazine of the same title. The De Stijl group included fine artists, architects, and designers, with its early outlook conditioned by the work and thought of the painter Piet Mondrian, who had been considerably influenced by the work of the French Cubist painters before the outbreak of war. The Dutch architect and designer H. P. Berlage, whose own manipulation of form and space revealed links with the American architect and designer Frank Lloyd Wright, was another formative influence on the movement. The De Stijl designers sought to explore an elemental design vocabulary in their search for a modern, harmonious aesthetic. Equilibrium was to be achieved through the balance of verticals and horizontals and the restriction of the design palette to the primary

14 Gerrit Rietveld

Interior of the Schröder House, Utrecht, 1924

Rietveld's first major architectural project was built in the same year that Van Doesburg set out his manifestos on architecture in the magazine *De Stijl*. Planned in conjunction with Mrs Truus Schröder-Schräder, who had commissioned the house from Rietveld, the interior demonstrated many of the aesthetic principles of De Stijl, and was a balance of interlocking planes and forms articulated by the primary colours—red, yellow, and blue—and black, white, and grey.

colours of red, yellow, and blue as well as black and white. Interior designs by Van Doesburg, including stained glass windows, tiled floors, and mosaics, textiles by Bart van der Leck and Vilmos Huszár and furniture by Gerrit Rietveld, including his famous experimental Red/Blue chair, typified the early agenda of the group. By the early 1920s, the De Stijl aesthetic took on a more international profile as modernism generally began to attract more critical attention: Rietveld's 1924 design for the Schröder House in Utrecht [**14**] was the most striking realization of its outlook where abstract, geometric forms, symbolically compatible with modern mass-production technology, were manipulated both with regard to external detailing and internal spaces and furniture.

This search for universal forms in Holland in many ways paralleled Muthesius' commitment to standardization in the debates at the Deutscher Werkbund before the First World War, although with an emphasis on its symbolism rather than its technological practicalities. This quest for modern, abstract form, symbolically reflective of the twentieth century [**15, 16**], was also taking place elsewhere, as in Russia, where Constructivism became an important focus in progressive design circles.

15 Gerrit Rietveld

15 Gerrit Rietveld
Exhibition at Metz & Co.
department store,
Amsterdam, showing
dining area and glass
sideboard, 1933

International modernism
in Holland was represented
by the Rotterdam-based de
Opbouw group (established
1920) and the Amsterdam
de 8 association (established
1927). The progressive
tendencies of this Nieuwe
Bouwen movement was
echoed in propaganda for
light, durable, and functional
furniture. Metz & Co. regularly
promoted modern furniture,
particularly after 1930,
commissioning work from
Rietveld, Van Der Leck,
Stam and Oud, and other
avant-garde designers.

Following the October Revolution of 1917 many Russian avant-garde artists and designers committed themselves to propaganda, including theatre and poster design. However, by 1920, rifts occurred amongst the avant-garde, with concern expressed about the way in which utilitarian concern was leading to the stifling of individual artistic creativity. Artists such as Wassily Kandinsky (who went on to work at the Bauhaus in Germany) believed in the primacy of the creative expression of the individual in art whereas others, including Alexander Rodchenko, his wife Varvara Stepanova [17], and Vladimir Tatlin, committed themselves to work with a more utilitarian bent, geared to the needs of society, employing forms compatible with the potential of modern mass-production technology [18, 19]. El Lissitsky was another highly influential Russian with a strong commitment to the establishment of an international vocabulary of form. Travelling extensively between Russia and other European countries in the 1920s, he forged links with De Stijl and other progressive groups and published in Berlin a journal *Vesch* (Object) in which he sought to reconcile art with mass-production.

The Bauhaus 1919–1933: Weimar, Dessau, Berlin

Perhaps surprisingly, given Walter Gropius's commitment at the Werkbund Exhibition at Cologne in 1914 to notions of standardization, the manipulation of modern materials, and an industrial aesthetic, the early years of the Bauhaus were closely linked with Expressionism. Such a radical change of outlook immediately after the war undoubtedly sprang from the subsequent antipathy of many designers (particularly on the left of the political spectrum) to large-

Giso Lamps poster, 1928
Gispen, a founder member
of de Opbouw, established
his metalware company in
Rotterdam in 1916, and in the
1920s increasingly promoted
modern lighting and furniture.
Typifying his progressive
aesthetic beliefs was the
famous Giso lamp seen in
this poster, fabricated from
standardized parts and in
serial production from 1927
onwards. Much of the
company's furniture
designs from the mid-1920s
onwards used chromium-
plated tubular steel.

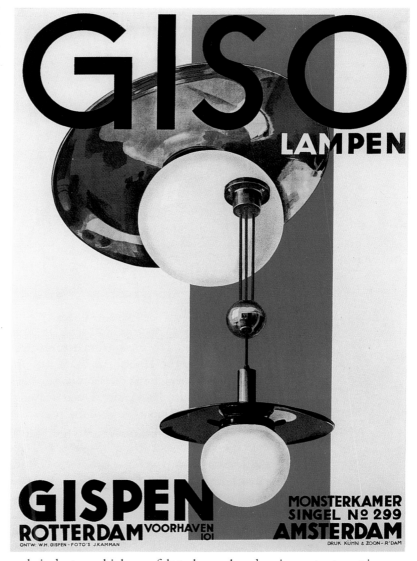

scale industry, which was felt to have played an important part in pre-
cipitating Germany's involvement in the First World War. In 1919
Gropius was the chairman of the radical Arbeitsrat für Kunst
(Worker's Council for Art), the programme of which embraced a commitment to crafts training and the unification of all the arts, undoubtedly influencing the spiritual intensity of the Bauhaus Founding
Manifesto of 1919. Something of this expressionist spirit may be seen
in one of the most important early Bauhaus projects, the wooden
Sommerfeld House.[14] Designed by Gropius and Hannes Meyer in
1921, it provided an early opportunity for design collaboration on a
large scale, embracing the architecture as a framework for all the fields
of design contained within it, including elaborate woodcarvings by

Sports clothes by Stepanova and graphics for *Dobrolyet* by Rodchenko from *LEF* magazine, Moscow, 1923

LEF (1923–5) was an important outlet for Russian Constructivist debate. Varvara Stepanova, renowned for her striking textile and clothing designs, and her husband Alexander Rodchenko were leading figures in the movement. Their concerns were to utilize art and design as potent and progressive forces in the construction of a new society, aligning symbolically the abstract forms of their artist vocabularly to the machine age.

Joost Schmidt with reference to folk art traditions in the detailing. But within two years a distinct shift of design outlook was discernible, no doubt engendered by the need to demonstrate the economic relevance of the school to the Thuringian State government which funded it, an authority with which the Bauhaus had an increasingly fraught political and ideological relationship. Once again a design aesthetic which explored forms compatible with the ethos of modern mass-production technology was clearly visible, even if its realisation was achieved by craft modes of construction. This could be seen in Gropius's own office [20], throughout which the contrast of horizontal and vertical articulated both furniture and fittings, particularly in the lighting fitting, which was designed by Gropius himself, echoed solutions by Constructivist designers in Russia and Hungary or De Stijl in Holland. This marked a much more international design orientation [21], itself stimulated by several events which took place in Weimar in the early 1920s: the arrival of Van Doesburg in 1921, the mounting of a Dada/Constructivist conference at which Van Doesburg, El Lissitsky, the Hungarian Constructivist Lázló Moholy-Nagy, and his wife Lucia participated, and the appointment to the Bauhaus staff of the Russian painter Wassily Kandinsky and Moholy-Nagy in 1922 and 1923 respectively. In 1923 the Bauhaus also mounted an exhibition in order to defend itself against increasing criticism from its funding authority and elsewhere. The centrepiece, a physical manifesto, was the 'functional' Haus am Horn, designed by Adolf Meyer and Georg Muche, for which the interior furniture, fittings, and equipment were produced as prototypes for industry by a number of the Bauhaus workshops. These were especially evident in the kitchen, the design of which was influenced by the weaver Benita Koche-Otte who, reinforcing the general expectations of women at the Bauhaus, was brought in to lend 'a woman's view' in the male arena of industrial design.[15] A new Bauhaus slogan, 'Art and Technology: a New Unity' was adopted by Gropius, a firm rejection of the handicraft ethos which he reiterated in a contemporary speech to the Werkbund conference also held in Weimar in the summer of 1923.

Gropius had recognized the importance of establishing links with industry as a vital means of helping to alleviate Bauhaus dependency on the Thuringian State government. To this end a business manager was appointed in 1923 but, particularly during the remaining years at Weimar, his task was fraught with problems, not the least being the incapacity of the various Bauhaus workshops to meet delivery deadlines. Displays at trade fairs were also poorly handled, with many goods overpriced. As a result the Bauhaus saw many of its potential outlets located at the more exclusive end of the market [**22**, **23**].[16]

The firm commitment to a fusion between art and technology was even more emphatically expressed in the new buildings, interiors, furniture, and fittings at Dessau, where the Bauhaus had been forced to move for political reasons in 1925–6. The commitment to industrial prototypes was more rigorously pursued in the later 1920s, despite the departure from the staff of Gropius and Moholy-Nagy in 1928, soon followed by two other influential teachers (and former Bauhaus graduates), the graphic designer Herbert Bayer and furniture designer Marcel Breuer. A number of lighting designs were put into production by the Leipzig manufacturers Körting and Mathiesen, wallpapers by Rasch Brothers & Co of Hanover, and textile designs by Polytextil-

Late 1920s textile, USSR
The design of this textile
blends the geometric
abstraction of the progressive
tendencies in Russian
Constructivism with
recognizable and politically
potent forms of symbolism.

Gesellschaft in Berlin, Pausa in Stuttgart, and the Deutschen Werkstätten in Dresden. In fact, the Weaving Workshop at the Dessau Bauhaus under the direction of Gunta Stötzl was one of the leading centres for training in the field and was the only one that qualified women graduates to work for industry.

The removal of the Bauhaus to Berlin in 1932, in the face of implacable opposition from the National Socialist City Council in Dessau, and its final demise in the following year have been widely documented and have perhaps increased its ideological cachet for later historians. Furthermore, many architects and designers working in Germany fled the increasingly oppressive Nazi regime and moved to Britain, the United States, and elsewhere, thus sharpening debates on, and knowledge of (at least in progressive circles), both the modernist aesthetic and Bauhaus educational practice.

The Bauhaus: some issues in interpretation and historical location

As indicated earlier, for many years the Bauhaus, formed in Weimar in 1919 under the directorship of Walter Gropius, has subsequently played a dominant role in considerations of the Modern Movement in Germany. Its lifespan almost directly coincided with the culturally fertile period of the Weimar Republic, established in 1919 and terminating with the election of the National Socialists under Adolf Hitler in 1933, and many of the wider social, economic, and political tensions engendered during those years mirrored the problems and successes of the institution. In addition to the Bauhaus's own considerable propagandist output concerning its own activities, there have been many subsequent useful published historical evaluations and collections of documentary material, as well as exhibitions celebrating the work of associated artists, architects and designers.[17]

As has been argued earlier, this notoriety has tended to obscure the achievements and concerns of other important art institutions in contemporary Germany, including those at Berlin, Breslau, Dusseldorf, Essen, Stuttgart, and Frankfurt. For example, the latter, formed in 1923 from an amalgamation of the existing School of Handicrafts and Institute of Art and Architecture, was also renowned in the 1920s and increasingly forged links with industry, particularly in printing and textiles. Like that of the Bauhaus its curriculum became progressively specialized and attracted onto its staff Bauhaus graduates such as Christian Dell, as well as eliciting contributions to its programme from leading designers and architects such as Ferdinand Kramer (also a Bauhaus graduate) and Ernst May (the Frankfurt City Architect).

The prominence of the Bauhaus has also tended to overshadow the activities of other culturally significant German organizations that had an important bearing on design production in the same years, most

Gropius's office was open to
the public as part of the 1923
Bauhaus exhibition, reflecting
other aspects of the modern
interior shown in the Haus am
Horn (see **26**). The geometric
character of the furniture,
designed by Gropius,
endorsed the modernist
preoccupation with an
aesthetic compatible,
at least symbolically,
with contemporary mass-
production technology.
The industrial character of
the light-fitting, also by Gropius
(closely following a 1922
design by the De Stijl designer,
Rietveld), the wall-hanging by
Else Mögelin, and the rug by
Gertrud Arndt, both students
in the Weaving Workshop,
were similarly conceived.

notably the Deutscher Werkbund. Considered by historians to be a
significant shaping influence on the roots of the Modern Movement, it
has generally received most scrutiny in the period from its foundation
in 1907 to the occurrence of the seminal Werkbund Exhibition in
Cologne in 1914, the culminating point of Pevsner's *Pioneers of Modern
Design*. Indeed, as the Canadian historian Joan Campbell argued in
the introduction to her authoritative publication, *The German
Werkbund: The Politics of Reform in the Applied Arts*:

the impressive achievements of the early Bauhaus are not sufficient reasons to
neglect the contributions of the Weimar Werkbund to the cause of modern
architecture and design. Moreover, because the Werkbund was one of the few

national cultural institutions to survive from the Second Reich into the Third, examination of its ideals can illuminate both the extraordinary flowering of the modern spirit commonly designated as "Weimar Culture" and the intellectual-cultural origins of National Socialism.[18]

However, it is also the case that such wider historical emphases on the commitment to modernism of both the Deutscher Werkbund and the Bauhaus have tended to overshadow the wider realities of design production and everyday consumption in contemporary Germany, considerations which have largely been overlooked in publications on the period.

More recently research into the structure and workings of the Bauhaus has addressed the role of women at the institution, the restrictions of which had far wider social and industrial implications in Germany (and elsewhere). Magdalene Droste, in an essay entitled 'Women in the Arts and Crafts and in Industrial Design 1890–1933' drew attention to the ways in which Walter Gropius sought to limit the number of female students at the Bauhaus through the introduction, from 1920, of a more rigorous entry policy, 'particularly for the female sex, whose number is excessive'.[19] Furthermore, in a climate in which there were clear male conceptions that arts and crafts practice (generally associated with women) might be seen to threaten the successful realization of the stated goal of the institution—architectural proficiency—he sought to restrict women's opportunities after completion of the foundation course to weaving, pottery, or bookbinding. Where women such as Marianne Brandt and Alma Büscher did emerge to a position of some prominence in other fields, metalwork and furniture respectively, this very much flew in the face of the general assumption that design for industry was a male preserve.

The wider climate of modern design in Germany in the 1920s

Just as the unambiguous prosecution of the modernist cause at the Bauhaus was evidenced by its 1923 exhibition and the move towards the production of industrial prototypes, the DWB re-emerged from a period of ideological confusion in the immediate postwar years. With a marked shift away from a position of economic impotence and affiliation with the idea of the cultural and economic significance of the crafts, it once again became a significant campaigning body for the reconciliation of design excellence with modern industry. This was intimately linked to the halting of the inflationary spiral at the end of 1923 and more invigorating future prospects for German industry.

During the mid-1920s the DWB became an important sponsor of

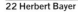
22 Herbert Bayer

Brochure advertising Bauhaus products, 1925

Bayer was in charge of the printing workshop at the Dessau Bauhaus from 1925 to 1928. The clarity of the design and structured layout of this brochure page was characteristic of progressive typographers of the period. The use of sans-serif letterforms, often accentuated by bold underlining, was favoured by Bayer who was influenced by the work of Moholy-Nagy, El Lissitsky, and Van Doesburg.

exhibitions promoting modern architecture and design, with an emphasis on many aspects of its wider social relevance. An important travelling exhibition reflecting this new spirit was entitled *Form ohne Ornament* (Form without Ornament).[20] First shown in Stuttgart in 1924, it included both craft- and machine-produced goods and embodied a broad commitment to the rejection of historical ornamentation and the individualism of postwar Expressionism. Furthermore it helped to ferment the idea of developing standardized forms compatible with modern modes of production. Such a functionalist outlook began to sound the alarm bells in traditional art industries where a premium was placed on traditional craft skills, an alarm which was to articulate itself far more vociferously at the Weissenhof housing exhibition of 1927. But in other ways the 1924 exhibition was rooted in the past since, in the accompanying publication, women were associated with the crafts and 'primitive' design whereas men were linked with 'technical' design, reinforcing their nineteenth-century stereotype-casting at the centre of cultural and industrial change.[21]

The DWB magazine *Die Form* resumed publication in 1925[22] and soon became a highly influential mouthpiece for progressive ideas, being read by the avant-garde at home and abroad. None the less, it is important not to underestimate the relative lack of enthusiasm of German industry for the widespread adoption of such ideas in the domestic marketplace. Indeed, opportunities to realize them were comparatively short-lived since, by the late 1920s, German industrial production began to decline with the lessening of foreign investment and the successive economic crises that followed the Wall Street Crash of 1929. As a result, the membership of the DWB dropped markedly, and in the polarized political climate of the times it found itself increasingly unable to defend itself against accusations of 'cultural bolshevism' from the political Right and cultural élitism from the Left.

Lighting by Wilhelm Wagenfeld
from *Das Frankfurter Register*,
17, 1931

In the later 1920s there were
concerted efforts to promote
Frankfurt as an emphatically
modern, twentieth-century
city, much stimulated by the
appointment of Ludwig
Landmann as
Oberbürgermeister in 1924.
The radical municipal
achievements in architecture
and design were furthered in
the pages of the monthly
journal *Das Neue Frankfurt*
which was published from
1926 to 1934. Its supplement,
the *Frankfurter Register*,
contained many examples
of modern design in everyday
life, and often included prices
and details of retail outlets.

DAS FRANKFURTER REGISTER 17

WEIMAR BAU- UND WOHNUNGSKUNST G.M.B.H.
Ehemalige Vertriebsorganisation der Staatl. Bauhochschule Weimar

TYPE:
M 42
TISCHLEUCHTER
mit Zeißspiegelreflektor
Metallteile: Messing vernickelt,
poliert. Gesamthöhe: ca. 42 cm

Entwürfe:
WILH. WAGENFELD
Oberweimar / Thüringen

TYPE:
M 30
**ZUGPENDEL-
LEUCHTER**
Messing, matt vernickelt. Mit
Cellon- od. Karton-Unterschirm
aus besonders lichtdurchlässig.
Material und innen mattweiß
lackiertem Metallreflektor.
Reflektor ⌀ 24 cm
Unterschirm ⌀ 48 cm

Fordern Sie Kataloge über Leuchten, Metallgeräte, Möbel, Bauteile,
Keramiken und Webereien von der

WEIMAR BAU- U. WOHNUNGSKUNST G.M.B.H.
WEIMAR · SCHILLERSTRASSE 14,I

Beilage zu „Das Neue Frankfurt" 1931, Heft 3 5. Verlag Englert und Schlosser, Frankfurt a. M.

Like the Bauhaus before it, the DWB eventually fell prey to the cultural repression of the National Socialists.

Municipal patronage also played an important role in the dissemination of modernist design and planning in Germany in the mid-1920s. This had originated in the general shift away from private to public patronage in the period of spiralling inflation of the early 1920s, and was considerably boosted by the greater economic stability in the mid-1920s brought about by substantial American investment. Progressive concepts such as the *Neue Gestaltung* (New Design), *Neue Bauen* (New Architecture) and the *Neues Wohnen* (New Lifestyle) became rallying calls for the avant-garde, reflecting a desire to embrace the material advantages which could result from the whole-hearted embrace of modern mass-production technology, new materials and, above all, the true spirit of the twentieth century. In this respect the world-shattering consequences of the First World War had marked a much more emphatic break with the past than had the literal passing of the old century in 1900. Magazines such as *Das Neue Frankfurt* and *Das Neue Berlin*, which commenced publication in 1926 and 1929 respectively, argued for the recognition of the social as well as aesthetic value of modern architecture and design. A related publication, the *Frank-*

furt Register was also an extremely telling vehicle for the dissemination of the modernist project. Effectively a sales catalogue for the promotion of modern design for everyday life, with sections devoted to lighting [**24**], furniture, and other facets of interior design, it pursued, from a municipal perspective, similar objectives to the *Deutsches Warenbuch* published jointly by the Dürerbund and the Deutscher Werkbund in 1915, to which reference has already been made [**13**]. Ernst May, in charge of Frankfurt's municipal housing programme, brought a number of modernist aspirations to life in the provision of mass-housing. Such dwellings saw the development of special building techniques and were equipped with functionalist furniture and fittings tailored to the practicalities of efficient living in small spaces (*Existenzminimum*). One of the most noteworthy solutions was the Frankfurt kitchen, the planning of which was achieved by a team working under the Viennese architect-designer Greta Schütte-Lihotsky.

The Frankfurt kitchen: a design solution for twentieth-century living

The planning of efficient, pleasant kitchens had been a concern of the women's movement in Germany for some time but, in the post-First World War period, was allied to a rethinking of the role of the housewife within the home. The growth of interest in the concept of 'scientific management' in the home was especially attractive as it afforded the role of housewife the prospect of acquiring status as well as 'professional' connotations through its adoption.[23]

Considerable impetus was given by the translation into German in 1922 of the American Christine Frederick's *Scientific Management in the Home* of 1915 in which considerable emphasis was placed on the kitchen. She argued for the removal from the kitchen of activities unrelated to the preparation of food in order that it could be made smaller and thus less wasteful in terms of movements around it. Another widely read text which promoted this new spirit in the domestic arena was Edna Meyer's *Der Neue Haushalt*. First published in 1926, it had gone into 40 editions by 1932. She collaborated with the Dutch architect-designer J. J. P. Oud on kitchen design at the Weissenhof Siedlungen exhibition of 1927, a feature which received considerable critical acclaim. Also important in this field of design was Greta Schütte-Lihotsky who had been influenced by Heinrich Tessenow, an important pioneer in the analysis of the design of small apartments, and was also well aware of Oud's work, having worked in Rotterdam where some of his most important schemes had evolved. Called in by the Frankfurt City Architect Ernst May, Greta Schütte-Lihotsky sought to bring about a fruitful collaboration between architects, housewives, and manufacturers to arrive at the most appropriate means of approaching housework.[24] Much more systematically conceived than the labour-saving kitchen of the Haus am Horn seen at the 1923 Bauhaus exhibition, the size and layout of the Frankfurt kitchen [**25**, **26**] was determined by time-and-motion studies, although the aim was also to produce a pleasant, as well as efficient, environment. To this end psychological considerations were also incorporated into the design, which took careful account of the use of colour as well as the sizes of the window and the opening into the adjoining family room. Costs were kept low by the use of factory prefabrication, and different versions of the kitchen were incorporated into a range of the new housing estates in 1920s Frankfurt and reflected the trends towards an increasing nationally instituted standardization of many household goods and kitchen equipment.

The concept of *Existenzminimum* (compact living) was discussed extensively at the 1929 Congrès Internationaux d'Architecture Moderne (CIAM) conference in Frankfurt, and many modernist designers explored ideas of space-saving. Such experiments were important facets of their social utopianist aims and were proposed in many European and Scandinavian countries. In Russia, for example, El Lissitsky designed a 'compartment kitchen' in Moscow in 1928; in Finland, at the 1930 Minimum Apartment Exhibition in Helsinki Town Hall, Aino Aalto designed a minimum kitchen, which included a rubbish bin on wheels and tables with extendable surfaces at which

25

Blueprint for the Frankfurt Kitchen, designed by Grete Schütte-Lihotzky, 1924

The ergonomic functionalism of the Frankfurt Kitchen reflected a desire to provide high standards of design in mass-housing. With built-in cupboards, storage units, and work-surfaces, the space-saving ideas looked back to the design of ship and railway galleys as well as to the highly influential *Scientific Management in the Home* (1915) by Christine Frederick. The practicality of the Frankfurt design was furthered by the provision of a swivel-stool from which the housewife could easily reach the sink, chopping board, and food storage.

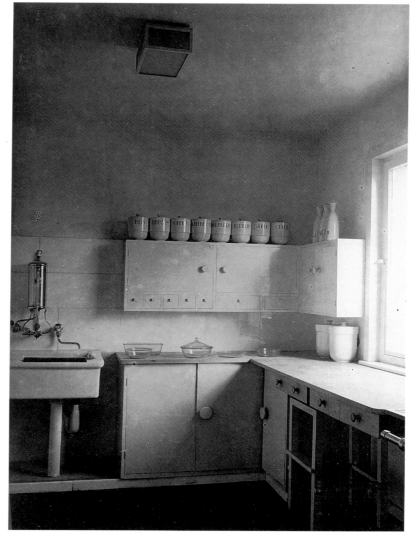

Haus am Horn kitchen, designed by Benita Otte and Ernst Gebhardt, Bauhaus Exhibition, 1923

The Haus am Horn marked an unambiguous commitment to a modernist vocabulary of form seen both in its stark, undecorated exterior and the clarity of internal spatial organization. The fitted kitchen units, built in the Bauhaus cabinet-making workshops, reveal a growing commitment to notions of standardization and economic mass-production technology, an outlook echoed in Theodor Bogler's earthenware containers seen above the cupboard, mass-produced by Velten-Vordamm, as well as the glassware on the work surface which was manufactured by Schott & Gen.

the person preparing meals could work; in the same year a Minimum Flat Exhibition was mounted in Warsaw; and in Britain in 1933–4 Wells Coates produced a galley-kitchen design for his 'Minimum Flats' at Lawn Road, London.

Die Wohnung: the Weissenhof Siedlungen exhibition, Stuttgart, 1927

Perhaps the most celebrated and unambiguous manifestation of modernism in Germany was the *Die Wohnung* (The Dwelling) exhibition held in Stuttgart in 1927, reflecting the high status afforded architecture in the modernist canon. Organized on behalf of the Deutscher Werkbund by the German architect and designer Ludwig Mies van der Rohe on the Weissenhof Estate, Stuttgart, it included about sixty housing designs by sixteen of the leading protagonists of the Modern Movement, including Le Corbusier from France, Mart Stam and J. J. P. Oud from Holland, Victor Bourgeois from Belgium, and Gropius and Mies himself from Germany. The modernist forms seen in the architecture, furniture, and fittings did much to establish the notion of an 'International Style' as critics were able to see that the work of architects and designers from a number of countries, including Germany, was stylistically homogeneous. This gave rise to growing hostility in Germany to an aesthetic which disregarded indigenous traditions: the flat roofs of the buildings were seen as incompatible with the German character. The exhibition was also a forum for the display of modern home furnishings and provoked conservative furniture manufacturers to attempt to prevent avant-garde furniture by Marcel Breuer and others being shown. The exhibition did much to centralize criticism of the avant-garde, and modernist designers and architects were increasingly portrayed as embodying harmful moral and political characteristics, often being associated with Bolshevist, Jewish, and other 'undesirable' or 'foreign' origins.

Although modern design was generally suppressed under the Nazis for such reasons as had become apparent at Stuttgart in 1927, the design historian John Heskett has argued that standardization and rationalization continued to exert an important impact on economic planning, particularly with regard to rearmament and militarization.[25] Despite the widespread adoption of an emphatically *völkisch* aesthetic under the Nazis guidelines were still produced for neat, functional design in housing, domestic furnishings, and equipment, and the work of many Modern Movement designers who had come to the fore in the 1920s, such as the metalware and glass designer Wilhelm Wagenfeld or the industrial ceramic designer, Hermann Gretsch, continued in production throughout the 1930s. Gretsch's porcelain service for Arzberg of 1931 [27] exemplified the clean-formed 'functional' aesthetic of the modernists which continued in production for more than fifty years. The extent to which the Modern Movement could still be seen in Germany as late as 1939 was apparent in the *Deutsche Warenkunde*, an official state publication of approved designs in current production.

Modernism in France: Le Corbusier and the UAM

In France Le Corbusier was undoubtedly the most prominent figure in modernist circles, having links with a number of the pioneers before 1914, most notably Peter Behrens, in whose Berlin office he worked in 1910–11. Corbusier remained at the forefront of modernism until after the Second World War. Active in many creative fields, including architecture and planning, design, and the Fine Arts, he also produced a number of important theoretical texts. *Vers une architecture* of 1923 in particular was an important vehicle for the dissemination of the modernism across Europe and beyond, drawing attention to the aesthetic significance of modern anonymously designed cars, aeroplanes, or grain silos.

The 1925 Exposition Internationale des Arts Décoratifs et Industriels in Paris has often been viewed by design historians as an important forum for the material embodiment of conflicting design ideologies in the interwar years. Here, the austere, modern aesthetic of Le Corbusier's celebrated Pavillon de l'Esprit Nouveau [**28**] clearly indicated the huge ideological gulf which lay between the decorative excesses of the expensive creations of the French *ensembliers*, which were predominant throughout much of the Exhibition, and the modernists' spiritual affinity with notions of standardization, the exploration of new materials, and firm embrace of the contemporary spirit.

28 Le Corbusier

Interior of Pavillon de l'Espirit Nouveau, Exposition Des Arts Décoratifs et Industriels, Paris, 1925

Corbusier's Pavilion was opposed to the major aim of the 1925 Paris Exposition, that of promoting French decorative arts and design. Instead, his design assumed an uncompromisingly modern aesthetic which the exhibition authorities sought to censor. Inspired by the economic use of space in ocean liners, the modular storage system (known as 'casiers') was designed by Corbusier and used here as a space divider. Even the paintings on the walls, in Purist style, were in keeping with the ethos of the machine age.

Corbusier's commitment to the poetics of the utilitarian object could be seen in the clean forms of the interior fittings and furniture, most of which was mass-produced.

As has already been noted, Le Corbusier's ideas relating to interior design were characterized in his book *L'Art décoratif d'aujourd'hui* of 1925, first published as a series of articles in his magazine *L'Esprit nouveau*. Here he argued that interior design and furniture should, like architecture, embrace notions of rationalization and standardization, concepts brought to life in the furniture, storage systems, and paintings (by himself and Fernand Léger) in his 1925 pavilion. Corbusier's ideas for furniture were developed further at the 1929 Salon d'Automne exhibition, at which Charlotte Perriand collaborated with him and his brother Pierre Jeanneret.[26] Their output included modular storage systems to define interior spaces, as well as the celebrated *Chaise Longue* and *Fauteuil Grand Confort* armchair, which have subsequently become design 'classics'.

The wider climate of design politics in France reflected similar oppositions to those evidenced at the 1925 Exposition, set against the retrospective historic encyclopaedism in design for the mass market. The latter, largely uncollected and under-researched on account of its perceived lack of cultural cachet, was unrepresented by the advocacy of the other main factions: the politically radical modernists, collectively represented by the Union des Artistes Modernes (UAM), which sought 'balance, logic, and purity' in its designs, and the more conservative Société des Artistes Décorateurs, from whom the founding members of the UAM had seceded in 1930. Under the directorship of René Herbst the UAM included Le Corbusier, Charlotte Perriand, Robert Mallet-Stevens, Eileen Gray, Louis Sognot, Charlotte Alix, and Pierre Chareau. But, despite the social utopianist commitment of such designers, the market for their design work, like that of many modernists, was largely restricted to the affluent tastes of a metropolitan cultural élite.

Modernism in Fascist Italy

The radical embrace of technological, social, and cultural change by the Futurists so evident in their manifestos of the years immediately following the foundation of the group in 1909 did not, as some art, architectural, and design historians have implied, fade out with the death of a number of its adherents in the First World War. This in part stemmed from Marinetti's close political links with Mussolini and Fascism, but also from the increasing marginalization of the movement in the architectural and design debates of the later 1920s and 1930s. Despite the efforts of Giacomo Balla, Enrico Prampolini, and Fortunato Depero to promote experimental Futurist interior design, furniture, and decorative objects in exhibitions in Rome and Milan in

29 Ufficio Tecnico Olivetti

Olivetti office at Ivrea with *Synthesis* tubular steel furniture, *c.*1935

The cantilevered tubular steel chairs reflect the company's adventurous design policy under Adriano Olivetti who became general manager in 1933. He brought in a number of Rationalist architects and designers before the Second World War, establishing a corporate tradition of design innovation in product, advertising, architectural, interior, and office design. The efficient appearance of the offices seen here perhaps reflects Adriano's experience of scientific management in the United States which he visited on an extended study tour in 1925–6.

1918 and 1919, the most potent expressions of this essentially metropolitan movement were to be found in dramatic graphic representations of futuristic cityscapes and poster designs. None the less, the Futurists' emphatic rejection of Italy's cultural heritage was paralleled in the work of the architects-designers of Group 7, which was formed in 1926 and was the first clear expression of the spirit and aesthetics of the Modern Movement in Italy.[27]

The leading figures of the group were Luigi Figini, Gino Pollini and Giuseppe Terragni. Known as Rationalists, their work embraced the prevailing modernist aesthetic of clean, abstract forms spiritually attuned to modern life, materials, and technology; committed to a spirit of dynamic cultural change, they hoped that Rationalism would be adopted as *the* official Fascist aesthetic. It has been suggested by a number of historians that their failure to achieve such an objective stemmed from their commitment to an internationalist outlook.[28]

The Rationalists gained only few commissions in the public sector, and their reputation is based in part on the critical attentions afforded private commissions in the late 1920s and early 1930s, such as Figini, Pollini, and Luciano Baldessari's interior for the Craja Bar in Milan (1930) or the Parker shop interiors (1934), also in Milan, by Edoardo Persico and Marcello Nizzoli. Magazines such as *Domus*, founded by Gio Ponti in 1928, and *Casabella*[29] provided further vehicles for the dissemination of their work. However, exhibitions provided the most potent means of expression for the avant-garde. The most significant were the Triennali, first held on a two-year cycle in Monza in 1923 under the title 'International Biennale of the Decorative Arts' before moving to Milan ten years later as the 'International Triennale of Decorative and Modern Industrial Art'.[30] These exhibitions provided progressive Italian designers with opportunities not only to put their ideas into practice in a number of one-off commissions but also to exhibit them alongside other leading foreign designers and architects: at the 1930 Triennale functionalist interiors were exhibited by the Berlin Werkbund, including lamps and fittings from the Dessau Bauhaus, chairs by Mies van der Rohe, and equipment by Siemens and AEG; the 1933 Trienale included photographs of CIAM work by Le Corbusier, Gropius, Mies, and Melnikov; and in 1936 the Finnish designer Aino Aalto was awarded a gold medal, the birchwood furniture by her husband Alvar also attracting interest. But the efforts of the Italian Rationalists at the Triennali and other exhibitions to place the modernist agenda within the public domain remained largely unsuccessful [**29**].

However, the Fascist regime's relationship with the modernist aesthetic was by no means as publicly hostile as that which prevailed in Nazi Germany, for there were a number of instances where Rationalist designers were directly involved with design which promoted the Fascist regime, whether at celebratory political exhibitions or Fascist buildings, their interiors and furnishings. The best known example of the latter is Giuseppe Terragni's House of Fascism of 1933–6. However, the difficulties of reconciling a modern, internationalizing aesthetic with the propagandist demands for visually accessible symbols of a political regime steeped in notions of a Roma Secunda were rarely overcome in the 1930s.

Scandinavian Modern

The term 'Scandinavian Modern' as a concept has tended to provide a stylistic umbrella for progressive designing in Sweden, Finland,

Norway, and Denmark. However, whilst there were undoubtedly common features in their aesthetic concerns—the value of craftsmanship, empathy with natural materials, and respect for the creative imagination of the designer—there were in fact clear political and cultural differences.[31]

The Svenska Slödföreningen (Swedish Society of Industrial Design) did much to promote the modernist cause in Sweden, tempered by a historic commitment to preserve the aesthetic and creative qualities of the crafts. Although the Society had been founded as far back as 1845, the demographic changes brought about by widespread migration from the countryside to the cities in the late nineteenth and early twentieth centuries led to a re-evaluation of its social role. As with the Deutscher Werkbund, with which Gregor Paulsson (later the Society's Director) had developed links before the First World War, the Svenska Slödföreningen sought to raise the quality of life by bringing about improved standards of design in everyday life. The Swedish design climate (like the Dutch) was not disrupted by involvement in the First World War and during this period bridges between art and industry continued to be developed. A key manifestation of this alliance of aesthetic awareness, manufacturing processes, and social purpose was the *Home* Exhibition put on by the Society in Stockholm in 1917. Often seen by design historians as a seminal show, it consisted of twenty-three fully furnished interiors, the results of a competition for the design of furnishings, fittings, and equipment for one- and two-bedroomed flats. Prizes were awarded right across the design spectrum, from carpets to domestic appliances. As was apparent in Gunnar Asplund's kitchen-living room, there was something of a compromise between the ethos of crafts production and the simplicity of form and decoration compatible with industrial production. As with

31 Wilhelm Kåge

Praktika I, model X, *Weekend* pattern dinner service for Gustavsberg, 1933

Kåge, the Art Director at the Gustavsberg ceramics factory from 1917 to 1947, introduced this dinner service at a time when there were strong ideological conflicts between functionalist and traditionalist designers in the wake of the austere modernism of the 1930 Stockholm Exhibition. The somewhat stark design lived up to the practicality of its title, with stackable cups and interchangeable lids. It was favoured by the critics and shunned by the public.

Wilhelm Kåge's *Blue Lily* tableware, also produced in 1917 and geared to the pockets of the working-class, such efforts to elevate standards of design in everyday life were in fact generally rejected by consumers in favour of traditional heavier, more decorative products [**30**].

Despite fresh initiatives such as the Svenska Slödföreningen's collaboration with AB Svenska Möbelfabrikerna, one of the largest furniture manufacturers in Sweden, in the production of 'beautiful' mass-produced furniture, there was an ambiguous commitment to modernism during the 1920s. Two major strands of Swedish design had emerged by the end of the decade: the first of these, promoted by the Svenska Slödföreningen, its director Gregor Paulsson, and Gunnar Asplund, was committed to a 'functionalist' aesthetic, blended with the social utopianism of the German modernists; the second embraced an aesthetic rooted in the arts and crafts, an outlook particularly evident in the glass and ceramics industries, the principal exponents of which were the glassmakers Orrefors and the Gustavsberg and Rörstrand porcelain manufactories.

The Stockholm 1930 Exhibition was a clear affirmation of faith in the contemporary spirit and attracted a considerable amount of attention abroad. Given shape by the tripartite alliance of Paulsson, Asplund, and the Svenska Slödföreningen, it sought to ally modern design with a sense of social purpose and presented an agenda relevant to the dynamics of twentieth-century life. Advertising, one of the most potent forms of expression of the latter, was at its core, together with transport, communications, and the urban environment: housing projects, furnished flats, and interiors were displayed alongside school and hospital exhibits, and the modernist commitment to ideas of standard-

32 Alvar Aalto

Paimio armchair, no. 41, 1931/2

Perhaps his most celebrated design, this elegant plywood chair for the Paimio Tuberculosis Sanatorium reveals Aalto's interpretation of the modernist canon. Using a natural material (wood) he endowed it with a more humanizing face than the uncompromising tubular steel essays of many modernists outside Scandinavia. Plywood proved an attractive medium on account both of its price and malleability.

ization and mass-production was highly visible. Opposition to the rather stark and austere qualities of the machine aesthetic which generally prevailed at the exhibition was animated and led to considerable debate between those representing *funkis* [31] (functionalism) and *tradis* (tradition). Amongst the factions which expressed particular concern were the conservative furniture manufacturers, who set out to suggest that standardized designs with a minimum of decoration would lead to unemployment in the industry and that innovation might lead to price inflation.

Following this there were a number of exhibitions during the 1930s which set out a less radical agenda, often in conjunction with the Svenska Möbelfabrikerna, including the display of interiors and furniture by Svenskt Tenn at the Galerie Moderne in 1931 and the Modern Home Exhibition of 1933, where the sharply articulated clarity of space in interior spaces was softened by furniture and equipment which blended modernism with more traditional forms. Natural materials played a far more prominent role, and this more humanizing interpretation of the modernist ideal, which became known as Swedish Modern, was evident in the work of Bruno Mathsson and the Viennese architect-designer Josef Frank, who settled in Sweden in the early 1930s and became increasingly familiar as a propagandist of this 'softer' modernism to a wider international audience through the design press, exhibitions and the export trade.

The more publicly acceptable face of modernism through this greater exploration of natural materials was also evident in other Scandinavian countries in the interwar years. In Finland the Arabia factory[32] established an international reputation for its ceramics and glass products, together with the Karhula glassworks. Individual designers, such as the Finnish architect Alvar Aalto [**32**, **33**], also began to attract international attention. His furnishing of the Paimio Sanatorium, through its custom-designed interiors, fittings, and fitments (embracing everything from lighting fixtures to drinking glasses), has been celebrated as an aesthetic unity. Aalto's sensitive and elegant use of plywood in furniture, architecture, and interior spaces also drew favourable comment and widespread notice in the displays in a number of international exhibitions, including the V and VI Triennali in Milan of 1933 and 1936, the Paris International Exhibition of 1937, and the New York World's Fair and San Francisco Golden Gate Exhibitions of 1939. In published accounts, like those dealing with the later work of the husband and wife team of American designers Charles and Ray Eames, the distinguished work of Alvar's wife Aino has tended to be overshadowed by that of her partner. Their work was marketed internationally through a number of organizations, most notably Artek, which they established with two partners in 1935.

Denmark was also prominent in attracting contemporary international attention in its own interpretation of the modernist aesthetic, particularly through many products of the Royal Copenhagen Porcelain factory, the anthropometrically considered furniture of Kaare Klint, and the austere forms of the silversmith Kay Bojesen, who had been trained by Georg Jensen, a dominant designer in the field. Bojesen was a key figure in the establishment in 1931 of the Copenhagen exhibition gallery and shop Den Permanente, a collective venture where the 'best' of Danish design was put on show—a forerunner of other design propagandist agencies set up elsewhere in Europe after the Second World War.

Britain and modernism

Although modernist design in Britain has received considerable attention from historians, its true significance, as opposed to the wider patterns of production and consumption, has perhaps been overvalued. It is clear that from the late 1920s onwards there was an increasing awareness of avant-garde developments in continental Europe, as reflected by an increasing number of articles devoted to them in magazines such as *The Architectural Review* and *The Architect and Building News*. However, rather as had been the case with the propagandist output of the Bauhaus in Germany, assessment has been influenced in favour of organizations which have left their legacy in archives, exhibition catalogues, and magazines. The Design and Industries Association (DIA), a pale reflection of its spiritual antecedent, the more politically and economically powerful Deutscher Werkbund, never impacted upon British manufacturing industry in the same way as its counterpart had in Germany in the mid-1920s. Many design historians have also argued that the British State was committed to promoting a greater

34 Marion Dorn

Hand-knotted wool rug, Wilton Royal Carpet Factory Ltd., c.1937

Marion Dorn was a leading textile and carpet designer in Britain in the interwar years, gaining important commissions for ocean liners and hotels. Many of her designs contain strong and bold geometric patterns but often also, as here, formalized natural motifs. This perhaps reflected the general unwillingness of her clients, albeit with adventurous taste, to accept the uncompromisingly abstract face of unadulterated modernism.

consciousness of design in manufacturing industry and the domestic marketplace through the setting up of the Gorell Committee by the Governmental Board of Trade, drawing attention to the report on *The Production and Exhibition of Articles of Good Design and Everyday Use* of 1932 as the first of a series of initiatives to promote modern design. The establishment by the Board of Trade of the Council for Art and Industry at the end of 1933 has also been cited. However, it should be remembered that the commissioning and publication of reports and the establishment of a state agency with very limited funding may be interpreted as acts of political defensiveness as much as marked positive intervention. This theme will be returned to in Chapter 6.

Historically, modernism in British design has been built around a number of key individuals and exemplars. For example, Wells Coates's Lawn Road Flats in Hampstead, London, may be seen as an important rallying point. Funded by Molly and Jack Pritchard of the progressive Venesta Plywood and Isokon furniture companies, its early tenants included a number of European modernist emigrés including Walter Gropius, Marcel Breuer, and Lázló Moholy-Nagy. Breuer and Gropius also designed furniture for Isokon before moving on to the United States.

Key exemplars in the public arena included the co-ordinated design policy of London Transport, which was apparent in the commissioning of posters, fabrics for the seating of its underground trains, sign-systems, litter-bins, and other manifestations of its corporate existence. The British Broadcasting Corporation (BBC) has also played a part, not only through the commissioning of leading modernists such as Serge Chermayeff, Wells Coates, and Raymond McGrath to design functional interiors and furniture for the new Broadcasting House in London, erected between 1928 and 1932, but also through the broadcasting of a series of talks and debates on design in daily life in the early 1930s.

However, despite the formation of avant-garde groups such as Unit One, founded in 1933 to promote modern art and architecture in Britain, and the publication of propagandist texts such as Herbert Read's *Art & Industry* of 1934, design which fully endorsed an uncompromisingly modern aesthetic [34] was never widely accepted in a country where the lure of the past, heritage, and Empire found much more visible expression in the widespread mock-Tudor architecture and interiors of the burgeoning suburbs than the sleek modernism of housing for the more wealthy.

Eastern European developments

Certain aspects of the Russian experiment with modernism between the October revolution of 1917 and the Social Realist repression under Stalin have already been addressed (and will be explored further in

Chapter 4). But, as was the case in other European countries, there were also marked tensions in Eastern Europe between those who looked to international developments in design and those who sought to define national identity through association with vernacular, peasant and craft traditions. Such tensions came to the fore in Poland in connection with her display at the Paris Exposition des Arts Décoratifs of 1925, where the craft-oriented, applied arts outlook of the Cracow Workshops was seen by progressive factions as irrelevant to the realities of modern twentieth-century life. After the First World War Warsaw had emerged as the centre of the avant-garde, with many of her designers having studied elsewhere in Europe, including Austria, Germany, and Russia. Aware of the outlook of De Stijl and Russian Constructivism, progressive artists rallied under the title Blok, also the name of their magazine, in 1924. Although lasting only two years, the group was increasingly riven by debates, similar to those which had taken place a few years earlier in Russia, in which the autonomy of artistic creativity and abstract form as agents of social and cultural change in their own right was posited against a commitment to harnessing modern forms to the possibilities of mass-production technology. Many of those representing a more functional outlook became members of Praesens, formed in 1926, an internationally oriented group focused around a journal of the same name. As with many of their modernist counterparts elsewhere in Europe, architecture was seen to be at the root of a social and aesthetic revolution. However, as in many other countries, the number of opportunities to implement the modernist agenda was limited by the prevailing economic conditions. Despite a number of noteworthy experiments in working-class

35 Adolf Syszko-Bohusz and Andrej Pronaszko

Boudoir furniture, Presidential Castle, Wisła, 1930

In the light of contemporary debates between progressive and traditionalist factions, the adoption of an emphatically modern aesthetic for an official commission caused considerable debate in the Polish architectural and design press. This confident use of chromium-plated tubular steel in furniture manufactured in Poland marked the influence of the Praesens group in avant-garde circles. However, such modernist designs were never put into large-scale industrial production and the modernist cause became more muted as the 1930s unfolded.

Hall and cloakroom
furniture, Presidential Castle,
Wisła, 1930

Like **35**, this illustration
featured in the magazine
Architektura i Budownikcwo.
However, the curved wooden
forms of the table end and
the cloak storage area are
rather less uncompromising
in their modernity than the
boudoir furniture, perhaps
revealing the stronger
design personality of the
more conservative Syszko-
Bohusz than his
co-designer Pronaszko,
a member of Praesens.

housing, the majority of achievements were confined to houses and apartments for the wealthy [**35**, **36**] and, as the 1930s unfolded, there was a move away from more 'internationalizing' tendencies towards a position in which the modernist spirit was tempered with a greater acknowledgement of vernacular and regional considerations.

Like the Bauhaus in Germany, educational establishments in Eastern Europe were also important vehicles for the spread of modernism. For example, in Russia the Constructivist outlook of the Moscow Vkhutemas school of design, founded in 1920, provided an important stimulus for the training of artists in industry, closely allied to the desire for cultural regeneration; in Poland the School of Architecture at Warsaw Polytechnic was a powerful advocate of the new spirit in design. Elsewhere there were other educational institutions which were modernizing in their educational philosophy as, for example, the Bratislava School of Applied Arts, founded in Czechoslovakia in 1928 under the directorship of Josef Vydra. Stressing a close relationship between architecture, the applied arts, and industrial production, its aim was to modernize, and raise standards of, domestic manufacture. However, as in Germany a few years earlier, the oppressive political climate of the late 1930s forced the school to close its doors in 1939.

Commerce, Consumerism, and Design

The United States: design and consumption as a way of life

As will be clear from the preceding chapters, a considerable gulf existed between the aspirations of progressive designers, theorists, and reforming organizations and the realities of mass-consumption. In 1920s Europe the attention of the avant-garde was largely directed towards a particular notion of the *Zeitgeist*, or 'spirit of the age', which looked to abstract forms and their symbolic, rather than functional, relationship with modernity together with the economic implications of standardization and mass-production technology. However, in the United States, notions of contemporaneity found material realization in popular perceptions of the power of technology to create exciting new products for mass consumption. There was also an intensification of consumers' levels of material expectation and aspiration through the calculated awakening of their latent desires by manufacturers, designers, and advertisers [**37**]. During this period the American advertising industry was transformed from a relatively unsophisticated medium to one which began to pay far greater attention to possibilities offered by an understanding of consumer psychology. Furthermore, the increasing influence on everyday life of the cinema, gramophone, the automobile, and the large-scale corporation did much to interest the general public in the dramatic utopias envisaged by many industrial designers in exhibitions, such as the Chicago Century of Progress Exhibition of 1933/4 and the New York World's Fair of 1939/40, or even in popularizing texts, such as Norman Bel Geddes's propagandist *Horizons* of 1932.

The First World War had had a considerable effect on US industrial capacity, leading to a doubling of industrial production and significant increases in purchasing power in the following decade. There were other factors which affected such changes: the end of mass immigration in 1921 further stimulated the growth in the mechanization of labour; the expansion of the electricity supply industry alongside a housing boom led to a dramatic increase in the volume and range of domestic appliances which themselves became consumerist symbols stylistically expressive of an ephemeral contemporary lifestyle; and the further adoption of new methods of factory management and the implications of rationalization, standardization, and scientific man-

Detail of 40

This roadside New Jersey restaurant, the first de luxe White Tower outlet, was an archetypal symbol of 1930s American commercial life, the name Marbett's being adopted to give the allusion of competition. The Deco-inspired glazed, curving windows, the striped horizontal decorative, and neon bands had, by the 1930s, a particularly American flavour. The rounded corners reflected the vogue for streamlining, and the prominent signage tower recognized the importance of communicating with passing automobile traffic. The usherettes' 'commander' performed his work on rollerskates.

agement embraced by the Taylorist and Fordist outlook of the pre-First World War era. However, despite such positive stimuli, the market had begun to reach saturation point by the mid-1920s, and the increasing employment of designers to boost sales through the restyling of the appearance of a wide variety of products had only a limited effect on the wider economic horizon, which was conditioned by a severe slump, culminating in the Wall Street Crash of 1929. Perhaps the most significant expression of the economic opportunities afforded by the implementation of a consumer-oriented design policy in the 1920s was in the automobile industry, particularly at General Motors, where the introduction of an annual body change and an increasing choice of colours did much to boost sales and encourage the acceptance of built-in obsolescence.

The growth of the industrial design profession in the United States

The Wall Street Crash of 1929 had a devastating impact on the American economy. It also brought about significant changes in the profession of the industrial designer, which moved away from concerns with the outward styling of products towards a more developed understanding of materials, manufacturing processes, marketing strategies, and consumer aspirations. In business circles, through the agency of such key texts as Roy Sheldon and Egmont Arens's *Consumer Engineering: A New Technique for Prosperity* of 1932,[1] increasing currency was also given to the idea that 'consumer engineering' was a potent means of shortening the cycle of consumption through its emphasis on the fashionability and ephemerality of everyday goods. Otherwise known as 'planned obsolescence', such an outlook was a significant factor in the recovery of the American industrial economy and achieved credibility as an important ingredient of business strategy through its utilization of studies in behavioural psychology and market research.

It was in such a milieu that the first generation of American industrial designers emerged as notable figures: Norman Bel Geddes, Harold Van Doren, Henry Dreyfuss, Lurelle Guild, Raymond Loewy, Walter Dorwin Teague, Harold Van Doren, and Russel Wright were amongst the better known. Since there was no vocationally-oriented training available to them,[2] they came from a diverse range of backgrounds including engineering, illustration, advertising, and theatre design. Many of them, particularly Bel Geddes and Loewy, were adroit self-publicists and were given further credibility by frequent discussions of the potential role of industrial design in the American business magazine *Fortune*. Founded in 1930 by the publisher Henry Luce, in addition to the promotion of design as an important adjunct of business the magazine set high standards in editorial design circles and featured many dramatic covers that articulated the progressive technological spirit with which many members of the American public identified in the 1930s. Norman Bel Geddes, in his highly propagandist and futuristic text of 1932, *Horizons in Industrial Design*, even went so far as to portray industrial design as the true art form of the twentieth century when he wrote:

When automobiles, railway cars, airships, steamships or other objects of an industrial nature stimulate you in the same way that you are stimulated when you look at the Parthenon, at the windows of Chartres, at the Moses of Michelangelo, or at the frescoes of Giotto, you will have every right to speak to them as works of art.

Just as surely as the artists of the fourteenth century are remembered by their cathedrals, so will those of the twentieth be remembered for their factories and the products of those factories.[3]

Raymond Loewy, who was accorded celebrity status after the Second World War through his appearance on the cover of *Time* magazine in 1949 [**38**], surrounded by many of the key products designed in his offices, had also done much to promote a mythical picture of himself as an individual who altered single-handedly the visible form of the material environment of North America. With a keen eye for publicity he was often portrayed in photographs standing on Loewy-designed railway locomotives, seated in Loewy-designed automobiles, or nonchalantly posed in a fictive, laboratory-like, industrial designer's studio, such as that shown at the Metropolitan Museum of Art's Contemporary Industrial Art Exposition of 1934.

38 Raymond Loewy

Cover of *Time* magazine,
31 October 1949

Rather like the pioneering engineers in nineteenth-century Britain, a number of first-generation American industrial designers enjoyed considerable public acclaim. Foremost amongst them was Raymond Loewy who defined 'good design' as 'an upward sales curve'. The constant portrayal of himself in publicity photographs alone in his studio, standing on, sitting in, or using Loewy-designed products played its part in creating the myth of the all-powerful industrial designer. In fact, in 1947, his studio had 150 employees contributing a variety of expertises to the success of the company.

DESIGNER RAYMOND LOEWY
He streamlines the sales curve.

American industrial design: the creation of myths

Much has been written about the visual impact on the everyday material environment exerted by a number of leading designers. As has been suggested, industrial designers themselves[4] did much to celebrate their role in the developing consumerist climate of the 1930s, a tendency subsequently carried further by many historians and museum exhibitions.[5] They were also featured in a number of publications, ranging from articles in the design and business press through to features in the Sunday supplements. Furthermore, leading industrial designers worked for major corporations thus rendering their output highly visible and pervasive: Teague's clients included Kodak, Ford, and Texaco, Loewy's Sears Roebuck, the Pennsylvania Railroad, and Studebaker, Bel Geddes's Standard Gas Equipment Company and General

Motors, and Dreyfuss's Bell Telephone and New York Central Railroad. Vacuum cleaners, cookers, refrigerators [**39**], radios, clocks, shops, packaging, furniture, office equipment, automobiles [**40**], trucks, and passenger coaches, railway locomotives and rolling stock, aircraft interiors and ocean liners were among the almost limitless range of commodities to which they helped give contemporary material expression [**41**].

However, as considered briefly in Chapter 1, an undue emphasis on the notion of 'Pioneers' and the achievements of individual celebrities tends to distort their importance. As Daniel Miller argued in his attack on what he saw to be prevalent design-historical practice in *Material Culture and Mass Consumption* of 1987, this could be seen as 'a form of pseudo art history, in which the task is to locate great individuals such

39 Raymond Loewy

Coldspot Refrigerator for Sears Roebuck, 1935

This was one of Loewy's most celebrated early commissions. Loewy was brought in by Sears Roebuck in 1932 to design a new refrigerator for its range, resulting in the Coldspot of 1935. As can be seen here, it was sold on far more than functional terms: the consumer is asked to 'Study its Beauty'. As well as many innovatory features like rustproof aluminium shelving, its rounded, streamlined form, complete with logo, exudes a spirit of contemporaneity, endowing a domestic object with the same qualities found in automobiles.

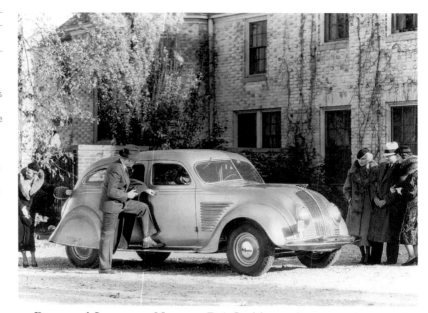

as Raymond Loewy or Norman Bel Geddes and portray them as the creators of modern mass culture'.[6] As an anthropologist Miller was arguing for greater recognition of the transformation of goods in consumption as a means of understanding material culture, but even from a more conventional historical perspective undue emphasis on the individual is somewhat misleading. Harold Van Doren in his 1940 text, *Industrial Design: A Practical Guide*,[7] stressed the importance of specialist collaboration as a means of achieving greater levels of effectiveness in the industrial design profession and suggested that a design team should include a designer, an engineer, a technical expert, a manufacturer, a merchandiser, and others with a knowledge of production planning and channels of distribution. Indeed, in the 1930s the offices of leading industrial designers were often quite sizeable: in 1934 Bel Geddes's office embraced design, drafting, modelling, and technical activities, employing about 30 with outside specialists being brought in as required; by 1937 Teague employed 25; and by the end of the decade the flamboyant Loewy employed 60. None the less, although much of the literature of American industrial design has tended to emphasize the positive achievements of the emergent design profession, this was not a representative picture of the ways in which it was recognized by industry at the time. Harold Van Doren, as late as 1940, was at pains to stress that the designer's position in industry was still tenuous, with the majority of manufacturers either unconvinced by, or unaware of, the efficacy of design as a business tool. He related that many of them were unused to budgeting appropriately for the implementation of a design programme and expected immediate results rather than the necessity of investment in longer-term strategies.

The mass media as stimuli for consumption

Like the highly influential mail-order catalogue, the radio did much to bring about a greater homogeneity in national patterns of taste, especially with the erosion of regional barriers through the formation of national radio networks by NBC and CBS, respectively in 1926 and 1927. During the 1930s the cost of radio purchase had fallen dramatically and small ('baby') radios retailed for as little as $10, making them widely accessible to most income groups. Just as the *Volksempfänger* ('People's Radio') was an important instrument of political propaganda in Germany under the Third Reich, so the radio in the United States was an important advertising medium for the goods and services of large-scale corporations. By the later 1930s radio advertising was highly significant in economic terms, and advertisers competed to promote all kinds of products at prime listening times. These included radios themselves, gramophones, domestic appliances, kitchen equipment, home furnishings, and automobiles, as well as foodstuffs and other domestic goods.

Several writers[8] have suggested strong parallels between the futurist Utopias of popularizing industrial designers such as Norman Bel Geddes and the visions described in contemporary science fiction, a genre which flourished in the late 1920s and early 1930s. The same years also saw the birth of the popular comic-strip heroes Buck Rogers, Flash Gordon, and Superman, and magazines such as Hugo Gernsback's *Amazing Stories, Astounding Stories*, and *Wonder Stories* collectively sold more than 1.5 million issues per annum at the height of their popularity in 1935. Concepts such as speed and change, and the exploration of the possibilities of new materials, together with the development of new modes of transport and appliances were also common to both the more extravagant futures portrayed by Bel Geddes and many science-fiction writers, illustrators, and film makers. There

41 Staubsauger

Champion vacuum cleaner, Type OK, Holland, late 1930s
The dramatic shape of this chromium-plated, streamlined vacuum cleaner reveals the extent to which American-inspired styling had permeated European markets, with the fascination for the aerodynamic forms of contemporary transport designs permeating the domestic arena.

was in addition a mutual faith in the power of technology as a means of transforming society for the better. In similar vein in the early 1930s, in the wake of the Wall Street Crash, the American Technocratic Party briefly commanded public interest through its emphasis on scientists and engineers as the potential agents of future national prosperity rather than those associated with the discredited business and financial sectors. Technological Utopian visions continued to be drawn to the public attention by events such as the Chicago Century of Progress Exhibition of 1933/4 which attracted a total of 48,769,227 visitors over the two seasons of its opening, and the very much larger, in terms of site, New York World's Fair of 1939/40 which enjoyed 44,932,978 visitors.

The original ambitions of the Chicago Century of Progress Exhibition were thwarted by the collapse of the economy, since few foreign countries were in a position to participate. The National Research Council, however, was able to organize a coherent exhibition on the theme of science, demonstrating both past achievements and future possibilities. The sheer volume of visitors attested to the Exhibition's popularity, and the general public were able to wonder at marvels such as the photo-electric cell, to inspect G. F. Keck's *House of Tomorrow* of steel frame and glass walls built around a central core containing utilities, complete with aeroplane hangar and garage, and to travel one-third of a mile on the *Sky Ride* in double-decker 'rocket-cars' suspended between two 628 feet tall towers. In the Exhibition's second season the public were able to view the latest streamlined trains, Union Pacific's M-10,000 (later renamed *The City of Salina*) and Burlington's *Zephyr*. The dramatic streamlined forms of both resulted from the exploration of the dramatic possibilities of new, lightweight materials and constructional techniques and offered new standards of comfort and design. Vividly catching the public imagination, both trains underwent extensive national tours and did much to transform railway-locomotive and rolling-stock design and stimulate popular interest in the streamlining of a wide range of consumer durables during the rest of the decade.

The New York World's Fair of 1939/40, centred on the theme of 'Design for Tomorrow', provided an unrivalled opportunity for industrial designers to harness themselves to the marketing ambitions of the larger American corporations since, as Walter Dorwin Teague remarked in 1939, they were 'supposed to understand public taste and be able to speak in the popular tongue, and because as a profession they are bound to disregard traditional forms and solutions and think in terms of today and tomorrow'.[9] The main themes of the World's Fair echoed the major developments which had been taking place in the 1930s: transportation, science, and communications.

On display were numerous examples of science-fiction as popularist

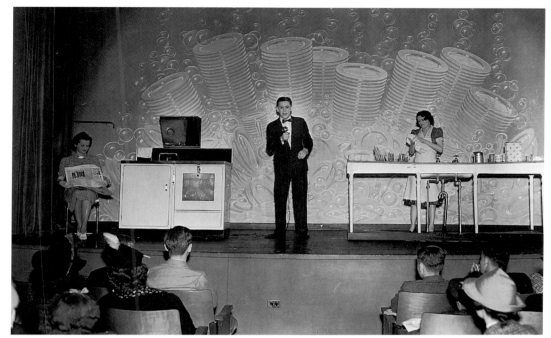

entertainment as, for example, in the Transportation Zone, where visitors could view Raymond Loewy's *Rocketport of the Future*. There, in *son et lumière*, travel from London to New York was portrayed in the form of a passenger rocket being fired from a gun, with a projected journey time of an hour. Moreover, in the Westinghouse Building visitors could marvel at the seven-feet-high robot Elektro and his robotic dog Sparko responding to a variety of spoken commands. Rather more down to earth in the specific promotion of domestic appliances, in the Fair's second season, visitors could follow Westinghouse's 'Battle of the Centuries' in which a dishwashing contest was held between Mrs Drudge, who washed by hand, and Mrs Modern, who used a 1940 model Westinghouse electric dishwasher [**42**]. Although a somewhat crude piece of marketing propaganda, many of the more large-scale and elaborate examples of exhibitions and displays mounted by the larger American corporations were ultimately little more than vehicles for the creation of a future public demand for new ranges of consumer goods, mediated through the agency of industrial designers.

Glimpses into the future were an important part of visitors' experience. A notable exhibit was Henry Dreyfuss's futuristic vision of Democracity, an imagined world of 2039 which was seen daily by 8,000 visitors; in the Consolidated Edison Building visitors could see Walter Dorwin Teague's and Frank J. Roorda's 'City of Light', the world's largest diorama, which portrayed the whole extent of New York from Westchester to Coney Island undergoing in the space of 12 minutes the changes in lighting experienced in 24 hours; inside the Ford Motor

General Motors Exhibit at the New York World's Fair 1939/40, showing envisaged street scene of 1960 with General Motors buses and cars

A major element of the General Motors 'Highways and Horizons' exhibit at the NYWF was Bel Geddes's *Futurama*. One of the most popular draws of the Fair, it featured a panoramic, futuristic vision of the world of 1960 which visitors viewed from moving chairs, as if from a low flying aircraft. Emerging from this seemingly vast perspective, visitors emerged on to this full-scale simulation of a street intersection of 1960 with segregated traffic and pedestrian flows. Needless to say, this particular 'World of Tomorrow' featured exclusively General Motors products.

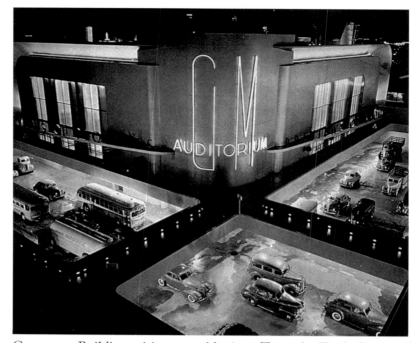

Company Building visitors could view Teague's 'Ford Cycle of Production', whilst outside they could road test Ford, Mercury, and Lincoln-Zephyr automobiles on the spiral 'Road of Tomorrow'. Visited by 5 million over the duration of the exhibition, the most popular exhibit was Norman Bel Geddes's *Futurama* which was located in the General Motors complex in the Transportation Zone. It consisted of a projected world of 1960 seen as if from a low-flying aircraft, with multi-lane highways carrying streamlined vehicles through a landscaped city of low and high-rise buildings, with views of zoned residential, commercial, and industrial districts, experimental farms, hydro-electric power plants, and spectacular countryside. In reality visitors were carried 500 metres by moving ramps and chairs at a simulated speed of 200 miles per hour. Visitors finally arrived at a full-scale intersection of the 1960 city [**43**], where road traffic was segregated from pedestrians, before being invited to inspect the latest General Motors products. Numerous other leading American corporations also promoted themselves in a forward-looking way, including the Radio Corporation of America (RCA), which promoted the new, but still very expensive, medium of television which commenced commercial broadcasting on the opening day of the Fair. Although many of these displays were promoted as glimpses of a future society in which American corporations, aided by the imaginative interpretations of industrial designers, helped to benefit society with a well-designed future they were perhaps more heavily geared towards increased profit margins and market share.

Contemporary critiques of industrial culture

A number of historians have drawn attention to the critics of the ethos of mass-production in contemporary America.[10] Some critics looked back to the past as representing a simpler, more moral existence, contrasting modern capitalist commercial society with a rural way of life. The photographer Doris Ulman, for example, through her early 1930s images of the communities of the Appalachian mountains focused attention on the values inherent in 'folk' culture, sustained by craftsmen and women working within their own cultural traditions. However, other more strident voices launched more direct attacks on contemporary industrial culture in the United States.

Henry Ford, whose assembly-line techniques were increasingly widely applied in factories throughout the industrialized world, was a particular target of those who saw life in the USA as 'shaped by the spiritual dictatorship of machinery, warfare and magazines and newspapers of large circulation'.[11] For example, in *Brave New World* of 1932 Aldous Huxley attacked wide-spread faith in the concepts of the large-scale and standardization which he saw as major ingredients of what he feared would become a loveless and emotionally arid society, a society in which Fordism was the dominant religion, with Ford replacing God and Ford's autobiography the Bible. The cinema also carried a number of anti-technological messages in films such as Fritz Lang's chilling vision of *Metropolis* of 1926, a hostile, futurist city in which its inhabitants were enslaved and dominated by technology; many of the sets were directly inspired by the Manhattan skyline which Lang had seen on a visit to New York in 1924. Over a decade later, in Chaplin's *Modern Times* of 1936, the relentless drive for ever-increasing efficiency in the production line (which Chaplin had experienced at first-hand at the Ford Factory in Detroit) eventually resulted in the insanity of the worker.

There were also critics within the wider reaches of the design world, perhaps the most articulate of whom was Richard Buckminster Fuller.[12] Very much opposed to what he saw as the complicity of industrial designers in the superficial styling and built-in obsolescence of an ever-increasing range of consumer goods, he had sought increasingly to propose design solutions that derived maximum human advantage from the minimum use of materials and energy. He wrote on this 'Dymaxion' theme and produced prototypes for his highly revolutionary Dymaxion cars (from 1933) and bathrooms (from 1930) [142], although for a variety of reasons these failed to find acceptance with manufacturers. Unwilling to compromise his beliefs, he remained highly sceptical of the grandiose claims of the burgeoning industrial-design profession to be able to take on everything from a fountain pen to an ocean liner. Fuller viewed industrial design as a close adjunct of advertising and marketing and, reflecting on such an outlook in the late 1950s, he declared;

industrial design is a very tarnished affair . . . I assure you that no aircraft company will let an industrial designer through its engineering front door. Industrial designers are considered to be pure interior and exterior decorators. And yet, I've listened to industrial designers assert that they designed the steamship, *United States*. If you were to exhibit schematically all the items that the industrial designers created for the *United States*, you would have sailing down New York Harbour an array of window curtains, chairs, paint clouds and bric-à-brac floating in space, with nothing to really hold it together. To assert that these men designed the *United States* could not have been more dishonest.[13]

The impact of European design

American interest in European design in the interwar years was bolstered by a number of European immigrant designers including Joseph Urban and Paul Frankl from Austria, Gustav Jensen from Denmark, Peter Muller-Munk from Germany, George Sakier, William Lescaze, and Raymond Loewy from France, and Paul Lazlo from Hungary. Furthermore the American Designers' Gallery and Contempora Inc. were both established in the later 1920s in order to promote modern decorative arts and design in the United States, much along the lines of European groups such as the Wiener Werkstätten and the Werkbunds in Austria and Germany or the Société des Artistes Décorateurs in France. Although the activities of such American propagandist organizations were seriously curtailed by the Wall Street Crash of 1929 they did much to foster a new climate for modern design in the United States in the years leading up to the Second World War. Far more significant, however, was the international Exposition des Arts Décoratifs et Industriels which was held in Paris in 1925.

Paris 1925: luxury, elegance, and commerce

As has been seen in connection with the New York World's Fair of 1939/40, international exhibitions were important vehicles for the promotion of national interests, whether propagandist or economic, most particularly for the host nation, whose industries and national displays assumed the greatest significance. The Paris Exposition des Arts Décoratifs et Industriels of 1925 was very much a matter of French national prestige since its explicit aim was to re-establish her preeminence as the leading force in the decorative arts. Even before the outbreak of hostilities in 1914 France's economic status in this respect had been increasingly called into question as a result of the growing international industrial competitiveness of other countries.

For various reasons—most particularly the intervention of the First World War—the idea of mounting an international exhibition to follow up the 1900 Paris Exposition Universelle was not realized until 1919 when it featured as part of the French postwar programme of industrial development and economic recovery. Sponsored by the

Ministries of Commerce and Fine Arts, the projected postwar exhibition was intended to encourage the establishment of a modern design vocabulary that would blend traditional French expertise in the design of luxury goods with the realities of modern mass-production technology. None the less, the kind of modernism embraced by the vast majority of French products and room settings was far from the ideas being discussed by Muthesius and others at the Deutscher Werkbund before the First World War. Apart from the austere modernism of Le Corbusier's Pavillon de l'Esprit Nouveau (discussed in Chapter 2, see **28**) a quality of unbridled luxuriousness and élitism characterized a significant proportion of the French exhibits, many of which were out of the financial reach of the everyday consumer. As a result the exhibition engendered a considerable amount of criticism. None the less, as will be discussed below, many of the stylistic characteristics on display, subsequently known as Art Deco, were widely influential in the United States, and made their presence firmly felt in many fields of design in Britain and elsewhere.

One of the pavilions at the Exposition which attracted most attention was Jacques-Emil Ruhlmann's Pavilion of a Wealthy Collector [**44**]. Even the title confirmed Ruhlmann's close links with high fashion, high prices, exclusivity, and a premium on craftsmanship rather than industry. Lacquered furniture by Dunand, decorative iron railings by Edgar Brandt, a blue and pink carpet by Gaudissard, and the celebrated exoticism of Jean Dupas's oil painting *The Parakeets* all sustained such an impression.

As at the Paris 1900 international exhibition, some of the most memorable displays a quarter of a century later were located in the pavilions of the great Parisian department stores, all of which were situated on favourable sites. Their presence in the French section together with the enticing Rue des Boutiques on the Pont Alexandre III, helped sustain the desired image of Paris as a city of shopping.[14] This street contained forty shop displays of haute couture, fashion accessories, perfumes, and other luxury goods.

The lavish displays of the Parisian department stores were driven by their desire to capitalize on a growing public interest in contemporary design. This spirit of commercial entrepreneurship had already brought about the establishment of their own design ateliers: 'Primavera' (under the directorship of René Guilleré and his wife Charlotte Chaucet-Guilleré) had been established at Printemps in 1912, La Maîtrise (under Maurice Dufrène) at Galeries Lafayette in 1921, Pomone (under Paul Follot) at Bon Marché in 1923, and Studium Louvre (under Étienne Kohlmann and Maurice Matet) at the Magasins du Louvre in 1924 [**45**].

The official desire to overwhelm visitors with the excellence of French decorative arts was revealed by the amount of space allocated to the French sections, which amounted to about two-thirds of the whole 57-acre site. Many of the most dazzling French displays were located in the displays of the Société des Artistes Décorateurs. Entitled 'Reception Rooms and Private Apartments of a French Embassy', it occupied twenty-five fully furnished rooms set round a three-sided courtyard. The Smoking Room by Jean Dunand, with its Cubist-inspired forms and decorative motifs, stepped silver ceiling set off against highlights of red lacquer, and wall facings of black lacquer, attracted considerable attention. However, its relevance to the average consumer was restricted to glamorous reinterpretations in Hollywood film sets, modernistic cinema foyers, and other public spaces intended to impress their occupants [**46**], such as restaurants, the interiors of ocean liners [**47**], or the foyers of important business enterprises.

Paris 1925 and the United States

Although not a participant at the 1925 Paris Exposition des Arts Décoratifs et Industriels,[15] the United States appointed a commission of over a hundred representatives drawn from a wide range of industries and institutions to visit it and report on the state of contemporary European design. Charles Richards, Director of the American Association of Museums, headed the commission and subsequently organized a touring exhibition of designs drawn from the 1925 exhibition which was shown in nine museums in the USA, commencing with the Metropolitan Museum in New York. Drawing on diverse sources such as Fauvism, Cubism, Purism, and African art, the Art Deco style was characterized by flat, geometric abstract motifs used in a decorative manner, often deriving from sunbursts, lightning flashes, fountains, flowers, and other organic forms. Such abstract forms soon became fashionable, and the style was actively promoted by leading stores throughout the country, many of whom also mounted exhibitions.[16] In New York, artists such as Erté and Raoul Dufy designed for the Amalgamated Silk and Onondaga Companies, and firms such as Cheney Brothers and F. Schumacher & Co marketed French textiles alongside other ranges.

45 André Fréchet

Lahalle and Lavard, reception hall for the Studium-Louvre Pavilion, Exposition des Arts Décoratifs et Industriels, Paris, 1925

Many of the qualities found in Ruhlmann's pavilion (**44**) are reflected here, but at more affordable prices. The Studium-Louvre was one of the major Parisian department stores with its own decorating studios. The 1925 Exposition offered them an unprecedented opportunity to show potential clients the fullest display of designs which could grace the fashionable Art Deco home.

Architecture and interiors, particularly in terms of detailing such as metalwork, lettering and signage, lighting and the geometric patterning of floor and wall surfaces, brought the Deco style very much to the public eye in the major cities of North America. In New York, William Van Alen's Chrysler Building of 1928–31, with its dramatic stainless steel cladding and roofline, external geometric frieze of wheels, radiator caps, and abstracted eagles, and striking lobby interior typified most vividly a stylistic trend which manifested itself throughout Manhattan. In Washington many Government buildings, particularly in the Federal Triangle, also adopted the style, which was equally widespread in the West, as in Los Angeles, or in the south, as in Miami Beach.

The Deco influence was also widely seen in interiors connected with the leisure and entertainment industries. The Rockefeller Center complex in New York provided an almost unprecedented opportunity for the exploration of the Deco style, particularly in the interiors of Radio City Music Hall (RCMH). The elaborative decorative schemes were overseen by Donald Deskey who did much to link European design with practice in the United States, having studied in Paris in the early 1920s and visited the 1925 Exposition. He collaborated with a number of leading American designers, painters, and sculptors in the design of the foyer, auditorium, smoking and powder rooms, and other public spaces, contributing designs for some of the wallpapers and cov-

46 Jaap Gidding

Foyer of the Tuschinki Cinema, Amsterdam, 1918–21

Superficially Gidding's dramatic and highly colourful designs have much in common with the decorative ethos of contemporary French decorative arts and the glitz of 1920s Hollywood film sets. However, the expressive possibilities afforded by the cinema's unified external and ornamental decorative schemes also had more in common with the expressive work of the Amsterdam School, a progressive strand of Dutch design opposed to the greater commitment to a modernist machine age aesthetic of contemporary De Stijl architects and designers.

47 Stanislaw Brukalski

Interior of the America
Bar, on the ocean liner *MS
Bathory*, 1936

The interior of this transatlantic
liner reveals the gradual
elision of the modernist and
'applied arts' factions in 1930s
Polish design. Here Brukalski,
who had been involved in the
more radically modern
factions of Polish design
in the later 1920s and early
1930s, perhaps
acknowledged the more
decorative tendencies of the
nationalistic Ład group which
drew heavily upon folk art
motifs and patterns.
None the less, the overall ethos
of the bar was more in line with
wider international
tendencies in the decorative
arts, reflecting the dual
role of the vessel as a
national carrier serving an
international clientele.

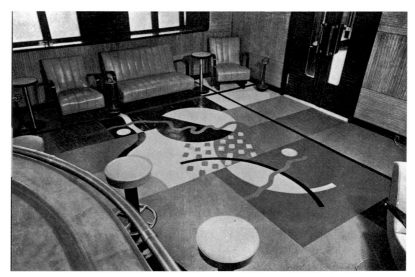

erings, carpets, furniture, and lighting designs. Many of the interiors exhibited a distinctly Deco (or Moderne as its American derivate was often referred to) flavour in their exploration of the decorative possibilities of aluminium, bakelite, mirrors, glass, lacquer, and even gold-leafed ceilings, all of which were reminiscent of the work of the French artistes-décorateurs of the 1920s from which such an outlook ultimately derived.

Just as the 1925 Paris Exposition was an important influence on RCMH, many of the more lavish ensembles can be seen to have exerted an influence on Hollywood film sets, which in turn did much to popularize the Deco style. For example, Van Nest Polglase designed the set for the Paramount film *The Magnificent Flirt* of 1928 which showed a number of interiors which were amongst the earliest examples of Art Deco on film. Studio publicity of the time proclaimed that the film showed 'the latest idea in interior architecture for the modern home'. Similar trends could be seen in many other film sets through the later 1920s and 1930s, including Richard Day's designs for MGM's *The Kiss*, starring Greta Garbo, of 1929 [**48**]. Furthermore, Cedric Gibbons, the leading Hollywood Art Director of the time, visited the 1925 exhibition, and its direct influence could be seen, in his design for the fountain scene from MGM's *Our Blushing Brides* of 1930. By the end of the decade there were about 40 million regular cinema-goers, underlining its potency as a medium for influencing patterns of taste and the consumption of particular products and lifestyles.

Wider patterns of taste: historical diversity

Not only was film instrumental in the promotion of luxurious Art Deco settings; it also drew on a huge variety of styles, periods, and geographical origins, ranging from ancient Egypt, Greece, and Rome through to the Middle Ages, the Renaissance and the Elizabethan era, and onwards to the present day. American cinemas themselves also took on a plethora of styles in their highly striking interiors, often competing for effect with the elaborate celluloid fantasies seen on screen.[17]

Stylistic diversity was also reflected in the homes, furniture, and furnishings of the majority of Americans. Although they willingly embraced notions of contemporaneity in the streamlined forms of their domestic appliances, kitchen equipment, and automobiles, admired the strikingly modern designs for public transport systems as seen in aircraft such as the Douglas DC-3, trains such as Dreyfuss's Twentieth Century Limited or Loewy's Greyhound bus, they generally looked to traditional styles in the decoration of their homes. The ubiquitous mail-order catalogues of the period unequivocally underline this affirmation of the traditional in the home. Manufacturers were generally conservative in their outlook, drawing on the past for commercial survival in the present, and consumers could purchase a variety of styles including Tudor, Queen Anne, Chippendale, and Louis XVI.

In their 1945 book *Tomorrow's House: A Complete Guide to the Home-Builder*, the modernist propagandists George Nelson and Henry Wright lamented the sentimental attachment of home-owners to the past. Considering the 'Home as a Psychological Fact' they wrote:

Home, in the American dream, is a quaint little white cottage, shyly nestled in a grove of old elms or maples, bathed in the perfume of lilacs, and equipped with at least one vine-covered wall.[18]

They also drew attention to such characteristics as 'a steep gabled roof', 'tiny dormers', 'shutters in soft blue or green', 'a replica of an oil lamp, wired for electricity', and 'a four-poster bed' and concluded that if people pursued this dream they would get either 'a cheap imitation or an outrageously expensive fake'.

The period styles in which many houses were built in the 1920s and 30s reflected a similar spirit of retrospection, although taking on a richer diversity and choice. As will be considered in the following chapter, a number of these styles were identified as specifically American in their origins and were promoted by a number of organizations intent on lessening dependency on European models through the establishment of a distinctive American style. For example, the restoration of Williamsburg in 1926, funded by the Rockefellers, reinforced interest in the Colonial style [**133**]; the Spanish Colonial style, deriving from traditions rooted in the Southwest, was also popular. The 'English Style', replete with half-timbering and pitched roof, also caught the imagination, and in the suburbs of Philadelphia German farmhouses were renovated.[19] By the late 1920s speculative builders were producing developments on a significant scale which were centred on specific historical themes.

Commerce and consumerism in Britain

Historians of design have often played down the popular and commercially successful in the interwar years, following the line of contemporary design reformers who have suggested that cheap historicist or modernistic mass-produced items were often purchased as a result of a lack of education in matters of taste. Yet for the consumer or user their forms and decoration were often laden with meaning and associations, whether or not Pevsner in his *Enquiry into Industrial Art* of 1937 condemned them as part of the 90 per cent of industrial products that he adjudged to be 'artistically objectionable', whether or not they were designed by a named designer or simply copied from, or variants on, long-standing precedents. With the exception of museums such as the Geffrye Museum in London or site museums such as Ironbridge Gorge or Beamish examples of this kind are rarely collected by museums, let alone located in the context of 'ordinary' rooms. Such objects are generally seen as artistically deficient rather than culturally significant; documentation concerning their use by consumers is hard to come by; often material concerning their design, production, and distribution has often simply been thrown away. However, research[20] into such areas has been slowly developing, with a steady stream of publications about methodology and possible approaches.[21] However, highly commercial styles often signify more than the fact that they are ephemeral trends and, in the case of Tudor, Elizabethan, and Jacobean formulae, can be seen to embrace notions of national identity in design, as will be discussed in Chapter 4. Similarly, the floral patterns adorning countless tea-cups and furnishing textiles may be interpreted as communicators of an 'essential' Englishness rather than summarily dismissed as hackneyed designs.

The Art Deco style exerted a significant impact in Britain across many design media and was a highly commercial style, including many items at the cheap, novelty end of the market. Its flat, coloured, geometric patterns could be found in the 'sunrise' motifs (contemporary symbols of health) on thousands of wooden garden gates, front doors, gable ends, packaging, fabric designs, carpets, tableware, jewellery, and other ornamental products. Its zig-zag, chevron, and other geometric patterns could also be found in typography, posters, and shop-fronts. The Deco vocabulary was widely adopted in both interior and exterior designs for cinemas, particularly those associated with Oscar Deutsch's Odeon chain. Other notable commissions included Ronald Atkinson's 1932 foyer of the Daily Express Building in Fleet Street, London, Oliver Bernard's foyers for the Strand Palace Hotel of 1929–30 and the J. Lyons and Company Ltd's New Oxford Street Corner House in central London, and Wallis, Gilbert, and Partners' Hoover factory in West London of 1931–2. There were also a number of potteries producing a wide range of artifacts, including tea and coffee services, bowls, vases, and ornaments at prices which many could afford. Among the more notable manufacturers were Carlton Ware, Foley Potteries, A. E. Gray, and Shelley Potteries [49]; women designers, including Susie Cooper, Clarice Cliff, and Charlotte Rhead, were also prominent in the field.

Other sites of commercial display: England and France

Barometers of commercial production and consumer interest in Britain may be found in trade catalogues and periodicals, as well as the range of home-making magazines which grew considerably after the war. The vast range of exhibits at the annual British Industries Fairs (which commenced on an annual basis in 1915 as a manufacturers' 'shopwindow') and the displays and show houses at the increasingly popular *Daily Mail* Ideal Home Exhibitions are also revealing. The latter commenced in 1908, with 160,000 visitors in its first year, and nearly 700,000 even in the depression of the early 1930s. In the 1950s and 1960s there were regularly more than 1 million visitors, tailing off in the later 1970s and early 1980s to an average of about 900,000. Many of the exhibitions were widely reported in the media, and catalogues and related ephemera, including visual material, are extant.[22]

In France the idea of domestic management caught the public imagination. Martine Segalen, social anthropologist, sociologist, and historian has described the Salon des Art Ménagers (SAM, Exhibition

49 Eric Slater

Vogue shape teaset, Shelley Potteries, Longton, 1930

The geometric forms and flat, colourful pattern of this popular teaset reflect the influences of both Cubism and Art Deco. Slater had been made design director in 1928, and through the introduction of a number of Deco-inspired designs, including *Mode*, *Eve*, and *Regent* in the early 1930s, firmly established Shelley as a popularizer of contemporary French styles.

of Domestic Science) held as public exhibitions in Paris between 1923 and 1983 as

the most vocal institution providing the French popular classes with information, norms, and education on all aspects of housing furnishing, home decoration and domestic management. As a producer and consumer society developed, in which producers undertook to develop goods geared towards the home, the SAM occupied an instrumental position between those who manufactured domestic goods and those who were expected to buy them.[23]

It began in the Champ de Mars in Paris in 1923 as the 'Salon des Appareils Ménagers' with a clear focus on domestic appliances, attracting over 100,000 visitors, and moved to the Grand Palais in 1926 where it was retitled the 'Salon des Arts Ménagers'. In the same year Paulette Bernège founded the Institut d'Organisation Ménagère (Institute for Household Organization) and in 1932 was a key figure in the establishment of the Ligue d'Organisation Ménagère (League for Household Organization). The prime mover behind the Salons themselves was Jules-Louis Breton, who had been Under-Secretary for State for inventions during the war, and who also coined the term 'arts ménagers'. Both Breton and Bernège were important figures in what was essentially an educational movement, one which attracted increasing public interest. (In Britain perhaps the nearest equivalent was the Council for Scientific Management in the Home—COSMITH—which had begun in 1931.) By the 1930s the Salons had embraced the exhibition of furniture and room settings, and the work of members of the UAM (Union des Artistes Modernes) was frequently featured. In 1939 the Salon attracted 608,000, a figure which rose in the postwar years to more than 1,400,000 in 1955. However, as patterns of consumption changed and marketing and retailing mechanisms became increasingly sophisticated, the socio-educational role of the Salons was diminished, leading to their final demise as public events in 1983.

Design and
National Identity

Paris 1925 and 1937: tradition, vernacular design, and national identity

The study of international exhibitions reveals much about the designing of national identity,[1] although the design and content of national pavilions were often constructed to portray particular facets of nation states [**50**] or political regimes. As such they may be seen as bearers of myths rather than accurate reflections of more deep-seated national traits. Having examined in Chapter 3 the intended focus of the projection of French decorative arts and craftsmanship at the 1925 Exposition des Arts Décoratifs et Industriels in Paris, we turn now to other dimensions of this and its 1937 successor.

Although the 1925 exhibition regulations had stipulated that only 'articles of modern aspiration and real originality should be shown', a stipulation which led to a certain amount of confusion before the exhibition and a considerable amount of criticism afterwards, a number of nations sought to stress their artistic heritage as a continuing and important ingredient of their current identity. Just as the French artistes-décorateurs had acknowledged past styles and traditions in their lavish room settings, furniture, and furnishings, so a number of other countries looked to their artistic roots in peasant and folk art traditions as an important feature of their exhibits. This was true of the Polish displays which were underwritten by the Polish government, eager to promote a positive national identity on the international stage.

Founded in Cracow in 1901, the Polish Applied Art Society (Towarzystwo Polska Sztuka Stosowana) had sought to identify specifically Polish characteristics in design as a unifying force in the face of the complex political and boundary shifts with which Poland was faced.[2] This nationalizing impetus was revived by the formation in 1913 of the Cracow Workshops, which also vigorously promoted a Polish style rooted in vernacular and peasant traditions. After the end of the First World War the aesthetic and ideological aspirations of Cracow School designers were increasingly influential, culminating in their dominance in the national exhibit at the Paris Exposition of 1925. The Polish Pavilion, designed by Józef Czajkowski, contained colourful murals (which drew upon peasant festivals and Slavic myths for

Detail of 60

50 Y. Utida and Y. Matsui

Interior of the Japanese Pavilion at the New York World's Fair, 1939

The Japanese Pavilion, set in a traditional Japanese garden, laid particular emphasis on the country's cultural heritage. The Grand Hall shown here exhibits many of the artistic traits associated with her past, styles increasingly recognized in the West since the mid-nineteenth century. Such a projection of national identity, complete with tea ceremony and kimono-clad attendants, avoided the political and economic problems engendered by Japanese manufacturers' cheap imitation of many western products in the 1920s and 1930s.

their subject matter), tapestries, furniture, and fittings which were every bit as coherent as the ensembles of the French artistes-décorateurs [**51**, **52**]. Reflecting the Arts and Crafts origins of many of the main exhibitors and wedding the vernacular with the contemporary, the display attracted favourable attention from the Exposition juries.

At the 1937 Exposition Internationale des Arts et des Techniques Appliqués à la Vie Moderne the importance of national projection through design was especially evident in the striking propagandist architecture and displays of the German, Soviet, and Italian Pavilions.[3] Josep Lluis Sert's Pavilion of the Spanish Republic, its very presence a symbol of anti-Fascism, was also highly politicized. The displays of the Fascist and totalitarian pavilions stressed industrial and technological achievements alongside overt visual propaganda reinforcing the mythological constructs which tied the present to long-standing traditions and heritage. The Spanish Pavilion, on the other hand, unambiguously laid stress on art and culture as powerful expressions of a free and democratic state.

In such a highly charged political and propagandist context it is unsurprising that some countries at the 1937 Exposition actually sought to suppress peasant handicraft in their displays, considering that they were symptomatic of a 'backward' past rather than stimulating contemporary reinterpretations of tradition. However, popular, peasant,

51 Józef Czajkowski

Chair for the office in the Polish Pavilion at the Paris Expositions des Arts Décoratifs et Industriels Modernes, 1925

The design of this chair embraced the beliefs of the Cracow School which sought to further the idea of a Polish national style, drawing inspiration from the forms and decorative motifs of peasant art. Although the carving of the arms and the patterned textile on the seat and back looked to vernacular traditions, it should not be seen as literally retrospective. For its designers it represented the modern re-affirmation of a culture which had been under political threat since before the Treaty of Versailles in 1919.

and folk art featured in more than sixty pavilions. A number of exhibiting countries chose to set such work within a modernizing context, whilst others sought to stress unambiguously national, and thus indigenous, characteristics in their crafts [**53**, **54**]. The Hungarian,[4] Rumanian, Polish, and Portuguese pavilions exhibited the most vital displays of peasant art. The Polish displays, set within a modernist setting, endorsed the vernacular as an important aspect of national culture. In addition to the luxury goods displayed by French designers in the main pavilions, French regional and historical styles were also shown in the Centre Régional. The more exotic decorative styles drawn from the different cultures of the French colonies could be seen in the Île de Cygnes, which included exhibits from French Equatorial Africa and the Cameroons, as well as Indochinese craft shops and Moroccan markets.

British identity in design: retrospection and ruralism

In the first sentence of her 1989 book on *British Design: Image and Identity*, the Dutch design historian Frederique Huygen characterized certain aspects of the projection of Britain:

British design: Burberry raincoats, floral interior fabrics, Jaguars, Shetland pullovers, Dunhill lighters, and Wedgwood pottery. Tradition, respectability and quality. This sort of Britishness forms but part of this book, for there are many more faces to British design than the clichés listed above.[5]

Writing over forty years earlier, John Gloag, a tireless campaigner for the acceptance of a modernist aesthetic in British industry, had identified another range of clichés in *The English Tradition in Design* when he railed against what he perceived as a false tradition in twentieth-century English design. He felt it was

submerged by a wave of faking and imitation, and the real English genius was marked by a false 'Olde England'—a shoddy and flimsy form of taste which still persists. Only very slowly is it being realised that 'ye olde England' is neither real nor English but a hollow sham.[6]

Whether a 'false' tradition or not, like the clichés identified by Huygen, 'Olde England' has played a significant role in the sociology of British design,[7] whether reflected in the style of housing and furnishings purchased by millions in the interwar years, or in many aspects of the official projection of British values, history, and heritage at home and abroad. The Tudor world evoked from the latter half of the nineteenth century onwards was emphatically rural in its composition. Many writers, commentators, and others believed that the true essence of England was to be found in the countryside, rather than the false, essentially 'un-English' values of urban life.[8] This emphasis on a pre-industrial heritage was also used in a number of international exhibitions for the official projection of Britain, from the Paris Universelle Exhibition of 1867 onwards. As Britain's industrial leadership came under increasing threat from other countries in the later nineteenth century, so it was considered important to display her imperial powers as significantly predating the industrialization process.

Such a retrospective profile continued to be developed in the public arena in the early twentieth century and was celebrated at the British Empire Exhibition held at Wembley in 1924/5. It is not an exhibition to which historians of British design[9] have devoted a great deal of attention, despite the fact that it covered 216 acres of North London, involved an expenditure in excess of £4.5 million, and attracted 17.5 million visitors in its first season.[10] This contrasts with the considerable design-historical attention devoted to the Paris Exposition Internationale des Arts Décoratifs et Industriels which attracted one-third of the number of visitors and was confined to a site of a quarter of the size. It should be remembered also that views of the declining potency of the British Empire as a force of popular significance between the wars were heavily influenced by writers such as Robert Graves, George Orwell, and other intellectuals whose opinions have been interpreted as widely representative.[11] The British Empire Exhibition at Wembley provided an important vehicle for reinforcing or moulding contemporary attitudes, since much of the imagery on display utilized archetypal symbols of power and authority and constantly evoked Britain's historical and imperial heritage. For many, in the economically turbulent climate of the 1920s, trading within the British Empire offered a route to future economic prosperity. In support of this idea the state-funded Empire Marketing Board (1926–33)

52 Józef Czajkowski and Wojciech Jastrzebowski

Office interior in the Polish Pavilion, Paris, 1925

Planned as an office for a government official this ensemble by leading members of the Cracow School represented a strong affirmation of national identity. In common with parallel debates in other countries, the display attracted hostility inside Poland where progressive factions argued for an unambiguously modern and international aesthetic rather than what was interpreted as passéist national romanticism. Such attacks were largely generated by those associated with Blok, a group founded in Warsaw in 1924.

53

The Tractor, textile design by
V. Maslov, USSR, late 1920s

The overt political message
of this textile print celebrated
the national importance of
agricultural progress as an
element of Stalinist ideology
and can be linked to the
heroization of the agricultural
worker in many posters of the
1930s. In line with the political
outlook of the late 1920s and
1930s such evocative cultural
propaganda paved the way for
Socialist Realism, spelling the
demise of the less obviously
didactic avant-garde forms of
the Constructivists.

displayed constantly changing displays of striking posters in prominent sites in the major towns and cities of Britain as a means of promoting imperial trade.

The conservative, historicizing tastes of the British consumer were
evident in many parts of the Wembley exhibition, including the Palace
of Industry, where the section devoted to furniture, floor coverings,
and textiles was seen to exemplify the belief that 'all modern decoration
must be more or less based on tradition'.[12] Whilst by no means all
rooms were devoted to past British styles and traditions, the Palace of
Arts contained a historical résumé of rooms decorated in the styles of
1750, the 1820s, 1852, 1888, and 1924, and the furniture and interior
design firm Waring & Gillow display rooms included a Georgian
library; many other traditional forms were to be found in furniture and
furnishings of the gas and electricity exhibits. Similar historicist inclinations were in evidence at the annual *Daily Mail* Ideal Home
Exhibitions, the British Industries Fairs, and in the majority of furniture stores. This sense of retrospection and identification with a pre-
industrial past was also evident in the many hundreds of thousands of
Mock-Tudor houses which were erected in the rapidly growing suburbs of the interwar years, replete with barge-boarded gables, leaded
windows, and heavy oak front doors with coloured stained-glass insets
of Elizabethan galleons and other references to bygone eras [**55**]. Much

of the furniture in the living areas of such houses also exuded a similar sense of historical retrospection, blending with wood-panelled halls and dining rooms, fireplaces with inglenook seats, and Jacobean style dining suites with machine-cut and stamped mouldings.

Another important aspect of British national identity promoted abroad related to leisure and recreation, a feature which was prominent in the British Section at the Monza exhibition of 1930 [**56**]. *The Studio* commented that 'the Englishman invented modern sport and stands supreme in the design and execution of its appliances, both for field and games, and the present group [of objects] symbolises a few of the things that find their way into a man's dressing room today'.[13] Included were golf clubs, tennis rackets, and boxing gloves, 'all of the finest workmanship', exhibited by Lillywhites, brightly coloured blazers by Ryder and Amies of Cambridge, and a sporting gun by Greener. The leather and sporting goods shown at the Exhibition were favourably reviewed. Sporting and leather goods were also singled out for praise at the British Industrial Art Exhibition held in Copenhagen the following year.

At the much larger Paris International Exhibition of 1937 the official British display concentrated on the theme of the English week-end, reinforcing the idea endorsed by a number of contemporary

54

Central Russian Folk Art, USSR Pavilion, Paris Internationale Exposition, 1937

Such traditional designs were at the root of a vernacular, peasant culture which the State sought to promote alongside the wider heroization of workers on the land.

Such oak furniture with 'an
authentic dark Antique finish'
was firmly associated with
an incontrovertibly British
historic past. Widely
affordable through hire
purchase schemes, it reflected
the retrospective outlook of
many British consumers in
the interwar years. A natural
counterpart to the countless
leaded-windowed
mock-Tudor houses which
were a significant feature of
speculatively built suburbia
of the 1930s, such designs
accorded with leanings
towards an economic
future vested in the British
Empire, rather than the
more competitive markets
of Europe.

writers and critics that the countryside was the essence of England.
Widely represented in contemporary photographs, paintings, posters,
and poems, the countryside was also seen as a location for shooting,
hunting, walking, and entertaining. In the British Pavilion the photo-
mural display included scenes of harvesting, ploughing, village cricket,
country houses, cathedrals, and landscape views. As Christopher
Hussey remarked in the Exhibition Catalogue:

Though circumstances may compel him to live and work in cities, the
Englishman is still in most cases a countryman at heart to the extent of prefer-
ring to take his pleasure in the country.

When he can afford it, he has his own weekend cottage, his ideal being a picturesque old yeoman's dwelling with an old-fashioned garden. There he can,
for two days a week, indulge the romantic dream that he is a country gentleman and be refreshed by the complete contrast to his everyday life.[14]

But, as at Monza and Copenhagen and other British exhibitions of
the period, at the Paris Exhibition there was also a considerable
emphasis on the significant display of sporting goods and equipment.
Cricket, golf, tennis, fishing, football, and darts were seen as embodi-
ments of the English spirit and heritage. Sport had also played an
important, though unofficial, part in imperial policy by exporting
notions of a 'British way of life' and 'fair play': cricket was a particular
conveyor of such ideals, bringing with it notions of green lawns, after-
noon tea, and reminiscences of the archetypal village green beside the
church. All such ideas represented a projection of national identity distinct from the overt and aggressive propagandist outlook of a number
of other countries at the 1937 Exhibition, especially Germany and the
USSR. As was remarked by a member of the organizing body for the

Gentleman's Sporting Equipment from the British Display at Monza, 1930

The association of the British with high-quality sporting goods was a feature of many displays of British goods abroad in the interwar years, most notably at Paris in 1937 where notions of 'fair play' were in marked contrast to the more overt political propaganda of Germany and the USSR. Included in this illustration is 'an appropriately simple chest of drawers', fashioned from Empire woods and designed by Betty Joel.

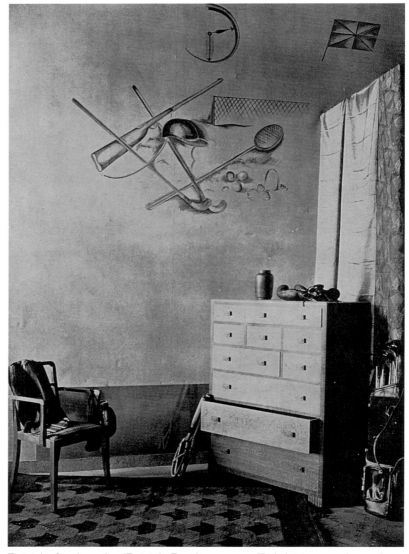

British display, the 'British Pavilion at an Exhibition ought to be a demonstration of the way of living in a non-totalitarian state and should not be a trade exhibit.'[15] As the photographic historian John Taylor has pointed out in his study *A Dream of England*,[16] images of the English countryside were particularly important aspects of propaganda. For example, in *Picture Post* of 13 July 1940, striking contrasts were made between photographs of the English and German ways of life. England was typically symbolized by a photograph of a country cottage which stood for 'England: where each one can work out his own life' or a half-timbered house representing 'England: where a man's home is still his castle'. Conversely, the German way of life was represented as regimented, mechanized, and totalitarian. On the cover 'the British way of life' was symbolized by a boy with a cricket bat, 'the German way of life' by a uniformed militaristic Hitler youth.

In 1932 an important document in terms of cultural propaganda was written by Stephen Tallents. Entitled *The Projection of England* [17] it invoked a number of British attributes such as 'a reputation for coolness' in national character, 'a reputation for disinterestedness' in international affairs, 'a reputation for fair dealing' in commerce, 'a reputation for quality' in manufacture, and 'a reputation for fair play' in sport. He also pointed to important 'institutions and excellencies' which included Oxford, Bond Street, the English countryside, the English home, English servants, football, foxhunting, gardening, and tailoring [**57**, **58**].

While many such traits were clearly in evidence at the British display in Paris 1937, they continued to be an important part of the projection of British national identity in the post-second World War era. Where the overseas promotion of British identity in design was concerned there were two very different standpoints, both funded by the Board of Trade. One represented the 'good design' ethos of the Council of Industrial Design, the other, more favoured, supported that of a historic heritage rooted in the past, paired with British inventiveness and scientific achievements such as the Dounreay reactor or the Jodrell Bank telescope. In general terms, historians of British design [18] have concentrated on the former to the virtual exclusion of the latter, which was even supported by a special Board of Trade display package for British weeks abroad, entitled *Past and Present*. [19] Even at an important international exhibition, such as that at Brussels in 1958, there was a commemorative wall-plaque in one of the courtyards of the official British display, proudly proclaiming that 'in Britain roses grow on tea cups and wallpapers'.

The close relationship between the countryside and 'Englishness' has been sustained in many areas of design. Perhaps most obviously,

ARRANGEMENT OF 56 SEATER DOUBLE DECK BUS (Central)
Approved Colour Scheme.

TYPE S.T.L II | DRAWING No. BP. 103/1

this can be seen in the output of the clothing and interior decoration company Laura Ashley which, since its origins in fabric prints in the 1950s, has become identified with an 'English country look' in clothing, wallpapers, and other cottage and chintz accessories. Its international outlets around the globe have all continued to promote this characteristic national identity. This is also evidenced in many other fields. In ceramics, for example, the *Old Country Roses* tableware range designed by Harold Holdcroft in 1962 for Royal Albert, has sold almost 100 million pieces around the world. It proves the enduring attraction of the 'country garden' theme [**138**], first introduced by the company in 1893.

Germany: the two faces of national identity in design in the 1930s

As the design historian John Heskett has argued in a number of publications[19] there has been an oversimplification of German design identity in the interwar years. This has often been characterized by the portrayal of the Weimar Republic as a period in which modernism flourished to the apparent exclusion of other styles and traditions; also by the view that its symbolically functional aesthetic was brought to an abrupt end with the appointment of Adolf Hitler as Chancellor in 1933, when an avowedly anti-modernist aesthetic was imposed. Some of the reasons for the heavy emphasis placed on modernism by art, architectural, and design historians have been addressed in Chapter 2. However, although a *völkisch* aesthetic can be discerned in many areas relating to the design for the home and other fields where tradition might be expected to play an evocative role, a rational, modernist aesthetic continued to prevail in many other, often economically significant, key areas of production in Germany under the Third Reich [**59**, **60**]. However, it may be argued, recent efforts to show that much design in Third Reich Germany formed a continuity with Weimar modernism[21] may now be swinging the pendulum away from a proper understanding of the true levels of production and consumption of vernacular, ordinary, types. The 'hidden traditions' of everyday consumption largely missing from historical evaluation of design in other countries may also be overlooked in accounts of Germany in the 1930s.

As has been seen in Chapter 2, tensions between the internationalizing spirit of the modernists and the increasingly nationalist tendencies of conservative manufacturers and the political right simmered uneasily in the 1920s, coming to the fore at the Weissenhof Siedlungen housing exhibition in Stuttgart in 1927. As the 1920s evolved craftsworkers saw their employment opportunities increasingly threatened by the widespread introduction of American-influenced standardized and rationalized methods of production in many industries, an efficiency drive furthered by the Reichskuratorium für Wirtschaftlichkeit (State Efficiency Board) which had been established in 1921. Their position became acute as the national economic

Illustrated cover of *Kampf der Gefahr* (Fight Against Danger), December 1939

This portrayal of a German family reflected the traditional values of home-making espoused by the National Socialists in the 1930s. Despite the homely qualities typified by the carved chairback and tablecloth, the unambiguously modernist design of Herman Gretsch's coffee pot on the tabletop (see **27**), first produced by Arzberg in 1931, also finds a place in such a propagandist image.

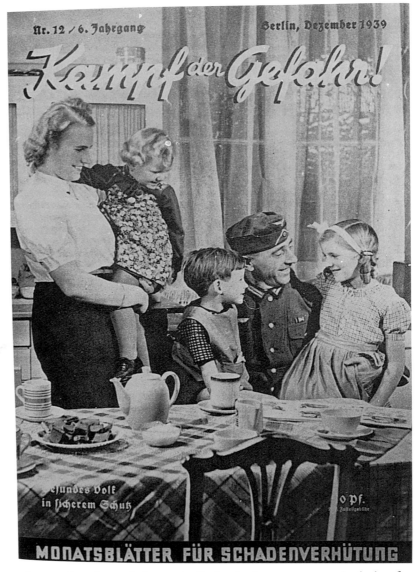

nr. 12 / 6. Jahrgang   Berlin, Dezember 1939

Kampf der Gefahr!

gesundes Volk in sicherem Schutz

MONATSBLÄTTER FÜR SCHADENVERHÜTUNG

climate deteriorated dramatically in the late 1920s, particularly after the Wall Street Crash of 1929. This led to a period of considerable volatility in which the National Socialist (Nazi) Party emerged as an increasingly powerful political force. Paul Schultze-Naumburg emerged as spokesman for the supremacy of 'authentic' German values, epitomized by folk crafts and traditions, and toured Germany advocating a true national art based on notions of *Blut und Boden* (blood and soil).

In February 1929 Alfred Rosenberg, a National Socialist, formed the Kampfbund für Deutsche Kultur (Militant League for German Culture) which denounced avant-garde culture as degenerate. It also

62

Traditional German interior, 1935

This wooden settle and occasional table, together with the woven wall-hanging and decorative motifs of the cushion and lampshade, typify the *völkisch* and *heimatlich* tendencies promoted by the National Socialists. Such designs drew upon roots in regional German folk culture and can be seen as important elements in the establishment of a particular kind of German national identity.

allied itself closely with the craftsworkers who, despite the propagandist activities of the Arbeitsgemeinschaft für Handwerkskultur (Council for Craft Culture) which had been founded in 1922, did not feel that they had significantly influential representation for their views. In fact, their support, actively encouraged by promises of a more influential role in the future, was significant in the emergence of the Nazi Party. Such an outlook was sustained for a brief period following Hitler's election as Chancellor in 1933 when *völkisch* and *heimatlich* ideals appeared to be politically favoured.

Such ideals found their fullest expression in public art and political propaganda, although they were also often followed through architecturally[22] by the utilization of traditional vernacular forms in housing and in hostels for the Hitler Youth. Such ideas were also taken up in many state commissions for furniture and furnishings for government buildings and party headquarters, as well as in domestic furniture, furnishings, and equipment. In design terms it was in the German home that the ethos of traditional forms was most fully and unambiguously exploited [**61**, **62**]. Sabine Weißler[23] emphasized the domestic role that women were expected to play in the Third Reich. They were portrayed as guardians of 'the home of the children, of old memories and of sacred ideas' with the added responsibility for its appearance. As Weißler argued, this meant the favouring of furniture produced from

63

Canteen crockery, 'Schönheit der Arbeit' ('Beauty in Work') model, 1937

The Amt Schönheit der Arbeit, founded in 1934 and led by Albert Speer, was responsible for the development of many prototypes for office furniture, leisure centres, and factory canteens. A number of designers associated with the organization were former members of the Werkbund and, despite the official inclination towards a more handicraft-oriented aesthetic, the functional simplicity of many Schönheit der Arbeit products can be related to modernist precedents in the Weimar years.

64

National Socialist Propaganda Exhibition, 'Gebt Mie Vier Jahre Zeit', May, 1937

Visitors to the Transport Section of the 'Give Me Four More Years' exhibition could see the technological modernism of the Third Reich realized in many of the forms included in the display, such as streamlined railway locomotives, aeroplanes, airships, and ocean liners. In many of these forms of transport, modernist furniture and fittings were to be found, revealing the official acceptance of modernism in contexts where international prestige was important.

German softwoods at the expense of 'bolshevik' tubular steel products, of hand-embroidered cushions rather than heavily upholstered chairs, and of crisp cotton clothing rather than French frippery. Thrift, orderliness, and simplicity were viewed as commendable virtues.

The Deutscher Werkbund, an active supporter of the *Neue Zeit* in the mid-1920s, found its position increasingly compromised both by the economic crisis in the late 1920s (which led to a significant fall in membership and thus funding) and by its relationship with the National Socialists. In fact, in 1933 it fell into the orbit of the National Socialism, linked to the Kampfbund für Deutsche Kultur, before being incorporated into the Reichskulturkammer (Reich Chamber of Culture) where its influence was gradually curtailed.[24]

In 1934 the Schönheit der Arbeit (Beauty in Work) division of the Labour Front was established in 1934, an important body for promoting German national identity in design. It sought to 'awaken joy in work and kindle in the worker the will to organize his working world in a beautiful and dignified and friendly manner'.[25] In this spirit the organization developed model designs for furniture, tableware [**63**], and lighting, and designed interiors for works canteens and offices and recreation centres. A number of historians have seen these as adhering to Bauhaus and Werkbund principles,[26] but in many instances such designs can also be related to traditional German vernacular forms.

None the less, there were a number of significant German designers who had worked for industry in the modernist idiom before the advent of the Third Reich and continued to do so during the 1930s. These included William Wagenfeld, well-known for his glassware, tableware, and lighting, the textile and wallpaper designer Margaret Hildebrand, Heinz Löffelhardt and Hermann Gretsch [**27**], who designed furniture ceramics and glass. Their products were seen to

NATIONALSOZIALIST... KRAFT SPORNTE EISENBAHN UND
LUFTVERKEHR ZU UNGEAHNT... ...RUNG DER GESCHWINDIGKEIT AN.
GLEICHZEITIG ERHÖHTE SICH DIE SICH... ALLER VERKEHRSMITTEL. GRÖSSTE
BEQUEMLICHKEIT MACHT DAS REISEN D... DIE SCHÖNEN DEUTSCHEN LANDE
BESONDERS REIZVOLL DEUTSC... ...EPPELINE UND FLUGZEUGE...
ÜBERBRÜCKEN... ...OZEANE.

BREMEN

65

Grande Salon of the *Normandie*, ocean liner, 1932–5

The 1920s had seen the proliferation of luxury liners, providing the opportunity to promote national prestige and design leadership. Many ships were subsidized by the French government, and like the 1925 Paris Exposition, provided the opportunity for the display of the best of national craftsmanship. The *Normandie*, with its predominantly Art Deco styling, involved many leading French practitioners.

have an important economic role in the drive to increase foreign exports, as well as promoting German taste as modern in its outlook. Many of their designs could be found in the 1939 *Deutsches Warenbüche*, a National Socialist Catalogue of commended designs in current production.

However, the concept of Schönheit der Technik' (the Beauty of Technology) was also an important element in national projection and identity, symbolizing the progressive nature of the regime at home and abroad, whether in such innovations as the streamlined *Flying Hamburger* diesel-electric train which entered service on the German State Railways in 1933, the network of sweeping autobahns, or giant airships such as the LZ 129 *Hindenburg* which sliced the time off transatlantic travel [**64**]. Fully embracing the modernist aesthetic as an appropriate counterpart to its own technological contemporaneity, its symbolically functional tubular steel furniture was a feature of the public areas. Other countries used design for travel for other nationalistic ends [**65**].

Italy: design and Fascism

Like Hitler's Germany, Mussolini's Italy was characterized by an ambivalence in the ways in which she was represented in the years following Mussolini's historic march on Rome in 1922. As has been shown in Chapter 2, there was a period when Italy's own version of the Modern Movement—Rationalism—aspired to become the material embodiment of Fascism. It never had the same opportunities as its German counterpart, which was adopted enthusiastically for a while in the mid-1920s by forward-looking municipalities such as Frankfurt and Stuttgart, with additional support from the industrially-oriented Deutscher Werkbund. None the less, it was adopted for a number of important Fascist exhibitions, as well as both private and public architectural commissions.

Many of the most obvious and striking symbols of Fascist iconography adopted the symbolism of power of Ancient Rome, linking past grandeur with contemporary ambitions and future aspirations [66]. The most instantly recognizable of these were the *fasci* (fasces) which were adopted as the official emblem of the Fascist regime in 1926. These were bundles of rods bound together, with or without an axe, which were carried ceremoniously before high-ranking Roman magistrates. These *fasci* could be seen everywhere, from their transmutation into the columns of triumphal arches such as the *Monumento alla Vittoria* war memorial (1925–8) at Bolzano by Marcello Piacentini,

66

'Radiorurale', built with slight variations by various companies, 1934

This standard model was manufactured especially for the farming communities, symbolized in the ear of corn curving round the speaker, itself emblazoned with an abstracted rendering in aluminium of the ceremonial fasci (bundles of rods, with axes, carried before the magistrates in Ancient Rome). Such propagandist symbols of the Fascist regime linked the past with the modern medium of broadcasting. These radios were sold through the Ente Radiorurale at a special political price, half the commercial rate in order to encourage the growth of a rural audience.

their appearance as decorative motifs on the *Fasci e Bandieri* (Fasces and Flags) patterned silk by Gio Ponti for the Vittorio Ferrari Company in 1930, their attachment to the egg-shaped radiator grilles of FIAT *littorine* trains, to their featuring as sleeve badges and publicity for the uniforms of the Gioventù Italiana di Littorio (the Fascist Youth Organization). Rationalist architects were given opportunities to incorporate them into settings for important exhibitions, such as that marking the tenth anniversary of the Fascist Revolution in Rome in 1932 [**67**]; the Palazzo dell'Esposizione was given a temporary façade by Adalberto Libera and Mario de Renzi which incorporated four twenty-five metres high *fasci*.

As in Germany, technological achievements were important elements in promoting the progressive nature of the regime. These could be seen both in the air and on the land. The S.55 twin-engined, twin-hulled seaplane captured the public imagination. It was designed by the aeronautical engineer Alessandro Marchetti, and became a symbol of Fascism after a number of highly publicized long-distance flights. Another field marked by notable Fascist achievement was the modernization and electrification of the railways, perhaps an unsurprising development given the fact that many early provincial Fascist leaders were former railway employees, usually either stationmasters or white-collar employees. A prototype of the Breda electric train ETR 200 was shown at the V Triennale of 1933 in Milan. Giuseppe Pagano designed the streamlined exterior and Gio Ponti the interior, which boasted high standards of comfort; a second design was commissioned from Ponti and Paolo Masera in 1935, and the ETR went into

69 Ruth Reeves

Manhattan, block-printed cotton for W. & J. Sloane, New York City, 1930

The Cubist-influenced vocabulary adopted by Reeves in this striking design is overshadowed by her exploration of the unambiguously American imagery of New York City, characterized by the everyday metropolitan images of skyscrapers, ocean liners, railway trains, factories, switchboard operators, and a secretary at her typewriter. Such a quest for an American identity in design was shared by many designers at the time.

service on the Milan–Rome line in 1936, travelling at speeds of up to 110 mph.

The autostrada network was another legacy of the Fascist era, accompanied by a dramatic rise in car ownership, from just over 47,000 in 1922 to 345,000 in 1938. The FIAT company had a virtual monopoly of automobile production, launching a number of celebrated models in the interwar years. One of the most famous of these was the 1936 Fiat 500 or *Topolino*, designed by Dante Giocosa. The smallest production car in the world, it was promoted in publicity as 'Bella, Comoda, Economica'—and continued in production until 1955. However, the Fascist ambivalence between an alliance with imagery which drew on the traditions of Ancient Rome (or *Romanità*) and that which was inextricably linked to modernity in the form of new technology is revealed in contemporary automobile advertising. For example, Mario Sironi's 1936 poster for the FIAT 500 as *La Vetturetta del Lavoro e del Risparmio* (the little car for work and economy) shows the automobile set against an image of the She-Wolf of Rome, suckling Romulus and Remus [**68**]. Four years earlier, Giuseppe Romano had designed a poster which represented a range of cars dwarfed by monumental stone letters spelling FIAT, assembled in the form of a triumphal arch.

The search for a national identity in interwar design in the United States.

The almost encyclopaedic variety of styles upon which American designers were able to draw in the interwar years in many ways reflected the cultural diversity of the population of the United States. References back to Hispanic heritage seen in Spanish Colonial Revival in the South-West or the American Colonial Style of the North-East were all part of the efforts of a number of organizations[27] to arrive at an

Up in the sky

Drink Coca-Cola
Delicious and Refreshing

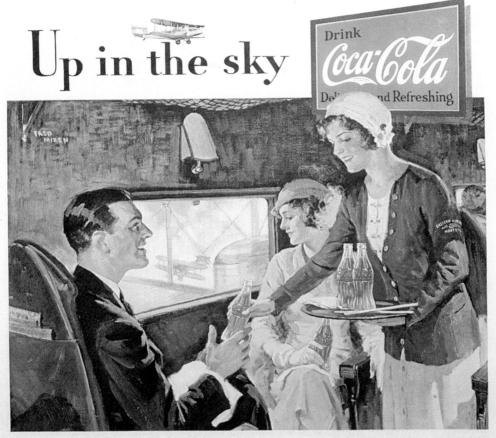

. . . the comfort and pleasure of
the pause that refreshes

On Eastern Air Transport's giant 18-passenger planes, flying between New York and Atlanta, charming hostesses offer ice-cold Coca-Cola and *the pause that refreshes*. This same comfort and pleasure is given on the big ships of other companies that fly from coast to coast and over other routes.

Thus through skyways, as on highways, railways and busy streets, ice-cold Coca-Cola is always ready to help speed you on your way—refreshed. Its tingling, delicious taste and cool, wholesome after-sense of refreshment add life to action or pleasure to leisure. The Coca-Cola Company, Atlanta, Ga.

LISTEN IN
Grantland Rice — Famous Sports Champions — Coca-Cola Orchestra. Every Wed. 10:30 p. m. Eastern Standard Time Coast-to-Coast NBC Network

OVER NINE MILLION A DAY . . . IT HAD TO BE GOOD TO GET WHERE IT IS

71

'Up in the Sky', Coca-Cola
advertisement from the
Saturday Evening Post,
USA, 1920s

Coca-Cola, invented in 1886, has become one of the most potent symbols of the American way of life. From the early years of the century its publicity campaigns were mounted on a sophisticated level, with all kinds of associated promotional material, as well as an annual budget exceeding $1 million by 1914. The distinctively shaped bottle seen here, designed by Alexander Samuelson, was adopted by the company in 1915. The company's association with modern transportation systems ('through skyways, as on highways, railways and busy streets') presages its growing international presence.

indigenous American style. However, a much more potent unifying force was provided by the increasing significance of the city, the inhabitants of which reflected much of the cultural diversity of the American population. Furthermore, in the years following the end of mass immigration in 1921, the preoccupations of American industrial designers were largely centred upon an essentially urban, industrialized experience. As a result, many designers explored different city themes as an iconographic basis for producing inherently American designs. For example, Paul T. Frankl produced a number of bookcases in the form of a skyscraper as part of this drive to establish an American-based iconography in the late 1920s. In fact, the skyscraper motif provided many other designers in a number of fields with a potent form of expression. For example, Harold Van Doren and John Gordon Rideout's plastic-cased radio of 1933 for Air-King Products Co. of Brooklyn follows the stepped form of skyscrapers; Ruth Reeves's celebrated block-printed cotton pattern of 1930 for the New York firm of W. & J. Sloane, *Manhattan*, is dominated by the verticality of many vistas of the New York skyline [**69**], a motif adopted by many other textile designers of the period. Although revealing French stylistic influences in its form of expression, it was the urban content that constituted a truly American dimension. The iconography of everyday life also provided a specifically American form of design [**70**]. For example, in 1926 Edward Steichen explored the possibilities of textile design using photographs of common objects such as cigarettes and matches as the basis for silk designs produced by the Stehli Silk Corporation of New York, an adventurous company which promoted work by a number of American designers. One of their best-known ranges consisted of the American Prints series of 1927, which featured such designs as Neyea McMein's *Hollywood*, Ralph Barton's *Gentlemen Prefer Blondes*, and Clayton Knight's *Manhattan*.

However, by the time that American industrial designers had begun to exert a widespread visual impact on everyday life in the 1930s, American national identity in design was increasingly associated with the symbolism of technological progress [**71**], a theme exploited to the full by the large American corporations at the New York World's Fair of 1939/40. This image continued to predominate for some years after the end of the Second World War, especially in those increasingly affluent European countries where ownership of all kinds of domestic appliances became the norm.

The Second World War: Reconstruction and Affluence

5

The United States after the war: technology and consumption

The Second World War did much to develop business organizational techniques and more efficient modes of production; between 1940 and 1945 the United States devoted 40 per cent of its productive economy to wartime needs, investing $25 billion in new plant and equipment in what the War Production Board called 'the greatest expansion of industry in the history of the country'. There were also notable advances in the production of new materials and machinery, with considerable developments in the chemical and electronic industries. However, as in Britain, restrictions were imposed on particular areas of production: MOMA in New York mounted a *Useful Objects in Wartime* exhibition in 1942, displaying areas of non-priority status such as pottery, glass, paper, and plywood. MOMA was not as influential as many histories of design have implied, but its 'Taste-Makers', as Russell Lynes[1] and others have styled them, preached a creed which was in some ways analogous to the Utility canon: anti-obsolescent and opposed to styling for profit; like the austere aesthetic associated with Utility, it also failed to capture the imagination of everyday consumers. On a wider front, the War Board also limited the range of products available to the public, with President Roosevelt placing a price ceiling on many goods. None the less, as in Britain, from about 1943 onwards, there was a growing emphasis on planning for the postwar period, with expectations of future prosperity dramatically captured in the Libby-Owens-Ford 'Day after Tomorrow's Kitchen', designed by H. Creston Dohner, which was shown in 'mock-up' form in many leading department stores across the United States. It was reported[2] that this 'dream kitchen' was 'a public sensation' and was visited by more than 1.6 million in the 15 months that three identical displays were on show. Complete with 'picture window', the futuristic design represented a move towards the flexibility of a work/living space and the General Motors/Frigidaire 'Kitchens of Tomorrow' which were frequently displayed in the following decade [76].

In a series of twelve articles published in 1953 and 1954, *Fortune* magazine identified a number of significant aspects of what it characterized as the 'Changing American Market' of the early 1950s and beyond. The authors, Gilbert Burck and Sanford Parker, summarized the key points of the investigation thus:

It has analyzed the unforeseen and amazing rise in the American birth rate. It has recorded the unparalleled rise in the nation's living standards, and the postwar rise of a 'great new moneyed middle class, growing larger, wealthier, more uniform, and yet more various'. It has described the economic implications of the phenomenal popularity of suburban life. It has examined individual markets, present and prospective, for cars, houses, food, appliances, clothes, luxuries and leisure-time spending.[3]

This analysis attracted interest in the design press, *Industrial Design* carrying an article on 'The Designer's Stake in the Changing American Market' in April 1954.[4] Much was made of the growth in what was seen as the middle-class market with its increased levels of disposable income and thus developing opportunities for the designer. Such opportunities were sustained by the rapid growth of suburbia, with a consequent rise in demand for labour-saving appliances, tableware, and utensils.

This phenomenal growth of suburbia in the postwar years was stimulated by the ambitions of the housebuilding and property-developing firm of Levitt & Sons, which set the pattern for many others. Between 1947 and 1951 William J. Levitt's company built nearly 17,500 houses in the first Levittown on Long Island and in the early 1950s expanded its activities into Pennsylvania and New Jersey. The houses combined the traditional styling of the Cape Cod cottage with modern constructional techniques and offered a whole range of enticing all-inclusive features, such as refrigerators, washing machines, built-in televisions, and white picket fences [**72**, **73**]. As *Harper's Magazine* reported in 1948:

'A dream house', Levitt wrote, for a GE ad, 'is a house the buyer and his family will want to live in a long time . . . an electric kitchen-laundry is the one big item that gives the homeowner all the advantages and conveniences that make his home truly livable'. To include a Bendix washer in the sales price may seem frivolous and extravagant, but it is worth every bit of the cost in sales appeal and publicity. 'And it will sell faster', Levitt added. His house is the Model-T equivalent of the rose covered cottage—or Cape Coddage, as someone has called it. It is meant to look like the Little Home of One's Own that was the subsidiary myth of the American Dream long before Charlie Chaplin put it into 'Modern Times'.[5]

Levittowners, as the inhabitants were known, were soon seen to represent the norm, one resident and his family being singled out as early as 1951 as 'the average American'. The social mores and attitudes of this group were recorded in the detailed two-year-long study made by Herbert Gans in his book, *Levittowners*, after moving into the third Levittown in Willingboro, New Jersey. However, as Betty Friedan made clear in *The Feminine Mystique*, published in 1963, for the American housewife the conventional picture of the suburban idyll, sustained by Lucy and Ricky's move from town to suburb in the popular television situation comedy *I Love Lucy*, proved highly problematic for many of the female inhabitants who had surrendered careers and independence in search of the American Dream. None the less, in the early 1950s there was a widespread perception that the suburban housewife

73

Component parts of a Levitt Home prior to on-site assembly, *c*.1950

Illustrated here are the basic components of the Levitt package prior to erection. The all-inclusive domestic equipment stands on the standardized concrete base, including cooker, washing-machine, refrigerator, storage systems, and sundry other elements, right down to the characteristic white picket fence. According to *Fortune* magazine of October, 1952, the Levitt factory on Long Island was producing materials for one four-roomed house every sixteen minutes.

Cadillac Fleetwood advertisement, late 1950s

The styling of this 1959 model reveals many qualities associated with the archetypal American 1950s car, symbolizing the conspicuous consumption of the period: a long, low body, curved 'wraparound' windscreen, and extensive 'sculptural' detailing in chrome on the radiator grille and rear end. The detailing of the latter relates to the contemporary fascination with the Jet Age, the rear lights simulating 'rocket-burn'. The rear tail 'fin' had first appeared on a Cadillac in 1948, inspired by Harly J. Earl, the General Motors director of styling.

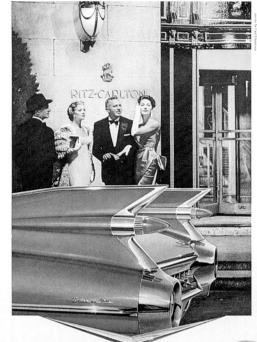

It would be difficult to recount all the wonderful things that a Cadillac car indicates about its owner. But it is readily apparent, we think, that it now speaks more eloquently than ever of his good taste and judgment. Cadillac's new beauty, for instance, is graceful and inspiring as never before. This new Cadillac refinement is equally evident in the car's interiors—in the rare quality of its fabrics, leathers and appointments . . . and in the care and skill of its Fleetwood tailoring and craftsmanship. And then, of course, there is the car's marvelous new performance and handling ease. We suggest you visit your Cadillac dealer soon. You'll quickly see why the new "car of cars" has been accorded the most brilliant reception in Cadillac history.

CADILLAC MOTOR CAR DIVISION • GENERAL MOTORS CORPORATION
EVERY WINDOW OF EVERY CADILLAC IS SAFETY PLATE GLASS

The world's most eloquent possession... *Cadillac*

was the dream image of the young American women and the envy, it was said, of women all over the world. The American housewife—freed by science and labour-saving appliances from the drudgery, the dangers of childbirth, and the illnesses of her grandmother. She was healthy, beautiful, educated, concerned only about her husband, her children, her home. As a housewife and mother, she was respected as a full and equal partner to man in his world. She was free to choose automobiles, clothes, appliances, supermarkets; she had everything that women ever dreamed of.[6]

The postwar suburban growth also saw the development of larger shopping centres and malls in place of the more conventional shopping 'strips', in which smaller shops were lined up alongside a supermarket which acted as an attraction. These had developed in the years following the First World War, when a number of much larger centres were built, accessible only by car. The first of these was the Country Club Plaza in Kansas City, Missouri, constructed by J. C. Nichols in 1922.

The post-Second World War pattern of much larger developments was set by the Northgate Shopping Centre, erected in a Seattle suburb in 1950. It was in the form of a mall of forty shops, centred around a Bon Marché department store, with segregated parking and underground access for delivery vehicles. The first covered mall, the Southdale Center, opened six years later in a suburb of Minneapolis, in many ways set the pattern for subsequent developments around the world.

Another essential ingredient of postwar suburban life was the possession of an automobile. Although production was extremely limited in the middle of the war, by 1949 it was running at over 5 million per annum. By 1950 it reached 8 million, with the figure rising until 1955, the apex of the boom. The automobile became an emblem of conspicuous consumption in itself, but also exerted a considerable impact on the ornament and signage of the urban environment, whether in terms of drive-in cinemas, restaurants, motels, shopping centres, car washes, or simply signs which could be read and absorbed quickly while travelling down the highway at speed, a semiotic phenomenon addressed in Robert Venturi and others' 1972 book, *Learning from Las Vegas*.[7] 'California Coffee Shop Modern'[8] did much to develop such an architectural currency in the 1950s, with raised roof-lines and elaborate neon signs. It was also at this time that the distinctive architecture and signage of McDonalds restaurants evolved, a striking corporate image of yellow parabolic arches integrated into the roadside hamburger bars and echoed in the roadside signs.

This era of conspicuous consumption has been seen as the age of

75

General Motors Show, Los Angeles, 1954

These motor shows were important publicity and sales showpieces for General Motors, showing a range of new models as well as futuristic non-production 'dream cars' against which consumer reactions could be tested. This was a similar outlook to that adopted by many major American corporations in the 'World of Tomorrow' seen at the New York World's Fair of 1939–40.

76

Frigidaire *Kitchen of Tomorrow*, 1956

Part of General Motors since 1919, Frigidaire began to exhibit 'dream kitchens' in 1956. Among many futuristic features seen here were an ultrasonic dishwasher, an IBM Electro-recipe file which automatically activated an ingredients dispenser, and rising storage cabinets. In the foreground is the cooking surface, a wipe-clean marble work-top punctuated with in-built heating elements, together with a Thermopane domed oven powered by quartz lamps. Behind the housewife is a Roto-storage system which could also be checked externally by tradespeople to facilitate automatic replenishment.

'Populuxe', a term employed by the critic Thomas Hine in his 1987 book of the same title[9] to denote populism, popularity, and luxury. He defined it further as 'not merely having things. It is having things in a way they'd never been had before, and it is an expression of outright vulgar joy in being able to live so well'.[10] This was epitomized most obviously in the styling of the American automobile in the 1950s, characterized by the extravagant chrome excesses of radiator grilles and tail-fins, both of which drew heavily on the symbolism of rocketry and jet engines [**74**, **75**]. The tail-fin had first appeared in a restrained form on a Harley Earl-designed Cadillac of 1948, but became a major feature of styling in the 1950s; the wrap-around windscreen which gave the feel of being in a cockpit was introduced by Oldsmobile in 1954; instrumentation became increasingly ostentatious in the range of dials and controls arranged round the driver; and the advertising language used to sell features became increasingly evocative of space. Key figures in this styling rivalry were Virgil Exner at Chrysler, George Walker at Ford, and Harley Earl at General Motors. The latter was the first designer in a major industry to become a corporate Vice-President and by the mid-1950s General Motors' Styling Section had grown to about 850, increasing to 1,400 by the time he retired in 1959. Earl was also involved in work in the Products and Exhibits studio, which was responsible for Frigidaire products as well as promotional exhibitions such as the 'Motoramas', the first of which was held at the Waldorf-

Astoria Hotel in New York in 1953. These exhibitions introduced 'dream cars' to the public, models which were never actually put into production but which carried futurist features to test, or condition, public opinion.

The control layouts of automobiles influenced the control panels of cookers, and other aspects of detailing could be found on many other domestic appliances, juke-boxes, and other products which relied on 'up-to-the-minute' styling for success in the market-place. In the buoyant consumer climate of 1953 the Frigidaire Division of General Motors adopted a similar strategy to that of the Motoramas in the first of their *Kitchen of Tomorrow* events, which was also mounted at the Waldorf-Astoria Hotel in New York. Three years later the Frigidaire *Kitchen of Tomorrow* [**76**] sought to seduce consumers with such futuristic equipment as a loudspeaker telephone able to be answered from anywhere in the kitchen, to record messages, and to send and receive written messages; a Roto-storage centre with dry, refrigerated, and frozen sections, which could be rotated with external access so that tradesmen could check and refill them with staple items as required; a laundry which would be activated automatically when the weight in any of three bins reached eight pounds; and an ultrasonic dishwasher/drier/sterilizer.

By the end of the decade doubts about many aspects of conspicuous consumption had begun to be voiced by organizations such as the Consumers Union, moralizing critics such as Vance Packard, ardent campaigners such as Ralph Nader, designers such as Richard Neutra, and economists such as J. K. Galbraith. A number of these questions are explored further in Chapter 10.

Britain: utility and beyond

As has been discussed in Chapters 2 and 3, there was a significant gulf in interwar Britain between the aspirations of those who sought to promote modernism and the realities of the market-place. Nikolaus Pevsner himself openly acknowledged the difficulties of changing patterns of design consumption without radical social change in his 1937 *Enquiry into Industrial Art in England*.[11] He believed that the causes of the prevalence of poorly designed goods were more deep-seated than indifference on the part of manufacturers, retailers, buyers, and consumers, and that a firm commitment to slum-clearance, rehousing, and improved standards of environmental planning was necessary in order to provide a climate in which design debates would have meaning.

It was perhaps ironic that it needed an outbreak of war in 1939 for a number of the design reformers of the interwar years to convert their ideals and aesthetic creeds into a wider material reality. This opportunity arose with the establishment by the Board of Trade of the Utility

Scheme in 1942, which was to affect many areas of design through state-imposed control of materials, specifications, and availability of a range of goods including furniture and furnishings, bedding, household textiles, glass, knitwear, clothing, hosiery, and footwear [**77**]. A Furniture Advisory Committee was soon established, the membership of which included stalwarts from the interwar design campaigns: Elizabeth Denby, John Gloag, and Gordon Russell. Also advising were three furniture manufacturers and a consumer. As was remarked at the time in an editorial in the *Architectural Review*, a sympathetic advocate of design reform, Utility offered

a social opportunity of the first order. If here, with all the force that government monopoly gives at present, something had been done that could have satisfied both the experienced and the discriminating, and the wide manifold public for which the furniture is intended, a step forward might have been taken of more importance than anything so far accomplished by DIA propaganda, exhibitions and the exhibitions of the few adventurous designers.[12]

The scope of design activities embraced by Utility was considerably enhanced in 1943 by the appointment of a Utility Design Panel under the chairmanship of Gordon Russell. This included his brother R. D. Russell and the furniture designers Edwin Clinch and H. T. Cutler who had produced designs for Utility furniture. They were subsequently joined by Enid Marx who designed furniture fabrics and Jacques Groag, former pupil of Adolf Loos. Despite efforts to enthuse the public through the mounting of promotional exhibitions and publication of catalogues and articles in the press, both the public and industry remained at best lukewarm to the idea of a state-imposed, standardized aesthetic in their everyday lives, even if for many it ensured standards of quality and economy—in other words a kind of consumer protection. However, as the Utility guidelines were increasingly relaxed in the later 1940s the fashion-conscious or historicizing qualities in design of the 1930s that those involved with Utility hoped would recede into the background of the public's desires in the postwar years soon assumed a highly desirable allure.[13] The public remained unconvinced by the modernist adage 'less is more', even when blended with British craftsmanship and humanizing materials. Instead they once more inclined towards what Anthony Bertram described in 1946 as 'The Enemies of Design': 'Indifference itself, the Hitler of the gang, Cheapness First, Unnecessary Novelty, Borrowed Glory, Mass Production, Articraftiness and Fashion Snobbery'.[14]

During the war years various other bodies were active in promoting design both as a social and as an economic force, particularly as optimism grew about the likely outcome of the war.[15] These included the Council for the Encouragement of Music and the Arts (CEMA) and the Central Institute of Art and Design (CIAD), both of which had

Utility living-room layout as revealed to the public in Board of Trade exhibition in London's West End, October, 1942

The exhibition lasted three weeks, attracting over 30,000 visitors and the favourable attention of the popular press. As can be seen here, the furniture was very austere in appearance, conforming to the design specifications laid down by the State Utility Furniture Advisory Committee. In many ways it conformed to the design reform ideals of the campaigners of the interwar years, unsurprising perhaps since the Committee included stalwarts such as Gordon Russell and John Gloag.

been established in 1939. The CIAD was particularly concerned with the development of postwar export trade and initiated contracts for design research in a range of industries, including cotton, wool, and plastics. The state was also concerned to promote industrial design as a positive force in the postwar market-place. The unpublished Weir *Report on Industrial Design and Art in Industry* of 1943 and the Meynell–Hoskins *Report on Art Training* of 1944 both supported the idea of establishing an independent design council. Late in 1944 Sir Hugh Dalton established the Council of Industrial Design (COID) under the chairmanship of the textile industrialist Sir Thomas Barlow, with S. C. Leslie as its first director.[16] However, the social formation of the COID was such that many provincial manufacturers felt suspicious about the supposed cultural élitism of a body firmly rooted in the metropolitan taste-making circles of the South-East of England.

From Britain Can Make it to the Festival of Britain

The most significant foray into the public domain was the COID's organization of the 'Britain Can Make It' (BCMI) Exhibition of 1946, held in London. Over 5,000 objects were shown in an effort to convince manufacturers, retailers, the public, and foreign buyers that design was of critical importance in the postwar period. As with much design history involving propagandist organizations with a vested interest in promoting themselves as successful in realizing their aims, it is difficult to disentangle myth from fact in the case of BCMI. Fortunately, the COID commissioned the Mass Observation organization to undertake a survey of the public's response to the exhibition[17] which, conducted around 2,523 interviews of exhibition visitors, revealed significant gaps between the COID's interpretation of the

78

Die-lines as issued to manufacturers participating in the Festival Pattern Group, c.1950

The Festival Pattern Group was conceived by Mark Hartland Thomas, the COID's industrial officer. Inspired by a paper he had heard at a 1949 conference which introduced designers to a range of visual sources from other arts and sciences, he decided to use crystallography diagrams as the basis of a new decorative scheme. It was launched at the Festival of Britain (Britain led the world in crystallography) and could be found on carpets, curtains, tableware, glass, and other surfaces capable of carrying pattern. Twenty-six manufacturers from different industries collaborated together as the Festival Pattern Group.

needs of rather crudely defined social groups and their actual perceptions. In fact, in September 1946, *The Economist* had already drawn attention to the need for systematic research into design, raising questions about the importance of sociology in the design process. The COID's *ad hoc* sociology was at its most apparent in the furnished room settings in the exhibition which, according to a Mass Observation survey, was one of the most popular sections of the show. Rather than any sociologically-informed display of the specific needs of particular social groups a sense of social paternalism was evident in the rooms designed for fictitious families, encapsulated in Nicholas Bentley's wiry line drawings in the catalogue, accompanied by prose thumbnail sketches by the poet John Betjeman.

When accounts of events are written mainly by their initiators, they tend to celebrate the most optimistic, ideal, and reassuring aspects. This was particularly so in relation to the Festival of Britain of 1951, where the COID, under its director Gordon Russell, was heavily involved in the selection of all goods seen at the main Festival sites in London, Glasgow, and Ulster. Much of the history of British design in the early postwar years has been constructed from published sources which not only centre on the COID but also support a positive view of the Council's achievements. Such sources include the *Annual Reports* (important vehicles for persuading the COID's paymaster, the Board of Trade, of its effectiveness), *Design* magazine, its mouthpiece to industry and the design profession, the autobiographies of key personnel such as Gordon Russell[18] and Paul Reilly,[19] written many years afterwards. The Festival Catalogue, *Design in the Festival*, published by the Design Council, sold 95,000 copies: its widespread availability has also furthered a particular interpretation of the COID position. However, a more complex view was broached in *A Tonic to the Nation: The Festival of Britain 1951*,[20] published in 1976, in which a number of myths about British design in the 1950s were dispelled. Two principal illusions were disposed of by Reyner Banham in his perceptive essay[21] in which he argued that it was untrue to maintain either that 'the Festival of Britain created a style that was new and valuably English' or that 'this style was influential, especially on popular taste'. However, there is another myth that needs to be dispelled, that of unequivocal support for state intervention in design matters. Within two years of the closure of the Festival officials within the Treasury were arguing that the COID, for all its aesthetic policing of design in 1951, should be closed down.

None the less, although the impact of the Festival Style or, as it was also known, the 'Contemporary Style' was comparatively short-lived, it made itself felt in a variety of everyday spheres from packaging design to plant pot holders and from sideboards to shopping plazas. Typified by the wiry linearity of Ernest Race's *Antelope* chair and a

79

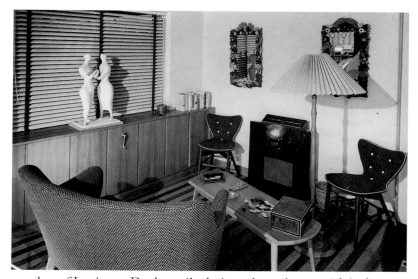

79

Parlour, designed by Eden and Bianca Minns from the Homes and Gardens Pavilion on the South Bank, London, at the Festival of Britain, 1951

One of many interiors showing examplars of modern British design selected by the COID, it reflects the modernizing tendencies supported by that organization in the postwar years: built-in units under the window, and lightweight furniture (particularly the parlour chairs and coffee table), suitable for living in smaller rooms. Behind the venetian blinds was a wind-up plate-glass window, working on the same principle as a car window.

number of Lucienne Day's textile designs the style was widely disseminated in magazines and stores geared towards the tastes of a middle-class market [**78**]. It is noteworthy that ten years later Gerald Barry, the Festival's Director General, saw its legacy as limited to the light industrial sector, particularly tableware, furniture, lighting, and textiles.[22] Indeed, the Festival Style has also been seen to mark the end of an era [**79**, **80**], rather than heralding a renaissance of British design [**81**]. For many ordinary consumers, however, the partiality for traditional patterns in tableware, carpets and wallpapers, and other artifacts of everyday living remained a significant aspect of the market-place. None the less, as will be shown in Chapter 8, higher levels of employment and disposable income made the alluring image of consumerism in the United States increasingly attractive both to theorists and the wider public in Britain, sustained by the American cinema, the advent of commercial television, glossy magazines, and popular music.

Italy: postwar ideals

Following the end of the war the Italian economy made an impressive recovery. In terms of exports this can be measured in comparative terms: between 1951 and 1962, whilst Britain's exports increased by 29 per cent, and France's by 86 per cent, West Germany's rose by 247 per cent and Italy's by 259 per cent. Only Japan, with a growth of 378 per cent, made more significant progress.

Italian design established a reputation for style and sophistication in a number of fields where design is a significant factor including automobiles, furniture and furnishings, lighting, interior design, and fashion. The concept of a truly Italian style became a reality during the 1950s, alongside the postwar regeneration of Italian industry.

At the end of the war, industrial output in Italy was scarcely a fifth

Füred and Lelle furniture
sets manufactured in the
Metal-Furniture Factory,
Hungary, 1950s

The Hungarian equivalent
of 1950s Contemporary Style
British furniture reflects a
similar preoccupation with
providing practical designs
which fitted easily into postwar housing developments
of the early 1950s. The bold,
abstract patterns of the
carpets reflect a parallel
commitment to modernity.

of what it had been in 1938. None the less, by 1948, the Italian economy
had recovered to its prewar level, aided both by protectionist policies
and the activities of the Istituto per la Riconstruzione Industriale (IRI)
which had been established under Mussolini in 1933 to stimulate
industrial growth. In 1946 there was a strong anti-fascist dimension to
Italy's coalition government, with significant representation of both
the socialist and communist parties. Many Italian intellectuals were
strongly committed to the political left and believed that they had a
potentially significant role in the reconstruction of a democratic society. This outlook was expressed materially at the RIMA (Riunione
Italiana per le Mostre di Arredamento) exhibition of popular furnishing in Milan in 1946 [**82**, **83**], where concepts of modernity, flexibility,
space-saving, and practicality predominated as well as a commitment
to designs which could be produced at prices which put them in the
reach of the majority. Ernesto Rogers, who had taken over the editorship of *Domus* in the same year, identified the main objectives of the
exhibition as 'economy, practicality and good taste', themes which also
ran through his magazine at the time. Similarly, the first postwar
Milan Triennale of 1947 was devoted to the theme of reconstruction,
with a particular emphasis on the working-class home. This preoccupation with 'democratic' design could be seen in a number of products
such as Corradino D'Ascanio's *Vespa* motor scooter for Piaggio of 1946
[**84**], Cesare Pallavicino's Lambretta Innocenti scooter of 1947, and,
though later, the 1953 Iso-Isetta mini-car and Dante Giocosa's *Nuova
500* (New Cinquecento) FIAT of 1957.

Italian style in the 1950s

As Andrea Branzi remarked in *The Hot House: Italian New Wave*

Design,[23] Italian design of the 1950s should really be seen to begin in 1948 and end in 1962, a period marked by centrist politics and an economic boom. It has been convincingly argued[24] that the United States not only played a significant role in re-invigorating the Italian economy but also, in the effort to increase production, recognized that design was a tool that could be used to develop new markets and promote new patterns of consumption in Italy. The 1948 elections marked a clear shift away from leftist politics towards the centre, a change of emphasis which was also seen in design with a move away from democratic idealism towards a more style-conscious aesthetic, geared to the pockets of the more affluent sectors of society. Gio Ponti resumed editorship of *Domus* in 1948 and did much to promote a new language of modern design.

The Italian design aesthetic that emerged at about this time was characterized by organic, sculptural forms which could be found in a diverse range of objects [**85**] including the 1946 *Vespa* motor scooter, Pininfarina's Cisitalia Berlinetta 202 automobile of 1947, Marcello Nizzoli's *Lexicon 80* typewriter for Olivetti of 1948, and Giulio Minoletti's ETR railway train and Gio Ponti's La Pavoni coffee machine, both of 1949. The flowing forms of such designs [**86**] shared a vocabulary with contemporary sculpture by Hans Arp, Max Bill, and Henry Moore, as well as design work by Charles Eames and Eero Saarinen in the United States which had been published in *Domus*. In the architectural field there were also similar interests in organic form, articulated by the APAO (Association for Organic Architecture,

81 Alec Issigonis

Austin Mini (1959) as seen in the Paramount Picture Corporation's film *The Italian Job*, 1969

Following the Suez crisis of 1956, the British Motor Corporation decided to design a small, economical family car, resulting in the production of the Mini in 1959. Its innovations included the space-saving transverse engine which provided a capacious interor in relation to its external dimensions. It was not particularly successful when launched but, following successes in the Monte Carlo Rally of 1964 and 1965, its sales passed one million in 1965. Its attractive price ensured widespread appeal, and it became a symbol both of British Pop and urban chic.

82 Ignazio Gardella

Apartment for three people, RIMA Exhibition, Milan, 1946

Held in the Palazzo d'Arte in Milan and curated by Carlo Pagani, this exhibition was devoted to the theme of 'arredamento populare' (popular furnishing). Exploring ideas such as practicality, economy, and good taste under the slogan 'casa migliore vuol dire vita migliore' ('a better house means a better life'), the designs were intended as prototypes for serial production. Ignazio Gardella was awarded the Grand Prix for his design for his hypothetical 'new' nuclear family, based on three people.

founded in Rome in 1944) and Bruno Zevi (who wrote *Verso un architettura organico* in 1945). Both saw organic form as offering a more humanizing face of modernism than that of the austere and standardized vocabulary of the Rationalists [**87**, **88**].

Links with the United States

The United States provided Italy with important financial aid through the Marshall Plan, providing knowledge of modern mass-production technology, which lay at the root of the dramatic increases in output in the automobile, textile, office equipment, and petrochemical industries. However, there were other important links between Italy and the United States which helped to promote an international awareness of Italian design at this period.

Many Italians had emigrated to Italy before the First World War and had maintained family links since then. These had been reinforced by many of the American armed forces in Europe during and after the Second World War and were further stimulated by the development of the postwar tourist trade. But of more specific importance for design promotion was the mounting by the Art Institute of America of the 1950 exhibition of 'Italy at Work: Her Renaissance in Design Today',[25] which toured a large number of major American museums. The show of about 2,500 items included prototypes for furniture, lighting, and other industrial products, as well as a wide range of current lines including a Lambretta motor scooter, items of office equipment, and coffee machines. All the exhibits were placed within special settings commissioned from Italian designers. The crafts too were prominent in the show not only because they represented a particularly important aspect of Italian design in the postwar period but also because the United States had done much to further their development. As a means of initiating this, Handicraft Development Incorporated in America had been set up in 1945 in the United States as a non-profit-making organization, and in 1947 it opened the House of Italian Handicrafts in New York as a means of linking Italian craftsworkers with American distributors.[26] In Italy the organization operated as CADMA (the Committee for Assistance and Distribution of Materials to Artisans) with representation in Florence, Milan, Venice, and Naples.

American knowledge of Italian design was also furthered by other exhibitions, such as MOMA's travelling show on the theme of 'The Modern Movement in Italy: Architecture and Design'. In fact, MOMA's patronage of modern Italian design both through shows and acquisitions did much to reinforce its cultural and artistic status.[27] M. Singer & Sons of New York also promoted furniture by Ponti, Mollino, and Parisi in the early 1950s, as did Altamira and Knoll. Italian fashion design also attracted increasing attention during the 1950s when leading American stores began to promote it.

Another important means of promoting developments and debates in Italian design to a wider international audience was afforded by the Milan Triennali. Those in 1951, 1954, and 1957 were all concerned with themes in industrial design: 'The Production of Art', 'Europe', and 'Compulsory Schooling'. At the X Triennale of 1951 the section entitled 'The Form of the Useful', organized by Ludovico Bellgioioso and Enrico Peressutti, concentrated on industrial aesthetics and gave rise to criticism that there was insufficient emphasis on the social and economic dimensions of design. However, experimentation was much in evidence, particularly in the work of Marco Zanuso, Carlo Mollino, and Franco Albini. Zanuso experimented with foam rubber furniture for Arflex, a subsidiary of Pirelli, winning the Medaglio d'Oro and

83 Ignazio Gardella

Little Sideboard (Piccola Credenza), RIMA Exhibition, Milan, 1946

This sideboard, which can be opened from both sides, and thus act as a spatial divider, is a neat and ingenious solution for the provision of utilitarian furniture of 'good taste', very different from the Utility furniture still being produced in Britain at the time (see **77**).

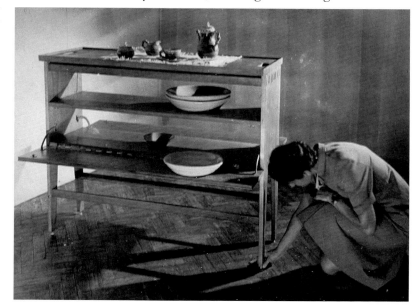

Workers riding Piaggio *Vespa* motor scooters designed by Corradino d'Ascanio at the Piaggio factory, Pontedera, January 1949

Designed in 1946, the streamlined styling of the *Vespa* was an aesthetically refined solution to the problem of providing an economic and practical form of transport in the period of *ricostruzione*. Without the gender-specific implication of traditional motorcyle design it later became a popular symbol of youth culture, particularly of the Mods in Britain in the 1960s, and remained in production until 1987. The sculptural quality of its styling was apparent in other transport products of the later 1940s, including Pininfarina's *Cisitalia* automobile (1946) and Minoletti's ETR railway train (1949).

Gran Premio; Mollino explored the possibilities of organic form in furniture; Albini experimented with combinations of modern forms and craft traditions, as in his *Margherita* wickerwork chair. This 'rediscovery' of craft traditions in the 1950s did much to unleash the creative potential of form in furniture, ceramics, glass, metal, and plastics.

Italian design was also promoted on the commercial front, particularly through the major department store La Rinascente which, as it had done in the autarchic climate of the 1930s, sought to influence Italian taste, commissioning leading designers such as Ponti and Albini to design for the mass market. Furthermore, after mounting a series of 'good design' exhibitions in the early 1950s the store launched the Compasso d'Oro award scheme in 1954 as a means of encouraging better technological and aesthetic standards. The awards did much to promote modern Italian design at home and abroad.

The Kartell Company can be identified closely with the rise of Italian design at this time. Founded by Giulio Castelli in Milan in 1949, it soon emerged as one of the leaders of stylish plastic products. Its first product was a ski rack for automobiles, designed by Carlo Barassi and Roberto Menghi, perhaps indicating the orientation of design-conscious companies towards an affluent middle-class clientele. During the 1950s Kartell manufactured a wide range of products: housewares, lighting, and industrial goods [89]. Gino Colombini was in charge of the company's technical office and did much to establish its reputation for design, particularly through the Compasso d'Oro awards in which he regularly featured, commencing with second prize in 1955. Other renowned designers for the company have included Joe

Colombo, Achille and Pier Castiglione, and Anna Castelli-Ferrieri. However, the company's success did not derive simply from a commitment to design. An essential element was an emphasis on research and technological innovation and in 1954 the company established a European pool for the exchange of technology and marketing analysis as a means of promoting plastics more widely.

By the end of the decade a number of innovative companies placing a premium on design had established a reputation. Typical of this trend were Arteluce (founded in 1939), Brion Vega (established 1945) [**90**], Tecno (established 1952), Gavina (established 1953), and Zanotta (established 1954). These joined larger companies with a much longer association with high standards of design such as Olivetti, Lancia, Alfa Romeo, and FIAT. The years from 1959 to 1962 marked the culmination of the postwar selective marketing strategies for domestic products, automobiles, and petrochemical products, as well as growing levels of affluence and conspicuous consumption. However, the emphasis on style, status, and product aesthetics on which the Italian design reputation was based in the European and North American markets began to attract an increasing amount of criticism from certain sectors of the Italian design profession which believed that social and environmental considerations were being sacrificed in the name of art. This conflict between socio-economic relevance and aesthetic contemplation, which had found particular focus at the Triennali, became increasingly acrimonious as the Italian economy began to run into difficulties in the early 1960s. The elections of 1963 saw a resurgence of leftist politics and the Communist Party, mirrored by the growing critique of the restrictive effects of a capitalist-dominated economy on the social and creative potential of design, a critique which found potent expression in the Radical or Anti-Design movement of the later 1960s.

Germany: reconstruction and Wirtschaftswunder (economic miracle)

The destruction of much of Germany's industrial base in the Second World War made possible radical innovation, and by the early 1950s the first signs of an 'economic miracle' were apparent: between 1950 and 1964 West Germany's gross national product (GNP) rose faster than in any other European country; in the same years industrial output increased sixfold; between 1949 and 1950 foreign trade doubled, and between 1954 and 64 it trebled. This was a period of considerable consumer demand which also saw the establishment of new industries to accommodate it.

American influence was a significant factor in Germany's postwar reorientation and many leading German industrialists, like their Japanese, French, and British counterparts, visited Detroit and other major manufacturing centres in the United States in order to study progressive management techniques and industrial organization. There are also a number of parallels which may be usefully drawn between the Germany of the 1920s and that of the 1950s. Both were periods of stabilization and economic recovery after a major war in which Germany had been on the losing side; both saw important injections of American finance and were accompanied by social and cultural readjustment. In the 1920s there had been a strong American influence in many sectors of German society:[28] Henry Ford's autobiography sold more than 200,000 copies, and Taylorism exerted a strong influence on industrial practice; wider everyday American values asserted them-

87

Citroën DS display at the Salon
d'Automobile, Paris, 1955

First seen publicly in France
at the 1955 Salon, the organic,
tapered form of the DS
(pronounced 'déesse',
meaning goddess) had been
shown without wheels at the
Turin Motor Show of 1953,
rendering it almost as a piece
of abstract sculpture. Very
much in keeping with wider
international interest in organic
form, the DS set new
standards of styling, comfort,
and ride. The interior styling,
particularly that of the
dashboard and the steering
column, exuded an aura of
technological progress.
Between 1955 and 1975
almost one and a half million
DS cars were manufactured.

selves in the spheres of culture, style, and material possessions. Similarly, in the 1950s, for some Germans, American models exuded a strong flavour of capitalist democracy, and the study of American management techniques and the approaches of the Harvard Business School were influential in the commercial and industrial sectors. Immediately after the war, magazines such as *Business Week* and *Time* were so sought after that there was a black market demand for them. Furthermore, by 1952 over 500 significant German companies were controlled by American capital, particularly in areas such as electrical products, automobiles, and chemicals. After the war, many American cultural values were also transmitted by the overwhelming presence of American troops, just as was the case in Japan under General MacArthur. Coca-Cola, which had first been produced in Germany in 1929, was relaunched there in 1949, and by the mid-1950s there were 96 bottling plants in West Germany. American films promoted the American way of life and many American brand names were widely recognized. It is perhaps unsurprising that, given such influences, streamlining was manifest in a wide range of domestic and other appliances as well as in automobile styling, such as that of the Hansa 1500 Borgward of 1949, which looked back to American car styling of the late 1930s [**91**], or the mid-1950s Kapitan, the tail-fins of which were clearly inspired by American precedent.

88 Arne Jacobsen

Cutlery, AJ pattern,
produced by A. Michelsen,
Copenhagen, 1957

The bold yet refined simplicity
of this Danish cutlery is an
elegant reconsideration of
everyday artefacts and typifies
what has become known as
Scandinavian Modern design.
Jacobsen's minimalist design
created a furore when it was
first introduced but has
subsequently become a
design 'classic'. The organic
character, particularly of the
spoon, allies it to essays in
sculptural form design in Italy,
France, and elsewhere.

However, there was also a strong desire amongst German designers to establish themselves on a sounder professional footing than had been the case in the interwar years. As one means of persuading commerce and industry of their economic worth designers placed an increased emphasis on the need to adopt a more systematic and scientific analysis of design problems. This also signalled a clear ideological shift away from the *völkisch* characteristics associated with the Third Reich. As will be investigated further in Chapter 7, this scientific approach was particularly associated with the development of the curriculum at the highly influential Hochschule für Gestaltung, where teaching commenced in 1953, as well as with products made by Braun in which notions of 'functional beauty' were emphasized. For many years the dominant trend amongst manufacturers was to place a premium on design, a trend sustained by official and industrially supported organizations promoting 'good design'. The Rat für Formgebung (German Design Council), the Neue Sammlung Gallery in Munich, the Deutscher Werkbund [**92**, **93**], the Institut für Neue Technische Form at Darmstadt, and Industrieform at Essen all sought to stress the economic and aesthetic benefits of rational design.

Opposed to this aesthetic associated with what became known as 'scientific operationalism' was an outlook that favoured the organic as the basis for furniture, textile, product, and architectural design. In the late 1940s it shared common ground with many designers in Italy,

89 Kartell

Cover page from the company magazine *Qualität*, no. 6, Winter 1957

This illustration shows a wide range of plastic domestic products manufactured by the Kartell company, founded by Guilio Castelli in Milan in 1949. These include the rectangular tub at the base of the 'tree' (Compasso d'Oro prizewinner, 1957) and the bucket hanging from the lowest 'branch' (Compasso d'Oro prizewinner, 1955), both designed by Gino Columbini who was head of Kartell's technical office. High standards of colourful design in everyday products soon expanded to plastic lighting and furniture for which the company became increasingly renowned internationally in the following decades.

Britain, Holland, France, and the United States, embracing notions of artistic creativity, individuality, freedom of inspiration, and an interest in the arts and crafts. Contemporary fine art practice also provided inspiration, particularly action painting, which appeared to offer the means of expression appropriate for a new, dynamic era in German life. Links with the organic work of Charles Eames in the United States could be discerned in the work of the German furniture designer Egon Eiermann, as in his 1953 Model SE18 folding chair manufactured by Wilde + Spieth, one of the best-selling wooden chairs of the 1950s, and much more obviously in Georg Leowald's stacking chair of 1954 for Wilkening + Hahne. In textile design the influence of abstract expressionism can be seen in Willi Baumeister's curtain fabric designs for Pausa AG in 1955, whilst in architecture Hans Scharoun's flowing forms for the Berlin Philharmonic of 1960–3 give it a dramatic realization.

Consumption in everyday life

One of the problems with developing a fuller history of design, as has been seen in many areas of this study, is to do justice to the wider patterns of consumption and everyday life. The difficulties of investigating sufficient material evidence in the face of archival and museological determinants of (high) cultural significance are still in the process of being addressed. Lorenz Eitner, in a 1958 article on 'Industrial design in Postwar Germany',[29] drew attention to a survey of home furnishings of German women of all classes and all age groups over 18 carried out in 1954. Its results were as follows: of all women questioned 2 per cent were still attached to the Wilhelminian grandeur of carved oak and potted palms; nearly 60 per cent were content with the flowered chintz, simulated wood grains, and heavy overstuffings of current department store best-sellers; while 30 per cent preferred the style which might be called 'subdued modern' or 'Swedish middle-brow', with its blond woods, chaste shapes, and unadorned surfaces. More advanced designs were favoured by a far smaller group, though of the younger women (under 30 years old) 10 per cent voted for what could be called 'Knoll International', a modernist aesthetic adopted in the public spaces of many corporate buildings. A further breakdown of the sample showed that the modern idiom ('Swedish' or 'International') was preferred by 44 per cent of women between 18 and 29 years, 28 per cent of working class wives, 44 per cent of self-employed women, and 54 per cent of female wage earners. It was most popular in towns of middle size, less so in metropolitan or rural areas.

Despite the emergence of the New Left and the economic recession of the mid-1960s, designers generally remained unmoved either by critiques of what J. K. Galbraith termed the 'affluent society' or the increasing sensitivity to social and environmental issues. In the 1970s, however, a number of designers in Germany began to question the continuing validity of the dominant rational, functionalist aesthetic. Among them was Luigi Colani, whose designs provoked fierce criticism from his peers. His work exhibited a pronounced biomorphic character, as in his Drop profile tea service for Rosenthal of 1974, sanitary-ware designs for Villeroy & Boch, or the T-90 range of cameras for Canon. In the 1980s the German design consultancy, Frogdesign, has also taken a line opposed to the quasi-scientific approach to design in a number of its brightly coloured, organic designs, even coining the phrase 'form follows fun' to underline its philosophy. By this time Berlin had emerged as an avant-garde centre of significance, becoming the nexus for what has been termed the New German Design. Essentially a critique of the functionalist tradition, whether in terms of the symbolic functionalism of Bauhaus design or post-Ulm rationalism, groups like Berlinetta and Stiletto [94] provided a radical opposition to the orthodoxy of Good Design.

Japanese design in the postwar period: myths and stereotypes

The post-Second World War period has marked a significant change in attitudes to Japanese design, both within Japanese manufacturing industry and abroad. There was a marked reconsideration of the dominant view of Japan, characterized by Pierre Loti in his best-selling novel *Madame Chrysanthemum* of 1887, where the country was portrayed as exotic and alluring, peopled by erotic women and devious and unethical men.[30] Further stereotypes had evolved in the twentieth century, particularly in reaction to the threat which Japan's economically priced exports increasingly posed to her Western competitors. The anxiety that the Japanese would flood the Western markets with cheap

90 Marco Zanuso & Richard Sapper

Television 201 for Brionvega, 1969

Brionvega, originally a radio manufacturing company, moved into the production of televisions in the early 1950s with the advent of the Italian television network. In the early 1960s the company commissioned Zanuso and Sapper to develop a number of innovative radios and televisions. As can be seen in this illustration the fact that this acrylic cube is a television is concealed when the set is not in use, resembling a stylish, if minimalist, black box.

91

Isabella coupé, Borgward, West Germany, 1956
Even though there was considerable debate about the distinctiveness of German design in the 1950s, American influence continued to exert a powerful allure on many aspects of everyday life. Just as late 1930s American automobile styling had influenced a number of late 1940s and early 1950s models, the *Isabella* coupé echoes a number of styling traits seen in the USA in the late 1940s.

goods was felt in a number of countries. In Britain, for example, this surfaced increasingly in the textile and pottery industries, with a number of accusations of Japanese sharp practice being raised in the House of Commons. In November 1950, A. Davies MP drew the attention of the President of the Board of Trade to what he saw as unfair competition, asking whether he was 'aware that I have in my hand a sample of British pottery which is being coloured, designed, produced and sold at eight times the price at which the Japanese copy is being marketed in Canada and the United States'.[31]

Similar views were held in the motor-cycle industry, as revealed by the remarks of the President of the British Cycle and Motor Manufacturers when visiting a large trade show in London in 1951. As experience has shown only too clearly, he vastly underestimated the capacity of the competition when he confidently declared that he did not think that 'the Japanese would be able to beat us in European markets . . . though [before the war] they had ousted us temporarily from South East Asian markets, the consumers seemed to have learnt that it was worth while to pay for a good quality British product'.[32]

From this time onwards many other stereotypical views were sustained in the West, particularly that of a people selflessly dedicated to the success of the companies for which they worked. Perhaps in response to Prime Minister Ikeda's 'national income doubling policy'

92 Käte Gläser

Model no. 1 Living Room
furnished by the Deutscher
Werkbund, Berlin, 1953

In common with State-funded
design organizations the
industry-financed Deutscher
Werkbund sought to 'improve'
levels of public taste. Boxed
sets of approved products
were made for parents, whilst
Werkbund kits were available
for schools. Advice on home
furnishings was offered from
1953: the lightness of the
design of the chair, table,
and standing lamp seen here
marks a distinct shift from
the heavier *völkisch*
tendencies in 1930s German
domestic design.

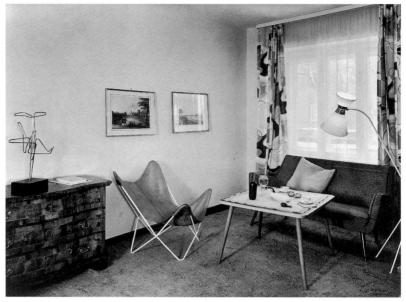

of 1960, such a view was given widespread prominence in the celebrated account in *Time* magazine in 1961 where it was reported that, at the start of each day's work, executives and workers together sang the following verse:

> For the building of a new Japan
> Let's put our strength and mind together,
> Doing our best to promote production,
> Sending our goods to the people of the world
> Endlessly and continuously,
> Like water gushing from a fountain.
> Grow industry, grow, grow, grow!
> Harmony and Sincerity!
> Matsushita Electric.[33]

By the early 1980s the development of the Japanese economy and manufacturing industry, as well as the high levels of investment in plant, equipment, and Research & Development, had been subjected to a much more serious analysis in other countries eager to learn from her economic success. Lawrence Franko, in his book *The Threat of Japanese Multinationals—How the West Can Respond*[34] of 1983, stressed a number of facts that were not widely realized: that the Japanese worked fewer hours on average in manufacturing than their counterparts in Britain, Switzerland, Germany, the Netherlands, and Finland; that there were many Japanese companies which in fact performed badly, went bankrupt, or needed to be rescued; that Japan was less strong in the fields of aerospace, agricultural machinery, custom machine tools and dies, precision and scientific instruments, and computer software; and that Japan had no significant lead over her Western competitors in

1950

93

One of the Bijenkorf department store displays from 'Pioneers of Today' display, Amsterdam, 1961

In 1948 the Bijenkorf store began a series of modern furnishing displays called *Ons Huis Ons Thuis (One's House is a Home)*, promoting designs by progressive Dutch manufacturers. The range became increasingly international in scope and this illustration shows one of nine historic settings where the work of design 'pioneers' was contrasted with more commercial products. Here the pioneering work of Eames (foreground) is contrasted with everyday 1950s design (background).

pharmaceuticals, civil engineering, construction, mass-transit systems, telecommunications, or computers. However, at the time that Franko's remarks were published, less than forty years from the end of the war, Japan had emerged with a powerful economy as well as a high reputation for design in a number of fields, from motor vehicles to electrical appliances, from office equipment to cameras and video-recorders, and from graphic design to high fashion. Although by the 1990s about half of the corporate identity programmes in Japan were executed by American consultancies (thus aiding global projection), since the 1950s there had been an increasing stress on design within companies such as Honda, Toyota, Matsushita, Canon, Sharp, Toshiba, or Sony where there were vast numbers of in-house designers; individual Japanese designers such as Issey Miyake and Rei Kawakubo in fashion, Masanori Umeda and Shiro Kuramata in furniture (both designing for Memphis in Milan), and Ikko Tanaka and Tadanori Yokoo in graphics all became internationally recognized; GK Industrial Design Associates, a pioneering Japanese design consultancy, grew from modest beginnings in 1957 as a group of six student graduates who had studied under Professor Iwataro Koike[35] at Tokyo National University of Fine Arts to a multinational enterprise with offices in the United States and the Netherlands.

The American occupation and influence

After her humiliating defeat in the Second World War, the major task facing the Japanese government was the reconstruction of the national economy. Many important social, economic, and political reforms initiated by the Allied Headquarters (GHQ) under General MacArthur

Stiletto Studios, Consumer's Rest, no. 11 lounge chair prototype, 1986 (prototype developed in 1983)
The 1980s saw the emergence of a number of new design groups in Germany. Initially inspired by experimentation in Italy, many of them challenged notions of good form promoted by the Rat für Formgebung (German Design Council) or the clinical rationalism associated with Ulm. This remodelled and varnished supermarket trolley in the form of a chair, produced by the Berlin-based design group Stiletto Studios, is characteristic of the 'New Design' movement in Germany, presenting familiar objects in a fresh perspective.

provided the planks upon which Japan's postwar recovery was built.[36] As in other countries where there had been a strong presence of American troops, many aspects of American packaging and consumer culture held a fascination for the indigenous population. Takeshi Inoue[37] recalled forty years later that, although he could not then appreciate design in any sophisticated way, he felt that he could 'smell the flavour of the American lifestyle' and its associations with democracy, together with the idea that ordinary people enjoyed a high standard of living.

The Japanese economic and industrial recovery received a considerable boost from the outbreak of the Korean War (called 'a gift from the gods' by Prime Minister Yoshida) in 1951, which provided a key market for Japanese industries at a critical time. However, the 1950s was also an important decade in the development of Japanese design, with continuing American influence on industrial design and business management techniques. Of particular significance was the number of prominent Japanese businessmen who (like a number of their German counterparts) went on organized tours of the United States to study business management techniques. Among them were Taizo Igishaki, Chairman of Hitachi, and Konosuke Matsushita, of Matsushita Electric, and Soichiro Honda, who were also able to acquaint themselves with the role of design in product development. American design expertise was also imported into Japan (see Chapter 7); Raymond Loewy was in the country for three weeks in the early 1950s, participating in a seminar on postwar Japanese product design attended by leading industrialists in which he suggested that with its own rich cultural heritage Japan could do more than copy other countries' ideas. On the invitation of the Japanese Monopoly Bureau he also designed a

95

TR 610 Pocket Transitor
Radio, Sony, 1958

Sony marketed the first
transistor radio in 1955,
establishing it as a company
in which innovative products
played an important part of its
success. The TR 610 pocket
radio, available in four fashion
colours, was one of the
company's early major
successes on the export
market. The text in this
American advertisement
makes it clear that, in its
own time, it was as liberating
a prospect as the Sony
Walkman (see **100**) was to be
twenty-one years later. 'Ideal at
home, at the office, when you
travel . . . *anywhere!*'

cigarette packet for the 'Peace' brand made by a nationalized company. Within a few years a new breed of industrial designers had emerged, including Jiro Kosugi (who had helped to resuscitate the fortunes of the Janome Sewing Machine Co. Ltd), Shozo Sato (who designed the first Datsun for the Nissan Motor Co.), and Yoshio Akioka.

In-house design in the Japanese corporation

Konosuke Matsushita (founder of Matsushita in 1918, the largest manufacturer of consumer electrical goods in the world, comprising the National, Panasonic, Technics, and Quasar brand-names) did much to establish the role of the industrial designer in Japanese companies. He had been influenced by American practice before the war, having in 1933 constituted the company on a divisional basis similar to that introduced in the American automobile industry by Alfred P. Sloan at General Motors in the 1920s. Although the extent of the impact which the United States made on Matsushita by his 1951 visit has perhaps assumed something of an apocryphal dimension in the construction of twentieth-century Japanese design history, he set up an industrial design department in his company, said to be the first in Japan. Initially consisting of a handful of designers, by the end of the decade it had grown to more than 50.

This initiative was soon taken up by other companies: in 1953 the Canon Company set up its industrial design department to develop the Canon V camera; Toshiba established its design department in the same year, followed by the Sharp Corporation in 1957; in 1958 Japanese National Railways set up a Design Committee; Sony, widely recognized for a consistent and enlightened design policy [**95**], appointed its first full-time designer in 1954 and seven years later established its design department under Norio Ohga with seventeen on the staff. However, although the field was gradually recognized in a number of enlightened firms, it was not always highly significant in their organization. At Ricoh, for example, there was no separate industrial design division: Yoko Uga, a design graduate in the mid-1950s worked on posters, displays, lettering, and packaging as well as product design. In fact, in most companies in-house designers had to make quick changes in design, responding to demand, with products often having a life-span of only a few months. Within thirty years of initiation many design departments were on a large scale: by the mid-1980s there were 200 designers at Sharp's Design Center in Osaka, creating about 2,000 new models a year under its Corporate Director, Kiyoshi Sakashita, who was also on the company Board; at the Sony Design Center there were about 120 designers; at Matsushita about 300, although they were decentralized across the various company divisions; at the Toshiba Corporation's Design Division there were about 140 designers. In

'You Meet the Nicest People on a Honda' advertising campaign in the USA, late 1950s

The Honda *Super Cub* motor cycle was launched in Japan in 1958, becoming an immediate success through its economy, practicality, and easy handling. It became an important weapon in establishing a base for Honda in the lucrative consumer markets of the USA. The American Honda Motor Co. Inc. was established in Los Angeles in 1959, working closely with Grey Advertising Inc. to change attitudes to motor cycles in a car-dominated country. The resulting slogan, 'You Meet the Nicest People on a Honda', was aimed at all walks of life and was succeeded by 'The Nicest Things Happen on a Honda'.

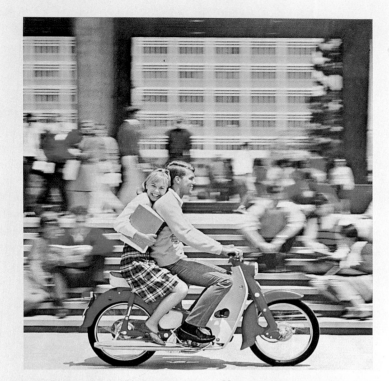

You meet the nicest people on a Honda. And the remarkable thing is the low cost of it all. Prices start about $215.* Insurance is painless. Upkeep negligible. Honda's four-stroke engine demands 200 miles from a gallon of gas. And gets it. Plenty of drive. That's how you stay at the top of the class. World's biggest seller. HONDA

addition to the increasing prevalence of design management in Japanese companies, Computer Aided Design (CAD) has been an important consideration, alongside Computer Aided Manufacture (CAM).

An important product in the establishment of the Japanese reputation in design was the Honda *Super Cub* motorcycle, which became the world's most successful model [**96**], leading to comparisons with the Volkswagen Beetle and Ford Model T. Launched in 1958, it set the standard for lightweight motorcycles until well into the 1960s—by 1967 five million had been sold. The *Super Cub* provided an opportunity to establish Honda on the American market in 1959. A dip in sales in the USA in 1966 was countered for a while by the introduction of a range of gaudily coloured, psychedelic patterned *Tiger Cubs*; the 'step-through' design, its light weight, and easy handling made it also easy for women to ride. The company produced cars from 1962 onwards, establishing itself with the highly successful front-wheel drive N360 mini-car of 1967 and the 1300 model of 1968, and gaining international recognition with the launch of the *Civic* in 1972.

The Tokyo Olympic Games of 1964 did much to open up a world-wide interest in Japan, stimulated by the media. The 1960s was also a period of rapid economic growth and liberalization. Since then Japanese industrial design has established itself in a number of fields, including the automobile and motorcycle industries, audiovisual equipment, domestic appliances, cameras, watches, office and factory automation systems, telecommunications, advanced medical electronics equipment, and a range of equipment within the heavy industrial sector.

Research & Development has played an important role for many Japanese companies as a means of achieving a strong market position. Its results can be seen in the miniaturization of many products from transistor radios and televisions to 'capsule' hotels. For Sony this was exemplified by the introduction of the Walkman in 1979 (which has since been given more than 350 variants by the company's designers); in 1981 the Profeel television was introduced; in 1982 the compact disc player was introduced jointly between CBS/Sony, Philips, and Deutsche Grammophon. All have been widely imitated.

By the 1980s, aided by a number of initiatives such as the launch of the biennial Osaka International Design Festival in 1983 (for further details of this and other initiatives see Chapter 7), Japan was recognized as an international centre for design, with many foreign architects and designers working in Tokyo and other major cities. These included Norman Foster, Michael Graves, Ernesto Rogers, and Nigel Coates, all of whom worked in genres with distinctive cultural values. However, much successful Japanese design has stemmed from its own technologically innovative qualities developed by individual companies, which are, in turn, swiftly imitated by numerous others. There are also significant design fields, such as furniture and tableware, where cultural resonance is important to consumers and in which, with the exception of the expensive output of 'New International Style' designers, Japan has made little impression abroad.

Multinational Corporations and Global Products

6

The corporate personality: invention and identity

From a critical perspective it may be argued that the idea of corporate identity or personality, as articulated by designers and consultancies, is often little more than a contradiction in terms [**97, 98**]. Some of the ways in which symbols and imagery from the past have been used to validate particular outlooks have been considered in the 1983 collection of essays edited by Eric Hobsbawm and Terence Ranger entitled *The Invention of Tradition*.[1]

Interestingly, at the end of the decade, this book was viewed by Wally Olins, a leading figure in corporate identity design and chairman of the design consultancy Wolff Olins, as 'fascinating' and 'brilliant', perhaps acknowledging the relevance of the two key words of the title for those working in his profession.[2] Furthermore, the power to communicate a very selective portrayal of company activity through a major element in corporate communication, the annual company report,[3] was also seen by Olins as a particular kind of invention:

In the world of the annual report there are many similarities with Lewis Carroll's *Alice in Wonderland*. Big things can look small and small things look big. The world is neatly parcelled up into sections that suit a company's organisation. Brazil, for example, disappears with most of South America and all of Africa into a place called 'Rest of the World'. All the people who work for the corporation have, of course, made major contributions to the business . . .

There are no divisions, no splits, no rifts. Everything in the garden is just lovely.[4]

Corporate projection and identity creation

The corporate identity creation business developed dramatically with the growth of multinational corporations and the emergence of global products such as Coca-Cola, McDonald's hamburgers [**99**] or the Sony Walkman [**100, 101**]. It was an aspect of the design profession that became increasingly significant in the post-Second World War period. F. H. K. Henrion, who established Henrion Design Associates (HDA) in 1951, was a pioneer in the field in Britain and, in 1967, defined corporate identity thus:

Detail of 99

CROSLAND FILTERS

CAV

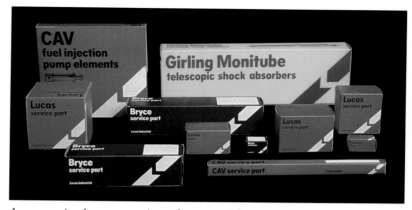

A corporation has many points of contact with various groups of people. It has premises, works, products, packaging, stationery, forms, vehicles, publications and uniforms, as well as the usual kind of promotional activities. These things are seen by customers, agents, suppliers, financiers, shareholders, competitors, the press, and the general public, as well as its own staff. The people in these groups build up their idea of the corporation from what they see and experience of it. An image is therefore an intangible and essentially complicated thing, involving the effect of many and varied factors on many and varied people with many and varied interests.[5]

In effect, Henrion was highlighting both the need to promote a clear and coherent image in the quest for corporate success and the abilities and expertise of design consultancies to bring such perceptions effectively into the public arena. However, with the growth of interest in the concept of design management in the 1970s and 1980s, it was suggested with increasing frequency that corporate identity initiatives should be closely integrated with company infrastructure and policy initiatives. In this evolving climate Wally Olins consistently argued strongly for such a linking of corporate personality with the painstaking analysis of management structures and marketing strategies. Writing in the late 1980s, he pronounced:

We are entering an epoch in which only those corporations making highly competitive products will survive. This means, in the longer term, that products from major companies around the world will become increasingly similar. Inevitably, this means that the whole of a company's personality, its identity, will become the most significant factor in making a choice between one company and its products and another.[6]

Problems of evaluation

Such a positive affirmation by a design consultant of the corporate need for the expression of individual personality in the face of increasing homogeneity of products indirectly highlights the difficulties inherent in a historical evaluation of the relative economic significance of corporate identity creation in the post-Second World War period.

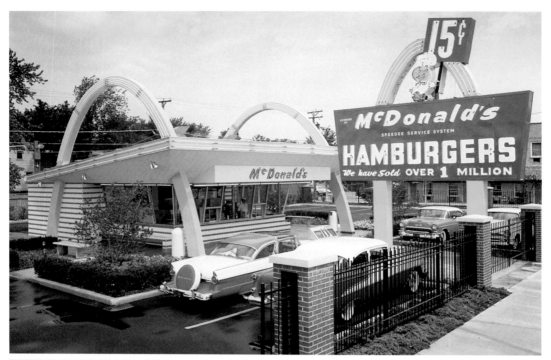

This is particularly problematic if the weight of evidence is drawn from the design profession itself since, as the twentieth century has unfolded and consumerism blossomed, it has become significantly more important for the growing ranks of design consultants and the burgeoning design press to convince the business and manufacturing sectors that design can play a critical economic role in the market-place. This perceived need for a positive portrayal of the effectiveness of corporate identity design has resulted in numerous articles and texts written by those in, or closely connected with, the design profession. The British design historian and theorist Steve Baker, in an extremely useful Olins-focused evaluation of historical approaches to corporate identity design published in 1989, highlighted the problem thus:

Olins is an aggressive publicist of his firm's approach to corporate identity; he claimed in 1988 that 'there's nobody else from Britain apart from us doing it properly'. His writings must, of course, be understood as inseparable from his business activities. In a 1981 article in *Designer* called 'Getting New Business', he suggested that any effective design consultant should ensure that they published articles in 'influential publications like *Management Today* or *The Director*'. He also explained that one of his firm's tactics for attracting a particular company's business was to send its chief executive a copy of *The Corporate Personality*.[7]

Furthermore, the design press, which flourished remarkably in the entrepreneurial, service- and distribution-oriented climate of the

1980s, has inevitably been dependent on advertising revenue from the design profession and its clients. Unsurprisingly, the majority of articles in this specialized sector of the media have tended towards the reportage of the output or ideology of successful individual designers, design practices, or companies embracing design as a visible aspect of their corporate life. However, such examples have provided much of the source material for the many celebratory, design-centred narrative corporate histories which have, in turn, been constructed in comparative isolation from the wider political, economic, social, and cultural complexities of the market-place.

Of greater potential value to the historian of twentieth-century design are company, institutional, organizational and individual designer archives, although these too are often problematic as evaluative tools. Much depends on the extent to which the sheer bulk of

100

Sony Walkman advertisement, 1980s

This advertisement, with its constituent images drawn from several countries, literally shows the global nature of the Walkman, now adopted as a generic name for a product type launched in July 1979. First marketed in the United States as the Soundabout, in Sweden as the Freestyle, and in Britain as the Stowaway, the Walkman has been a phenomenal international success. It demonstrated typical Japanese ingenuity in producing a highly innovative product without a commensurately large investment in new technology.

material in particular archives has been given over to editing, selection, or even destruction of potentially damaging evidence. Indeed, corporate confidential policies relating to boardroom minutes and sensitive policy decisions have in some cases resulted in the excising from the records of controversial or unfavourable comment.

Critiques of corporate power and influence

Writing from less design-oriented perspectives many other writers[8] have presented a different view of the power of the multinational corporation to influence social, economic, and political life. As the American economist J. K. Galbraith argued in his introduction to the 1974 British edition of his widely-read book, *The New Industrial State*:

It is central to my case that power in modern industrial society resides with the large producing organisations—the corporations. So, far from being safely and resignedly subordinate to the market, as the neo-classical argument holds, they fix prices, and go on extensively to accommodate the consumer to their needs. And they also obtain from the state such further action as is needed to ensure a benign and stable environment for their operations.[9]

This, Galbraith argued, was brought about through the economic power of the large-scale corporation to compete with the state in terms of planning and influence. In 1968, General Motors had a gross revenue of $22.8 billion, equivalent to about one-eighth of the total receipts of Federal Government in the United States. It accorded with Galbraith's model of large-scale American capitalism in its ability, through sheer size, to influence government, control markets, and dictate prices and wage settlements for the whole automobile industry (only one element of its industrial activities), as well as establishing patterns of consumer taste.

Such critiques often assumed a more overt political dimension with the global marketing of products which were increasingly identified with a particular way of life. This assumed particular strength in the immediate post-1945 period when products such as Coca-Cola [102] and Levi's jeans became emblems of a 'democratic', essentially American, lifestyle in countries such as Japan [103] and Germany which were seeking to throw off their recent associations with oppressive political regimes. This process has intensified in the post-Berlin Wall era of the 1990s with the proliferation in the former Eastern bloc of McDonald's restaurants and other outlets and products identified with the overt values of consumerism and at least symbolic 'freedom of choice'.

Critiques of what has been termed American 'cultural imperialism' were often highly politicized, as in Ariel Dorfman and Armand

102

Cover of *Time* magazine showing Coca-Cola as the 'World's Friend', 15 May 1950

This celebrated illustration confirmed the way in which Coca-Cola had become a truly global product by the mid-century, much stimulated by its popularity amongst American troops stationed across the world during the Second World War and its aftermath. It came to be readily associated with the material values and desires of American consumer society, a symbol of material affluence.

WORLD & FRIEND
Love that piaster, that lira, that tickey, and that American way of life.

Although jeans originated in the mid-nineteenth century as Californian workers' clothing made by Levi Strauss they have since become potent and expressive emblems of widely differing values throughout the twentieth century. Associated with teenage rebellion in the 1950s on the one hand, or expensive 'Designer' brand names in the late 1970s and early 1980s on the other, their changing meanings paralleled those of the T-shirt which successfully made the transition from working vest to emblematic carrier of slogans and images.

Mattelart's controversial text of 1971 *Para Leer al Pato Donald* (*How to Read Donald Duck*),[10] which was written in the volatile climate of the Chilean revolution. An ideology associated with the consumerist nirvana of wealth and leisure, epitomized by the extensive range of American comics, films, and television programmes which sustained such an outlook, was denounced by the authors as irrelevant to the real needs of under-developed countries, particularly Chile, which they saw as having become fundamentally dependent, in economic and cultural terms, on the United States.

The highly visible presence internationally of logotypes and branding associated with specific products and companies has been a powerful testimony to the perceived ability of design to communicate particular cultural values, as well as to engender corporate profitability. In a later text Mattelart also drew attention to widespread perceptions that multinational corporations, and their products, were seen increasingly as threats to national sovereignty. However, there was evidence that this was recognized by business itself:

... in April 1975, the President of the large North American publicity agency Doyle–Dane–Bernbach[11] asserted before students of a Canadian University that 'Multinational corporations could solve a part of their image problem through the establishment of global universities'. And, he added, going further into the description of his project, that by adopting this formula companies such as Exxon, Texaco or General Electric would have much less need for support by Government, trades union circles and consumers from accusations made against them of violating national sovereignty. The proposal is very simple: the companies would open a university course of two years for students from both industrialised and underdeveloped countries, with the requirement only 'that they spoke perfect English'. These courses could deal with the history of the company, the analysis of concrete examples of market-ing, management, international law, the relationship of the enterprise with the community, its social responsibility. Provided with a diploma granted by the company, the students would return to their respective countries and would constitute 'a kind of common denominator of understanding' around the world.[12]

Early manifestations of corporate identity: a historical overview

Although corporate identity has assumed an increasingly high profile in the post-1945 era, it has manifested itself over a far longer period through the formation, organization, and visual projection of groups as varied as armies,[13] political regimes,[14] and railway companies. In Britain, for example, the great railway companies of the nineteenth century made concerted attempts to project their own individual iden-tities across many aspects of their visible presence, from railway ter-mini through to coach livery, uniforms, and dining-car tableware. Design historians have laid particular emphasis on the corporate iden-tity work of designers such as Peter Behrens at the Allgemeine Elektrizitäts-Gesellschaft in the early years of the twentieth century in Germany, as discussed in Chapter 1. Significant examples of corporate identity policies can be found in many other countries, as in Britain in the buildings, locomotives, rolling stock, buses, signage, advertising, fittings, and fabrics of the London Passenger Transport Board under the operational direction of Frank Pick in the 1930s, or in the United States with Walter Dorwin Teague's striking designs for Texaco petrol stations.

Other notable examples prior to the Second World War include the Olivetti office equipment company in Italy, where a corporate identity policy emerged in the wake of Adriano Olivetti's initiatives in modern-izing the firm's business and production methods in the later 1920s. Much of the impetus had derived from a visit to the United States in 1926, and an advertising office was established in 1928. Following his appointment as general manager in 1933, a wide range of initiatives were adopted in the projection of the public, and also internal, identity of the company, sustained by the employment of a number of leading modernist architects and designers who worked on all aspects of the company's visible appearance, from brochures, advertising and office machines through to factory buildings and workers' housing. A Bauhaus graduate, Alexander Schawinsky, worked on graphic and product design from 1933 to 1936; Marcello Nizzoli, a renowned exhi-bition and graphic designer, became the company's chief consultant in 1936; in the same year Giovanni Pintori also joined the company and, like Nizzoli, added to Olivetti's reputation through publicity, product, and architectural design. This very much set the scene for the further development of an enlightened corporate policy in the post-Second

World War era with the employment of designers of the stature of Ettore Sottsass Jr. and Mario Bellini and the increasingly significant role given to cultural projection. The company's commitment to corporate identity design was recognized in 1974 when the American Institute of Architects awarded Olivetti the Industrial Arts Medal 'for a history of excellence in communicating its image through product design, corporate communications, architecturally distinguished manufacturing and merchandising facilities, and sponsorship of numerous social, educational, recreational, and cultural programs for both its employees and the public at large'.

In the United States corporate identity design also assumed increasing importance in the interwar years. The Container Corporation of America (CCA) was an important pioneer in this respect in the 1930s, largely through the enlightened patronage of the company's founder, the Chicago industrialist Walter P. Paepke. In 1936, wishing to communicate the company's commitment to a modern outlook and product quality, he employed the N. W. Ayer advertising agency as a means of bringing this about. In the same year he also appointed Egbert Jacobsen as Director of the company's new Design Department. Amongst those designers commissioned to produce advertisements were the French designers A. M. Cassandre and Fernand Léger, the former Bauhaus tutors Lázló Moholy-Nagy and Herbert Bayer, Herbert Matter, the Swiss emigré designer and poster artist, and the Hungarian-born graphic designer, Gyorgy Kepes. Combinations of photomontage with typography and other techniques associated with the European avant-garde were incorporated into company publicity, strongly influencing the outlook of other designers working for the company. Such strong links with European modernism were sustained by the establishment, in 1937, of the New Bauhaus in Chicago under Lázló Moholy-Nagy. Later becoming the School of Design, then School of Design in Chicago, and finally the Institute of Design,[15] a number of former Bauhaus graduates and masters were employed on the staff.

In the post-Second World War period Walter Paepke, Egbert Jacobsen, and Herbert Bayer were at the forefront of moves which sought to further understanding in business circles of the significant economic potential of design in industry. In 1951 Paepke inaugurated the first Design Conference at the Aspen Institute of Humanistic Studies in Colorado.[16] Initiating debate about the wider social, cultural, and philosophical implications of design it sought to bring together leading figures from design, industry, government, and education. At the 1951 meeting both Olivetti and the Container Corporation of America were cited as exemplars of the implementation of a consistent design policy in industry. Held annually, in 1954 it became incorporated as the International Design Conference in

Aspen (IDCA) and was soon established as a major forum for design debate, with contributions from leading designers, intellectuals, and industrialists from all over the world.

Design and the multinational corporation after 1945

As has been discussed in Chapter 4, the aspirations of those seeking to implement the modernist creed in the interwar years had been severely blunted by the rising tide of national identity in the increasingly difficult political and economic circumstances of the times. However, after the Second World War, with the widespread discrediting of totalitarian regimes and the waning of the power of imperialism in the Western industrialized world, the internationalizing values inherent in modernism no longer carried the same threat to national identity. With the postwar reorientation of traditional trading patterns and the need to develop new outlets many large-scale companies viewed the penetration of global markets as an increasingly important goal. As part of this strategy multinational corporations assumed the mantle of modernism, their international presence marked by efficient-looking buildings, products, and co-ordinated corporate design programmes.

As has been suggested earlier, the Olivetti company epitomized high standards for corporate identity design and implementation. It was particularly influential on the outlook of International Business Machines (IBM), a company which emerged as a world leader in the field of office equipment after the end of the Second World War. IBM's distinctive corporate style, which embraced everything from brochures and sign systems to dictating machines and company buildings, emerged after the appointment of the architect-designer Eliot Noyes as Consultant Director of Design in 1956 [**104**]. He had first worked on the IBM account in Norman Bel Geddes's office ten years earlier, continuing to work on a company retainer after setting up his own design practice in 1947. He brought in Paul Rand as Graphics Co-ordinator as well as a number of other design consultants including Charles Eames, George Nelson, and Edgar Kaufmann Jr. They were all heavily influenced by European modernism: Noyes had worked with the former Bauhaus masters Walter Gropius and Marcel Breuer at Harvard in the 1930s, and was Director of the Department of Industrial Design at the Museum of Modern Art (MOMA) in New York from 1940–2 and 1945–6; Paul Rand was well aware of European modernism in the interwar years, an interest stimulated by magazines such as the German *Gebrauchsgraphik*[17] and *Advertising Arts*; George Nelson had studied in Rome in the 1930s and, with the designer Henry Wright, co-edited *Architectural Forum*, a magazine which strongly promoted the modernist cause and frequently featured many aspects of corporate design; after a brief interregnum by Suzanne Wasson-Tucker, Edgar Kaufmann Jr. had succeeded Noyes as Director of the

104 Eliot Noyes

Selectric typewriter, IBM, 1961
Noyes, who had worked for
Gropius and Breuer in the
1930s, had also been director
of industrial design at MOMA,
New York. He was brought in
as design consultant to IBM in
1956 by the corporation's
President, Thomas Watson,
and soon gave the company
a modern, international
corporate image. This
pervaded its buildings, graphic
communications, and
products, much in the way that
previously the image for the
Olivetti company had done.
This particular typewriter also
introduced the 'golfball' as a
replacement for type-bars.

Department of Industrial Design at MOMA, a strong advocate of modernism and promoter of the annual Good Design Exhibitions held at the Museum between 1950 and 1955. Marcel Breuer and Eero Saarinen, an American architect-designer with Scandinavian roots, were also commissioned to design buildings for IBM.

The IBM design outlook was enshrined in its Design Practice Manual, written by Noyes. The company soon became renowned for a corporate identity which symbolized advanced technology and organizational efficiency through its crisp graphics (as in Rand's logotype of 1956, see **105**), the neat, clean lines of such office products as the 1961 *Selectric* typewriter, and the efficient, functional, yet pleasant, ethos of its architecture and interiors. Such an outlook (also promoted by Olivetti and other companies) additionally endowed the office environment with notions of status and aesthetic sensitivity and did much to help persuade potential employees that clerical work was an attractive alternative to the often more lucrative wage potential of competing factory work in the 1950s and 1960s.[18] IBM's policy of design co-ordination throughout the corporation was continued in the following decades, resulting in official recognition from the American design profession: in 1980 IBM was awarded both the Design Leadership Award by the American Institute of Graphic Arts and an award for long-term excellence in design by the Industrial Designers of America (IDSA).

Other large American companies were also significant exponents of corporate identity in the decades following the Second World War. By the mid-1950s the Westinghouse Electric Corporation had become increasingly concerned with its design image, with frequent complaints by retailers that the company was not oriented clearly enough towards the consumer and could not keep up with its competitors in terms of product development. Its position was further affected by a

105

Corporate logos: Paul Rand for IBM (1956) and Westinghouse (1960), Henrion Design for KLM (1964), Wolff Olins for BT (1991)

Corporate design was an important part of the armoury of national and multinational corporations in the post-Second World War period. These particular symbols and their designers are celebrated in their field.

series of strikes and the radical dropping of prices in 1956 by General Electric, the market leader in consumer appliances. Following detailed analysis of the position, Eliot Noyes was brought in to Westinghouse in 1960 in order to improve standards. In turn he brought in Paul Rand, who produced a striking logotype, based on electric circuitry and the letter 'W'. Noyes's other consultancies have included Mobil (1964) and Pan-Am (1969–72), whilst Rand has also produced logos for ABC Television and United Parcels Service.

The interiors of many large corporations were also endowed with an internationalizing modernist aesthetic, sustained by the furniture of companies such as Herman Miller and Knoll. Although Herman Miller had begun to explore a modernist outlook in the 1930s through the enlightened appointment of Gilbert Rohde as the company's designer, it was not until the appointment of George Nelson as director of design in 1944 that the company began to orient itself towards the architectural, and thus largely corporate, market. Nelson also brought in Charles Eames as a consultant to the company, reinforcing the modernist ethos in furniture production. There was considerable activity in the field of office furniture, most notably the Action Office, which was developed from the late 1950s by Nelson and Robert Propst, and marketed in its first version from 1964.

Knoll Associates, founded by the German-born Hans Knoll and his wife Florence in New York in 1946, also did much to support the modernist corporate environment through its furniture and furnishings, which could be found in many of the impressive foyers of large corporations [**106**]. Florence had studied at the Cranbrook Academy of Art and at the Illinois Institute of Technology, both institutions with strong European affiliations. She also knew Mies van der Rohe and worked with Gropius and Breuer. Building on such links, the Knolls marketed designs by leading Europeans, many of them being seen as 'classics' of modern design, especially those by Breuer, Saarinen, and Mies, who granted the company the production rights of his designs of the 1920s.

Other companies gained considerable recognition for their identity in the same period. In Germany, for example, the Braun company set high standards of a coherent rational design aesthetic with the introduction of Otl Aicher and Hans Gugelot from the pioneering Hochschule für Gestaltung at Ulm alongside the industrial designer, Dieter Rams, in the mid-1950s. In 1956 the company's design department was established, coming under Rams's direction in 1960. During his lengthy association with the company a clear identity emerged, characterized by the white, sculptural form of the KM2 Kitchen Machine designed by G. A. Müller in 1957 [**107**] or the HLD 4 Hairdryer designed by Rams in 1970. The austere, efficient lines of the company's domestic appliances were complemented by the rational

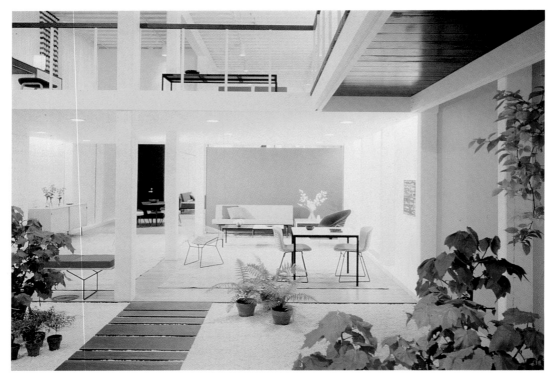

106

Knoll International furniture showroom, USA, 1950s

The styling of the furniture and spatial organization of this interior typifies the international modernism projected by multinational corporations after 1945. This could be seen in the work for Knoll by Eero Saarinen, Harry Bertoia (whose famous lattice steel wire Diamond chair (1952) can be seen in the centre of the floor) and by Florence Knoll herself, whose sideboard can be seen on the extreme left. Hans and Florence Knoll also forged links with other leading American and European designers, producing furniture under licence by Mies and Breuer. The company established a reputation for Good Design much in line with the aesthetic principles espoused by Kaufmann at MOMA, New York.

spirit underlying its corporate graphics, advertising, and packaging. It should be considered, in passing, that a coherent design programme did not in itself ensure market success: American Gillette took Braun over, and further difficulties were experienced in the competitive market-place of the early 1990s.

The work of a wide range of influential corporate identity consultancies such as Chermayeff & Geismar Inc. of New York, Pentagram of London or Total Design of Holland might be enumerated in this context, along with many instances of a multinational corporate design policy, such as those adopted by Philips,[19] Coca-Cola,[20] or Sony.[21] However, there are other mechanisms worthy of attention which have done much to support the globalization of specific products or cultural values, many of them enshrined in the corporate ethos of companies already discussed.

The role of museums and exhibitions in promoting a global sesign culture

While a growing number of museums are beginning to embrace wider definitions of design culture in the twentieth century, the majority have endorsed a policy which is centred on celebrated products or the output of specific designers whose work is seen to embrace high standards of aesthetic distinction or cultural status. The twentieth-century design galleries of many museums around the world have their roots in the collection and display of objects which, it was originally felt, would 'improve' standards of taste and enhance the cultural well-being of their visitors. Furthermore, those charged with selection policies and the acquisition of material were generally drawn from a narrow social and cultural spectrum and, when they were bold enough to step outside their own national conventions of artistic excellence, often favoured objects which conformed to the modernist canon. The meanings of such clean, abstract forms, stripped of superfluous ornamentation and symbolically compatible with the modern machine-age production technology, have changed alongside the reshaping of cultural and political perspectives both before and after the Second World War, as has been discussed in Chapter 2 (and will be examined further in Chapter 8). As has been argued, modernist products became increasingly associated with notions of 'Good Design', opposed both to retrospective indulgence in historicizing ornament in domestic products on the one hand and to the science-fiction-inspired futuristic chrome fantasies and tail-fins of automobiles on the other. Modernist products were also seen as oppositional to notions of built-in obsolescence and ephemerality and thus, particularly when placed in a spotlit, pedestalized museum—rather than a social—context, assumed something of the status of 'design classic'.

Modernism and MOMA, New York

MOMA, founded in New York in 1929 'to encourage and develop the study of the modern arts and the application of such arts to manufacture and public life', did much to establish such an outlook. Its Department of Architecture and Industrial Art was established in 1932

107 Gerd Alfred Muller and Robert Oberheim

Kitchen Machine KM 32, Braun, 1957

By the mid-1950s Braun emerged as a company with high aesthetic principles in product design, having forged links with the nationalist Hochschule für Gestaltung at Ulm. A design department was established at the company in 1956, the KM3 of the following year epitomizing the geometric clarity which was to be associated with Braun products for many years, particularly after 1960 when Dieter Rams became Braun's chief designer. A permanent display of Braun products was put on display at MOMA, New York, in 1958.

and mounted a series of didactic design exhibitions promoting modernism, commencing with the *Machine Art* show of 1934 which was curated by Philip Johnston. It was in the same year that MOMA's Design Collection was formally inaugurated, commencing with a selection from the *Machine Art* exhibition [12]. Two criteria were identified for the selection of objects—'quality' and 'historical' significance:

An object is chosen for its quality because it is thought to achieve, or have originated, those formal ideals of beauty which have become the major style concepts of our time.

Historical significance is a more flexible criterion. It applies to objects which may not resolve problems of aesthetics and function with total success, but which nevertheless have contributed importantly—or may yet contribute—to the development of design.[22]

In 1939 the Museum held a ten-year retrospective exhibition in which industrial design played a comparatively minor role. MOMA's stance against the ephemeral styling of American products was revealed by the inclusion of only one American designer, Richard Buckminster Fuller, a fierce critic of contemporary American industrial design. The more favoured European and Scandinavian modernism was represented through chairs by Breuer, Mies Van Der Rohe, Le Corbusier, and Alvar Aalto. This design creed was continued by Eliot Noyes and Edgar Kaufmann Jr., in charge of MOMA's Department of Industrial Design in the 1940s and 1950s. Kaufmann also mounted a series of *Good Design* exhibitions between 1950 and 1955 [108, cf. 109], the precepts for which were largely enumerated in his definitive text, *What Is*

108

'Good Design Show' organized by Edgar Kaufmann Jr. for MOMA, NY, 1951

Kaufmann's 'Good Design' programme was underpinned by a collaboration between MOMA, New York, and The Merchandise Mart, Chicago, representing respectively the interests of art and commerce. It was aimed at museum audiences and the wholesale buyers who represented the retail trade, seeking to educate both the public and manufacturing industry. The pronounced emphasis on form rather than decoration seen in this installation by Finn Juhl reflected the modernist credo followed by Kaufmann.

109 Frank Gehry

Interior of the Vitra Design Museum at Weil am Rhein, 1989

This innovative museum was built largely as a gallery for the chair collection of Rolf Fehlbaum of the Vitra furniture manufacturing company. Pictured here are a number of classic designs including Charlotte Perrier and Le Corbusier's Chaise Longue (1929), Breuer's B3 Wassily chair (1925), Jacobsen's *Ant* chair (1953), and Eames's lounge chair (1958). Pedestalized and removed from their primary function, they are to be viewed as art and symbols of aesthetic status.

Modern Design? of 1950.[23] Consolidating such a morally-charged approach to design, the exhibition 'Olivetti: Design in Industry' was put on in 1952, the first time a European manufacturer had been invited to display its products and graphic design at the Museum. Coming two years after the establishment of the Olivetti Corporation of America in New York, the show exemplified what was felt to be good practice, a practice which the company had itself done much to validate through external promotion. As was written at the time in MOMA's *Bulletin*,

The Olivetti company, many critics agree, is the leading corporation in the western world in the field of design. For patronage in architecture, product design and advertising, it would only be difficult to name a second . ., It is not only the aesthetic quality of these achievements that is remarkable. More important as a lesson in our industrial world of today is the organisation of all the visual aspects of an industry, unified under a single high standard of taste.[24]

The postwar inheritance of a form of European modernism was further consolidated when Braun products were put on permanent display at MOMA from 1958, following growing approbation of the German company's new design policy at the 1957 Milan Triennale, the Frankfurt Radio and Television Exposition, and the Berlin

110

Publicity for Scenicruiser Greyhound bus, designed by Raymond Loewy Associates, 1954

Loewy devoted considerable attention to new transportation designs, endowing them with style and panache. He had worked with the Greyhound company since 1940, when he designed the Silversides motor coach. It was replaced by the sleek, streamlined, and obviously American Scenicruiser, and its high standards of passenger comfort, together with the development of the US highway system, were intended to attract inter-city travellers in the face of competition from rail and the air.

International Building Exhibition, where its products were seen in the majority of show houses.

There was a similar institutionalization of the notion of Good Design in Europe, often with support from the State, as with the Council of Industrial Design (COID), established in Britain in 1944 or the Rat für Formgebung (Design Council) in Germany, which, following a 1951 mandate in the German Parliament, was inaugurated in 1953. The COID was charged from the outset with 'improving' standards of design in the consumer and manufacturing sectors and initiated a Good Design Award Scheme for selected products in 1957, the year after opening its own Design Centre in the Haymarket, London. The awards generally recognized products which conformed to the modernist canon—genteel and restrained, and devoid of excessive ornamentation or ephemeral styling. Similar awards reflecting parallel aesthetic priorities were offered in other European countries, including the Compasso d'Oro scheme, initiated by La Rinascente department store in Italy in 1954, and the Beauté France award, made through the French Ministry of Commerce.

That there was an established international canon of 'taste' in the 1950s can be argued further through the evidence collected by Jay

Doblin, Director of the Institute of Design at the Illinois Institute of Technology, in 1958.[25] He wrote to 100 of the 'leading' designers, architects, and design teachers around the world, asking them to identify the ten 'best designed mass-produced products of modern times'. About 80 ballots were returned and, after the issue of further questionnaires, a final order was drawn up. Although the overall ranking was significantly more accommodating with regard to ephemeral styling than would have been the case with MOMA, the COID, and comparable organizations with a commitment to the concept of Good Design, the top three products were the Olivetti Lettera 22 portable typewriter of 1950, designed by Marcello Nizzoli, the Eames side-chair of 1947, produced by Herman Miller, and Mies Van Der Rohe's Barcelona Chair, originally designed in 1929, produced by Knoll Associates. Raymond Loewy Associates-designed products were featured six times (including the Coldspot refrigerator for Sears Roebuck, a 1948 vacuum cleaner for Singer, and the 1954 *Scenicruiser* greyhound bus [**110**]), but overall the favoured products generally looked to modernism, with a particular leaning towards designs from Europe and Scandinavia, including designs by Aalto, Barnack, Breuer, D'Ascanio, Ghia, Gretsch, Nizzoli, Pinin Farina, Ponti, Porsche, Thonet Brothers, and Wegner.

The corporation and cultural heritage

As has been seen in the case of Herman Miller and Knoll International in the United States, a significant number of companies were active in the promotion of the international style through the marketing of high-quality furniture with a heavy premium on aesthetic distinction. Cassina, the Milan-based furniture company, played a similar role, moving into the field of architect-designed furniture from the late 1940s onwards, with a particular emphasis on Italian designers, such as Franco Albini, Gio Ponti, Vico Magistretti, and Mario Bellini. From 1965 it also initiated a policy of producing a range of past classics from the late nineteenth and earlier twentieth centuries. Entitled the 'Masters' series, it commenced with manufacture, to the original design, of the 1929 chaise longue by Le Corbusier, Charlotte Perriand, and Pierre Jeanneret. Later, particularly in the heritage-aware 1980s when the pervasive fashionability of Post-Modernism cast many aspects of modernist design into a historical perspective, the 'Masters' range included the resurrection of furniture by Gunnar Asplund, Breuer, Frank Lloyd Wright, Gerrit Rietveld, and Charles Rennie Mackintosh.

Also important in the wider projection of companies has been their involvement in cultural activities, a sphere in which Olivetti has been particularly prominent. Exhibitions specifically centred upon the company's own products and designers were widely disseminated, typified by such shows as *Olivetti: Form and Concept* put on at the Musée des Arts Decoratifs in Paris (as well as at venues in Barcelona, Madrid, Edinburgh, London, and Tokyo between 1969 and 1971) and *Os Artistas e a Olivetti* (The Artists and Olivetti) shown in Sao Paolo, Brazil in 1976. However, wider aspects of Italian artistic heritage were celebrated in a series of art-historical films by Carlo Ludovico Ragghianti in the 1950s, as well as in exhibitions such as the Italian Modern Art Exhibition 1910–35, drawn from the Mattioli Collection, which was shown in New York and Europe in the late 1960s and early 1970s. Film and photography have also been a potent vehicle for the projection of company ethos, environment, design practice, and social policy, with commissions from, and about, other countries, cultures, ecology, and the environment. Even gifts, souvenirs, desk diaries, and company calendars, first introduced in 1951, were a part of the process of establishing the company's personality as cultural. Corporate gifts and souvenirs have included melamine paper knives by Marcello Nizzoli (1960), a melamine desk tidy by Bruno Munari (1960), a canvas brief case by Giorgio Soavi (1965), and an enamelled-iron pencil tray (1966) and electric table clock (1968) by Ettore Sottsass Jr., many of which became extremely sought after as status symbols by business executives and managers.

'The New International Style'

Globalization of the designed object accelerated significantly in the 1980s with the emergence of design groups such as Memphis. It originated in 1981 in Milan and, centred around Ettore Sottsass Jr., effectively set on a commercial footing many ideas which had originated in the studio-based experimentation of 1970s Italy. Memphis furniture, lighting, ceramic, glass, and jewellery designs drew upon the symbols, forms, materials, and decorative motifs of mass culture; it utilized seemingly mundane materials such as plastic laminates, and emphasized surface decoration, colour, and layers of meaning at the expense of apparent function. Such products radically undermined both the architectonic principles of the modernist aesthetic inherent in international style furniture and the linear gracefulness that had generally characterized design-conscious Italian products since the Second World War. In addition to Sottsass, the group had a strong international range of contributors to its output, including Andrea Branzi, Michele De Lucchi, Matheo Thun, and Marco Zanini from Italy, Michael Graves and Peter Shire from the United States, Hans Hollein from Austria, Xavier Mariscal from Spain, and Shiro Kuramata and Arata Isozaki from Japan. During the 1980s, shows of the group's work were held in the major museums in many capital cities around the world and its products marketed under the banner of the 'New International Style'.[26] This notion of a 'New International Style' indi-

111 Philippe Starck

Toothbrush for L'Oréal/Goupil Laboratories, France, 1990

With greater emphasis on health, fitness, and hygiene in the 1970s, the bathrooms of the wealthier sectors of society were increasingly characterized as places for leisure and relaxation rather than functional necessity. During the 1980s many associated 'designer' products were introduced to this sphere of domestic life. The Starck toothbrush, with its Brancusi-like sculptural form and conical 'pedestal' has become an icon of an emergent 'designer' culture.

cated the commodification of particular cultural concepts within a global context. Endowed with the immediate cultural status conferred through featuring widely in exhibitions and the more image-oriented media across the world, Memphis products were the preserve of an affluent élite who saw them essentially as works of art.

This notion of 'design as art', where design was generally collected for its visual identity and implicit cultural values rather than any premium on function or practicality [**111**], was also reinforced by the outlook of companies such as Officina Alessi[27] from Italy or the New York-based Swid Powell [**112**]. Specializing in what has been termed 'the tabletop industry' or 'micro-architecture',[28] both companies focused on the commissioning of small-scale pieces of decorative art by well-known architects and designers, whose buildings, interiors, tastes, personalities, and exhibitions were increasingly widely covered in the media.

Officina Alessi launched a series of *Tea and Coffee Piazzas*[29] which were commissioned from eleven internationally recognized architects [**113**], including Robert Venturi, Michael Graves, and Charles Jencks from the United States, Alessandro Mendini and Paolo Portoghesi from Italy, Oscar Tusquets from Spain, and Hans Hollein from Austria. The eleven sets were each produced in limited editions of 99, priced individually at about £12,000, and galleries in Milan and New York simultaneously hosted their launch in 1983, reinforcing the cultural status and economic exclusivity of the objects.

Swid Powell was founded in 1982 by Nan Swid and Addie Powell, significantly both previous employees of Knoll International, the former as design director in product design development, the latter a sales vice-president. Swid Powell's first range of architect-designed pieces, including porcelain dinnerware, glassware, and silverplate, was launched in 1984 in six American cities, proving an instant commercial success in the upper echelons of the market-place. The company continued to maintain a fashionable aura throughout the decade, sustained by such high-profile events as the striking window displays in the Bergdorf Goodman department store which were planned to coincide with the American Institute of Architects' 1988 convention in New York. Many of the displays incorporated Swid Powell artefacts,

112 Robert Venturi

Village, 4-piece tea and coffee set, Swid Powell, 1986

Drawing on an eclectic range of references—historic, high art, and the everyday—this tea set for the highly fashionable Swid Powell company reflected Venturi's Post-Modernist inclinations. The teapot decoration and domed lid with oculus refers to the Pantheon in Rome; the coffee pot derives from the form of a Tuscan tower, the milk jug from a Renaissance palazzo and the sugar bowl from a peasant's cottage.

113 Kazumasa Yamashita

5-piece tea and coffee set,
Tea and Coffee Piazza series,
Alessi, 1983

This coffee set was one of
eleven limited editions of the
scheme marketed by Officina
Alessi and the two venues
from which they were
launched—the Brera Gallery,
Milan, and the Max Protech
Gallery, New York—mark out
the company's cultural and
artistic intentions.
Commissioned from high-
profile designers and
architects, these objects
of high fashion, destined for
museums or the coffee tables
of the very wealthy, signified
the global nature of 1980s
design culture.

their fashionability and status considerably enhanced by the featuring
of a number of Swid Powell-commissioned architect-designers alongside celebrated fashion designers. These pairings included Michael
Graves and Giorgio Armani, Robert Venturi and Christian Lacroix,
and Richard Meier and Calvin Klein. This international dimension
was reinforced by the commissioning by Swid Powell of other high-
profile designers including Ettore Sottsass Jr., Paolo Portoghesi,
Vittorio Gregotti, and the British-born George Sowden from Italy,
the Austrian Hans Hollein, and Arata Isozaki from Japan. The
metaphorical distance from the tabletops of an affluent international
design-conscious clientèle to cultural re-affirmation in the displays of
leading museums such as MOMA and the Metropolitan Museum in
New York, the Museum Boysmans-van Beuningen in Rotterdam, or
the Design Museum and Victoria and Albert Museum in London
was small. It is also clear when reviewing the names of many of the
designers working for Memphis, Officina Alessi, and Swid Powell and
other such enterprises that they and their designs have become global
commodities just as have the more anonymous products of IBM,
Philips, Sony, or Benetton.

Design Promotion, Profession, and Management

7

The nineteenth and early twentieth centuries had seen the proliferation of many societies which sought to promote design as a significant activity, whether from a social, cultural, political, or economic point of view [114]. These included such diverse bodies as the Swedish Society of Industrial Design (Svenska Slödförinengen), which had been established in 1845 to encourage and promote handicraft in industry, the Finnish Society of Crafts and Design of 1879, the Art Workers' Guild and the Arts and Crafts Exhibition Society, founded in Britain in 1884 and 1888 respectively, the Hungarian Decorative Art Society (Magyar Iparmüvészeti Társulat) of 1885, the Polish Applied Arts Society of 1901, the Netherlands Association for Crafts and Industrial Art (Nederlandsche Vereeniging voor Ambachts en Nijverheidskunst), the Danish Society of Arts and Crafts and Industrial Design of 1907, and the National Alliance of Art and Industry in the United States of 1912. The more significant impact in Germany of the activities of the Deutscher Werkbund in the twenty-five years following its foundation in 1907 has already been discussed in Chapters 1 and 2. Like other similar less influential bodies formed in its wake, such as the British Design and Industries Association (DIA) founded in 1915, it sought to achieve recognition of the economic significance of design in manufacturing industry and thus indirectly helped to enhance the professional status of the designer.

The long-term difficulties inherent in efforts to achieve recognition of the design profession in manufacturing industry can be seen to reside partially in the conflict between notions of the individual artistic personality and the economic and technological realities of manufacturing industry. Indeed, for much of the twentieth century there has been considerable reservation about designers in manufacturing circles. Several instances of such suspicion early in the century can be detected in the debates about design and standardization in industry. But there was also considerable disagreement amongst designers and their propagandists themselves, centering on opposition of individuality and standardization, subjectivity and objectivity, and artistic licence and social responsibility. Notable examples of such ideological differences already encountered include those between Henry van de

Detail of 119

Velde and Hermann Muthesius at the Deutscher Werkbund before 1914 or between Wassily Kandinsky and Alexander Rodchenko, his wife Varvara Stepanova, and Vladimir Tatlin around 1920. Although these rifts have been accorded a high historical profile on account of the dominance of personality-centred design-historical writing, resonances of such concerns were felt in many countries in the boardrooms of everyday manufacturing industry, where the spectre of the artistic personality, oblivious of the realities of production technology, consumer preferences and market strategies, haunted the thoughts of many industrialists and businessmen. In Britain, for example, the Council for Art and Industry's 1937 report on *Design and the Designer in British Industry* stated that a key 'difficulty which has to be overcome is the existence of a mutual distrust between artists and manufacturers'.[1]

Design-historical writing has often obscured much of the wider picture of the professional status of the designer and the role of design in industry through its general focus on successful partnerships between designers and industry: attention is drawn to Sweden, for example, where Wilhelm Kåge worked as Art Director for the ceramics manufacturer Gustavsberg, and Simon Gate and Edward Hald helped to establish the artistic reputation of the glass manufacturer Orrefors; to Italy, where Marcello Nizzoli designed for Olivetti and Gio Ponti for the ceramics manufacturer Richard-Ginori and the furniture maker Fontana; and to the United States, where the first generation of industrial designers such as Raymond Loewy, Henry Dreyfuss, and Walter Dorwin Teague worked for large, well-known corporate clients.

However, the widely-felt uncertainty of the connotations of terms commonly used in the interwar years such as 'commercial art' or 'graphic design', 'industrial art' or 'industrial design' reflected the inability of designers to establish a clearcut professional identity or status. Indeed, the use of such terms can lend insights into the changing politics of professional validation. For example, the Chartered Society of Designers (CSD) in London, the leading professional organization for designers in Britain, began life in 1930 as the Society of Industrial Artists (SIA) and despite a radical reorganization at the end of the Second World War, did not actually incorporate the word 'design' into its title until 1965, when it became the Society of Industrial Artists and Designers. The last change of title, to Chartered Society of Designers, reflected the continuing drive for more widespread professional recognition by the business and manufacturing community: the omission of the word 'Artists', together with any notion of the idiosyncracies that such a term might still have been thought to imply, was perhaps as significant as the word 'Chartered', with all of its professional connotations.

The design profession in interwar Britain

The Society of Artists (SIA) was established with two distinct aims, the first of which was

to establish the profession of the Designer on a sounder basis by forming a controlling authority to advance and protect the interests of all engaged in the production of Design for Industry, Publishing and Advertising. The second purpose is to assemble the resources of Design as a vital factor in British Industry and so to assist the advancement of British Trade, both at home and abroad.[2]

The founding of the SIA appeared to presage a flurry of official design activity in Britain in succeeding years: a Board of Trade Committee under the Chairmanship of Lord Gorell was appointed in the following year, 1931, to report on Art and Industry;[3] late in 1933 the Council for Art and Industry was established under the auspices of the Board of Trade, making its mark through the publication of a number of design-centred reports (including *Design and the Designer* of 1937), the organization of exhibitions, liaison with industry, and involvement in design education; in 1936 a National Register of Industrial Art Designers was established, and the Royal Society of Arts appointed ten members to act as a new select faculty of Designers for Industry (upgraded by the Home Office to Royal Designers for Industry (RDI) in the following year). It was also a decade which heralded a number of BBC radio programmes devoted to design matters, saw the publication of Herbert Read's celebrated pro-modernist text, *Art and Industry* (1934),[4] and Nikolaus Pevsner's *Pioneers of the Modern Movement* (1936)[5] and *An Enquiry into Industrial Art in England* (1937),[6] as well as the mounting of a number of widely reported exhibitions[7] including the large-scale 'British Art in Industry' show at the Royal Academy, with 2,223 exhibits on show. The Design and Industries Association (DIA) was also active at the time in its promotion of the design cause, publishing its own magazines, newsletters, books, and other design propaganda, as well as organizing public exhibitions. But, as has been suggested in 'Britain and Modernism' in Chapter 2, such apparently clear-cut evidence, though cited by many historians of British design,[8] can be misleading in its portrayal of a real sea change in terms of recognition of the designer in industry. The long history of British design has often embraced the establishment of many official design-related committees, particularly in times of economic difficulty, when the government or its agencies wish to be seen to be working towards improving the position. An early instance of this was the Select Committee on Art and Manufactures which was appointed in 1836 in the light of worries about increasingly strong competition from foreign manufacturers. Almost 150 years later, in not dissimilar circumstances, and indicating in some ways how little the picture had really changed, the Department of Education and Science and the Design Council commissioned a report on *The Industrial Design Requirements of Industry* which came to the conclusion that foreign companies generally

value more highly the contribution made by design to market success, they spend more money on industrial design and give the designer considerably more say in the final selection of the design for manufacture. As a result they appear to attract and motivate designers who are generally very competent and highly creative.[9]

The DIA has left a considerable legacy for historians in its Yearbooks, magazines, and the prolific writings of its key members. None the less, its influence should not be overestimated: its attitude to industrial design in the 1920s was ambivalent, its membership was small by comparison with the Deutscher Werkbund (in 1930 Werkbund membership stood at 3,000 and the DIA's at 820), and its magazines had an extremely difficult time in the difficult economic climate of the 1930s. *Design in Industry* launched in 1932 lasted for only two issues, the lifespan of *Trend in Everyday Things* of 1936 was equally brief, with only *Design for Today* lasting for any length of time, between 1933 and 1935. Similarly, although the state-funded Council for Art and Industry, and its predecessor the British Institute of Industrial Art (founded in 1920), may be researched easily through their published reports and the papers lodged in the Public Record Office at Kew, their contemporary impact is more difficult to evaluate. The *Design and the Designer in Industry* report of 1937, claimed by one British historian to be 'by far the most influential'[10] of the Council for Art and Industry's publications, may well have been read in official circles, but the publisher, His Majesty's Stationery Office, was concerned a year after issue that only 1,594 of its 5,000 print run had been purchased.

However, the interwar years saw the emergence of a small number of significant advertising agencies, such as S. H. Benson (established in 1893) and W. S. Crawford (established in 1914). Ashley Havinden joined Crawfords in the early 1920s, becoming director of art and design in 1929, and did much to gain recognition for the firm as one of the leaders of the field in Britain. Multidisciplinary design consultancies along the lines of the American model, as discussed in Chapter 3, were slow to emerge in Britain. Early instances included the Bassett-Gray Group of Artists and Writers which became the Industrial Design Partnership (1935–40). The founders were Milner Gray, Misha Black, and Walter Landor: Gray and Black were significantly involved in the establishment of the Design Research Unit (DRU) in 1943, a consultancy aimed at providing the necessary design expertise for postwar industry; Landor founded the internationally renowned consultancy, Landor Associates, in San Francisco in 1941 after emigrating to the United States in the previous year. None the less the American model of industrial design consultancy did emerge on the British stage with the opening of the London office of Raymond Loewy. This was launched in London in 1936 under the management of Carl Otto, who had worked at General Motors and with Bel Geddes, and employed Beresford Evans and Douglas Scott as designers. Before its closure in 1939 its clients included Allied Ironfounders, Electrolux, General Electric Company, and Rootes, the motor manufacturers.

The design profession: fresh opportunities after 1945

The post-1945 period saw many significant shifts in design practice and approach: fresh attitudes were engendered by the implications of changing technologies, which were in turn stimulated by widespread European and American involvement in the Second World War; by an increasing reconsideration of the extent to which the methods and approaches adopted by designers in the interwar years were still appropriate for postwar needs; and by the growing perception in design circles that there was a fresh opportunity to establish in business circles a clearer perception of the importance, or professional status, of the designer than had generally been the case in the 1920s and 1930s.[11] There was a clear move away from faith in the primacy of intuition and individuality towards the recognition that the increasingly complex problems of an increasingly technologically-dependent society could only be solved by a coalition of a range of skills and expertise. Ironically, the individual celebrity status which a number of the emergent breed of industrial designers in the United States had sought to cultivate in the 1930s, in order to gain both public recognition and commercial advantage, tended to reinforce doubts in business circles about individual designers' abilities to grasp the wider manufacturing, marketing, advertising, retailing, social, and economic implications of product development. The principles of teamwork upon which the larger American practices were in fact organized pointed towards the basis upon which many postwar consultancies were to be organized. This notion of teamwork had been strengthened by the wartime experience of many designers who worked alongside engineers and scientists in the war effort, gaining a more complete understanding of new materials and processes. Examples of this multidisciplinary approach may be seen in consultancies such as the Japanese GK Industrial Design Associates which, from its modest beginnings in 1957, has grown to embrace product design, communication design, architectural and environmental design, research, planning and development, and design studies; Pentagram, founded in London in 1972 from a range of different types of expertise capable of catering for the complex demands of large corporations which were placing an increasing premium on design, was similarly able to deal with a broad range of commissions. Other examples include Total Design, founded in the Netherlands in 1963, Minale Tattersfield, founded in Britain in 1964, and Plan Créatif, founded in Paris in 1985.

State initiatives in design promotion

The potential of design as a means of gaining a market edge was acknowledged by a number of governments in their establishment of official design bodies to promote its value to industry and the public. The most significant of these was the Council of Industrial Design (COID) established in London in 1944 on an initial grant of £55,000, ready to assist in the anticipated postwar export drive. Its specific aims were to promote good design in industry; to disseminate design advice and information to manufacturers, government departments, and others; to organize design exhibitions and advise on design education and training; and to educate the public in the importance of good design. Amongst its most important early initiatives was the organization of the 1946 *Britain Can Make It* Exhibition. Providing a sweeping vista of the benefits that design could provide for the home, work, and leisure this large-scale exhibition in the Victoria and Albert Museum attracted 1,432,369 visitors and included a display designed by Misha Black of the DRU entitled 'What Industrial Design Means'. Centred on the problem of designing an egg-cup for mass-production, Black showed how the industrial designer consulted with management, engineers, and salesmen in order to determine such matters as proportion, practicality, colour, and decoration, and how he needed to have an understanding of materials and mass-production technology. As well as advising industry through its industrial officers and library and information service, the COID organized regional conferences and exhibitions, furnished show houses, commissioned reports, and published books and, from 1949 onwards, its own magazine, *Design*. It has undergone many changes of fortune since then, often due to wider economic problems which at some times have threatened its grant-in-aid from government and at others have enhanced its profile, as with the widely publicized design initiatives of the Conservative government under Mrs Thatcher in the 1980s. The COID established a Design Centre in central London in 1956, an information centre and showroom for exhibitions of well-designed goods. During the 1960s its centre of gravity shifted away from consumer goods towards engineering, and in 1972 it was renamed the Design Council in recognition of its aim 'to wed engineering and industrial design in one body dedicated to improving design throughout all sections of British industry'. In 1994 the Design Council was dramatically cut in size, resulting in the closure of the Design Centre and all regional offices, and leading to a complete re-appraisal of its role.[12]

Similar state-funded organizations were established in a number of other countries in the postwar years. In Poland the Buiro Nadzoru

Estetyki Producji (BNEP/Office for the Supervision of Aesthetic Production) was established in 1947 within the Ministry of Culture and Art under the directorship of Wanda Telakowska. Its aim was to invigorate the design profession in the immediate postwar years, to improve standards of design in industry through the provision of models and prototypes, and to promote greater aesthetic awareness in everyday life. However, its ambitions were soon thwarted by the Stalinist reorientation of the State of the late 1940s.[13] Later, in 1960, the Council of Design and Aesthetics of Industrial Production was established to promote industrial design activity although its effective impact was very limited. Elsewhere in eastern Europe, state initiatives were equally problematic. In the USSR, VNIITE (the All-Union Scientific Research Institute for Technical Aesthetics) was set up under the directorship of Yuri Soloviev in 1962, but its subsequent achievements were considerably constrained by high levels of official bureaucracy and planning.[14] Its greatest strengths lay in ergonomics and engineering design.

In West Germany, the German Parliament voted in 1951 to establish a Rat für Formgebung (Design Council) which was inaugurated in 1953 to further the understanding of design in manufacture. Although it received attention in the Milan Triennali it was not highly effective in the 1960s and 1970s, but with support from the Ministry of Economic Affairs it has played a continuing role in promoting greater awareness of design in German industry, a task of considerably greater complexity in the wake of the unification of the FDR and GDR. In France, the picture of state support for design has been more ambivalent, although the state has provided architects and designers with many high-profile commissions which during the 1980s included furniture at the Elysée Palace, furnishing of the French Embassy in Washington, the interior design of the Musée d'Orsay, and redecoration work at the Louvre and the Ministry of Finance. The Centre de Création Industrielle (CCI), first established in 1969, was funded by the Ministry of Culture from 1973 in order to promote the cultural dimensions of French design. In 1975 the Ministry of Industrial and Scientific Development set up the Conseil Superieur de la Création Esthétique Industrielle, to complement in economic terms the CCI's cultural role, but following widespread lack of interest and support, as well as antipathy to any notions of intervention from the industrial sector, was soon wound up.

Other European initiatives include the commissioning in 1960 by the Irish Government's Exports Board of a panel of Scandinavian design experts to report on potential design strategies that the Republic might adopt.[15] Their deliberations may be seen to have resulted in the Government's establishment of the Kilkenny Design Workshops (KDW) in 1965. Following Scandinavian models the KDW sought to develop the design potential of crafts-based indus-

115

Toshiba Rice Cooker, 1957
The aesthetic of this product—
clean and austere—firmly
links it to the international
canon of Good Design being
promoted in the USA by
MOMA, New York, in Britain by
the COID, in Germany by the
Rat Für Formgebung, and Italy
by La Rinascente. It was one
of the first recipients of the G-
Mark, an award for aesthetic
excellence in design
instituted in 1957 by the
Design Promotion Council
of the Japanese Ministry of
Trade and Industry.

tries, moving into the field of engineering design in the 1970s. In
Scandinavia itself, although the Swedish government set up a Design
Centre in Stockholm in 1984 and issued a White Paper on design three
years later, the Danish Design Council and Design Centre, founded in
1977 and 1987 respectively, are perhaps the best known design promotional bodies. Although independent they are supported by the
Ministry of Industry and work with it and the Ministry of Education
and Research to develop design education policy guidelines.

In Japan there was also a modest investment by the state in the promotion of design. In the 1950s JETRO (Japan Export Trade
Organization) sent five or six students a year to study design abroad,
principally to the United States, but with a number studying in
Germany and Italy, a scheme which was jointly funded by state and
industry. From 1956 onwards JETRO was also responsible for inviting
American and European designers to participate in design seminars
which lasted for between two and three weeks. In the first five years of
their existence almost four-fifths of the 35 designers who participated
were American, a clear indication of the commercial efficacy of
American design practice. In 1957 the Design Promotion Council of
the Ministry of Trade and Industry (MITI) initiated a Design Awards
Scheme, known as the G-Mark, as a stimulus to industry [**115**, **116**].
This was followed in 1959 by MITI's establishment of a Design
Division, and in the following year the Japan Design House was set up
as a permanent information centre for well-designed Japanese prod-

116 GK Design

Soy sauce bottle for Kikkoman Corporation, Japan, late 1950s
This design did much to establish the reputation of the GK Design consultancy as well as the Kikkoman company which grew rapidly from its origins as a family firm to a large national company. Although the elegant form of the bottle in many ways conforms to an international modernist aesthetic it also marks an effective design solution to the marketing of soy sauce in a table-top container, much in the manner of the ubiquitous tomato ketchup bottle in the USA. Initially Kikkoman was extremely sceptical that this would be effective in a market-place dominated by tradition, but it became a market leader.

ucts. This had been inspired both by the COID's London Design Centre and the Den Permanente (established in 1931) exhibitions of Danish Design, which received international prominence in 1958 through its receipt of the Italian Compasso d'Oro award. Finally, in 1969 the Japan Industrial Design Promotion Organization (JIDPO) was established along the lines of the British Council of Industrial Design. From 1975 it also became responsible for the Design Development Programme for regional industries, funded both by national and regional governments, which laid particular stress on design as a management resource. A further initiative was the establishment in 1981 of the Japan Design Foundation (JDF), funded by national and local government as well as commerce and industry.

Under the directorship of Kazuo Kimura, it aimed to promote Japanese design to the forefront of the international stage. It organized the Biennial Design Festival and Competition at Osaka, the first of which was held in 1983 and attracted considerable attention through the granting of the First International Honorary Award for the Encouragement of Design Activities to the British Prime Minister, Margaret Thatcher. More recently, in 1992, the International Design Centre Nagoya Inc. was established with a capital of $100 million as a quasi-governmental corporation with funding from national, regional, and local government as well as the business sector. The largest centre of its kind in Japan, its aims were to bring together community, industry, and the design profession, establishing an R & D centre, a design resource centre, and a design museum with a shopping mart open to the profession, industry, and the public.

Elsewhere in the Far East, Korea has a design promotion policy dating back to 1966, although the government's investment has been more heavily directed towards design education and exhibitions, bringing in educationalists from Japan and West Germany and funding overseas training and study tours. In 1970 the Korea Design and Packaging Center (DKPC) was established and a GD mark for 'good design' instituted in 1986, although it was largely funded by industry. The Taiwan Design Promotion Centre was founded in 1979 to raise the levels of industrial design in Taiwan and to improve perceptions of its products abroad, much of its budget deriving from the Ministry of Economic Affairs. In Singapore, the Singapore Trade Development Board has included design promotion amongst its activities since 1984 and, following the British Design Council's model of the early 1980s, paid for up to 75 per cent of a design consultancy's fees for firms using such expertise for the first time.

Professional design organizations

From the 1940s onwards there has been a significant increase in the number of design organizations, reflecting the growing number of professionals in the field as well as their perceived need to campaign collectively for greater recognition of their value to business, commerce, and society.

In the United States the Society of Industrial Designers was established in New York in 1944, initially with fourteen members (including Loewy, Bel Geddes, Teague, Deskey, Van Doren, and Russel Wright) but growing to almost 100 members by 1949. It aimed 'to improve the vocation of industrial design, by providing the mechanism through which the members of the profession can agree and take action on every type of common problem' as well as to promote better standards of industrial design education and to improve public and industrial understanding of their work. In order to provide a showcase for many examples of their members' work from 1949 onwards it produced an annual publication entitled *US Industrial Design*. In 1955 the organization changed its name to the American Society of Industrial Designers, merging in 1965 with two other bodies to become the Industrial Designers Society of America (IDSA). According to an article in the American business magazine *Fortune*,[16] by the late 1950s there were about 300 design consultancies in the United States, a fact that also reflected the growing number of in-house design departments in manufacturing industry. Many of them increasingly moved into the broader arena of design management rather than dealing with products or graphic design in isolation. Many of these changes can be followed in the pages of *Industrial Design* which, founded in 1954, was the leading magazine for design professionals in the United States; in 1980 it was retitled *ID Magazine of Industrial Design*.

In Italy in the 1950s the names of designers were important selling tools, but their role in industry was generally much more concerned with product aesthetics than with the wider concerns occupying American and, to an increasing extent, British consultancies. In 1956 the Italian Association for Industrial Designers (ADI) was founded and many of their concerns can be discerned in the magazine *Stile Industria* which was launched in 1954 and edited by Alberto Roselli. Published in Italian and English, it was an important vehicle for growing international interest in the theory and practice of Italian design, although it closed in the difficult economic climate of 1963.

In 1951 the Japan Advertising Artists Club was founded, followed by the Japanese Industrial Designers Association (JIDA) which was founded in the following year with 25 members. It has grown considerably since then, in tandem with the growing recognition of design in manufacturing industry discussed in Chapter 5, with 601 full members in 1985 (284 being employed by companies, 258 being freelance, and 59 drawn from education). It also published its own magazine *Industrial Design*, which by 1985 had about 3,000 subscribers, although there were only about twenty subscribing from abroad.

Throughout the 1950s and 1960s many other national design associations were formed[17] and there was an increased awareness of the wider international climate, stimulated by the growing number of professional design magazines and the holding of international conferences, as at Aspen, Colorado, from the early 1950s. The International Council of Societies of Industrial Design (ICSID) was established in 1957, mounting conferences biennially at various locations around the world, followed in 1963 by the International Council of Graphic Design Associations (ICOGRADA). Designers of many nationalities increasingly shared many concerns, and in 1981 ICOGRADA, ICSID and IFI (the International Federation of Interior Designers) held a joint conference in Helsinki, examining design issues on a world scale.

A rational approach to design: the Hochschule für Gestaltung at Ulm: 1953–1969

Penny Sparke suggested in her book *Consultant Design*:

While Germany sells design in the name of science, Italy in the name of art, Scandinavia in the name of craft and the USA in the name of business, all these national images of design were necessary strategies in the highly competitive markets of the immediate post war years. The role of the designer was to help develop a marketing strategy which would give his product a special place in that market.[18]

The scientific, rational, and efficient outlook associated with German design in the later 1950s, as typified in the austere aesthetic of Braun products of the period, was very much bound up with the innovative curriculum at the Hochschule für Gestaltung at Ulm (HfG).

Inge Scholl, whose brother and sister had been executed by the Nazis in 1943, wanted to establish a new international school of design as part of an express commitment to social and moral reconstruction in the postwar years. In fact many German universities had shown considerable continuity in personnel and outlook with the prewar years, and so the envisaged school was intended to reflect a distinctive alternative personality. Scholl established a foundation in 1950 in order to bring the school into being, and funding was also secured from the US government, German federal and regional government, and the business sector in the Federal Republic. Opening its doors in 1953 as a private institution, and thus free from the constraints of the local and national education system, its original impetus was focused on the idea of a new Bauhaus: visiting teachers included Johannes Itten, Josef Albers, and Mies van der Rohe, all of whom had contributed to the original Bauhaus ethos in the 1920s. In 1955 the HfG moved into new buildings designed by Max Bill, who had been installed as director in the previous year. Students and staff were involved in their construction and furnishing, much as the Bauhaus students had been under Gropius at Dessau in the mid-1920s.

However, within a short space of time ideological differences between Bill and several of his younger colleagues began to emerge. These centred on their strong desire to emphasize the theoretical dimensions of the curriculum at the expense of the studio- and workshop-based studies upon which Bill placed a much higher priority. He resigned as director in 1956, and the running of the school was placed in the hands of a rectoral board of five (later three) members, renewable on an annual basis. From then there was an increasing emphasis on science and other disciplines which cast a fresh perspective on design thinking and practice, leading to Bill's resignation from the school in 1957. His departure was also exacerbated by personal as well as curricular conflicts with Tomás Maldonado who had joined the staff in 1956.

Maldonado played a key role in theoretical debates, particularly through his many contributions to, and editorship of, the HfG's magazine *Ulm*, which was published between 1958 and 1959 and from 1962 to 1968. Other HfG theorists included Claude Schnaidt and Giu Bonsiepe who, following the closure of the school, became an important figure in South American design.

Richard Hamilton, who had visited the HfG in 1959, put into words the distinctiveness of the institution thus:

> The major difference between the HfG and any other school of design in the world is precisely in the rejection of those principles which gave the Bauhaus its meaning and almost every school now available for the design student.[19]

By the later 1950s mathematical, statistical, and analytical methods, together with sociology, anthropology, physical and behavioural psychology, and twentieth-century cultural history, were considered sufficiently important elements to rank alongside the more practical aspects of the curriculum. In the early 1960s methodology and theory assumed a dominant role in many areas of work, creating further tensions with those who placed a greater priority on the practical elements. This state of relative ideological confusion led to the creation of a new constitution for the school in 1962, when once more its direction fell under the control of a single person, initially Otl Aicher. It was also in this period that the radicalism of the institution came under attack in the press, accompanied by a funding crisis. The regional government served the school with an ultimatum to amend its constitution in 1963, which it duly did, and further political problems were averted until 1967 when there was renewed pressure to bring the school into

117 Hans Gugelot *et al.*

M125 Furniture system, 1957
Gugelot began to explore furniture systems for the Wohnbedarf company in Zurich in 1950, before working for the Braun electrical appliance company. He was appointed professor at the Hochschule für Gestaltung at Ulm in 1956, and the rational, systematized approach to furniture seen here (without doors) reflected the scientific approach to design increasingly adopted in the curriculum. The M125 range was put into large-scale production by the Wilhelm Bofinger company.

King's Fund Mark I Hospital Bed, manufactured by J. Nesbit-Evans & Co., 1960s

The Hospital Bed Project derived from a dissatisfaction with the poor design and wide variety of types of hospital beds used by different health authorities throughout Britain. Existing types were unversatile and uneconomic to manufacture. A scientific approach to the problem was explored by L. Bruce Archer, Kenneth Agnew, and their team at the Royal College of Art, and was externally funded. The project involved a global search for existing data on hospital bed design, followed by a systematic analysis of, and possible solutions to, the desired multiple functions. Prototypes were extensively field-tested and exhaustively monitored.

line with the regional educational system. This coincided with a financial crisis for the Geschwister-Scholl Foundation which had helped to set up and sustain the institution, together with the withdrawal of funding from federal government which deemed that education was a matter for regional government. Furthermore the regional government of Baden-Württemberg decreed that the HfG should amalgamate with a low-level engineering college also in Ulm. Faced with loss of status and autonomy the staff and students at the Hochschule chose to close the institution in 1968.

Interpreting the HfG

Robin Kinross, in a very useful survey of literature[20] on the HfG published in the 1980s considers that it is perhaps too soon to be able to evaluate the institution's true significance. He drew a number of parallels between Ulm in the 1980s and the position of the Bauhaus in the late 1930s: most of those involved in both institutions were still alive, there was self-representing documentation in the form of the *Ulm* magazine and the Bauhaus Books, as well as a number of self-representing exhibitions put on by members of both institutions.

None the less it is quite clear that the HfG made a considerable impact on design education and led to a greater acceptance of designers in German industry as well as an expansion of design education.[21] The institution's own links with industry were limited: the volume of work from Braun, the electrical appliance manufacturer, was modest and other commissions, such as that for the corporate identity scheme for the West German national airline, Lufthansa, were sporadic. None the less, the HfG curriculum, with its balance of theory and practice, embraced a move away from intuition to method, from component to system [**117**], from product to process, and from the individual to an interdisciplinary design team as an appropriate means of solving problems. Such a definition of the designer's role anticipated the outlook of many of the larger consultancies which were to place an increasing premium on design management.

Design methods

The significance of design methods as a means of solving problems systematically emerged as an area of great interest and concern to the more progressive factions of the design profession from the early 1960s. The first conference in the field, entitled 'Systematic and Intuitive Methods in Engineering, Industrial Design, Architecture and Communications', was held at Imperial College, London, in 1962. Literature on the subject had begun to appear during the late 1950s and 1960s, with frequent articles in the COID periodical *Design*, the ever-increasing publication of conference papers in Britain and the United States, and a proliferation of books. These included L. Bruce Archer's *Systematic Method for Designers*[22] of 1965, revealing links with the HfG where Archer had taught industrial design before becoming a Research Fellow at the Royal College of Art [**118**].[23]

Ergonomics and anthropometrics: data for designers

In the early 1960s there was an increasing range of potential tools to aid the rationality of the decision-making process in design. As a result many designers were eager to reconcile emergent disciplines such as ergonomics, anthropometrics, cybernetics, marketing, and management science with design thinking. In such shifts away from the intuitive, micro- rather than macro-, means of problem-solving designers increasingly began to make use of interaction charts and matrices. Such a rational outlook had its roots in the application of scientific techniques known as OR (Operational Research) which had been used for problem-solving in the Second World War, having evolved alongside developments in ergonomics. Both British and American armed forces had produced extensive guides for their designers, with American versions being published for general use in 1954.[24] Ergonomics, 'human engineering' as it was known in the United States, or 'biotechnics' on the continent, was of considerable interest to design and industry around the world, resulting in a proliferation of societies, university courses, and international conferences within a short space of time.[25] The field of anthropometrics—the systematic study of measurement of the human form—was also of increasing interest and value to designers as was emphasized by Henry Dreyfuss

119 Henry Dreyfuss

Joe and Josephine
anthropometrics charts, 1960s
Anthropometrics (the
scientific measurement of
human form) and ergonomics
(the systematic analysis of
work efficiency relating the
user to his or her environment)
became increasingly important
tools for the designer after
1945. Publishing the
influential *Measure of Man:
Human Factors in Design*
(1959), Dreyfuss was
important in this movement
which developed alongside
a desire in professional
design circles to move away
from individual, intuitive, and
artistic approaches to
design problems towards
more collaborative and
systematic solutions.

in *Designing for People*[26] of 1955 [**119**]. Another well-known text which examined the problem of designing for cleanliness and hygiene was Alexander Kira's *The Bathroom Book*.[27] First published in the United States in 1966, it was based upon a seven-year research project at Cornell University and included anthropometric, ergonomic, and many other factors in his analysis.

In some respects related to this growing concern for method and system in design was the emergent field of design management, which has been touched upon in relation to the increasing depth of expertise offered by consultancies. In Britain it was recognized by the Royal Society of Arts in its Presidential Awards for Design Management, which were initiated in 1965: Heals, Hille, London Transport, and Conran were among the early recipients. An early exponent in the field was Michael Farr, who set up his own design management consultancy, Michael Farr (Design Integration) Ltd., in Tottenham Court Road, London, writing *Design Management*[28] in 1966. Increasingly many of the larger consultancies around the world have subsumed managerial, financial, and business analysis as an aspect of their work for large corporate clients.

Pop to Post-Modernism: Changing Values

8

With a discernible shift of emphasis from production towards consumption[1] in the changing market conditions of the postwar period, questions were raised whether either the monolithic Fordist model, which had hitherto dominated approaches to manufacture for the mass market for much of the twentieth century, or the modernist aesthetic could cater adequately for the increasingly variegated tastes and desires of the consumer [**120**, **121**, **122**]. In this connection a number of critics, theorists, and designers became interested in the relationship between visual and linguistic 'signs', the correlation between the two being embraced in what has been termed semiotics. Writers such as the French sociologist Raymond Barthes, in his seminal text *Mythologies* of 1957,[2] the Italian theorist, critic, and design historian Gillo Dorfles, in *Il disegno industriale e la sua estetica*[3] (*Industrial Design and Its Aesthetic*) of 1963, and the American Robert Venturi, in *Complexity and Contradiction in Architecture*[4] of 1966 did much to open up debates about the perceived shortcomings of the modernist aesthetic.

Theoretical and critical reorientation

In the early 1950s Reyner Banham began working on his doctoral thesis, later published as *Theory and Design in the First Machine Age*.[5] It is an important text for design historians as it marks a very different approach to modernism from that of his doctoral supervisor, Nikolaus Pevsner, in his *Pioneers of the Modern Movement*.[6] Representing a shift in critical and theoretical circles, particularly that centred on the Independent Group[7] in London, with which Banham was closely associated, it was written at a time when modernist architecture, design, and theory began to be challenged by those who felt that the new postwar era was one which should embrace mass culture and advanced technology. An era of passenger jet transportation, growing affluence and consumer aspirations, expendability and obsolescence, the 1950s was also, according to Banham, 'the Second Machine Age, the age of domestic electronics and synthetic chemicals'.[8] He also clearly differentiated it from the First Machine Age, the era of modernism:

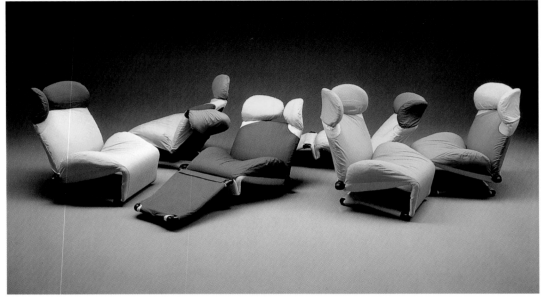

120 Toshiyuki Kita

Wink Chair, Cassina, 1980

This colourful and versatile seating can be transformed from armchair to *chaise longue* by tilting the base forward, whilst the back rest can be adjusted by the knobs at its base. The headrests can also be independently adjusted. Like many Post-Modern products it draws upon a range of sources, whether the ethos of Pop through the brightly coloured covers (which can be pulled over the frame like a T-shirt), 'Mickey Mouse' ear-like forms of the headrests, or the automobile world of adjustable seats and headrests.

[in] the Second, highly developed mass production methods have distributed electronic devices and synthetic chemicals broadcast over a large part of society—television, the symbolic machine of the Second Machine Age, has become a means of mass-communication dispensing popular entertainment. In the First, however, only cinema was available to a broad public, whose home life was otherwise barely touched and it was in the upper middle-class homes that the First Machine Age made its greatest impact, the homes that could afford these new, convenient and expensive aids to gracious living, the homes that tend to breed architects, painters, poets, journalists, the creators of the myths and symbols by which a culture recognises itself.[9]

In the early 1950s, in the first phase of meetings of what became known as the Independent Group, considerable interest was expressed in science, technology, and the history of design, an emphasis which underlay Banham's firm belief in the liberating force of technology and his stress in *Theory and Design* on Futurism, which he saw as 'a turning point in theories of design' (unlike his doctoral supervisor, Pevsner, who considerably downplayed its significance in *Pioneers*). At the 1954-5 meetings of the Group—which included Peter and Mary Banham, Lawrence Alloway, Eduardo Paolozzi, Richard and Terry Hamilton, John McHale, Nigel Henderson, and Toni del Renzio—there was considerable interest in popular culture, advertising, and the media in the United States, exemplified in talks such as Banham's 'Borax or the Thousand Horse-Power Mink' of 1955, which considered the extravagant styling, sensuous advertising, and sexual symbolism of the American automobile. Technologically-inspired iconography influenced the styling of many other appliances as well as the seductive language which helped to advertise them, as recounted by John

McHale in a special Americana issue of the Royal College of Art magazine, *Ark* in 1956.

References to 'aquamatic action', 'jet spray', 'centrifugal clutch drive' in the washing machine, figure well in General Electric's new cooking range names—the Stratoliner and the Liberator. A quote like 'New Extra Hi-Speed Giant 2,600 Calrod Unit is 20 per cent faster than gas—by actual test' is straight out of '56 auto ad-speak, and with push-button control, 'a flick of your finger selects your cooking heat' as well as your gear change. Automatic 'cut-offs', 'oventimers', 'circuit-breakers', 'washer and sediment swirl-out' signalled the general preoccupation with robotics, and the 'WondR dial automatically pre-selects' everything from defrosting to the year's breakfasts.[10]

Twelve members of the IG were involved with the *This is Tomorrow* exhibition held at the Whitechapel Gallery in London in 1956. Many art historians, encouraged by particular reinterpretations by Banham and Alloway,[11] have seen this show as the genesis of Pop Art. They have placed particular emphasis on the environment created by John McHale, John Voelker, and Richard Hamilton, which included an American jukebox playing pop music, a publicity blow-up of Robbie the Robot from the film *The Forbidden Planet*, and a cut-out of Marilyn Monroe from *The Seven Year Itch*. However, Anne Massey has convincingly underlined the importance of design as 'the overarching con-

121 James Dyson

G-Force Cyclonic Vacuum Cleaner manufactured by Apex Inc., Tokyo, 1986

Designed in 1979, the striking colours of this sculptural, high-tech design mark it out as more than a functional object. Rather as the styling of food mixers in the 1950s (see **107**) increasingly demarcated them as objects to be displayed on kitchen work surfaces rather than stored in cupboards, so this product endowed the mundaneity of housework with associations of designer-chic in the icon-conscious 1980s. Unlike the kitchen appliance seen in **107**, this design is redolent with imagery and associations.

cept'[12] of the exhibition. *This Is Tomorrow* was visited by more than 19,000, was widely reported in the media, and thus brought some of these design-centred ideas before a wider audience.

That the potential liberating power of technology was not restricted to theoretical discussions amongst an educated artistic coterie, the interests of the art gallery-going public, or the prurient focus of the media was exemplified in Alison and Peter Smithson's design for a 'House of the Future' [**123**] which was shown at the *Daily Mail* Ideal Home Exhibition in Olympia, London, in 1956. During the mid-1950s these annual exhibitions were regularly visited by more than 1 million visitors. In 1956 in the Smithsons' vision of the early 1980s they could see a wide range of futuristic appliances and equipment, including remote-controlled radio-television and controls for raising sections of the floor for coffee or dining tables in the living room; an eye-level refrigerator, two eye-level ovens, one of which was microwave, and a dishwasher.

Another London-based group which embraced notions of expendability, obsolescence, and change as a sign of a vibrant, healthy society was Archigram which received its first public exposure at an exhibition at the Institute of the Contemporary Arts in 1963. Members of the group, disillusioned by the restrictive nature of contemporary architectural practice in Britain, looked to the world of science fiction for a prophetic insight into the future and, like Banham, placed their faith in

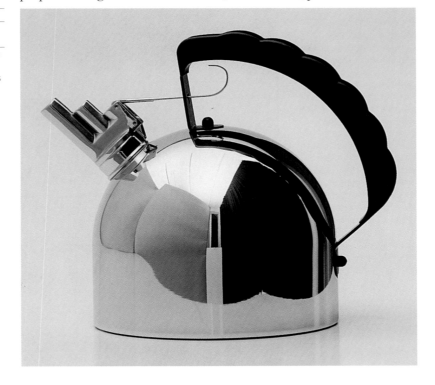

122 Richard Sapper

Kettle with bronze whistle, Alessi, 1983

Like the vacuum cleaner seen in **121**, this kettle became a cult icon in fashionable circles in the 1980s. Considerable attention was paid to design for the status-conscious kitchen, with products being made from high-quality materials. Sapper worked on several products for Alessi, including an extensive range of pans and kitchen utensils which was developed in conjunction with leading French and Italian chefs. It was manufactured in 1986 under the name *La Cintura di Orione*.

the latest technology—the space capsule, the rocket, the bathyscope, and the handypack. They rejected traditional forms of building and very much looked to a form of architecture which was determined by consumer need. Flexibility, individual choice, and an affinity with popular culture underlay many of their Utopian schemes such as the Walking City of 1964 and the Instant City of 1968.

In Establishment circles there was a clear difference of opinion about what was an appropriate form for modern design. American arbiters of taste, such as Edgar Kaufmann Jr. of the Museum of Modern Art in New York, had placed a very different interpretation of definitions of the requirements that modern design should fulfil from those in the Independent Group or Archigram in Britain. Kaufmann, who had warned British architects and designers about what he saw as the moral dangers of streamlining and styling for the sake of change in his celebrated 1948 article on 'Borax, or the Chromium-Plated Calf',[13] opined that modern design 'is the planning and making of objects suited to our way of life, our abilities, our ideals', that it should 'express the spirit of our times', and that it should 'serve as wide a public as possible, considering modest needs and limited costs no less challenging than the requirements of pomp and luxury'.[14] Clearly notions such as 'our way of life' or 'our ideals' epitomized a particular social and cultural sector of society.

At the Council of Industrial Design (COID) there was a similar resistance to American ideas of built-in obsolescence, 'style follows sales', and the lure of gadgetry, with a number of admonitory articles in the organization's magazine, *Design*. Richard Hamilton, painter and member of the Independent Group, was also a significant writer on design and, when he wrote about American practice in a 1960 *Design* article entitled 'Persuading Image',[15] John E. Blake wrote an accompanying editorial, 'Consumers in Danger',[16] in which he likened what

John Stephen attending the opening of Carnaby House in Via Margutti, Rome, 1967

John Stephen had opened his first shop in Carnaby Street in 1957, and in succeeding years did much to enliven men's fashion, drawing on Italian styling. By the mid-1960s he owned several shops in Carnaby Street which by then was at the centre of so-called 'Swinging London'. He opened a number of shops elsewhere in Britain and the USA, as well as twenty-one in Europe of which Carnaby House was one. This photograph shows John Stephen attending the opening in May 1967, accompanied by a typically mini-skirted companion with the almost inevitable *Vespa* motor scooter parked alongside.

he saw as the manipulative techniques of American industry to 'a form of economic totalitarianism not dissimilar from Orwell's terrifying prophecy'. There are many other layers of what has been termed 'the Spectre of Americanisation' which have been recounted by writers such as Dick Hebdige in 'Towards a Cartography of Taste, 1935–1962'[17] and which include concerns about the homogenizing effects of pervasive American culture, much like those expressed by many writers in the United States in the 1920s. In Britain the writer Richard Hoggart, in his constantly-reprinted text *The Uses of Literacy* of 1957, examined three facets of this phenomenon in a chapter entitled 'The Newer Mass Art: Sex in Shiny Packets'. He referred to the British 'Juke-Box Boys' with an 'American slouch', listening to American tunes on the 'nickelodeon' in 'milk-bars':

The young men waggle one shoulder or stare, as desperately as Humphrey Bogart, across the tubular chairs.[18]

Compared even with the pub around the corner, this is all a peculiarly thin and pallid form of dissipation, a sort of spiritual dry-rot amid the odour of boiled milk. Many of the customers—their clothes, their hair-styles, their facial expressions all indicate—are living to a large extent in a myth world compounded of a few simple elements which they take to be those of American way of life.[19]

None the less, other social, cultural, and aesthetic shifts were taking place in Britain in the late 1950s and 1960s which, although embracing many aspects of American-inspired consumer culture, also took on particular dimensions of Italian style, particularly in those sectors of the market-place catering for the young.

Pop culture in Britain

Much has been made by design historians[20] of the growth of youth culture and the potential economic significance of the teenage consumer from the late 1950s evidenced by Mark Abrams's two-part market research study for the London Press Exchange, *The Teenage Consumer*,[21] of 1959–60. A number of designers and manufacturers responded to the values embraced in the increasing acceptance of change and expendability as a way of life in this emergent market sector. Fashion designers such as Mary Quant and John Stephen [124] who had established their business in the 1950s became media-worthy figures in the Pop era of the 1960s, when an ever-increasing range of boutiques catered for the rapidly changing lifestyles of a 'throwaway society'. Bright colours and boldly patterned motifs covered the surfaces of shirts, shopfronts, and shopping bags, as well as everyday domestic items such as coffee mugs. Shirley Craven at Hull Traders Ltd. of Lancashire reflected such trends in her textiles of the 1960s; Hull Traders also marketed Bernard Holdaway's 1966 range of cheap,

125 Vivienne Westwood

Savages collection, 1981

A highly influential fashion designer over more than twenty years, Westwood was an important force in the re-establishment of London as a major fashion centre, drawing on a wide range of influences, from the ethnic—as seen here—to historic re-interpretation and street-style.

expendable, brightly coloured, simply shaped *Tomotom* furniture, the epitome of Pop.

In a number of design-historical accounts[22] of British Pop there has been a tendency to position the vibrant, youthful market-place of the 1960s alongside the aesthetic predilections of the Council of Industrial Design in order to demonstrate the increasing ideological gulf between the two. The position is sustained by reference to the COID director Paul Reilly's 1967 article on 'The Challenge of Pop'[23] in which the modernist-inspired aesthetic tenets of this organization may be seen to be about to be modified in the light of external change. It has also been suggested that the COID was faced with the dilemma either of accepting the implications of Pop or, through their rejection, of undermining those values that the organization had promoted since its inception. Whilst this is largely self-evident[24] it is also clear that, for the everyday consumer, the policies of the COID were completely unknown and irrelevant. However, like MOMA, being an organization that was seen to represent a particular, and increasingly outmoded, ideological stance, its modernist outlook provided a useful target for those design theorists, writers, and practitioners who were associated with the formulation of the concept of Post-Modernism.

Cultural pluralism and the mass media

As has been indicated in earlier discussion of the Independent Group and Archigram in Britain, for many professionals involved in the fields of design and architecture the seemingly restrictive vocabulary of the modernist aesthetic was felt to offer an impoverished means of expression in an age when the mass media were able to introduce images and cultures, past and present, from all over the globe at virtually the touch of a button. Such visual encyclopaedism provided designers and consumers with a rich visual syntax upon which to draw, bringing about a greater sense of freedom to express, through clothes, furniture, or even housing itself, affinities with particular ways of living, or 'lifestyles' as the market-oriented entrepreneurs of the 1970s and 1980s were to define it. The fashion designer Vivienne Westwood epitomized the ways in which designers could move, almost effortlessly, through a wide range of stylistic vocabularies in a comparatively short span of time: Punk was promoted through her London shop Seditionaries in the 1970s; in 1981 she launched both her Pirates Collection, 'plundering' the styles and images conjured up by the age of buccaneering, and the Savage Collection [**125**], with its references to a range of ethnic cultures; the following year saw her Buffalo Collection, which drew on American folk culture for inspiration, the same year in which she launched her London SW1 Nostalgia of Mud Shop, which drew upon Africa; her work has continued to draw upon a diversity of forms of inspiration.

The genesis of Post-Modernism

As indicated at the outset of this chapter, the designer-architect Robert Venturi was an important theorist for what was later to become known as Post-Modernism, and in *Complexity and Contradiction in Architecture*, published in 1966 (though written in 1962), he made what has subsequently become a widely used definition of many of its characteristics:

elements which are hybrid rather than 'pure', compromising rather than 'clear', distorted rather than 'straightforward', ambiguous rather than 'articulated', perverse as well as 'impersonal', conventional rather than 'designed', accommodating rather than 'excluding', redundant rather than simple, vestigial as well as innovating, inconsistent and equivocal rather than direct and clear.[25]

Architecture and planning were fields which attracted considerable critical attention at the time since, for many writers and consumers, they most vividly exemplified the ways in which the modernist vision had failed those for whom it was intended to provide a better living and working environment.[26] Thus, although there have been a number of debates about the exact origins of the term 'Post-Modernism' in the fields of design and architecture it is not surprising that it should appear in the title of an architectural text, Charles Jencks's book *The Language of Post-Modern Architecture*,[27] published in 1977. It came to be seen as a term which usefully embraced those characteristics—such as eclecticism, ornamentation, kitsch, wit, and irony—which most typified the diversity of contemporary culture in a pluralist society.

The Italian avant-garde: creativity in the face of industrialized capitalism

In the increasingly contested debates at the Milan Triennali of the 1950s and 1960s, many members of the Italian avant-garde reacted strongly against notions of 'Italian Style' as the bedrock of Italian design, despite the cultural approbation that the 'Linea Italiana' or 'Bel Disegno' had gained in Europe and the United States. They saw the stylized elegance of the furniture, domestic artifacts, and dress of fashionable society, or the design-as-art collections of the Museum of Modern Art in New York, as manifestations of a capitalist society in which the manufacturer was responding to the economic dictates of the market-place rather than the imaginative and creative possibilities of design as a means of enhancing the quality of life. As a result, many avant-garde Italian architects and designers looked to the exploration of the expressive possibilities of popular styling, eclecticism, kitsch, and nostalgia as a means of undermining the connotations of 'canons of taste' and elegance in the work of such mainstream designers as Vico Magistretti, Gio Ponti, and Mario Bellini. The Italian theorist,

126

Zanotta stand at the
Eurodomus 3, Turin, featuring
the *Blow* inflatable chair,
designed by Jonathan De Pas,
Donato D'Urbino, Paolo
Lomazzi, and Carla Scolari,
1967

In the mid-1960s the Zanotta
furniture company began to
commission work from avant-
garde designers, often
experimenting with new
materials. The *Blow* chair
was extremely fashionable
and emerged from the Pop
ethos of the 1964 Biennale.
Although inflatable furniture
had been seen in Britain in
the 1940s, it was not seriously
developed until the 1960s
when it was taken up by
several European designers.

designer, and founder-member of Archizoom Associati, Andrea
Branzi, subsequently described the impact of pop culture in 1960s
Italy:

> The whole of the Modern Movement's culture of design had denied con-
> sumption any autonomous value, considering it to be entirely covered by the
> canons of correct and rational planning. This rationality appeared to corre-
> spond to the nature of the whole industrial cycle from machine to factory to
> market. Now the contents of the project had to be completely altered so that
> the product could absorb all the mechanisms for inducement of consumption,
> commercial promotion and advertising communication. This meant mass
> languages instead of the strict canons of Rationalism; spiced up and contrived
> designs in place of the logical designs of the modern movement.[28]

Typical of this new language was the *Blow* inflatable chair designed by
De Pas, D'Urbino, and Lomazzi for the Zanotta furniture company in
1967 [**126**], which embodied notions of flexibility, expendability, and
the possibilities inherent in new materials.

Two avant-garde groups which had an important role in what
became known as the Radical Design and Anti-Design movements

were Archizoom Associati [**127**] and Superstudio, both founded in
Florence in 1966. Concerned with the implications of the total environment rather than the aesthetically-charged individual object, they
sought to undermine the profit-nexus of capitalism through their por-
trayals of a Utopian world in which the needs of everyday life were provided by self-sustaining technology, thus allowing the individual to
rediscover her or his own innate creative potential. Freed (theoretically) from the constraints of conspicuous consumption and the economics of the market-place they sought, through exhibitions,
manifestos, or staged environments, to explore the potential resonances of a wide range of cultural references. Other important contemporary Italian groups working along parallel lines included UFO
and Gruppo 9999, both formed in Florence in 1967, and Gruppo
Strum, established in Turin in the early 1970s. However, in some
instances, such groups did not feel that they could effect social change
through involvement in the design process itself and sought to communicate their ideas through the issuing of manifestos and staging of
performances.

Many of the radical propositions of Italian designers in the 1960s
and early 1970s were exhibited in the landmark exhibition at the
Museum of Modern Art, New York, entitled *Italy: the New Domestic
Landscape*. Its director was Emilio Ambasz, Curator of Design at
MOMA since 1969, who had previously taught at Princeton, the
Carnegie Institute of Technology, and the HfG at Ulm. He was also
the editor of the substantial catalogue, which contains much that is

128 Ettore Sottsass

Carlton Bookcase, Memphis, 1981

This striking example of Sottsass's early work for Memphis reveals a deeply anti-functionalist attitude through its premium on colour, decoration, and experimentation with form and surface. Evolving from the experimentation of the Milanese avant-garde of the late 1970s, its visual richness ran counter to the wider contemporary inclinations of furniture production which stressed elegance and refinement.

extremely useful about contemporary design issues in Italy. The large exhibition was highly significant, not only for staging important debates about the sociocultural implications of design but because it marked a fundamental change of perspective for MOMA, which previously had tended to focus on the aesthetics of the individual object or celebrated designer.

Ettore Sottsass Jr. played a pivotal role in this changing avant-garde climate of the late 1960s and 1970s, having a wealth of experience in experimental as well as mainstream industrial design. Not only had he exhibited at the first postwar Triennale in 1947, but in 1956 he worked in the studio of the American designer George Nelson, before beginning a longstanding relationship as a consultant to Olivetti in the following year. After responding to the possibilities afforded by kitsch and American Pop in the early 1960s, Sottsass drew on an increasingly wide range of cultural references, exploring ideas relating to meditation and love as well as reconciling aspects of ancient mythology and symbolism with imagery drawn from the contemporary world. This drawing on other cultures was partly reinforced by his visit to India in 1961 and was particularly evident in his ceramic work of the period including the 'Ceramics of Darkness' and the 'Ceramics to Shiva' series of 1963 and 1964. Like a number of his contemporaries, he also explored the status and meaning of objects in a series of furniture designs and rooms for Poltranova from the mid-1960s, using the symbolism of mass culture. Furthermore, allying himself to the Utopian spirit of Radical Design he envisaged in his drawings and text for the *Planet as Festival* series of 1973 a world in which consumerism and the work ethic had no place but provided the launching point for a voyage of imaginative self-discovery.

From Studio Alchymia to Memphis

Studio Alchymia was founded by Alessandro and Adriana Guerriero in Milan in 1979. Its chief spokesman was the designer-writer Alessandro Mendini, and its main protagonists included Ettore Sottsass Jr., Paola Navone, Andrea Branzi, and Michele de Lucchi. The practice of 'Alchemy' implied a pursuit of the quest to turn base substances into gold, a philosophy which evoked considerable controversy and critical attention in much of the group's work which centred on the idea of 'banality': ordinary, everyday consumer objects were transformed, or re-designed, into objects of aesthetic contemplation through the application of colour, pattern, and additional elements. Through this process they harnessed the potential of what Sottsass described as 'non-cultural imagery', that is, imagery without conventional aesthetic status. Their output ranged from individual items of furniture through to total environments or performances and was often highly decorative, drawing upon references from Braun to Bauhaus and from kitsch to Kandinsky in the exploration of the communicative boundaries of design.

However, as the 1970s drew to a close there were increasing tensions between Mendini and Sottsass. Sottsass wished to explore the potential impact of a richer design syntax than Mendini's concerns with 're-design' appeared to allow, as they were confined to what might be seen as the laboratory-like isolation of the experimental studio and confines of the exhibition gallery. For Sottsass the use of imagination and a rich visual language in design was both a means of enhancing the consumer experience and of persuading manufacturers to re-examine their understanding of the aesthetic possibilities inherent in everyday products. Notions of homogenization, standardization, and the production of universal models for global markets had been very much bound up in the notion of Fordism. In the Post-Fordist era, designers and manufacturers could turn their attention to the opportunities afforded by batch production, flexible manufacturing systems (FMS), or computer-aided manufacture (CAM). This allowed for a greater diversity of product types and enabled producers to satisfy more easily the varied cultural inclinations and semantic values of different consumer groups.

The Memphis design group was founded by Sottsass [**128**] and Michele De Lucchi in Milan in 1981, with the help of a Milanese cabinet-maker, Renzo Brugola, and Mario and Brunella Godani, who had a showroom. Financial backing was provided by the lighting designer and president of Artemide, Ernesto Gismondi, together with the industrialist, Fausto Celati. The group's activities and exhibitions provided a vital fulcrum for experimental design debate for two or three years, stimulating the design world in a positive fashion. Apart from Sottsass himself none of the founder members was over 30 years of age. Like a number of other Italian twentieth-century avant-garde design groups, Memphis was originally Milan-based, but it went on to include members from other countries including Japan, the United States, Austria, Britain, and France thus becoming a standard-bearer of the 'New International Style', as was discussed in relation to the globalization of culture in Chapter 6.

The title 'Memphis' has many perhaps apocryphal stories attached to it. For instance, it has been claimed by Barbara Radice, a founder member of the group, that it stemmed from the repeated playing on Sottsass's record player of a Bob Dylan song, *Stick Inside of Mobile with the Memphis Blues Again*. She maintained that the formative members of the group present felt that the name Memphis reflected the rich creative possibilities afforded by the ability to draw on cultural experiences of all kinds, whether the American blues, Tennessee, and rock' n' roll, or ancient Egypt and the capital of the Pharaohs. Whether or not Radice's account is entirely accurate such diverse cultural provenances contribute to the vitality of form, surface, and vocabulary associated with the group.

Memphis patterns derived from the mundane printed plastic laminated surfaces of counters in suburban coffee bars, from American consumer culture, Art Deco, Hollywood or ancient civilizations; materials could range from the cheap and ordinary to the expensive; colour was another vital ingredient and, like the surface decoration deployed, was a linguistic and expressive means of indicating references to cultural experience of all kinds. The significance of Memphis lay in the ways in which many different elements came together in fresh and surprising ways, reminiscent in many ways of Isadore Ducasse/Comte de Lautréamont's Surrealist adage, 'the chance encounter of a sewing machine and an umbrella on a dissection table': Memphis embraced the meeting of cheap and expensive materials, of mass- and high-cultural references, of invigorating colour combinations and new forms. Furthermore, as Radice wrote in 1984:

Memphis, like fashion, works on the fabric of contemporaneity, and contemporaneity means computers, electronics, videogames, science-fiction comics, Blade Runner, Space Shuttle, biogenetics, laser bombs, a new awareness of the body, exotic diets and banquets, mass exercise and tourism. Mobility is perhaps the most macroscopic novelty of this culture. Not only physical mobility but also and above all mobility of hierarchies and values; and mobility of interpretations which has liquefied the contours and solidity of things, shrinking the long, lazy waves of our 'Weltanschauung' to increasingly high frequencies until they burst and evaporate in a dust of hypotheses, in a world of events. What matters to us is not their substance but their appearance, their virtual image.[29]

The group worked across a range of media and products: clocks, textiles, furniture, glass, ceramics, flooring, and interiors all attracted their attention. Its members also believed that design was part of the fashion process. As the catalogue to the group's first exhibition of September 1981 stated: 'We are all sure that Memphis furniture will soon go out of style.' However, its very success ensured that many of its ideas were taken up by countless imitators, thus engendering the very commercial conformity from which its participants had sought to escape. Indeed, as one trenchant critic wrote in the late 1980s:

The visual promise of simplicity—though the ideological and technical bases of Memphis designs are far from simple—has since the early eighties spawned a multitude of imitators who consider themselves to be 'designers'. Designers obsessed with the total *objet d'art*, with the renaissance of the craftsman, though they themselves have had little or no training, bodge together chairs and lamps, sofas and beds, which, as long as they are eccentric and brightly coloured, are 'Memphis' style. The accompanying media circus is usually more interested in the anti-bourgeois atmosphere of this design environment than in the designs *per se*. Hence the important and far reaching changes introduced by Memphis in the concept of design have increasingly faded into the background.[30]

The role of the crafts within the Post-Modern project

For many Post-Modernists the organization of large-scale industry was perceived as a barrier to individual expression and creativity, a late twentieth-century inheritance of the long-standing tension between the constraints of mass-production and artistic integrity which had constantly resurfaced from the early phases of the Industrial Revolution. Ever since the English poet William Blake attacked Sir Joshua Reynolds's 'world of reason' in the late eighteenth century a succession of articulate writers have attacked the spiritual and creative consequences of the division of labour. William Morris's misgivings about many aspects of the industrialization process in the mid-nineteenth century helped sustain the enduring belief held by many that the hand-made article is superior to the machine-made, both in terms of aesthetics and function. The crafts provided an experimental arena in which new possibilities could be explored, avenues of investigation which were generally closed down by the structure and outlook of manufacturing industry.

All Memphis pieces were, with the exception of blown glass, intended as prototypes for industrial production, and the group always allied itself to the potentiality of industrial production to produce goods on a scale capable of satisfying the respective desires and imaginations of a variety of consumers. But craft skills were seen as an important vehicle for experimentation and exploration of materials, surfaces, and forms. To this end Sottsass had brought into the Memphis circle his Milanese cabinet-making friend, Renzo Brugola, who was encouraged to help lend material substance to the new ideas of Sottsass and his colleagues. However, this emphasis on craft was not a phenomenon confined to Italy, as elsewhere in Europe and the United States in the 1970s and 1980s a new breed of designers redefined the boundaries and explored the visual possibilities of the crafts. In Britain in 1986, for example, John Thackera wrote about designers who had

given up hope of finding sympathetic partners in industry and are exploring ways of manufacturing and distributing their own products. To some of this group the Italian experience is an inspiration; that country's success in furniture, lighting and clothing has been due, in part, to the survival of a lively artisan tradition, based in a small-scale workshop infrastructure, which makes it possible to produce, in small batches, products which could not economically be made in huge factories.[31]

Post-Modernism: the wider picture

Reaction against the semantic limitations of modernism was not restricted to industrial design, the decorative and applied arts, and architecture [129]. Similar experimentation in typography, letter-spacing, and the expressive possibilities of photolithography could be seen in the work of the influential graphic designer Wolfgang Weingart who, having reacted against the studied clarity of Swiss International Style typography, became associated with American New Wave design in the 1970s [**130**, **131**]. Such an emphasis on individual expression was taken up by April Greiman, a leading figure in such developments in California in the late 1970s and 1980s,[32] and others associated with the style magazine *Emigré*, launched by Rudy VanderLans in Berkeley in 1982. Similar tendencies can be discerned in the graphic work of Javier Mariscal in Spain, although his work also extended into other design media such as textiles, lighting, interiors, and furniture, in connection with which Ettore Sottsass invited him to participate in the Memphis exhibition of 1981.

A radical spirit could also be discerned in British street-style magazines such as *i-D*, published, edited, and art-directed by Terry Jones from 1980, and *The Face*, art-directed by Neville Brody between 1981 and 1986. Both designers were highly influential in their abandonment of conventional grid-base layouts, combining all kinds of surface marks with varieties of type and letter-forms and exploring the expressive possibilities of different textures and decorative motifs. Initially motivated by the vitality and crudeness of Punk, Neville Brody, in the eclectic manner of post-modern design, also drew upon the collagiste, photomontage, and typographic experimentation of Dada, Russian Constructivism, the Bauhaus, De Stijl, and other avant-garde trends of interwar modernism as a means of revitalizing the page. In keeping with the design cultism of the 1980s his work was celebrated in an exhibition entitled *The Graphic Language of Neville Brody*[33] at the Victoria and Albert Museum, London, in 1988 and has been extremely influential [**132**]: pale imitations of much of his early 1980s works were incorporated into the signage and design of many fashionable shops, record stores, packaging, and magazines. He has been commissioned by many important clients in Europe, the United States and the Far

THE GRAPHIX MAGAZINE THAT LOST ITS FAITH IN NIHILISM

130 Gary Panter

Raw magazine cover,
no. 3, 1981

The crude, brash styling of this cover marks it out as a manifestation of the experimental climate of the late 1970s and 1980s. Like much New Wave American graphic design of the time it represented a reaction against conventional, carefully structured approaches to typography and layout.

131 Tom van den Haspel and Henk Elenga

Front cover of *Lecturis*, 1981

Both designers were members of the Hard Werken design group which has become renowned for experimentation and freedom in graphic communication. Designers associated with the group have explored combinations of surface, image, and typography in an invigorating fashion.

East—Japanese retailers such as Men's Bigi and Parco, Dutch Telecom, PTT, Bloomingdales in New York, and the Body Shop in England—reinforcing the concept of global potency of style in affluent industrialized societies.

Pop, punk, and Post-Modernism: an afterword

Pop in the early 1960s has often been interpreted as a youthful challenge to many traditionally accepted values,[34] and the vibrant, expendable consumer values that it furthered were not seen as a serious threat to the social status quo. However, from 1966, when hallucinogenic drugs, free love, and interest in eastern religions assumed an increasingly significant profile, the outlook began to change. Psychedelic patterns and imagery, associated with vividly colourful experience of

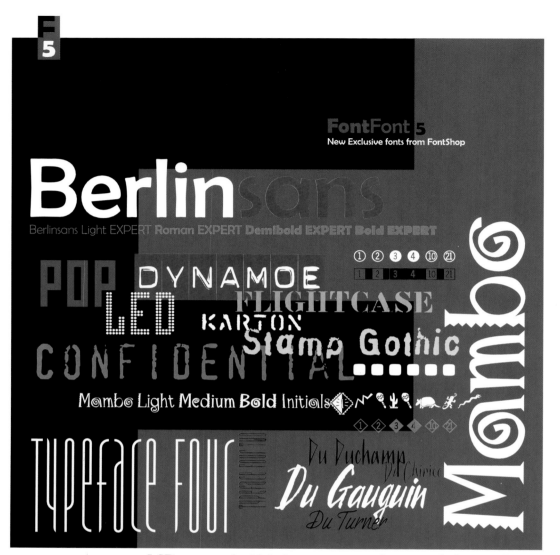

LSD, appeared widely in posters, record covers, clothing and other surfaces, including shop fronts. Originating in West Coast America Psychedelic art was associated with alternative or 'hippy' lifestyles and found expression in the widely disseminated posters of Rick Griffin, Wes Wilson, and Victor Moscoso. Their counterparts in Britain included Martin Sharp, illustrator for the notorious magazine *Oz*,[35] and the partnership of Nigel Weymouth and Michael English (known as Hapsash and the Coloured Coat), best known for their mural and shop-front work. However, any perceived social or cultural threat which such design might be seen to embody was undermined by the high levels of commercialization of the style, which ceased to embrace any genuine fundamentals of an alternative lifestyle as soon as it became readily available 'off-the-peg' in a wide variety of retail outlets. A similar transformation can be seen to have taken place with Punk,

132 Neville Brody

Brochure cover for *FontFont 5*, Fontshop International, 1992
The first FontShop was set up in Germany in 1989 in the belief that digital typefaces could be more successfully developed by designers themselves rather than by a limited number of major companies which were unwilling to accommodate radical design solutions. In 1990 Brody established FontWorks UK, part of an expanding international franchising network which invigorated the global typographic imagination much as radical young designers had the appearance of independent record covers more than a decade earlier.

which some writers have seen as an affirmation of the working-class urban reality of unemployment, expressed through ripped, zipped, and 'dirty' dress that was 'the sartorial equivalent of swear words', or personal ornamentation and body-piercing associated with overtones of 'deviancy'. Ideas and information about music and events were communicated crudely through small-scale 'newsheets'. Often typed with hand-written deletions and insertions and photocopied such 'fanzines' were stapled together and produced in very small runs for local networks: better known examples include *Sniffin Glue* and *Ripped and Torn* which began in 1976. The impact of such work has been significant and within five years became a mainstream element of commercialized street style in the graphic work of Jamie Reid, Michael Garret, Peter Saville, and Neville Brody. The immediate impact of Punk's outcry against establishment was relatively short-lived as 'offensiveness' was soon incorporated into mainstream cultural expression, with ripped and torn clothing soon mass-produced and available in fashionable boutiques. None the less, as a number of writers have argued, it did reassert Britain as a centre for new and original ideas in design.

But the rapid move from innovation to orthodoxy was not confined to street style. Many critics also drew attention to the ways in which positive and conscious moves to enrich the design and architectural vocabulary, as seen in the origins of the 'New International Style', might become devalued in what might be termed 'simplistic, reach-me-down formulae'. For example, in the book accompanying *The Design Now* exhibition in Frankfurt in 1988, Volker Fischer wrote of such formulae:

At three or four removes they may degenerate into a new form of kitsch, easy on the eye, tailor made for the suburban bungalow, with oriels and columnettes adorning facades across the land! Post-Modernism is basically characterised by the rediscovery of ornament, colour, symbolic connections and the treasure trove of the history of form.[36]

Nostalgia, Heritage, and Design

9

Nostalgia has played a significant role in the production and consumption of design throughout the twentieth century, whether in the late 1940s and 1950s mass-produced suburban developments by Levitt & Sons in traditional clapper-boarded American Cape Cod cottage style, the reaffirmation of 1950s and 1960s American motorcycle heritage in the Harley-Davidson Springer Softail and Heritage Softail Classic production models of the late 1980s,[1] Barbara Hulanicki's Biba boutiques and department store in London in the 1960s and 1970s (drawing on a changing panorama of sources from Victoriana and Art Nouveau to Art Deco and Hollywood), or the 'English Country Cottage' chintz-inspired interior décor promoted by Laura Ashley in the 1970s and 1980s. This 'sentimental longing for past times' is also closely bound up with notions of tradition and national identity, a number of which already have been addressed in Chapter 4. Furthermore, the variety of ways in which historical references can be harnessed is further complicated by the free use of, and potentially fresh meanings afforded by, quotations from the past by post-modern designers such as Philippe Starck in his *Richard III* armchair, a three-legged pastiche of the archetypal Club armchair of the 1930s or Robert Venturi in his *Chippendale Chair (with Grandmother Pattern)* produced by Knoll International of 1984.

Aspects of American heritage and Colonial Revival

Large-scale exhibitions were important vehicles for the reinforcing of ideas about identity and heritage in the twentieth century, just as they had been in the nineteenth. For example, the six million visitors to the Sesquicentennial Exhibition at Philadelphia, open from June to November 1926, could see a recreation of the main street of Philadelphia in 1776, complete with the Franklin Print Shop, the Paul Revere Forge and a Friends Meeting House. Even at the 1933 Chicago Century of Progress Exhibition reconstruction of the past also played a significant role, much as had been the case in large-scale imperial and colonial exhibitions in Europe such as the British Empire Exhibition at Wembley, London, of 1924 and the Exposition Coloniale in Paris of 1931. At Chicago in 1933 an important element of the display was the

Detail of 138

133

Colonial Williamsburg's
Ayscough's Cabinet Making
Shop, 1937

This was one of a number
of craft workshops at
Williamsburg which promoted
the Colonial Revival style.
Others included a forge and
pewter shop where
costumed craftsworkers
explained their work to visitors.
The carefully researched
restoration of Colonial
Williamsburg was conceived
as a means of establishing a
consciousness of a past
centred on the historic capital
of Virginia, promoting a set
of essentially Anglo-Saxon
and 'patriotic' values.

reconstruction of Fort Dearborn of 1833 and a replica of the log-cabin where Abraham Lincoln was born.[2] Furthermore, at the futuristic New York World's Fair of 1939, the governing Board of Design allowed traditional forms to be used in the Court of States which celebrated historical heritage: the New England states of Connecticut, Massachusetts, New Hampshire, Rhode Island, and Vermont collaborated on a joint exhibit featuring a replica of a sea-going schooner and a reproduction wharf and dockside which looked back to earlier trading days; in similar vein the Pennsylvania building was a replica of Independence Hall in Philadelphia, and the New Jersey building reproduced the Old Barracks where Hessian mercenaries in the service of Britain were overcome by Washington's forces at the Battle of Trenton in 1787.

Particular notions of American heritage had been prompted by a number of other concerns in the interwar years, including the setting up of the American Wing of the Metropolitan Museum of Art, New York, in 1924 and the Philadelphia Sesquicentennial Exhibition (celebrating the 150th anniversary of the signing of the Declaration of Independence) of 1926. In fact 1926 was a significant year as it saw the establishment of Greenfield village by the industrialist Henry Ford in Dearborn, Michigan, and the commencement of the restoration (funded by John D. Rockefeller Jr.) of colonial Williamsburg. The Index of American Design, sponsored by the Federal Arts Project[3] between 1935 and 1941 and originally co-ordinated by the textile designer Ruth Reeves, was a further important impetus in documenting a much more broad-based and inclusive portrayal of the heritage of the United States.

The Greenfield Village heritage concept was a means both of focusing contemporary attention on renowned American inventors and products and of clearly identifying their part in the shaping of what he saw as everyday American life from its origins in the colonial era. Much of the site was devoted to the reconstruction of an early American village that included a variety of archetypal buildings which symbolized, through their form and contents, the achievements and outlook of ordinary American people. Also incorporated into Ford's Greenfield Village scheme were a number of other buildings associated with major figures of American history, such as the Illinois courthouse where Abraham Lincoln first practised law. More significant in terms of the history of technology and invention in the United States, a field which Ford sought to emphasize in his particular portrayal of American history, were the reconstructions of Thomas Edison's Menlo Park, New Jersey, laboratory and the Wright Brothers' bicycle shop. Many other historical determinants in the shaping of American life were shown at the Henry Ford Museum, also on site, including Ford's collections of domestic appliances, furniture, clocks, and automobiles.

C 13.95

A 109.95

B 64.95

E 44.95

D 89.95

Western-styled Sofa-Bed Groups

FURNISH YOUR HOME IN THE RICH TRADITION OF THE AMERICAN WEST. These distinctive pieces offer frontier styling in the strong, practical construction of modern craftsmanship. Rounded "time-worn" effect edges, peg-effect trim and plank-top tables give authentic appearance—ideal for living room, den, basement or game room. Solid Hardwood construction—dowelled, corner-braced, hot-glued at points of strain to give added rigidity. Cotton and sisal padding for extra comfort.

DU PONT FABRILITE UPHOLSTERY—a Vinyl Plastic on strong fabric back for extra long wear on both Sofa-Bed groups. Highly resistant to peeling or cracking. Vinyl cleans easily with a damp cloth. You may choose from four striking colors: Chartreuse, Green, Saddle Tan or Deep Red.

BOTH SOFA BEDS open like (DGHJ), Pg. 505. Become 72x45-in. beds. 162 double-cone coil-springs in seat and back over No-Sag steel springs. Cotton and Steel padding eliminates "coil-feel." Bedding compartment. Ht. 33 in. Seat 72x22½ in. Rear of back is Cotton Velourette in matching color.

BOTH LOUNGE CHAIRS: Covered all around with Plastic—fit into any room arrangement. Removable coil-spring 21x23½-in. seat cushion rests on No-Sag steel spring base for added comfort. Coil-springs in padded back. Height 32½ in.

BOTH PLATFORM ROCKERS: Rock with steel spring on stationary platform. Attached 22x22½-in. coil-spring seat cushion, No-Sag spring base. Coil-spring back. Height 32 in.

DURABLE PLASTIC-COVERED PIECES—BUY SINGLY OR SAVE ON 5-PIECE GROUP ... ONLY 219.95

A B Combination of two finishes—"Driftwood," a gray natural finish contrasting with Light Walnut finish—both rubbed to a satiny smoothness. Authentic adaptations of old ox-yokes form arms. Handsome trapunto embossed steer heads on 80-in. long Sofa-Bed, a horse's head on both Lounge Chair and Platform Rocker. Note the unique Cocktail Table, inspired by buckboard seat on wagon springs — extra large planked top, 40x22 in. Height 16½ in. End Table top 22x13½ in. Height 21 in. Pay shipping charge from Austin, Texas Factory. Allow two weeks extra at Factory.*

C WESTERN TABLE LAMP. Hand-decorated cowboy-and-steer design on composition base. Ht. 28 in. Wt. ea. 9 lbs. Mailable. 66 A 247 M—Natural-color paper Parchment shade, 16-inch diameter. Use with either group. Pair $26.95; Each .. $13.95

66 A 4985 F—State Items or Groups and Upholstery Color wanted: Chartreuse, Green, Saddle Tan or Deep Red.
(A) SOFA-BED. Ship. wt. 165 lbs. $17 Down......Cash $109.95
(B) PLATFORM ROCKER. Ship. wt. 90 lbs. $10.50 Dn. Cash 64.95
SOFA-BED (A) AND LOUNGE CHAIR (above). Ship. wt. 235 lbs. $26.50 Down on Wards Credit Terms........or Cash $169.95
5-Pc. GROUP: Consists of Sofa-Bed, Lounge Chair, One Cocktail Table and Two End Tables. Shipping weight 330 lbs. Only $34 Down on Convenient Terms........or Cash $219.95

RANCH-STYLE SOFA-BED 89.95   SOFA-BED AND PLATFORM ROCKER 134.95   5-PIECE GROUP 164.95

D E Light Gray finish—resembling the textured, yet smooth finish of Limed Oak. Handsome trapunto embossed heads of horses on 85-inch long Sofa-Bed—extra wide arms, so convenient for resting books. Chair backs not embossed. Cocktail Table has 30x16 in. top. Height 16 in. Buy pieces singly or in low-price groups. Lamp (C) sold above is ideal with this group. Pay shipping charges from Factory in Austin, Texas. Allow two weeks extra at Factory.*

66 A 4986 F—State Items or Groups and Upholstery Color: Chartreuse, Green, Saddle Tan or Deep Red.
(D) SOFA-BED. Shipping weight 155 lbs. $14 Down, Cash $89.95
(E) LOUNGE CHAIR. Ship. wt. 70 lbs. $4.50 Down, Cash 44.95
SOFA-BED (D) AND PLATFORM ROCKER (below). Wt. 245 lbs. 134.95
5-Pc. GROUP: Consists of Sofa-Bed, Platform Rocker, 1 Cocktail Table and Two End Tables. Ship. wt. 310 lbs........$164.95

*SOFA-BEDS AND CHAIRS on this page are covered to your order and shipped to you from the Factory. This elimination of handling expense results in lower prices for you. For details on Wards Convenient Monthly Payment Plan, see Page 968.

506 WARDS FED

These designs from a
Montgomery Ward catalogue
draw on a very different notion
of American heritage from that
seen at Williamsburg.
Promoted as reflecting 'the
rich tradition of the American
West' together with 'frontier
styling', they also exhibit
'rounded "time-worn" edges,
peg-effect trim, and plank-top
tables' which afford an
'authentic appearance'.

The restoration of Williamsburg came to fruition with its formal opening in 1935, an event which was widely reported in the press and generated considerable public interest. Enthusiasm for the Colonial Revival had fluctuated since the Philadelphia Centennial International Exhibition of 1876, but was reawakened almost sixty years later by numerous features in magazines devoted to domestic interiors and decoration. Such a revival of interest in Colonial crafts was further invigorated by the opening in 1937 of the first of Williamsburg's reconstructed shops where crafts workers worked in the public gaze [133], explaining to visitors the processes and significance of their activities.[4] Furthermore, Williamsburg also supported the large-scale manufacture of Colonial reproductions through its Programme for the Promotion of Crafts which enabled manufacturers to reproduce a wide range of artifacts for the home to be put on sale at the Craft House in Williamsburg, selected retail outlets across the United States, and through mail-order. As has been shown by William Rhoads,[5] both the Williamsburg reconstruction and the phenomenon of Colonial revival were recognized as significant barriers to the wider acceptance of modernism in the United States. This attachment to the past was seen to be embraced by many in the interwar years, resurfacing with renewed vigour after 1945 when national identity and 'American values' once more became significant areas for concern [134].

The Index of American Design was largely a response to the campaigning activity of those who sought to revive interest in the Spanish Colonial style[6] and Hispanic crafts, to preserve the heritage of Indian tribal crafts, and to document a wider perspective of American decorative arts from the Colonial period onwards. This comprehensive survey consisted of more than 22,000 plates made by over 500 unemployed artists. Its multicultural embrace was far more wide-reaching than the monocultural and partial outlook of the Colonial Revival. More complex debates about identity and multiculturalism surfaced more potently in the post-1945 era, a difficult yet rewarding field of study which falls outside the scope of this particular volume on twentieth-century design. It is also an area of developing importance in the study of such concerns in the history of European design of the same period.

None the less, historical styles endured in the domestic sphere in the postwar years, as they did in Europe and elsewhere [135]. Even in the field of American diners,[7] archetypal heritage symbols of the streamlined era of the later 1930s, such historicizing design considerations began to assert themselves by the early 1960s. For example, the Kulman Dining Car Company of Newark, New Jersey, built its first diner in Colonial Revival style in Ocean City in 1962, marking a move away from the dominant stainless steel modernity of earlier models. Such an aesthetic, embracing such characteristics as wood-panelling, shaded lights on horizontally-suspended traditional wooden wagon wheels, and wall-mounted rifles, saddles, and gun belts, remained popular into the 1970s. Colonial Revivalism also featured in the home and business environment of the period when nostalgia became a more pronounced feature of middle-class houses and apartments. Historical styles were widely purchased across the economic spectrum, featuring in a wide range of contemporary magazines as well as in the products of named designers, such as William Baldwin, who explored the expressive possibilities of traditional forms in designs for furniture and interiors.

As interest in American folk art began to gain more widespread currency in this period, so a number of indigenous traditions such as stencilling, which had flourished from the late eighteenth to mid-nineteenth century, were reintroduced, particularly in period homes.

Other related folk-art traditions, such as painted floors and floor-cloths, were also re-explored, along with a revival of interest in the traditional forms of Amish, Mennonite, and other designs for patchwork quilts.

Nostalgia and the invention of tradition

Much nostalgic imagery in the packaging for, and surface decoration applied to, so many products is tied to a past which is characterized by non-specific space and time. In his discussion of nostalgia, *Yearning for Yesterday*,[8] Fred Davis drew attention to an article in the *New York Times* in February 1975 in which the spirit of contemporary nostalgia was described thus:

> . . . today's nostalgia is at worst bittersweet, at least designed to bring some pleasure. Our fashions, decor and happenings evoke the thirties without the Depression, the forties sans the war, the fifties minus MacCarthyism. These harmless activities deserve no monopoly of the past.[9]

Davis also drew attention to the confusion that seemingly 'accurate' films could generate in their relentless search for authentic historical flavour. In relation to the enormously successful film, *The Sting*, he wrote:

> . . . the problem of hypernaturalism's artificiality is further confounded by the cavalier imposition of pre-World War I rag-time music and 'big-store' con games onto the chic gangsterism of the twenties and the social protest atmosphere of the thirties. In short, the film was a historical mess, despite the apparently obsessive care taken by the makers to have everything look extra-real.[10]

Similarly, the apparent historical origins upon which many designs evocative of the past are based have little real foundation in fact. This theme is absorbingly explored in a variety of regional, cultural, and 'ethnic' contexts in Eric Hobsbawm and Terence Ranger's text of 1983, *The Invention of Tradition*,[11] which offers design historians a number of models which might usefully be explored further in their own field. The 'invention' of the naturally-based toiletries and quality foods firm of Crabtree & Evelyn in 1972[12] provides a parallel case in point, exuding as it did the spirit of Olde England through the historicist design of its shops. A strong scent of the past was also given off by its products and packaging [136] as well as the feeling of historical credibility afforded by the choice of names for the company's fictitious London 'proprietors' with their specific roots in English history: John Evelyn was a celebrated English diarist of the seventeenth century who wrote on food, was a horticulturist, and planned English country parks; George Crabtree, an English horticulturist, was a figure of the same period with an archetypally English name. However, Crabtree & Evelyn was in fact an American company, the founder of which, Cyrus

Harvey, sought out an English identity for the sale of its products in
the USA. This was supplied by the English designer Peter Windett
who was approached by Harvey before either the name or the company
logotype was arrived at: Windett's design solution for the logo was
based on a seventeenth-century woodcut of an apple tree. When the
company moved into direct retailing in the late 1970s the first shop that
Windett designed for it was based on the idea of the English apothe-
cary. Built in England, it was shipped out to Philadelphia, complete
with English cabinets, glass, brass fittings, wallpaper, and carpet; it was
later moved to the Crabtree & Evelyn outlet on Madison Avenue,
New York. As the company expanded, design of the American stores
was handed over to an American company, with design for the
European outlets being carried out by the London-based Prosper
Devas. In the mid-1980s Devas also designed an 'authentically English'
shop within the Matsuya department store in Tokyo.

Nostalgic packaging, with a high illustrative content, has provided a
fundamental aspect of the 'invented tradition' of the company's corporate identity. As Windett said:

The illustrations—particularly with food—tend to tell a story, to portray an
image, not just of the products, but of their history. To depict the origin of ginger in a ginger biscuit, for instance, we can do a very good, authentic drawing
of the West Indies, evoking an image of the quality and integrity of the product. And then the text will have anecdotes, historical quotes.[13]

To help consolidate the 'manufactured' authenticity of its designs the
company looked to cottage industries and old family firms to supply its

products, a recipe which, combined with the other aesthetically-charged ingredients of shop design, packaging, and advertising, proved a highly successful formula in the 1970s and 1980s—the invention of tradition turned out to be a highly profitable marketing enterprise. By the late 1980s the company had 170 licensed or company-owned shops in North America, with eight in Britain and a small number of others in Europe and Japan. It also had almost 2,500 points of sale in 23 countries.

Design and the past in Britain in the post-1945 era

The notion that certain aspects of the past were lost for ever took on particular resonances from the late 1940s onwards, a feeling that was reinforced by the destruction of the Second World War and the realization that British Empire, previously a significant ingredient of the national historical and educational make-up, was coming inexorably to an end. A number of writers have viewed this period as a battleground for the reassertion of particular cultural positions.[14] Against such a backcloth there was a heightened spirit of self-consciousness about the national past. At the same time that the recently founded Council of Industrial Design (COID) was seeking to promote a modern aesthetic[15] and technological innovations were being promoted overseas there was a resurgence of interest in the traditions of British popular art and the rural crafts. This manifested itself in a variety of ways, ranging from books to exhibitions. Important texts included Charles Marriott's *British Handicrafts*, first published in 1943[16] as part of the British Council's series on British Life and Thought. The author sought to reconcile surviving handicrafts with contemporary needs since he felt that they 'encourage that use of the hand which is the crying need of a mechanical civilisation . . . and, above all, they bring into play the basic native qualities on which artistic excellence in the crafts ultimately depends.'[17] Margaret Lambert and the designer-illustrator Enid Marx contributed to the field of the history of popular art, producing an illustrated text on *English Popular and Traditional Arts* in 1946,[18] followed up by a far more detailed study in 1951.[19] The latter expressed the firm belief that a strong tradition of British cultural creativity was being lost to the postwar generation, a tradition which Lambert and Marx wished to preserve for posterity as a field of study. In the same year Barbara Jones's *The Unsophisticated Arts*[20] was published, described at the time as 'the first substantial publication on British popular art'.[21] Included in its scope were such miscellaneous elements as fairground roundabouts, the decoration of canal boats and their equipment, the design of rustic porches executed by a late nineteenth-century craftsman, and the picturesque detailing of riverside bungalows. In this, the Festival of Britain year, Barbara Jones and Tom Ingram also organized an exhibition of British Popular and Traditional

Art at the Whitechapel Gallery, London. Entitled 'Black Eyes and Lemonade', it celebrated the heritage of everyday life, including souvenirs of all kinds, football memorabilia, traditional shaped loaves, sweets, and other foodstuffs, as well as miscellaneous artifacts connected with the home, such as Toby Jugs and thatched cottage teapots.

There were other tangible elements of change which enhanced this renewed consciousness of the past. Following the disappearance of the regional companies with the nationalization of the railways in 1948, steam trains were gradually replaced with diesel and electric systems. Such developments encouraged the formation of railway preservation societies and led to the growth of interest in British railway history. Furthermore, the preservation of folk songs and a growing sense of the importance of oral history helped to maintain a sense of continuity with the past, an understanding of which was further enhanced by the emergence of industrial archaeology as a field of academic study. Conservation and preservation also became important rallying points for those who were opposed to the widespread speculative building developments which irretrievably changed the face of many cityscapes throughout Britain in the 1960s. A growing sense of 'Heritage in Danger' was articulated by Malcolm MacEwan and others during the 1970s,[22] a very different interpretation of 'heritage' from the adoption of Victorian values by Margaret Thatcher and her Conservative government in the 1980s.

In his thought-provoking book of 1985, *On Living in an Old Country: The National Past in Contemporary Britain*, Patrick Wright viewed the emergence of heritage as a concern which took on a very distinct character after 1979 when Margaret Thatcher came to power. He drew attention to her aim of 'restoring national pride and other old values back to the country at large' and the great patriotic fervour with which the National Heritage Bill of 1980 was greeted on its introduction in Parliament. He also viewed the National Heritage Memorial Fund as one of the Conservative government's first attempts 'to revive the spirit of the Second World War and to set up its own patriotic measure against that long-drawn-out betrayal known in more polite circles as the post-war settlement'.[23] Although Wright did not suggest that the conservation of heritage was crudely class-determined, he drew attention to the prevailing cultural values endorsed by the National Trust.

Founded in 1895, by 1985 the Trust boasted a membership of over one million and was one of the largest landowners in Britain. Concern for the landscape, identified with the essence of England, and the preservation of monuments were seen to be linked with a desire to preserve the social order. In the light of Peter Windett's choice of the apple tree as summarizing Englishness for the historically-vibrant, yet myth-creating, logotype for Crabtree & Evelyn in the 1970s, it is perhaps interesting to note that when the National Trust was seeking to promote itself more forcibly through the creation of its own identity in the mid-1930s it eventually ran an invitation-only competition[24] in which the six preselected designers were only allowed to incorporate a lion, a rose, or a tree in their designs. The winning design by Joseph Armitage incorporated the oak-leaf as an effective communicator of the spirit of national heritage, a symbol which has endured to the present day.

The National Trust, like many more straightforwardly commercial companies, also entered into the market-place, selling traditional toiletries, foodstuffs, and many other products exuding a strong sense of national heritage and history. The first National Trust shop opened in a country house in Saltram, Devon, in the late 1960s. Following the appointment of Roy Hallet as the Trust's Sales and Marketing Organizer in 1970 there was a rapid expansion of this commercial dimension: within 12 months there were 30 new retail outlets, all of which proved profitable; designers, notably the textile designer Pat Albeck, were brought in to develop such potential. In less than twenty years National Trust Enterprises had a turnover of £20 million with profits in excess of £3 million. During the same period the commercial possibilities of marketing the past have been taken up as an increasingly significant part of the museum economy, whether through the activities of such concerns as V & A Enterprises at the Victoria and Albert Museum or the souvenir shops of the vast number of heritage sites throughout Britain.

As has been seen from the above, as well as in Chapter 4, there has been a long-standing belief that the quintessential England lay in the countryside rather than the city. The traditional 'unpolluted' values of a rural heritage and a spirit of nostalgia located in a seemingly familiar yet historically unspecified past were frequently extolled in advertisements, packaging (particularly of foodstuffs), and a wide range of artifacts. In the decades following the company's modest beginnings in the early 1950s as a producer of fabric prints in the Ashleys' Pimlico, London, flat the products of Laura Ashley fully embraced such ideals. The company became increasingly concerned with the marketing of a 'lifestyle' drawing strongly on the imagery associated with the countryside, commencing with clothing in 1967. A rapid expansion of the company's activities followed the opening of its shop in London's Fulham Road, the location of Terence Conran's first Habitat store, which had opened in 1964. In the late 1970s and 1980s Laura Ashley began to market ideas for complete interiors, retailing co-ordinating fabrics, wallpapers, and paints. The rural imagery employed, evocative of the idyllic country cottage and its surroundings, also proved attractive to overseas markets: by the early 1980s there were twelve retailing

137

Baroque service in porcelain, no. 9355, Zsolnay Ceramics Factory Hungary, 1945 onwards

This historicizing design reflects the potency of the past in many countries. Conforming to the affinity of many consumers to the reassuring nature of traditional artefacts, the *Baroque* service sold between 50,000 and 60,000 sets each year for several decades.

outlets in the United States as well as a number of others in major cities in Canada, Australia, and Germany; in addition there were mail-order facilities in several European and Scandinavian countries. The co-ordinated orthodoxy of cotton and chintz seen in the wallpapers, Country Furnishing fabrics and frills were evocatively promoted through the Laura Ashley *Catalogue*, an idea initiated in 1981 and further consolidated by the publication of a glossy ideas book, the *Laura Ashley Book of Interior Decoration*. The literally rose-tinted visions evoked by catalogue texts were exemplified by Laura Ashley's preface to the 1982 *Catalogue*, in which she declared:

Our aim each year is to study and review our prints and colours in the light of changing moods of lifestyle. Happily romanticism is more in the air than ever. If you bicycle from Chelsea to Hampstead the gardens are overflowing with roses and lavender . . .

In addition to the Chintz Collection so successfully introduced last year, we are launching a new Decorator Collection printed on Satin. These extra fine fabrics have enabled us to engrave flower prints as well as the more sophisticated geometric prints in a way never seen in our collections before.[25]

The marketing of retrospection was by no means confined to Laura Ashley and found expression in the output of ceramic manufacturers [**137**, **138**], wallpaper producers, textile companies, and others [**139**]. On both sides of the Atlantic the idea of the country house interior, first explored by (Sybil) Colefax & (John) Fowler in the 1930s, became a significant source of inspiration in the 1970s and 1980s, leading to a frequent sourcing of a range of patterns from the archives of long-established textile and wallpaper manufacturers: Arthur Sanderson & Co, who owned the original blocks for a range of Morris & Co designs, marketed a range of Arts and Crafts patterns; Tissunique of London,

Brunschwig & Fils, New York, and F. Schumacher & Co, USA, were among other notable exponents of such trends.

The past was also evoked in a revival of interest in traditional decorative techniques, fostered not only by the significant growth in the number of magazines devoted to interior design and decoration but by a continuing growth of Do-It-Yourself as a leisure activity. Techniques such as stencil work, rag rolling, and marbling were often featured in popular homemaking magazines, as well as advice notes in paint manufacturers catalogues aimed for the general public.

The heritage industry

During the 1980s there were other facets of the marketing of history which took on very specific forms, exploring aspects of the past which were seen to embody British national heritage. Such ideas have been discussed by Robert Hewison in his controversial book *The Heritage Industry*[26] of 1987. At that time heritage was reported to be the largest growth 'industry' in Britain, with a new museum opening every two weeks. The concept also found political support from the Conservative

138 Harold Holdcroft

Old Country Roses bone china tableware, Royal Albert (Royal Doulton), 1962 onwards

The world's best-selling tableware design, *Old Country Roses* has sold more than 100 million pieces all over the world since its introduction in 1962. Such was its popularity that in 1975 the range was extended from tableware to include vases, candlesticks, and other ornaments; later, other manufacturers produced the pattern on tablecloths and napkins. The fact that one pattern has been a high-selling range for more than thirty-five years should counsel against easy categorizations of taste and period.

139

'Victorian' designs from *Past Times* catalogue, Autumn, 1995

The Past Times company, launched in 1986, has more than 60 outlets in the UK and Ireland. In many overseas countries its products are also available by mail order, marketed from warehouses in the appropriate language and currency, including Japan, Germany, France, the United States, and Australia. The fact that a company can draw upon many historic styles and cultures, and achieve such a high volume of sales internationally shows the enduring appeal of the past for contemporary consumers.

government of the day, with English Heritage, an offshoot of the Department of the Environment, setting out to make the past 'marketable'. As has been seen above, this was paralleled by a number of demonstrably successful private enterprises, and it was therefore unsurprising that an All-Party Committee on the Environment should conclude that heritage could pay its own way. Proponents of the 'heritage industry' argued that the cultural end of the leisure industry would outgrow museum design as a medium for the interpretation of the past and that its efforts to interpret events, objects, and locations were sincere and highly organized. Giles Velarde, a heritage consultant, asserted:

heritage design, together with our heritage, is here to stay. It is a discipline we can export, it benefits the public and it can be profitable. The UK has a singular history and I, for one, am happy to see it in the safe hands of the designers currently operating in the field.[27]

None the less, there was considerable debate about the ways in which the 'heritage industry' was funded and promoted. Indeed, concern about the lack of regulation and professionalism in the field led the Carnegie UK Trust, an important body in the early days of heritage development, to withdraw from a front-line role and limit its funding to an investigation into standards and codes of practice within the field. Other bodies, such as the Centre for Environmental

Interpretation and the Society for the Interpretation of Britain's Heritage (founded in 1987), were similarly concerned.

Gillian Darley, writing in the *Financial Times* in 1989 drew attention to the high fees commanded by heritage consultants, as well as their ability to package the past for a wide range of clients, unconstrained by any sense of history tied to specific places. The chief target of her critique was the national-award-winning Mountfichet Castle and Norman Village at Stansted, Essex, which was promoted as 'the castle that time forget' and 'the 1066 village'.[28] The lack of historical specificity was similar to that of many designed artifacts of the nostalgia boom of the 1970s and 1980s. Darley drew attention to the obviously 'machine-cut timber' and 'modern cement' in the huts in the stockade, whilst

in the chapel, a calming tape of mediaeval choral music plays—only three hundred years ahead of itself. For this travesty of history the promoters have received more than their fair share of commendations and awards, including a British Tourist Authority trophy in 1986, a London Tourist Board Award in 1987, and a Carnegie Foundation commendation last year [1988].[29]

Kevin Walsh, in his 1992 book, *The Representation of the Past*, followed such criticism through into the financial sector which he saw as an underpinning element in heritage enterprise:

heritage organisations have no qualms in seeing their historical resources as a product to be marketed. Their target is the members of the ABC1 socio-economic groups. Such organisations judge success, not through how the public perceives or develops an understanding of the past, but by purely financial criteria. The columns of documents detailing performance of a site are headed with the labels 'Total Retail Sales', 'Target Income Achieved', 'Average Spend Per Head' (English Heritage Spread Sheet 1990). There seem to be only restricted attempts at assessing the educational quality or academic credibility of historic representations.

Success in a market, which is perceived as the natural benign context within which all human activity occurs, is complicit with a belief that the representation of the past is a practice devoid of politics.[30]

As will be seen in Chapter 10, environmental and ecological concerns also became increasingly important areas of contestation and debate in the design arena from the 1960s onwards. Just as concepts such as heritage, conservation, and preservation were balanced between the often conflicting pressures of ethics and enterprise, they too were subject to identification with marketing considerations and opportunities.

Design and Social Responsibility

10

The USA: design and consumer organizations

Although consumer rights have gradually evolved through the twentieth century it can be argued that their significance in any widespread societal sense emerged after the end of the Second World War. None the less, they evolved in a less structured way over a longer period of time, particularly in the United States. In the last quarter of the nineteenth century there were large population increases, significant moves from rural areas to the city, and dramatic improvements in transport and communication systems. A number of organizations were founded in the same period, including the pioneering Consumers' League in New York City in 1891 and the National Consumers' League in 1898 which, within five years, boasted 64 branches in 20 states. They came into being at a time when consumers were faced with an increasingly wide range of products, together with changes in shopping patterns: premium stamps were introduced by Sperry & Hutchinson in 1896, the A & P Company (the Great Atlantic and Pacific Tea Company) had launched its cash-and-carry 'Economy Stores' at around the turn of the century, and the first self-service grocery store, a Piggly-Wiggly, opened in Memphis, Tennessee in 1916.[1]

The majority of the most significant early steps in consumer protection were enacted in the area of food and hygiene.[2] However, as has been seen in Chapter 3, by the 1920s there was a rapid growth in sales of all kinds of goods, sustained by widespread advertising both on the radio and in printed media. Attention has already been drawn to a number of critical reactions to the commercialization of American life at this time; in the consumer sphere in 1927 Stuart Chase and Frederick J. Schlink published *Your Money's Worth: A Study in the Waste of the Consumers' Dollar*, an attack on contemporary advertising practices and the phenomenon of pressure selling. Schlink went on to found a Consumers' Club in White Plains, New York, which undertook product testing, leading to the establishment of Consumers' Research Inc. which did this on a much wider scale. Financed by its users, its recommendations covered a wide range of products across the whole consumer spectrum; lists of both approved and disapproved items were published. The Good Housekeeping Institute, the Delineator

140

Cover *Consumer Reports*,
Issue no. 1, May, 1936, USA

This magazine was published
by the Consumers Union,
founded in 1936. Initially
launched at a time of
economic uncertainty, its
testing of products and brand-
name goods provided the
increasingly bewildered
consumer with an informed
view about 'value-for-money'.
It sought to provide views
about a wide range of social,
health, safety, and
environmental concerns,
and came into its own as a
major campaigning body after
the Second World War.

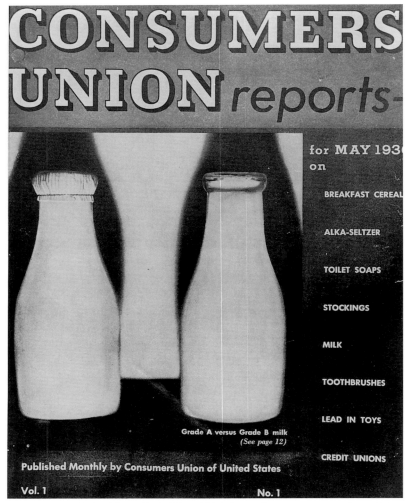

Institute, and the New York Herald Tribune Institute, together with a number of women's periodicals,[3] were also involved in the field of consumer advice and protection. They had their testing laboratories and often mounted exhibitions of home furnishings and kitchens which local readers could visit. Indeed, many manufacturers used the Good Housekeeping star, a symbol of product approval, as a means of promoting their products. None the less, such developments should be put into perspective. As one commentator, writing in 1934, remarked:

Only in recent years have there been any extensive studies of the ultimate consumer as such. A university library may contain 600,000 books, with ten directly classified under consumer. Of these, seven or eight will have been written by advertising men or marketing agents interested in the consumer only as a potential consumer. The consumer is . . . seldom considered.[4]

Contemporary consumer choice in America was considerable and potentially confusing, with department stores and mail-order catalogues providing an enticing array of goods. In 1933, for example, in the field of domestic appliances alone sales figures exceeded 2 million clocks, 1 million refrigerators, 1 million washing machines, 800,000 electric toasters, 500,000 vacuum cleaners, and 350,000 food mixers.

In 1936 the Consumers' Union was founded in New York with an initial membership of about 4,000, soon emerging as a key pressure group for educated consumers. It sought to test products and supply the consumer with appropriate information about competing products as well as advice about social, economic, health, and environmental issues, and its findings were reported in its magazine *Consumer Reports* [140].

In the five years immediately following the end of the Second World War, the circulation of the *Reports* rose tenfold, reaching 500,000 in 1950. It continued to grow through the decade together with the reality of what J. K. Galbraith termed the 'Affluent Society', and by 1961 the Consumers' Union was publishing almost a million copies of the *Reports* with an estimated readership of four million. By 1970 the circulation had reached 1,800,000 which, together with other Consumers' Union publications, gave the organization an operating budget of about $10 million and enabled the employment of a staff of 300 at its Mount Vernon, New York, headquarters. Despite attaining a position of such apparent widespread social relevance it was, like its British counterpart the Consumers' Association, an organization which was supported mainly by the managerial, professional, and better-paid sectors of society—in other words, those who were best equipped to take care of themselves.

Britain: design and the consumer from the 1940s to the early 1960s

As has been seen in Chapter 5, in the immediate postwar years the State-imposed Utility Scheme for a wide range of goods produced to particular design specifications was felt to guarantee certain standards of quality, durability, and value-for-money. However, in reality this was increasingly open to question since manufacturers were given progressively more flexibility through a gradual relaxation of Utility manufacturing requirements. As a result they often sought to exploit the preferential tax treatment accorded Utility goods by keeping within the decreed price ceiling at the expense of quality materials and fabrication. The Government appointed the Douglas Committee to examine the implications of such practices. In its report of 1952[5] it concluded that consumers had a real need for advice that would assist them in distinguishing between genuine value-for-money and cheapness which simply represented false economy.

The Cunliffe Committee on the Organization and Constitution of

Cover from *Which?* magazine, no. 1, 1957 (reprinted 1960)

Which? was the voice of the Consumers' Association, aiming to aid the consumer by 'encouraging the efficient manufacturer and exposing the producer of shoddy goods for the home and export markets'. The first issue featured the testing of ten electric kettles: five of them were condemned as having serious drawbacks, and only three recommended. Aesthetics played no part in the recommendation, the report stating as an afterthought that 'one big advantage of the chromium kettle is its appearance and only the buyer can decide whether it is worth paying the extra'.

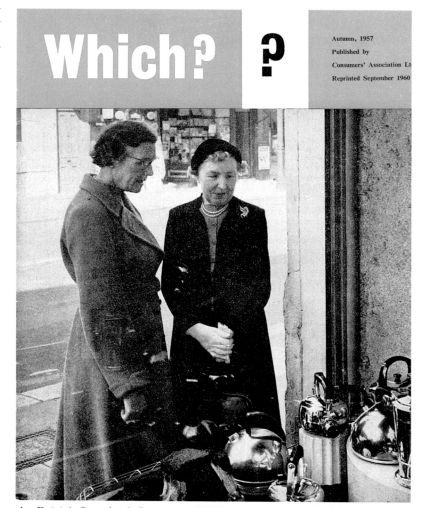

Which? **?**

Autumn, 1957

Published by

Consumers' Association Lt

Reprinted September 1960

the British Standards Institute[6] (BSI) of 1950 had argued for the adoption of a product certification scheme which would protect consumers from substandard goods. Public representation in consumer affairs had been slight, particularly on the various committees of the BSI. It was argued that women's organizations should play an important role in order that the implications of consumer standards should be communicated more effectively to the general public for, although these bodies (such as the Good Housekeeping Institute[7] and the Electrical Association for Women) had played a significant role in the field of domestic design in the interwar years,[8] their impact had been limited in this sphere. Accordingly, in 1951, the BSI established its Women's Advisory Committee as a means of facilitating collaboration between consumers, manufacturers, and retailers. This was followed by the founding in 1955 of the BSI's Consumer Advisory Council (CAC)[9] which, within two years, was informed by an Advisory Committee with delegates from 24 women's organizations, effectively representing the views of three million women.[10]

In 1957 an independent organization, the Association for Consumer Research (soon retitled the Consumers' Association) launched the consumer magazine *Which?* [141] in competition with the BSI's CAC and its magazine *Shopper's Guide*, which also commenced publication in the same year. Rather like the Consumers' Union in the USA, *Which?* found an audience eager to assimilate its investigations into consumer goods: within twelve months its membership[11] had reached 84,000, rising to 434,000 within ten years.

Other early postwar developments in consumer awareness and design

Similar developments were taking place elsewhere, although often the emphasis was much more fully laid upon consumer education than consumer protection *per se*. For example, in Sweden consumer awareness had developed through a collaboration of state, industry, and the public. In the war years two pioneering bodies laid the foundations for later developments: Activ Hushallning (Active Housekeeping) was established in 1940 as a state body to advise on rationing, and the Hemmens Forskningsinstitut (HFI—Home Research Institute) in 1944 as an organization for research into all aspects of everyday life in the home. In its early researches the HFI worked on kitchen planning, a field which the Svenska Slödföreninigen (Swedish Society of Industrial Design) had previously examined, and kitchen tools. Such initiatives resulted in a standardized kitchen design and innovative designs for kitchen tools which were put into industrial production and marketed. In 1954 Aktiv Hushallning was taken over by the HFI, which in turn was renamed the National Institute for Consumer Information in 1957. There were four major divisions of the organization: domestic equipment; textiles; food, chemicals and technical items; and information. As well as producing reports, guides, and educational film strips, lectures, and material for the media the Institute produced three regular publications: *Köprad*, each issue of which was devoted to the testing of particular product types; *Räd Och Rön*, a newsletter; and *Konsumeninstitut Meddelar*, a technical publication about testing methodology aimed at industry. The National Institute also had a permanent exhibition on *The Home—Its Layout and Equipment* which sought to explain the scope of its work.

As had been the case in Britain from the late 1940s onwards there was also increasing concern about standards in manufacture and perception of them by the general public. In 1951 the Varudeklarationsnämden (VDN—the Institute for Informative Labelling) was established. The D-mark, as the labelling scheme became known, was different from the BSI's Kitemark in that it gave the consumers a much fuller and more intelligible insight into product characteristics, with information on function, materials, and durability. Like the National Institute for Consumer Information, it also worked with the Svenska Slödföreninigen (Swedish Society of Industrial Design), the furniture research committee of which had also worked since 1948 on the testing and labelling of furniture.

In the early 1950s the Swedish example influenced developments in West Germany, particularly in the establishment of the Wohnberatung, advice and exhibition centres for the public to gain information on all aspects of home furnishing. The first of these was established by the Deutscher Werkbund in Mannheim in 1953, stimulated by the homes advice centres seen in the Swedish section of the 1949 Cologne Exhibition.

Critiques of industrialization and consumerism

A mere account of the evolution of consumer organizations and debate, however, gives a misleadingly simple picture of the position of design and the consumer in the fifteen years following the end of the Second World War. As will be seen below, the consumer's voice was comparatively muted in the wider context of increased levels of consumption in the Western industrialized world, with the advent of what the French termed the 'civilisation des gadgets'. It was not until the 1960s that significant shifts in consumer legislation began to acknowledge more fully the importance of individual consumer rights and of clarification of the responsibilities of the large-scale producers. Much of this shift was brought about through the strident writings of individuals such as Vance Packard, effective consumer campaigning by Ralph Nader, and the growing public disaffection with the ethics of the large-scale corporation. However, there had also been a long-standing tradition of assaults on the consequences of industrialization, a tradition which found many echoes in the postwar years, whether in debates about the social purpose of design surfacing at the Milan Triennali of the 1950s and 1960s, interest in the notion of 'small is beautiful' as articulated by Eugene Schumacher in the early 1970s, and growing public concerns about the wider environmental and ecological consequences of design, manufacture and consumption.

Ever since the early years of the Industrial Revolution there have been evident tensions between the material consequences of the development of industrialized capitalism and considerations of artistic and creative integrity. Although from the 1760s onwards there were a number of painters, such as Joseph Wright of Derby, who lucidly portrayed contemporary excitement at scientific discoveries,[12] by the late eighteenth century there were others, such as the English poet William Blake, who saw such developments as thwarting the freedom of the imagination and the senses through the imposition of rules and systems. Blake frequently denounced what he saw as the restrictiveness of the world of science and reason, symbolized in his 1795 colour print of Sir Isaac Newton where the scientist was depicted at the bottom of the sea, immersed in the waters of materialism. Newton was wielding a pair of compasses, symbols of measurement and regulation but also, in Blake's eyes, rational barriers to the exploration of the unconfined realms of the spiritually elevating world of the imagination. As the industrialization process gathered pace during the nineteenth century there were frequent, often eloquent attacks on its concomitants, particularly the division of labour and the cultural disruptiveness of technological development. A particular line of thought which contrasted medieval and nineteenth-century societies can be traced through writings such as Thomas Carlyle's *Signs of the Times* of 1829, the designer A. W. N. Pugin's *Contrasts* of 1836, and John Ruskin's *The Stones of Venice* of the early 1850s. In comparison with the spiritual wholesomeness of the Middle Ages Ruskin characterized Victorian society as oppressively materialistic, an outlook which was symbolized by the ostentatious and 'inappropriate' ornamentation which covered the surfaces of much contemporary, machine-produced design. His commitment to the values of 'truth to materials', honest workmanship, and the 'joy of making' lay at the philosophical roots of William Morris and his Arts and Crafts followers. As has been suggested in Chapter 1, this was a problematic outlook in so far as its social, cultural, and economic relevance was extremely limited for those most adversely affected by industrialization—unless its theoretical premises were reconciled with the realities of mass-production on a large scale. Similar lines of thought which attacked the consequences of industrialization, urbanization, and the anonymity of the large scale have continued throughout the twentieth century, albeit from a wider range of perspectives.

Consumerism, design, and critical perspectives in 1950s USA

In the 1950s the readership of *Consumer Reports*, generally drawn from the professional, educated sectors of society, were no doubt wary of the seductive advertisements and marketing techniques of those powerful motivators of material desires, the advertising agencies of Madison Avenue, New York, which increasingly explored the possibilities of motivational analysis in their quest to increase sales of products and services. It was this glossy allure that Vance Packard so vehemently attacked in his celebrated text of 1957, *The Hidden Persuaders*.[13] The first of a series of attacks on the profligacy and pretensions of consumer society, including *The Status Seekers* (1959) and *The Wastemakers* (1961), this colourful indictment of consumerism attracted considerable media attention. However, there were other aspects of everyday life which gave rise to wider consumer concerns. That key icon and status symbol of American material values in the 1950s, the large, heavily tail-finned automobile [**74**], replete with quasi-baroque chrome fantasies masquerading as radiator grilles, began to fall under the increasingly suspicious gaze of consumer groups, campaigners such as Ralph Nader, and, somewhat belatedly, federal government. At this time, as J. K. Galbraith and others observed, the very size, economic muscle, and social influence of automobile producers such as General Motors allowed them to use design in ways which were of questionable benefit to society at large.

The phenomenon of rapid obsolescence, in the form of the annual model change, was a fundamental aspect of the buoyant automobile market of the 1950s as well as a key factor in maximizing profitability since even superficial changes (or styling) in design could lead to increasing sales. The 'newness' of models was often literally 'skin-deep'. The annual model change also meant that many rapid changes to automobile design were not thoroughly analysed in terms of their effects on performance, leading to a whole spectrum of deficiencies which were criticized by many involved in the infrastructure of the transport industry: insurers, mechanics, federal investigators, and others. Such design deficiencies included problems with visibility, steering, braking, and ease of maintenance and should be viewed in the context of an apparent lack of independence of the highway safety lobby. For example, in 1954 the President's Action Committee for Traffic Safety was established with Harlow K. Curtice, President of General Motors, as its first chairman, whilst the Vice-Presidents of General Motors and Ford sat on the Business Advisory Board.

Harley Earl's design innovation of the 'wrap-around' windscreen, inspired by the Lockheed P38 fighter plane, was first incorporated into the Oldsmobile division of General Motors mass-production lines from 1954, immediately catching the public imagination. However, ophthalmologists reported on the distortions to which its curvature gave rise, as well as problems of increased glare and double vision which could arise from its sculpted surfaces. Other windscreen innovations introduced by General Motors included the tinted windscreen, billed as a 'safety feature' and optimistically named 'E-Z-Eye'. It was heavily criticized in *Consumer Reports* in 1952 as well as specialist periodicals such as the *Journal of the Optical Society*, which in 1955 reported it as a hazard in night driving, although it continued to be promoted as a safety feature in General Motors publicity as late as 1965. During this period critical literature was increasing rapidly in volume, the most celebrated example being Ralph Nader's *Unsafe at Any Speed: the Designed-In Dangers of the American Automobile*.[14] As an indicator of corporate commitment to automobile safety at General Motors it was estimated that styling accounted for $700 per automobile as opposed to 23 cents for safety or, framed alternatively, in 1964 the corporation spent $1.25 million dollars on safety research whilst accruing $1,700 million in profits. At this stage it was estimated that General Motors was grossing $2.3 million per hour, more than any government outside the United States, with the exception of Britain and the USSR.[15] However, with the appointment of the Ribicoff Committee in 1965 to investigate automobile safety, such imbalances were addressed and a process set in train that resulted in the 1966 National Traffic and Motor Vehicle Safety Act, which impacted upon production models from 1968 onwards.

Growing recognition of the consumer voice in the United States

It was in the climate of such attacks on the consumerist, corporate-led way of life in the United States, articulated by Packard, Nader, and others that consumerism emerged as an important facet of the political agenda. President Kennedy's 1962 Consumer Message to Congress expressed a commitment to the establishment of a number of clear principles for the protection of basic consumer rights: the right to safety, the right to be informed (thus ensuring that the economic interests of the consumer were protected), the right to choose (ensuring fair competition), and the right to be heard (as a means of ensuring that the consumer's voice would be heard in the formulation of federal policy). Such a commitment resulted in the fierce opposition of the business lobby, particularly in the early stages of the Johnson administration, which was more conciliatory to such concerns than Kennedy had been. However, by the later 1960s the climate had changed, with consumer legislation again seen as a likely popular vote-winner rather than simply an impediment to support from the business sector. This period saw the enactment of legislation affecting not only automobile safety (1966) but also such areas as 'truth-in-packaging' (1966), 'truth-in-lending' (1968), as well as tighter controls over the production and advertising of food and drugs. Despite its centrality in the American economy and way of life, there has been a long-standing lack of public faith in the ethics of the large-scale corporation, a conclusion which was supported by the conclusions of a wide range of opinion polls carried out in the 1960s, 1970s, and 1980s. For example, Gallup revealed that between 1973 and 1986 an average of only 29 per cent of those polled had confidence in big business, making it one of the least trusted of American institutions.[16] Harris too showed that the US population between 1966 and 1986, had little confidence in the leadership of such concerns. Although 55 per cent expressed confidence in 1966, the next highest figure was 29 per cent in 1973, settling down to a figure of less than 20 per cent in the 1980s.

Design and the consumer in Britain from the 1960s.

Despite the moves which took place in the consumer area in Britain in the 1940s and 1950s it was not until the publication of the *Molony*

Report on Consumer Protection[17] of 1962 that matters began to take on a more critical edge. Many of the seemingly positive developments of the 1950s were criticized in the 214 recommendations contained within the Report. The periodical *Shopper's Guide* was considered suspect because of its sponsorship by the BSI which in turn received backing from manufacturers whose products might be criticized in its pages. Criticism was also directed at the Consumers' Association's *Which?* on account of its restriction to member-subscribers, who also tended to be drawn from the already well-informed sectors of society, and at the Good Housekeeping Institute, which had campaigned for better standards in consumer products in the interwar years. Molony had 'little confidence in the Institute, in the quality of its standards, in the reliability of its testing—or, therefore, in the value of its seal of approval'.[18] The British Standards 'Kitemark', a leading quality mark, was also found unsatisfactory on account of widespread consumers' ignorance of what it represented; also that BSI Consumer Standards were mainly concerned with safety rather than quality, performance, or durability.

The Council of Industrial Design (COID) was approved by Molony for its promotion of 'good design' but was seen as having limited relevance for the consumer since COID product approval, either through inclusion in the *Design Index* or the award of the Design Centre Label, was not based on any rigorous standards relating to considerations such as value-for-money, efficiency, durability, or even the routine checking of manufacturers' production to ensure maintenance of quality. There was also the danger that many consumers might feel the label had greater significance than its testing warranted, especially since there were no controls for its inappropriate use by manufacturers on their publicity. For Molony, attractive or 'good' design without sound performance was of little value for consumers.

Steps were taken by the COID to remedy such shortcomings in the following decade, with the imposition of more rigorous testing procedures and the establishment of closer relationships with a number of consumer groups.[19] As had been the case in the United States, the government undertook a more active role with the establishment of a national Consumer Council in 1963 and the passing of the Trades Description Act in 1968. Despite a number of hiccups, the position of the consumer was further consolidated in the 1970s.

The response of the design profession
In the post-Second World War era one of the main problems facing the design profession in terms of assuming a more responsible role in relation to society was its intrinsic economic dependence on business, manufacturing industry, and the retail sector. Furthermore, in their quest to establish wider professional recognition in such circles (as discussed in Chapter 7) any wider commitment on the part of designers to

Patent drawing from the
Dymaxion Bathroom, 1937

Buckminster Fuller was one of the leading inventor-designers of the twentieth century and a strong critic of what he regarded as the wasteful practices of industrial design, the encouragement of obselescence and inessential use of materials and resources. The Dymaxion Bathroom, complete with all fixtures, equipment, and plumbing, was intended for mass-production and consisted of two major components: the washbasin and toilet, and the bath and shower. Covering a floor space of 5 feet square, it weighed 420 pounds and was intended to be extremely economical in terms of cost and use of resources.

Nov. 5, 1940.

R. B. FULLER

2,220,482

PREFABRICATED BATHROOM

Filed May 12, 1938

7 Sheets—Sheet 7

FIG. 9.

FIG. 10.

INVENTOR
RICHARD BUCKMINSTER FULLER

BY

ATTORNEY

social, environmental, and moral concerns was inevitably tempered by the ideological thrust of their employers, actual and potential.

As has been seen earlier, the design theorist and inventor Richard Buckminster Fuller had been highly critical of the outlook of the American industrial design profession of the interwar years as well as the superficial 'fashion inoculation' of Bauhaus modernism.[20] He also expressed concern for the considerable wastage of energy in the Western industrialized contemporary world [142], suggesting that since only about 25 per cent of energy generated was actually utilized there were, at least theoretically, sufficient reserves to sustain three more societies. Such radical design thinking proved increasingly attractive to young designers and architects in the later 1950s and 1960s when there was a strong drive to explore alternative approaches to the solving of design problems. Accordingly, Buckminster Fuller travelled widely, lecturing on a variety of challenging themes to professional audiences around the world.[21] Another important figure who attacked

Cutlery designed for people with single-hand function, Ergonomi Design Gruppen, Sweden, c.1980

Ergonomi Design Gruppen (EDG), founded in Sweden in 1979 by Maria Benktzon and Sven-Eric Juhlin, specializes in ergonomic design, whether in the industrial sector or for everyday life, particularly for those with disabilities. With regard to the latter category one of the consultancy's aims was to produce design solutions with a high aesthetic content and style, rather than producing designs which were obviously demarcated as catering for 'special needs'. Although the cutlery shown here was available commercially it was part-funded by public agencies.

8050 1003
Skärhjälp
Slicing aid
Schneidehilfe
Planche à découper

8050 1002
Kniv med slätt blad (svart)
Smooth blade knife
Messer mit geradem blatt
Couteau coudé

8050 1001
Kniv med tandat blad (gul)
Serrated knife
Messer mit gezahntem blatt
Couteau long manche

8050 1101
Förskärare, vinklad
Angled carving knife
Messer, abgewinkelt
Couteau à découper coude

8050 1016
Kniv inställbar
Knife, adjustable angle
Messer, einstellbar
Couteau, angle réglable

8040 2004
Sked RA
Spoon
Löffel
Cuillère

8040 2002
Gaffel RA
Fork
Gabel
Fourchette

8040 2007
Dessertsked RA
Spoon, for dessert
Löffel, klein
Cuiller, petit

8040 2006
Kniv RA
Knife
Messer
Couteau

the commercially-centred consumer drive of contemporary society, making a particular plea for a more broad-based redirection of design thinking, was Richard Neutra, who published *Survival Through Design* in 1954.

As has been seen in Chapter 8, there was a small but significant number of design groups in Italy which had pursued the idea of Anti- or Counter-Design, firmly rejecting involvement with mainstream commercial design. However, in the wider context of the design profession as a whole, a number of papers at the annual Aspen International Design Conferences took up several themes that challenged the design status quo, and these were followed through at the ICSID (International Council of Societies of Industrial Design) conference held in London in 1969 on the topic 'Design, Society and the Future' in which designers looked to the wider consequences of their actions. Important also was Victor Papanek's widely read text *Design for the Real World: Human Ecology and Social Change* of 1971, published in the United States only after being turned down by twelve publishers.[22] Since then the book has been the subject of many reprints and two revised editions and has been widely read by designers in many countries. However, in an extremely useful review of related literature, Pauline Madge noted that although 'it has long been considered the one book which looks at the environment and the Third World from a design point of view, the subject matter is much wider than that and it is in fact much more about design in the "first" world and about consumerism than what would now be considered key environmental issues.'[23] Its moralizing, yet somewhat shrill, tone very much followed in the tradition of Vance Packard's anti-consumerist diatribes of the late 1950s and early 1960s and appealed far more to the idealism of many young designers than to those more firmly established in their profession who saw it as an attack on their integrity.

However, the design profession continued to respond (not least in the arena of theoretical debate) to the wider climate of opinion which had increasingly voiced concerns about the social, environmental, and ecological consequences of industrial and technological progress. Such thinking had been further prompted by concerns about energy heightened by the Middle Eastern War of 1973 and the conspicuous failure of the United States to win the Vietnam War despite vastly superior technological resources. In April 1976 the Royal College of Art in London hosted the ICSID conference on the theme 'Design for Need'[24] where a range of such concerns were (often provocatively) discussed, including design in the Third World and the possibilities of alternative technology, as well as wider political and social issues such as design for disability, one of six fields which Papanek had previously prioritized in *Design for the Real World*.[25]

There had been a growing professional involvement with design for the disabled and handicapped from the 1960s onwards,[26] and among those designers who emerged as recognized specialists within the field were the Swedes Maria Benktzon and Sven-Eric Juhlin who founded the Ergonomi Design Gruppen consultancy in 1979. Their best-known designs have included tableware, cutlery, and a cutting board and knife for the physically handicapped [**143**]. These provided design solutions which were marked not only by their capacity to address specific design problems, but also by their high aesthetic content which did much to rehabilitate them into the mainstream of everyday

144 Peter Opsvik and Hans Christian Menghshoel

Balans chair, 1979, Norway

This design represents a solution to the problems of providing beneficial posture for everyday tasks. Rather than simply conforming to the standardized notion of a conventional office chair (left), the *Balans* (right) has been worked out on ergonomic principles.

145 John Habraken

Prototypes of WOBO bottle and WOBO House, early 1960s

An early experiment in secondary-use design, the WOBO (WOrld BOttle) scheme was envisaged by Alfred Heineken, head of the Heineken brewery. Lager bottles were uneconomic to return over certain distances, often simply littering the environment after consumption. Heineken commissoned Habraken for the design of a bottle which could be used as a brick after the consumption of the contents. This resulted in the design of a prototype house for marketing to Third World countries; but, despite its ambitions, the project was taken no further than the summer house in Habraken's garden seen here, although a second WOBO project was taken up some years later.

consumption [**144**]. In Britain groups working in this sector have included UDAP (Unit for the Development of Alternative Products), SCEPTRE (the Sheffield Centre for Product Development and Technological Resources), and LICT (the London Innovation Charitable Trust).[27]

Parallel concerns and design perspectives

The 1950s and 1960s had seen the emergence of a number of 'alternatives' to the conventional material values and social mores of consumer society [**145**]. An important manifestation was the hippy movement which took off on the West Coast of the United States, emerging from the 'beat'[28] and 'acid'[29] subcultures of the late 1950s and early 1960s. Key characteristics included a distaste for consumer society and commitment to 'doing one's own thing', resourcefulness, and creativity. In a number of ways, the hippies were responding to the wastefulness of society, an idea also articulated by Buckminster Fuller with particular reference to energy. For example, in the realm of housing many hippie dwellings were built from the waste of affluent society, as at Drop City [**146**], where significant use was made of discarded automobile panels.

The dome-like forms of many of these houses loosely echoed the dome constructions which Buckminster Fuller had evolved in the 1950s as well as being oppositional to the cube-like forms of conventionally constructed dwellings. Much of this thinking took on a more tangible form in publications such as *The Last Whole Earth Catalogue* of 1971, which was a practical guide to alternative living, advising the user/designer on everything from equipment to education which could be bought via mail-order. In Britain Peter Harper and Geoffrey Boyle edited a similar book, *Radical Technology*, which argued 'for the growth of small-scale techniques suitable for use by individuals and communities, in a wider social context of humanised production under workers' and consumers' control.'[30] Some of these ideas were explored and codified by the design and architectural critic and historian Charles Jencks together with Nathan Silver in *Adhocism: The Case for Improvisation* of 1972.[31] Embracing the underlying tenets of hippy philosophy they saw Adhocist design as a means of avoiding the delays engendered by specialization, bureaucracy, and hierarchical organizations, thus enabling the 'designer' to take immediate and purposeful action through the utilization of materials readily to hand. Although Jencks and Silver considered the use of catalogues as significant tools for the Adhoc 'designer' they appreciated their limitations in that they could not list all the products of a society nor present them in a way that pointed to uses for such artifacts out of their conventional context: what was needed was a 'resourceful' computer, cross-indexed to search out for the 'designer' the best component for the job. The aim of such thinking was to decentralize the design process, counteracting the restrictions imposed by advanced industrial systems. The social benefits of small-scale production were also emphasized in such influential texts as Eugene Schumacher's *Small is Beautiful: A Study of Economics as if People Mattered*[32] and Ivan Illich's *Tools for Conviviality*,[33] both published in 1973.

Other potent critiques of the preoccupations of mainstream design, in terms of profession, preoccupations, or social marginalization, emerged during the same years. Highly significant were feminist critiques committed to a more effective and user-centred approach to design which emerged in opposition to the celebration of design personalities and to the glossy, mythological worlds of advertising. At the root of such critiques was an assault on society's fundamentally patriarchal organization and outlook. As Cheryl Buckley, an important design historical contributor to such debates, argued in 1986:

Patriarchy has circumscribed women's opportunities to participate fully in all areas of society and, more specifically, in all sectors of design, through a variety of means—institutional, social, economic, psychological, and historical. The resulting female stereotypes delineate certain modes of behaviour as being appropriate for women. Certain occupations and social roles are designated female, and a physical and intellectual ideal is created for women to aspire to. These stereotypes have had enormous impact on the physical spaces—whether at home or at work—which women occupy, their occupations, and their relationship with design.[34]

Feminist writers sought to redress the balance, drawing attention to the ways in which gender stereotyping has informed the design of clothing, toys, tools, and many other consumer products, has resulted in inadequate designs for women users, and has afforded women few opportunities in many sectors of the design profession which have traditionally been dominated by men.[35] A number of feminist groups, such as the Matrix collective, formed in 1980, sought to promote a feminist approach to architectural practice, involving consultation and the dissemination of information, advice, and design thinking. An exposition of their thinking was published in 1984, entitled *Making Space: Women and the Man-Made Environment*. As the title suggests, it argued that patriarchal values dominated in the design of domestic space and the urban environment, necessarily defining the role which women were to play within that context. Other women's groups of the period which involved design within their remit included the Women's Design Service (WDS) and the Women's Environmental Network (WEN), founded in 1988.

Green design

By the mid-1980s the concept of 'green design' began to gain increasing currency in the design press, evolving from the broader-based environmental and ecological concerns which had commanded attention in the previous decade. By this time the concept had emerged from its relatively marginalized position as an 'alternative' outlook to one which was increasingly recognized by the design profession, including large-scale consultancies such as the Michael Peters Group and Wolf Olins

146

Drop City, USA, 1960s

Drop City provided the venue for an 'alternative' lifestyle for hippies who 'dropped out' of mainstream society. Dome housing was often fabricated from the tops of cars purchased from scrapyards for 25 cents each, literally re-using the waste materials jettisoned by consumer society. Its form, loosely derived from the geodesic dome structures explored by Buckminster Fuller, was opposed to the box-like structures which typified suburban housing norms.

Founded in 1976, the Body Shop has been a powerful advocate of ethical consumption in the High Street, with an emphasis on natural products and the use of re-fillable containers. By 1996 the company had over 1,400 shops world-wide, including 71 in Japan and 21 in Malaysia, as well as outlets in Singapore and Indonesia. The scale of the company's operations highlights the implicit contradiction in 'green' consumption since the act of consumption is still encouraged, albeit moderated by wider ethical considerations.

which considered it to be an important ingredient of design policy in the late twentieth century.

In the 1970s and 1980s in Britain the business success and high media profile of the toiletries and cosmetics company the Body Shop, founded by Anita Roddick in 1976, provided something of a public barometer against which to gauge the growing potency of ecological concerns in the market-place. Concepts such as the use of natural and recycled materials and refillable containers caught the public imagination [147].

The late 1980s saw a flurry of activity in exhibitions and publications centred on the concept of 'green design', including the mounting of the 'Green Designer' exhibition at the Design Centre, London, in 1986. John Elkington was involved in its organization and was the author and co-author of a number of texts which helped to articulate contemporary debate, both from the point of view of the consumer and business. These included *The Green Consumer Guide* of 1988,[36] and *The Green Capitalists* of the following year.[37] The 1990s continued to see frequent publication in the field, with texts such as Dorothy Mackenzie's *Green Design: Design for the Environment*,[38] Paul Burall's *Green Design*,[39] and Brenda and Robert Vale's *Green Architecture: Design for a Sustainable Future*,[40] all of 1991.

A survey on *European Management Attitudes to Environmental Issues* carried out in 1990 by the management consultants Touche Ross revealed that West German, Dutch, and Danish companies placed an increasing premium on the management of environmental concerns, with a significant percentage of companies committed to the alteration of product ranges in response to environmental considerations. Large-scale multinational corporations such as Philips and IBM endorsed such policies at senior management levels, whilst appliance manufacturers such as Zanussi moved to the adoption of a significant number

148 Neville Brody

Men's Bigi frisbee, 1990

Although much of Brody's earlier design work for the street-style magazine *The Face* and independent record companies supported the consumerist ethos of the earlier 1980s, his work from the late 1980s onwards often took up environmental concerns. His designs for the Japanese Bigi Group used many symbols linked with an emerging Japanese interest in wider global and environmental concerns. However, as with the message 'Stop Global Destruction Now' emblazoned on this frisbee, such concerns often remained largely on the surface.

of key components in recyclable materials and energy-saving programmes in their washing machines.[41] Such developments, together with the availability of ethical, environmental, and ecologically-sound investment trusts on the Stock Market, contributed to the impression of an increasingly widespread commitment to environmental responsibility in the industrial sector. Furthermore, in a number of countries product-labelling schemes emerged as a means of marking out ecologically-sound goods: the best known of these was the German Blue Angel which was introduced in 1978; by 1990 its logo was carried on about 3,000 products that met specific environmental criteria, manufacturers paying for the right to use it. Similar schemes were introduced in Canada and Japan in the 1980s, the latter accompanying its logo with brief explanations as to the reasons for its endorsement.

However, the wider picture was often ambivalent, as a number of critics have pointed out. For example, in his celebrated book *On Living in an Old Country* of 1985[42] Patrick Wright pointed to the contradictions inherent in the Shell oil company's long-standing association with the English countryside, sustained through the publication of its *County Guides* in the interwar years, its later *Discover Britain* television advertisements, and Shell-National Trust Nature Trails of the 1970s and 1980s. He saw it as remarkable that such images should be associated with the preservation of the countryside whilst at the same time the company was implicitly threatening rural integrity through the pollution and environmental damage that would be engendered by the automobiles which it encouraged to tour. The association continued in the later 1980s with the advertising of 'lead-free' petrol stations: one particular advertisement featured a remote Shell petrol station in the Scottish Highlands, accompanied by the textual claim that the company had 'introduced 1,287 conservation areas in Britain'. In Britain in the late 1980s even the colour green was often simply harnessed to the ecological cause, with the design consultants Addison Associates using it as a key element in their identity schemes for BP petrol stations, the Michael Peters Group deploying it as an important element of the visible face of the corporate identity for the newly-created Powergen electricity generating company, and John McConnell of Pentagram using the colour as a vital aspect of the newly-privatized electricity distribution network, the National Grid Company, symbolizing according to contemporary publicity 'both the environment and the vibrancy of the company's business'.

By this time it was clear that, in addition to the potential social and environmental benefits which might accrue, the whole field of green design also offered another marketing niche for designers to explore. As Elkington, Burke and Hailes remarked in *Green Pages: The Business of Saving the World* of 1988:

The green consumer is likely to be an increasingly important influence in the world of product design. Designers who ignore the fact, or who allow their clients to ignore it, risk losing out on some of the most exciting marketing opportunities of the eighties and nineties.[43]

Similar views from a design consultancy perspective were expressed by Wally Olins in *Corporate Identity: Making Business Strategy Visible through Design*, of 1989.[44]

None the less, there was at the same time a growing anxiety on the part of many campaigners for whom ecological and ethical concerns were of primary importance that many contemporary advocates of 'green design' were in fact still encouraging consumption: 'green capitalism' and 'green consumerism' were merely particular elements in the wider phenomenon of consumerism [**148**], albeit modified by ethical considerations. Such critiques were explored in Britain in Sandy Irvine's 1989 discussion pamphlet *Beyond Green Consumerism*[45] and in the United States in the 1991 publication *Green Business: Hope or Hoax?*[46] and have been subsumed into more radical propositions for the implementation of a more fundamentally ecological design policy. As Pauline Madge suggested in 1993:

While the first generation of publications on green design were 'how to do it' guides, written quickly to meet the demand for basic information, the next generation of publications in the 1990s is likely to be more considered and carefully researched, more critical and synergistic, more aware of the full complexity of design and sustainable development in both the developed and developing worlds.[47]

Notes

Introduction

1. A useful introductory text is John A. Walker, *Design History and the History of Design* (Pluto Press, London, 1989). Key articles which have evaluated particular ways in which the history of design may be approached include Clive Dilnot, 'The State of Design History, Part I: Mapping the Field' and 'The State of Design History Part II: Problems and Possibilities', *Design Issues* (MIT), 1.1 (Spring 1984), 3–23, and 1.2 (Fall 1984), 3–20, and Cheryl Buckley, 'Made in Patriarchy: Towards a Feminist Analysis of Women and Design', *Design Issues*, 3.2 (Fall 1986), 3–14. More recently, *Design Issues* devoted a whole issue (11.1 (Spring 1995)) to considering the place of design history as a distinct field of academic study.

2. First published as *Pioneers of Modern Design* by Faber & Faber, London, 1936.

3. N. Pevsner, *Pioneers of the Modern Movement: From William Morris to Walter Gropius* (Penguin, Harmondsworth, 1977).

4. (Oxford University Press).

5. (Studio Vista, London).

6. (Thames & Hudson, London, 1986).

7. D. Miller, *Material Culture and Mass Consumption* (Blackwell, Oxford, 1987). Although he described design history as 'bizarre' in this text, perhaps due to a lack of awareness of contemporary research and debate in the field, a number of anthropological studies have been influential in more recent design-historical research and publication. For example, T. Putnam & C. Newton (eds.), *Household Choices* (Futures Publications, London, 1990), moved significantly away from the design, manufacture, and development of products towards concepts of choice, reception, and understanding.

8. See e.g. A. Callen, *Angel in the Studio: Women in the Arts and Crafts Movement* (London, 1979), R. Parker and G. Pollock, *Old Mistresses: Women, Art and Ideology* (London, 1981).

9. See R. Parker, *The Subversive Stitch: Embroidery and the Making of the Feminine* (London, 1984) or M. Droste, 'Women in the Arts and Crafts and in Industrial Design 1890–1933' in *Frauen im Design: Berufsbilder und Lebenswege seit 1900/Women in Design: Careers and Life Histories since 1900* (Design Center, Stuttgart, 1989), 174–202.

10. Key texts include J. Attfield and P. Kirkham (eds.), *A View from the Interior: Feminism, Women and Design* (Women's Press, London, 1989; rev. edn. 1995), C. Buckley, *Potters and Paintresses: Women Designers and the Pottery Industry 1870–1955* (Women's Press, 1990) and *Frauen im Design* (n. 9 above).

Chapter 1

1. As e.g. in the period immediately following the First World War, which saw the establishment of the British Institute of Industrial Art; the economic difficulties encountered in the early 1930s led to the establishment of the Council for Art and Industry in 1933; the perceived problems of competitiveness in the post-Second World War export markets resulted in the establishment of the Council of Industrial Design; the 1980s saw the Thatcher Government's 'Design for Profit' initiatives.

2. See e.g. N. Pevsner, op. cit., F. MacCarthy, *A History of British Design 1830–1979* (Allen & Unwin, London, 1979), J. De Noblet (ed.), *Design: Miroir du Siècle* (Flammarion/APCI, Paris, 1993), and W. Kaplan (ed.), *Designing Modernity: The Arts of Reform and Persuasion 1885–1945* (Thames & Hudson/Wolfsonian Foundation, London/Miami, 1995).

3. Key texts include M. B. Miller, *The Bon Marché, Bourgeois Culture and the Department Store 1869–1920* (Allen & Unwin, London, 1891); R. M. Hower, *History of Macy's of New York 1858–1919: Chapters in the Evolution of a Department Store* (Harvard University Press, Cambridge., Mass., 1943); and R. W. Twyman, *History of Marshall Field and Co.,*

1852–1906 (University of Pennsylvania Press, Philadelphia, 1954).

4. B. Lancaster, *The Department Store: A Social History* (Leicester University Press, London, 1995), presents an extremely useful analysis of the subject which, although British-centred, takes account of wider historical and theoretical perspectives.

5. See e.g. W. Leach, *Land of Desire: Merchants, Power and the Rise of a New American Culture* (Pantheon, New York, 1993).

6. J. Heskett singled out this company as an indicator of wider patterns of consumption in Germany in *Design in Germany 1870–1918* (Trefoil, London, 1986), 86–92. Stukenbrok's *Illustrierte Hauptkatalog* of 1912 was reprinted in Heidelberg in 1973.

7. There had been earlier organizations with many common aspirations, including the Dürerbund founded by Ferdinand Avenarius in 1902 to promote art in everyday life and the Bund für Heimatschutz (Society for the Protection of the Homeland), founded in 1904.

8. *A Proposal for the Foundation of a Design and Industries Association* (DIA, London, 1915), 3.

9. Ibid.

10. Although its Treasury grants ceased within two years due to the economic slump of 1921.

11. This came about in response to the writings of Count Léon de Laborde. He abhorred the propensity of French manufacturers to celebrate an encyclopaedic historicism in their products.

Chapter 2

1. This key text was first published by Faber & Faber (London) in 1936. Its historical significance was considerably enhanced with the second edition which was published by the Museum of Modern Art, New York, in 1949, itself a key propagandist of the modernist cause. The most striking change of this redesigned volume was the increase in the number of illustrations from 84 to 137. It was further revised and partly rewritten when published as *The Pioneers of Modern Design: From William Morris to Walter Gropius* by Penguin Books (Harmondsworth) in 1960 and has subsequently undergone many reprints.

2. Despite the wide range of material already published in the field, modernism is an area about which there is still much to research. A very useful publication is P. Greenhalgh (ed.), *Modernism in Design* (Reaktion, London, 1990).

3. The aesthetic and symbolic aspects of modernism, as exemplified in its manipulation of abstract forms, adoption of new materials, and compatibility with the *zeitgeist* or 'spirit of the age' have often been underplayed, with considerable emphasis on the mechanistic notion that 'form follows function'. Tim Benton, in an extremely useful essay on 'The Myth of Function', in Paul Greenhalgh (ed.) (above, n. 2), 41–53, argued forcefully that this simplistic association of modernism with functionalism has done much to reinforce the perceptions of those who have portrayed it as 'dehumanizing'.

4. For studies in material culture see e.g. D. Miller (above, Introd. n. 7), M. Douglas and B. Isherwood, *The World of Goods: Towards an Anthropology of Consumption* (Allen Lane, London, 1975), and G. McCracken, *New Approaches to the Symbolic Character of Consumer Goods and Activities* (Indiana University Press, Bloomington, 1988).

5. *Frauen im Design* (above, Introd. n. 9) contains some very useful essays which open up fresh avenues of research in relation to women and modernism. Various approaches to the study of women and design are considered in J. Attfield and P. Kirkham (eds.), *A View from the Interior* (above, Introd. n. 10).

6. R. Lynes, *Good Old Modern: An Intimate Portrait of the Museum of Modern Art* (Athenaeum, New York, 1973), considers the museum's opposition to commercial styling and preference for 'purist' forms. See also, J. Mashek, 'Embalmed Objects: Design at the Modern', *Artforum*, February 1975, 49–55.

7. Certain aspects of the heritage of the Bauhaus in Dessau are discussed succinctly by J. Aynsley, 'News from Elsewhere: Leipzig/Berlin', *Journal of Design History*, 4.1. (1991), 43–7.

8. G. Berghaus, '*Girlkultur*—Feminism, Americanism, and Popular Entertainment in Weimar Germany', *Journal of Design History*, 1.2/3 (1988), 1, 3–4 gives a perspective on many wider aspects of consumer attitudes, together with a wide range of useful references. Useful also is J. Heskett, 'Design in Inter-War Germany', in W. Kaplan, (ed.), *Designing Modernity* (above, n. 1.2), 257–85.

9. Loos's essay is discussed at some length by Reyner Banham in 'Adolf Loos and the Problem of Ornament', *Theory and Design in the First Machine Age* (London: Architectural Press, 1960), ch. 7.

10. Trans. J. Dunnett (London: Architectural Association, 1987), 87–8.

11. H.-R. Hitchcock Jr. and P. Johnson, *Modern Architecture: International Exhibition*

and *The International Style: Architecture Since 1922* (both published in New York: Museum of Modern Art, 1932).

12. The arguments at the Werkbund congress of 1914 were far more complex than this in terms of the internal politics of the Werkbund, the desire to create a modern, German style closely linked with industry, and differing perceptions of the nature of the export markets to which these goods were ultimately directed. This is articulated in some depth in Joan Campbell, *The German Werkbund: The Politics of Reform in the Applied Arts* (Princeton University Press, Princeton and Guildford, 1978), particularly in ch. 3, 'Cologne in 1914', 58–81.

13. Founded in 1902 by the writer and poet Ferdinand Avenarius, the Dürerbund sought to promote art in everyday life.

14. Some writers, most notably Marcel Franciscono, *Walter Gropius and the Creation of the Bauhaus in Weimar: The Ideals and Artistic Theories of Its Founding Years* (University of Illinois, Urbana, 1971), have argued that Gropius had never fully abdicated his functionalist tenets, and that shortages of money and industrial materials at the school, together with the energies he expended in promoting the school at the expense of a heavy personal involvement in the curriculum, have tended to disguise this fact.

15. Magdalene Droste, 'Women in the Arts and Crafts and in Industrial Design 1890–1933', in *Frauen im Design* (above, Introd. n. 9), 174–202.

16. This aspect of Bauhaus activity prior to the move to Dessau in 1925 is fully discussed in Anna Rowland, 'Business Management at the Weimar Bauhaus', *Journal of Design History* (1988), 153–75.

17. These include G. Naylor, *The Bauhaus Reassessed* (Herbert Press, St Neots, 1985), and H. Wingler, *The Bauhaus—Weimar, Dessau, Berlin, Chicago* (1962; new edn., MIT Press, Cambridge, Mass., 1977).

18. Op. cit. (above, n. 12), 5.

19. Droste (above, n. 15).

20. The complexities of this are discussed in Campbell (above, n. 12), 176–179.

21. Droste (above, n. 15), 197.

22. It was first published briefly in 1922, but the economic climate was too difficult to sustain it.

23. This is extensively considered by Nicholas Bullock, 'First the Kitchen—Then the Facade', *AA Files* (London, May, 1984), 59 ff.

24. Lihotsky and the Frankfurt kitchen are also usefully discussed in 'The Frankfurt Kitchen: Contemporary Criticism and Perspectives',

in *Frauen im Design*, (above, Introd. n. 9), pp. 160–9.

25. See J. Heskett, 'Modernism and Archaism in Design in the Third Reich', *Block*, 3 (1980) 13 ff. and 'Art and Design in the Third Reich', *History Workshop Journal*, 6 (1979), 139–53.

26. For further discussion of Corbusier's furniture designs see C. Benton, 'Le Corbusier: Furniture and the Interior', *Journal of Design History*, 3. 2/3 (1990), 103–24.

27. Although A. Branzi, *The Hot House: Italian New Wave Design* (Thames & Hudson, London, 1984), claims that the first Rationalist interior was in fact Ivo Pannaggi's Casa Zampini.

28. See e.g. B. Zevi, 'The Italian Rationalists', in D. Sharp (ed.), *The Rationalists: Theory and Design in the Modern Movement* (Architectural Press, London, 1978), 118–29.

29. Founded in Milan as *Casa Bella* in 1928 with an intended readership of women it became more progressively oriented under its new title, launched in 1934.

30. This title was first taken up at Monza in 1930.

31. These are usefully discussed in the introduction to *Scandinavia: Ceramics and Glass of the 20th Century* (Victoria and Albert Museum, London, 1989).

32. Originally founded under the Swedish parent company Rörstrand in 1874.

Chapter 3

1. (Harper, New York).

2. Charles Richards stated in his report on *Art in Industry* of 1929 that there were 55 schools teaching 'industrial design' in the United States, but that this was often linked to the use of museums as providers of exemplars and very much dominated by stylistic influences from the past, such as Art Nouveau or Arts and Crafts.

3. (1932; Dover reprint, New York, 1977), 21–3.

4. Autobiographical texts by industrial designers include R. Loewy, *Never Leave Well Enough Alone* (Simon & Schuster, New York, 1951), and *Industrial Design* (Faber, London, 1980), and H. Dreyfuss, *Designing for People* (Simon & Schuster, New York, 1955). N. Bel Geddes, *Horizons in Industrial Design* (above, n. 3), and R. Loewy, *The Locomotive: Its Esthetics* (The Studio, New York, 1937) are expansive and optimistic statements about the power of the industrial designer to alter the consumer's outlook, to improve the quality of life—and at the same time to increase sales. Rather more measured accounts of the profession may be found in W. D. Teague,

Design This Day: The Techniques of Order in the Machine Age (Harcourt Brace, New York, 1940), and H. Van Doren, *Industrial Design: A Practical Guide* (McGraw-Hill, New York, 1940).

5. Such historical accounts include Donald J. Bush's eulogistic *The Streamlined Decade* (George Braziller, New York, 1975) which centres on the stylistic rather than economic aspects of industrial design; there are many historical texts which focus on the achievements of individuals, such as *The Designs of Raymond Loewy* (exhibition catalogue, Smithsonian Institute, Washington, 1975) or A. Schönberger (ed.), *Raymond Loewy: Pioneer of American Industrial Design* (Internationales Design Zentrum, Berlin, 1990). A balanced account of the period may be found in J. Meikle, *Twentieth Century Limited: Industrial Design in America, 1925–1939* (Temple University Press, Philadelphia, 1979), in which relationships between design, business, and society are evaluated.

6. Miller (above, Introd. n. 7), 142.

7. (above, n. 4).

8. Such as K. C. Plummer, 'The Streamlined Moderne', *Art in America*, January/February 1974, 46–54, D. Gebhard, 'The Moderne in the US, 1920–1941', *Architecture Association Quarterly*, July 1970, 4–20, and D. J. Bush (above, n. 5).

9. W. D. Teague, 'Building the World of Tomorrow', *Art & Industry*, April 1939, 126.

10. See e.g. D. A. Hounshell, *From the American System to Mass-Production 1800–1932* (Johns Hopkins University Press, Baltimore, 1984).

11. E. J. O'Brian, *The Dance of the Machines: The American Short Story and the Industrial Age* (Jonathan Cape, London, 1929), 115.

12. A number of his writings are collected in J. Meller (ed.), *The Buckminster Fuller Reader* (Penguin, Harmondsworth, 1971).

13. 'The Comprehensive Man', revised text of a lecture given at the University of Oregon in 1959, in J. Meller (ed.) (above, n. 12), 134.

14. This is usefully and lucidly discussed in T. Gronberg, 'Cascades of Light: the 1925 Exhibition as *Ville Lumière*', *Apollo*, July 1995, 12–16.

15. The official reason given was that there were insufficient American goods which conformed to the official guidelines for the exhibition, which required designs displaying 'modern aspiration and real originality'. However, it is more likely that the lack of participation was due to the distance, cost, and lack of clear economic advantage.

16. These included Lord & Taylor and Macy's in New York in 1928.

17. D. Naylor, *American Picture Palaces: The Architecture of Fantasy* (Van Nostrand Reinhold, New York, 1981), provides a useful account of this striking genre.

18. (Architectural Press, London, 1945), 4.

19. Many such developments are discussed in G. Wright, *Building the Dream: A Social History of Housing in America* (University of Chicago Press, 1981).

20. See e.g. S. Worden, 'Furniture for the Living Room: An Investigation of the Interaction between Society and Design in Britain from 1919 to 1939' (unpublished Ph.D. thesis, University of Brighton, 1980), and J. Attfield, 'The Role of Design within the Relationship between Furniture Manufacture and its Retailing (1935–65) with Initial Reference to the Firm of J. Clarke' (unpublished Ph.D. thesis, University of Brighton, 1992). Of more general interest, but providing useful starting points, are A. A. Jackson, *Semi-Detached London* (Allen & Unwin, London, 1973), and P. Oliver *et al.*, *Dunroamin: The Suburban Semi and Its Enemies* (Barrie & Jenkins, London, 1981). A useful introduction to the problems of interpreting the 'ordinary' room is by J. Porter and S. Macdonald, 'Fabricating Interiors: Approaches to the History of Domestic Furnishing at the Geffrye Museum', *Journal of Design History*, 3. 2–3 (1990), 175–82.

21. Perhaps the most significant attempt to examine furnishings and home decoration from a consumer's point of view is to be found in T. Putnam and C. Newton (eds.), *Household Choices* (Futures Publications, London, 1990).

22. The archives of the Ideal Home Exhibition are located in the Archive of Art & Design at Olympia, an outpost of the National Art Library (Victoria and Albert Museum).

23. 'The Salon des Arts Ménagers, 1923–83: A French Effort to Instil the Virtues of Home and the Norms of Good Taste', *Journal of Design History*, 7. 4 (1994), 267–75. This is also discussed in R.-H. Guerrand, 'Comfort', in J. de Noblet (ed.), *Design: Mirror of a Century* (Flammarion, Paris, 1993) 74–82.

Chapter 4

1. For a general reading of the significance of international exhibitions see P. Greenhalgh, *Ephemeral Vistas: the Expositions Universelles, Great Exhibitions and World's Fairs, 1851–1939* (Manchester University Press, 1988).

2. For the only authoritative account in

English of Polish design and vernacular traditions see D. Crowley, *National Style and Nation State: Design in Poland from the Vernacular Revival to the International Style* (Manchester University Press, 1992).

3. Some of these key issues are taken up in the exhibition catalogue *Art and Power: Europe under the Dictators 1930–45* (Hayward Gallery, London, 1995).

4. Hungary, like Poland sought to utilize a 'national' style derived from vernacular roots early in the century. See e.g. Katalin Keserü, 'The Workshops of Gödöllö: Transformations of a Morrisian Theme', *Journal of Design History*, 1.1 (1988), 1–23.

5. (Thames & Hudson, London), 15.

6. J. Gloag *The English Tradition in Design* (Penguin, London, 1947), 35.

7. The distinction that perhaps should be made between 'English' or 'British' involves a complex area of debate. For the purposes of this brief summary of British/English national identity I have tended to adopt the terminology adopted by contemporary commentators.

8. See e.g. A. Howkins, 'The Discovery of Rural England', in R. Colls and P. Dodd (eds.), *Englishness: Politics and Culture 1880/1920* (Croom Helm, London, 1986).

9. F. MacCarthy, e.g., *All Things Bright and Beautiful: Design in Britain from 1830 to Today* (Allen & Unwin, London, 1972), doesn't even mention it. See J. Woodham, 'Design and Empire: British Design in the 1920s', *Art History*, June 1980, 229–40, 'Images of Africa and Design at the British Empire Exhibitions between the Wars', *Journal of Design History*, 2.1 (1989), 15–33, or *The Industrial Designer and the Public* (Pembridge, London, 1983), for discussion of the field.

10. It attracted almost a further 10 million visitors in the following year.

11. See J. M. Mackenzie, *Propaganda and Empire: The Manipulation of British Public Opinion 1880–1960* (Manchester University Press, 1985) and id. (ed.), *Imperialism and Popular Culture* (Manchester University Press, 1986).

12. L. Weaver, *Exhibitions and the Arts of Display* (Country Life, London, 1925), 42.

13. [G. S. Holme], 'Where there is Non-Vision the People Perish', *Studio*, July, 1930.

14. C. Hussey, 'The Week-end House', *Guide des objects exposés dans le pavillon du Royaume Uni: 1937 Exposition Internationale Paris* (HMSO, London, 1937), 507.

15. Sir Thomas Barlow, speaking at the Council for Art and Industry meeting of 11 November 1937, file BT 60/40/2 at the Public Record Office, Kew.

16. *A Dream of England: Landscape, Photography and the Tourist's Imagination* (Manchester University Press, 1994); for the reference to *Picture Post* see the section 'Landscape for Everyone', 198–205.

17. (Faber, London).

18. A notable exception is Paddy Maguire, whose important article on 'Craft Capitalism and the Projection of British Industry in the 1950s and 1960s', *Journal of Design History*, 6.2 (1993), 97–114, includes some splendid examples of heritage props for the support of British displays abroad.

19. *Board of Trade Journal*, 13 April 1962.

20. 'Modernism and Archaism in Design in the Third Reich', *Block* (Middlesex Polytechnic), no. 3 (1980), 17–20, and 'Design in Interwar Germany', in W. Kaplan (ed.), *Designing Modernity* (above, n. 1.2), 257–85.

21. Seen also in the essay on 'Functionalism in Nazi Germany: Neoclassicism 1933–1945', in H. Fuchs and F. Burkhardt, *Product—Design—History: German Design from 1820 down to the Present Era* (Institute for Foreign Cultural Relations, Stuttgart, 1986).

22. Although a grandiose, updated form of Neo-Classicism was the favoured official style for all significant buildings and architectural schema.

23. S. Weissler, 'Imprisoned Within a Role: An Assessment of Arts and Crafts Production by Women Under National Socialism', in *Frauen im Design* (above, Introd. n. 9), 234–43.

24. For a full discussion of the political complexities of the DWB's activities after 1933, see ch. IX, 'The Werkbund and National Socialism', in J. Campbell, *The German Werkbund: The Politics of Reform in the Applied Arts* (Princeton University Press, 1979) 243–87.

25. Ibid. 275.

26. H. Fuchs and F. Burkhardt (above, n. 20).

27. Such as the Association of Decorative Arts and Industries, founded in 1920.

Chapter 5

1. R. Lynes, *The Taste-Makers: the Shaping of American Popular Taste* (1954; Dover, New York, 1980).

2. S. Giedion, *Mechanization Takes Command: A Contribution to Anonymous History* (1948; Norton, New York, 1969), 617–19.

3. 'The Consumer Markets: 1954–1959', *Fortune*, August 1954, 82. This was the last of the twelve articles.

4. pp. 96–101.

5. E. Larrabee, 'The Six Thousand Houses That Levitt Built', *Harper's Magazine*, 197 (1948), 82.

6. B. Friedan, *The Feminine Mystique* (1963; Penguin, Harmondsworth, 1972), 15–16.

7. R. Venturi, D. Scott Brown, and S. Izenour (MIT, Cambridge, Mass.), 1972.

8. See e.g. A. Hess, *Googie: Fifties Coffee Shop Architecture* (Chronicle, San Francisco, 1985).

9. (Bloomsbury, London).

10. Ibid. 4.

11. (Cambridge University Press).

12. 'Utility or Austerity', *Architectural Review*, January 1943, 3.

13. For fuller discussion see J. M. Woodham, 'Design Promotion 1946 and After', in P. Sparke (ed.), *Did Britain Make It: British Design in Context 1946–1986* (Design Council, London, 1986), 23–37, and 'The Post-War Consumer: Design Propaganda and Awareness, 1945–1965', in N. Hamilton (ed.), *From the Spitfire to the Microchip: Studies in the History of Design* (Design Council, London, 1985), 6–11.

14. *The Enemies of Design* (Design & Industries Association), 3.

15. For further discussion of this see e.g. ch. 5, 'Propaganda and Organisation of Modern Design', in J. M. Woodham, *The Industrial Designer and the Public* (Pembridge, London, 1983).

16. Many aspects of the cultural orientation of the early years have been discussed in J. M. Woodham, 'Managing British Design Reform I: Fresh Perspectives on the Early Years of the Council of Industrial Design', *Journal of Design History*, 9.1. (1996), pp. 55–65. See also J. M. Woodham, 'Managing British Design Reform II', *Journal of Design History*, 9, 2, 101–15.

17. In addition to the BCMI Reports, an extensive range of COID/Mass Observation-related material can be consulted in the Design Council Archive in the Design History Research Centre, the University of Brighton, and at the Mass-Observation Archive at the University of Sussex.

18. *A Designer's Trade* (Allen & Unwin, London, 1986).

19. *An Eye for Design* (Max Reinhardt, London, 1987).

20. Ed. M. Banham and B. Hillier (Thames & Hudson, London 1951).

21. 'The Style: Flimsy . . . Effeminate?' in M. Banham and B. Hillier, op. cit. 190–8.

22. 'The influence of the Festival of Britain on design today', *Journal of the Royal Society of Arts*, June 1961, 503–15.

23. (above, n. 2. 27), 39.

24. D. P. Doordan, 'National Agendas for Italian Design after 1945', paper given at 'Design, Industry and Government Initiatives: Past, Present and Future' international conference at the University of Brighton, November 1995 (to be published).

25. A catalogue was also produced: R. M. Rogers, *Italy at Work: Her Renaissance in Design Today* (Istituto Poligrafico dello Stato, Rome, 1950).

26. In 1948 Handicraft Development Inc. and CADMA were reorganized as the Compagna Nazionale Artigiania (CNA).

27. An exhibition of Olivetti products and graphics was put on in 1952, two years before the company opened its striking New York showroom on Fifth Avenue.

28. This is discussed in G. Berghaus, '*Girlkultur* (above, n. 2.8), 193 ff.

29. *Design Quarterly*, 40 (1958), 1–27.

30. E. Wilkinson, *Japan versus Europe* (Penguin, Harmondsworth, 1983), offers a very useful insight into changing perceptions of Japan in Europe over the previous hundred years or more.

31. *Hansard* (London), 23 November 1950, 500.

32. The quotation relates to a visit by the President of the British Cycle and Motor Manufacturers to Earl's Court in November 1951: Board of Trade Records, Public Record Office, Kew, File BT 11/4452. It is significant, however, that pencilled in the margin is the comment of a Board of Trade official who declared 'Far too complacent. Quality has improved.'

33. *Time*, 23 February 1961.

34. (Wiley, Chichester).

35. The initials of the consultancy stood for Group Koike, in honour of their professor who had done much to stimulate their interest in the emergent discipline of industrial design.

36. A very useful detailed account of all the major developments is contained in JETRO, *Japan's Post War Industrial Policy: Economic Programs in the Reconstruction and Expansion Periods* (Japan External Trade Organization, Tokyo, Japan, 1985). For some aspects of export history see JETRO, *A History of Japan's Postwar Export Policy: Japanese Experience* (Japan External Trade Organization, Tokyo, 1983).

37. Interviewed by the author in Tokyo, November, 1985 when Takeshi Inoue was Director of the Overseas Division of GK Industrial Design.

Chapter 6

1. (Cambridge University Press (first edition 1983), 1992. That six editions were needed in under ten years perhaps points to its particular applicability to such concepts in 1980s Britain.

2. W. Olins, *Corporate Identity: Making Business Strategy Visible through Design* (Thames & Hudson, London, 1989), 13.

3. That this was seen as an increasingly important aspect of the opportunity for corporate communication is evidenced by texts such as J. Grinling, *The Annual Report: A Guide to Planning, Producing and Promoting Company Reports* (Gower, London, 1986).

4. (above n. 2), 132.

5. F. H. K. Henrion and A. Parkin, *Design Co-ordination and Corporate Image* (Studio Vista, London, 1967), 7.

6. (above, n. 2), 9.

7. S. Baker, 'Re-reading *The Corporate Personality*', *Journal of Design History*, 2.4 (1989), 275–6.

8. These include J. K. Galbraith, *The New Industrial State* (Hamish Hamilton, London, 1967), G. Bannock, *The Juggernauts: the Age of the Big Corporation* (Penguin, Harmondsworth, 1973), and A. Mattelart, *Multinational Corporations and the Control of Culture: the Ideological Apparatuses of Imperialism* (Harvester, Brighton, 1979).

9. (Penguin, Harmondsworth), 12.

10. (Ediciones Universitarias de Valparaíso, Chile). An English edition, *How to Read Donald Duck: Imperialist Imagery in the Disney Comic*, with a foreword by David Kunzle, was published by International General, New York, 1975.

11. Doyle Dane Bernbach was founded in New York in 1949 and soon expanded with offices worldwide. Highly successful, it set new standards of co-operation between copywriters and art directors, with visual elements carrying equal editorial weight to that of advertising copy.

12. A. Mattelart, *Multinational Corporations and the Control of Culture* (above, n. 8).

13. The corporate implications of armies are considered in L. Mumford, *Technics and Civilisation* (1934; Routledge & Kegan Paul, London, 1962).

14. The overt symbolism of regimes such as Mussolini's conception of a 'Roma Secunda' and Hitler's Third Reich have been considered in Chapter 3. Wally Olins considers the latter in *The Corporate Personality* (Design Council, 1962). One might look back considerably further to, e.g., the city states and courts of the Renaissance, with the institution of programmes for building and cultural patronage as a means of projecting particular notions of corporate identity.

15. From 1949 it became part of the Illinois Institute of Technology. For further discussion of the early debates and politics of the institution see A. Findeli, 'Design Education and Industry: the Laborious Beginnings of the Institute of Design in Chicago in 1944', *Journal of Design History*, 4.2 (1991), 97–115.

16. Discussed more fully in ch. 9, 'The Aspen Muse and the Twilight of Modernism', in J. Sloan Allen, *The Romance of Commerce and Culture* (University of Chicago Press, 1983).

17. For an extremely useful discussion of the form, content, and influence of this magazine see J. Aynsley '*Gebrauchsgraphik* as an Early Graphic Design Journal, 1924–1938', *Journal of Design History*, 5.1 (1992), 53–72.

18. This has been discussed interestingly in ch. 6, 'Design in the Office', by A. Forty, *Objects of Desire: Design and Society 1750–1980* (Thames and Hudson, London, 1986).

19. See J. Heskett, *Philips: A Study of the Corporate Management of Design* (Trefoil, London, 1989).

20. S. Bayley, *Coke! Coca-Cola 1886–1986: Designing a Megabrand* (Conran Foundation, London, 1986).

21. S. Bayley (ed.), *Sony: Design* (Conran Foundation, London 1982).

22. A. Drexler, 'Introduction' to *Charles Eames: Furniture from the Design Collection* (MOMA, New York, 1973), 3.

23. (MOMA, New York, 1950).

24. Quoted in *Design Process Olivetti 1908–1978*, exhibition catalogue, Frederick S. Wight Art Gallery (Olivetti, Ivrea, 1979), 19.

25. The findings were published and illustrated in 'The 100 "Best Designed" Products', *Fortune*, April 1959, 135–41. This was subsequently enlarged and published as J. Doblin, *100 Great Product Designs* (Van Nostrand Reinhold, New York, 1970).

26. As in B. Radice, *Memphis: the New International Style* (Electa, Milan, 1981); I. Vercelloni, 'A New International Style', *House and Garden*, February 1982, 108–17; H. Cumming, and A. Van Tulleken, 'Memphis Design and Other International Styles', *Art and Design* (London), March 1986, 50–7.

27. The Officina was launched in 1983 as the experimental arm of the metal goods manufacturer, Alessi.

28. See e.g. Volker Fischer (ed.), 'Micro-Architecture', in *Design Now: Industry or Art?* (Prestel Verlag, Munich, 1989), 207–40.

29. (Wright Art Gallery, University of California, Los Angeles, 1979, 19). The term *Piazza* implied architectural structures and spatial relationships: these were defined by the forms of the tea and coffee pots, sugar bowl, and milk jug, set within the spatial definitions of their tray.

Chapter 7

1. (HMSO, London).
2. M. Gray, 'SIAD: The First Forty Years', *The Designer*, October 1970, 4.
3. Board of Trade, *Report of the Committee appointed by the Board of Trade under the Chairmanship of Lord Gorell on the Production and Exhibition of Articles of Good Design and Everyday Use* (HMSO, London, 1932).
4. *Art and Industry: The Principles of Industrial Design* (Faber & Faber, London, 1934).
5. (Faber & Faber, London).
6. (Cambridge University Press).
7. The most important of these were Industrial Art in relation to the Home, held at Dorland Hall, London in 1933, and Contemporary Industrial Design, held at the same venue in 1934.
8. e.g. N. Carrington, *Industrial Design in Britain* (Allen & Unwin, London, 1976), F. MacCarthy, (above, n. 1.2), J. Woodham, *The Industrial Designer and the Public* (Pembridge, London, 1983), and R. Stewart, *Design and British Industry* (John Murray, London, 1987).
9. (Design Council, London, 1983), 36.
10. R. Stewart (above, n. 8).
11. This was reflected in the growing amount of literature in the field, ranging from texts which sought to validate the profession to those which were to act almost as handbooks for those involved: e.g. F. A. Mercer, *The Industrial Design Consultant: Who He Is and What He Does* (Studio, London, 1947), J. Gordon Lippincott, *Design for Business* (Paul Theobald, Chicago, 1954), F. Ashford, *Designing for Industry: Some Aspects of the Product Designer's Work* (Sir Isaac Pitman, London, 1955), J. Pilditch and D. Scott, *The Business of Product Design* (Business Publications Ltd, London, 1965), and D. Goslett *The Professional Practice of Design* (1960; rev. edn., Batsford, London, 1971).
12. See e.g. J. Sorrell, *The Future Design Council* (Design Council, London, 1994). This, and much of the surrounding debate, is covered by Charlotte Benton in her review of the book in the *Journal of Design History*, 7.4 (1994), 310–12.
13. For further discussion of the State's involvement with design in Poland see

D. Crowley, 'Building the World Anew: Design in Stalinist and Post-Stalinist Poland', *Journal of Design History*, 7.3 (1994), 187–203.
14. See e.g. M.H., 'Design in Russia', *Industrial Design*, April 1963, 72–5, R. Hutchings, 'USSR', *Design*, January 1976, 48–9, J. Woudhuysen, 'Soviet Design: Quality Consumer Goods at Last', *Design*, January 1978, 27, and J. Lott, 'Trying to Sort Out the Soviet Union', *Design*, October 1981, 36–7.
15. *Design in Ireland: Report of the Scandinavian Design Group in Ireland* (Irish Export Board, Dublin, 1961).
16. S. Freedgood, 'Odd Business, This Industrial Design', *Fortune* (New York), February 1959.
17. This is a process which has continued as many emerging industrialized nations have given an increasing priority to design.
18. (Pembridge, London, 1981), 48.
19. 'Overseas Review: Ulm', *Design*, June 1959, 53–6.
20. 'Review Article: Hochschule für Gestaltung Ulm: Recent Literature', *Journal of Design History*, 1.3–4 (1988), 249–56.
21. H. Jacob, 'HfG: A Personal View of an Experiment in Democracy and Design Education', *Journal of Design History*, 1.3–4 (1988), 221–34. Other views may be found in B. Meurer, 'Modernity and the Ulm School', in J. De Noblet (ed.), *Design: Reflections of a Century* (Flammarion, 1993). For a women's perspective see G. Müller-Krauspe, 'There Were 26 of Us: Women at the HfG' in *Frauen im Design* (above, Introd. n. 9), 254 ff.
22. (Council of Industrial Design, London).
23. The use of design methods can be studied in the hospital bed project carried out at the Industrial Design (Engineering) Research Unit at the Royal College. This is examined in *Industrial Design and the Community* (Lund Humphries, London, 1967), 17–56.
24. W. E. Woodson, *Human Engineering for Equipment Designers* (University of California Press, Berkeley, 1954).
25. See e.g. H. Murrell, 'How Ergonomics Became Part of Design', in N. Hamilton (ed.), *From Spitfire to the Microchip* (above, n. 5.13), 72–6.
26. (above, n. 3.4).
27. (1966; rev. edn., Penguin, Harmondsworth, 1976).
28. (Hodder & Stoughton, London).

Chapter 8

1. This was noted by the sociologist David Riesman in *The Lonely Crowd* (1950; Yale University Press, New Haven, 1961).

2. (Éditions du Seuil, Paris, 1957). An English translation by A. Lavers was published by Jonathan Cape, London, 1972.

3. (Capeli Editore, Bologna).

4. (Museum of Modern Art, New York).

5. *Theory and Design in the First Machine Age* (Architectural Press, London, 1960).

6. See above, Introd. n. 3.

7. In a recent publication it has been argued forcibly that the history of the IG has been 'mythologised' and that the role of design in the Group's activities has been unduly overshadowed by the emphasis on fine arts. See A. Massey, *The Independent Group: Modernism and Mass Culture in Britain 1945–59* (Manchester University Press, 1995). See also A. Massey and P. Sparke, 'The Myth of the Independent Group', *Block*, 10 (1985), 48–56.

8. (above, n. 5, 7th impression, 1977), 10.

9. Ibid.

10. 'Technology and the Home', *Ark*, 19 (1956), 26.

11. See esp. ch. 8, 'The Myth of the Independent Group: Historiography and Hagiography' in A. Massey (above, n. 7), 109–27.

12. Ibid. 98.

13. *Architectural Review*, August 1948, 88–93.

14. *What is Modern Design?* (Museum of Modern Art, New York, 1950), 7. However, he began to accept a wider canon of taste by the end of the decade in his article 'The Design Shift 1950-1960', *Industrial Design*, 7 (August 1960), 50–1.

15. *Design*, 134 (1960), 28–32. A number of his views on design are contained in his *Collected Words* (Thames & Hudson, London, 1992).

16. *Design*, 134 (1960), 25.

17. *Block*, 4 (1981), 44 ff.

18. This rather indicates that the homogenizing effects of US culture are only one aspect of Hoggart's concerns about the erosion of the British way of life since the tubular steel chair was, at least in its origins, an emblem of modernism, or the International Style which many reacted against in the interwar years as it did not embrace national characteristics.

19. *The Uses of Literacy* (Penguin, Harmondsworth, 1977 edn.), 248.

20. See e.g. N. Whiteley, *Pop Design: Modernism to Mod* (Design Council, London, 1987), or C. McDermott, *Street Style: British Design in the 80s* (Design Council, London, 1987).

21. Part 1, 1959, and Part 2, 1960 (London Press Exchange, London).

22. See e.g. N. Whiteley (above, n. 20).

23. *Architectural Review*, October 1967, 255–7.

24. The organization was undergoing something of a shift away from its concentration on consumer goods towards capital goods and engineering, a shift which was endorsed in its reconstitution as the Design Council, 1972.

25. (above, n. 4), 22. Although published in 1966 it was written in 1962.

26. J. Jacobs, *The Death and Life of Great American Cities: the Failure of Town Planning* (Random House, New York, 1961), and P. Blake, in the rather more sensational *Form Follows Fiasco: Why Modern Architecture Hasn't Worked* (Little, Brown and Company, Boston, 1977), are typical examples of such critiques.

27. (Academy, London).

28. *The Hot House* (above, Ch. 2, n. 27), .

29. 'Memphis and Fashion', from *Memphis: Research, Experiences, Results, Failures and Successes of New Design* (Thames & Hudson, London, 1984), 187.

30. V. Fischer (ed.), *Design Now: Industry or Art?* (Prestel-Verlag, Munich, 1989), 74.

31. J. Thackera, (ed.), *New British Design* (Thames & Hudson, London, 1986), 11.

32. A. Greiman, *Hybrid Imagery: the Fusion of Technology and Graphic Design* (Architecture Design and Technology Press, London, 1990), provides a résumé of her work from the late 1970s onwards.

33. J. Wozencroft, *The Graphic Language of Neville Brody* (Thames & Hudson, London, 1988). For more recent discussion of his work see J. Wozencroft, *The Graphic Language of Neville Brody 2* (Thames & Hudson, London, 1994).

34. See e.g. N. Whiteley (above, n. 20).

35. T. Palmer, *The Trials of Oz* (Blond & Briggs, London, 1971).

36. (above, n. 30), 87.

Chapter 9

1. See P. Stanfield, 'Heritage Design: the Harley-Davidson Motor Company', *Journal of Design History*, 5.2 (1992) 141–55.

2. These instances and others are discussed in Jeffrey Meikle's useful essay, 'Domesticating Modernity: Ambivalence and Appropriation, 1920-1940', in W. Kaplan (ed.), *Designing Modernity* (above, n. 1.2), 143–67.

3. Which was in turn funded by the Works Progress Administration (WPA), established under Roosevelt.

4. In many ways this paralleled the use of crafts workers in British imperial exhibitions.

However, there were often ideological distinctions to be made, as at Wembley 1924, where (black) African crafts workers were working under the public gaze. The message of British imperialism was that Britain was the centre of industrial manufacture and that the colonies provided her with raw materials. In general colonial output was on a scale that was not seen as economically threatening but which none the less held an exotic allure.

5. See William B. Rhoads, 'Colonial Revival in American Craft: Nationalism and the Opposition to Multicultural and Regional Traditions', in J. Kardon (ed.), *Revivals! Diverse Traditions 1920–1945: The History of Twentieth Century Craft* (Abrams, New York, 1994), 41–54. A number of other essays in this volume are very useful, particularly in relation to wider ethnic and cultural concerns. However, in this more limited discussion of (white, Anglo-Saxon Protestant) heritage see especially Harvey Green 'Culture and Crisis: Americans and the Craft Revival', pp. 31–40.

6. Seen in the foundation of the Society for the Revival of Spanish-Colonial Arts in 1925 (renamed the Spanish Colonial Arts Society in 1929). It also promoted a Spanish Arts Shop to market traditional crafts.

7. The streamlined 'Modern Diner' in Pawtucket, RI, of *c.*1940, manufactured by Sterling Diners of Merrimac, Mass., was placed on the National Register of Historic Places.

8. *Yearning for Yesterday: A Sociology of Nostalgia* (Collier Macmillan, London, 1979).

9. Ibid. 109.

10. Ibid. 90.

11. (Cambridge University Press, Cambridge, 1992).

12. Although, prior to taking up the name of Crabtree & Evelyn, the company marketed soaps in a small shop in Cambridge, Mass., in the 1960s.

13. T. Reese, 'When More Is More', *Print*, March–April 1987, 84.

14. These included K. Walsh, *The Representation of the Past: Museums and Heritage in the Post-Modern World* (Routledge, London, 1992). He considered that the war had posed a threat to the status of the ruling classes and that in its aftermath there was a perceived need to preserve what they stood for.

15. Although there was a period in the 1950s when the COID worked with the Rural Industries Bureau and embraced certain aspects of the crafts within its orbit.

16. (British Council/Longmans Green & Co., London).

17. Ibid. 22.

18. (Collins, London).

19. *English Popular Art* (Batsford, London).

20. (Architectural Press, London, 1951). This publication was the culmination of a series of articles which Jones had been producing for the *Architectural Review* since 1944.

21. *Burlington Magazine* (London), September 1952, 203.

22. Such as P. Cormack, *Heritage in Danger* (New English Library, London, 1976).

23. In other words, the Welfare State implemented by Clement Attlee's Labour Government in the later 1940s.

24. The original competition attracted about 300 entries, none of which was felt to be appropriate.

25. Preface by Laura Ashley to the *Laura Ashley Home Furnishings Catalogue 1982* (Laura Ashley, Carno, Powys, 1982).

26. *The Heritage Industry: Britain in a Climate of Design* (Methuen, London).

27. 'Time Will Tell', *Design Week*, November 1990.

28. Other examples are cited in P. J. Fowler, *The Past in Contemporary Society: Then, Now* (Routledge, London, 1992), particularly in ch. 11, 'Exploiting the Past', 129–38.

29. G. Darley, 'History as Bunk', *Financial Times* (London), 2 December 1989, p. xvii. However, the criteria employed included such issues as catering, car parking, and toilet facilities, as well as sales literature. Authenticity and intelligence of historical presentation was subject to no factual or qualitative assessment.

30. (above, n. 14), 129.

Chapter 10

1. This was an innovation of Clarence Saunders who patented the idea in 1917.

2. The 1906 Pure Food Bill, spurred on by Upton Sinclair's horrific account of the malpractice of the American meat-packing industry in his publication, *The Jungle*, was passed despite the opposition of the powerful Chicago-based industrial lobby.

3. Such as the *Ladies Home Journal* and the *Woman's Home Companion*.

4. J. G. Brainerd, 'Introduction', *The Ultimate Consumer: A Study in Economic Illiteracy* (The Annals of the American Academy of Political and Social Science, Philadelphia, May 1934, p. ix.

5. *Report of the Purchase Tax/Utility Committee* (HMSO, London, 1952).

6. Originally established in 1901 as the British Engineering Standards Committee. For further historical details see C. Douglas Woodward, *BSI: The Story of Standards* (British Standards Institute, London, 1972).

7. The British Good Housekeeping Institute was started in 1924, later than its American counterpart, together with its magazine *Good Housekeeping*.

8. Many aspects of such developments have been discussed by S. Worden, 'A Voice for Whose Choice? Advice for Consumers in the Late 1930s', in T. Bishop (ed.), *Design History: Fad or Function?* (Design Council, London, 1978), 41–8.

9. Originally known by the more long-winded title of Advisory Council on Standards for Consumer Goods.

10. For a fuller discussion of women's consumer groups in postwar Britain see ch. 7, 'Consumer Awareness', in Jonathan M. Woodham, *The Industrial Designer and the Public* (above, n. 7.8), 90–8.

11. *Which?* was available by subscription only, unlike the American *Consumer Reports* which could be purchased off the shelf.

12. See, e.g., the discussion of such work in F. Klingender, *Art and the Industrial Revolution* (1947; Paladin, St Albans, 1972). Although scholarship in relation to many of the artists has moved on from the 1968 revised and enlarged edition of the original text, it remains an important contribution to discussions of scientific and cultural change in the 18th and 19th centuries.

13. (1957; Penguin, Harmondsworth, 1960).

14. (Grossman, New York, 1965). For further detailed criticisms and bibliographic references see also J. W. Eastman, *Styling vs. Safety* (University Press of America, 1984).

15. According to Nader in his address to the National Consumer Assembly, Washington, DC, in November 1967, reprinted in G. S. McClelland, *The Consuming Public* (H. W. Wilson, New York, 1968), 102 ff.

16. These and other poll statistics are drawn from ch. 11, 'Morality and the Marketplace', in P. Blumberg, *The Predatory Society: Deception in the American Marketplace* (Oxford University Press, 1989).

17. *Final Report on Consumer Protection* (HMSO, London, 1962).

18. Ibid. 112.

19. See above, n. 10.

20. As discussed in his article of 1961 on 'Influences on My Work' reprinted in J. Meller, (ed.), *The Buckminster Fuller Reader* (above, n. 3.12) 44–68.

21. Many of these lectures are reprinted in J. Meller, op. cit.

22. It had been first published in Stockholm, Sweden in 1970 under the title *Miljon och Miljonera* (*The Milieu and the Millions*). It was published in paperback in Britain by Granada, St Albans, in 1974. The revised editions came out in 1984 and 1991, the latter published by Thames & Hudson, London.

23. P. Madge, 'Design, Ecology, Technology: A Historiographical Review', *Journal of Design History*, 6.3 (1993), 149–66. See also Frank Jackson's review of the 1991 edition, also in the *Journal of Design History*, 6.4 (1993), 307–10.

24. The papers were published by J. Bicknell and L. McQuiston (eds.), *Design for Need: The Social Contribution of Design* (Pergamon Press, Oxford, 1977).

25. e.g. the design of teaching and training devices for the retarded, handicapped, and disabled; also design for medicine, surgery, dentistry, and hospital equipment.

26. See e.g. S. Goldsmith, *Designing for the Disabled* (2nd edn., McGraw-Hill, New York, 1967). A number of aspects relating to bathrooms and related equipment are discussed in chs. 20 and 21 in A. Kira, *The Bathroom* (rev. edn., Penguin, Harmondsworth, 1976).

27. The outlooks of these groups are described in N. Whiteley, *Design for Society* (Reaktion, London, 1993), 110–13.

28. In 1967 Ettore Sottsass Jr. described the houses of the Beat poets as places free of objects and books—what he saw as 'parking spaces' from which life might be reinvented.

29. LSD, one of a number of hallucinogenic drugs favoured by such countercultures.

30. P. Harper, G. Boyle, and the editors of Undercurrents, *Radical Technology* (Wildwood, London, 1976), 5.

31. (Secker & Warburg, London).

32. (Blond & Briggs, London).

33. (Calder & Boyars, London).

34. 'Made in Patriarchy: Toward a Feminist Analysis of Women and Design', *Design Issues*, 3.2 (1986), 4.

35. For further discussion of such issues see e.g. C. Buckley, op. cit.; J. Attfield and P. Kirkham (eds.), *A View from the Interior* (above, Introd. n. 10); and ch. 4, 'Feminist Perspectives', in N. Whitely, *Design for Society* (above, n. 27). The latter provides a basic run-through of a number of key texts and approaches.

36. J. Elkington and J. Hailes, *The Green Consumer Guide: From Shampoo to*

*Champagne—High Street Shopping for a
Better Environment* (Victor Gollancz,
London, 1988).
37. J. Elkington and T. Burke, *The Green
Capitalists: How Industry Can Make Money
and Protect the Environment* (2nd edn., Victor
Gollancz, London, 1989).
38. (Lawrence King, London).
39. (Design Council, London).
40. (Thames & Hudson, London).

41. Such as the Zanussi Nexus 'Jetstream RS'
washing machine.
42. *On Living in an Old Country: The National
Past in Contemporary Britain* (Verso, London).
43. (Routledge, London).
44. (above, n. 6.2), ch. 8, 205–6.
45. Discussion paper No. 1 (Friends of the
Earth, London).
46. C. and J. Plant (eds.) (Green Books).
47. (above, n. 23), 161.

List of Illustrations

The publisher would like to thank the following individuals and institutions who have kindly given permission to reproduce the illustrations listed below.

1. Giacomo Balla: Futurist clothing from the *Manifesto Futurista*, 1914. © Giacomo Balla Estate, Rome.

2. Cover of Sears Roebuck Catalogue, *Consumers Guide*, no. 108, 1899. Sears, Roebuck & Co., Hoffman Estates, IL.

3. Parlour Suites from the Sears Roebuck Catalogue, 1897. Sears, Roebuck & Co., Hoffman Estates, IL.

4. Hermann Haas: Stoneware tableware, tea and coffee service and children's playset for Villeroy & Boch, shown at the Deutscher Werkbund Exhibition at Cologne, 1914. Bauhaus-Archiv, Museum für Gestaltung, Berlin (from Deutscher Werkbund Jahrbuch, 1915).

5. Fritz Hellmut Ehmcke: Deutscher Werkbund cigar box, 1914. Die Neue Sammlung, Staatliches Museum für Angewandte Kunst, Munich.

6. The Hamburg Room at the Deutscher Werkbund Exhibition at Cologne, 1914. Werkbund-Archiv, Museum der Alltagskultur des 20. Jahrhunderts, Berlin (from Deutscher Werkbund Jahrbuch, 1915).

7. Peter Behrens: AEG Showroom, Berlin, *c.*1912. Werkbund-Archiv, Museum der Alltagskultur des 20. Jahrhunderts, Berlin (from Deutscher Werkbund Jahrbuch, 1913).

8. Peter Behrens: 1912 brochure advertising nickel-plated and brass AEG Kettles, designed 1909. Tilmann Buddensieg, Berlin.

9. Edward Johnston: Signage for London Underground Electric Railways, post-1916. London Transport Museum.

10. Cover for *RED* magazine, Czechoslovakia, 1928.

11. Qian Jun-tao: *Ahead of the Times*, published by Ahead of the Times Magazine Association, Shanghai, January 1931.

12. Installation view of the *Machine Art* exhibition, Museum of Modern Art, New York, March 5 through April 29, 1934/photo Wurts Brother, © 1996 Museum of Modern Art, New York.

13. Tea and Coffee Service from the *Deutsches Warenbuch*, 1915. Werkbund-Archiv, Museum der Alltagskultur des 20. Jahrhunderts, Berlin.

14. Gerrit Rietveld: Interior of the Schröder House, Utrecht, 1924. © Centraal Museum, Utrecht/photo Ernst Moritz.

15. Gerrit Rietveld: Exhibition at Metz & Co. department store, Amsterdam, showing dining area and glass sideboard, 1933. Centraal Museum, Utrecht, © Beeldrecht Amsterdam/photo RSA.

16. W. H. Gispen/J. Kamman: Giso Lamps poster, 1928. Stedelijk Museum, Amsterdam.

17. Sports clothes by Stepanova and graphics for *Dobrolyet* by Rodchenko from *LEF* magazine, Moscow, 1923. David King Collection, London.

18. Textile designs by Popova, from *LEF* magazine, Moscow, 1923. David King Collection, London.

19. Late 1920s textile, USSR. David King Collection, London.

20. Walter Gropius: Director's Office at the Bauhaus, Weimar, 1923: Bauhaus-Archiv, Museum für Gestaltung, Berlin/photo F. Karsten, London.

21. Ruth Hollós: tapestry, Dessau, 1926. Bauhaus-Archiv, Museum für Gestaltung, Berlin/photo H.-J. Bartsch.

22. Herbert Bayer: brochure advertising Bauhaus products, 1925. Torsten Bröhan GmbH, Düsseldorf. Benedikt Taschen Verlag GmbH, Cologne.

23. Marianne Brandt: Teamaker, 1928/30. Brass and ebony. Torsten Bröhan GmbH, Düsseldorf.

24. Wilhelm Wagenfeld: Lighting from *Das Frankfurter Register*, 17, 1931. Bauhaus-Archiv, Museum für Gestaltung, Berlin.

25. Grete Schütte-Lihotzky: Blueprint for

the Frankfurt Kitchen, 1924. Germanisches Nationalmuseum, Nuremberg.

26. Benita Otte and Ernst Gebhardt: Haus am Horn kitchen, Bauhaus Exhibition, 1923. Bauhaus-Archiv, Museum für Gestaltung, Berlin.

27. Hermann Gretsch: Model 1382 service, Porzellanfabrik Arzberg, 1931. Die Neue Sammlung, Staatliches Museum für Angewandte Kunst, Munich.

28. Le Corbusier: Interior of Pavillon de l'Esprit Nouveau, Exposition Des Arts Décoratifs et Industriels, Paris, 1925. Museum des Art Décoratifs, Paris/Editions A. Lévy.

29. Ufficio Tecnico Olivetti: Olivetti office at Ivrea with *Synthesis* tubular steel furniture, c.1935. Cantilevered tubular steel. Archivio Olivetti, Milan.

30. Salon furniture, Nordiska Kompaniet, 1917. Kungliga Biblioteket, Stockholm (from Svenska Slödföreningens Tidskrift, 1927).

31. Wilhelm Kåge: *Praktika I*, model X, *Weekend* pattern dinner service for Gustavsberg, 1933. Gustavsberg Porslin (Keramiskt Centrum), Gustavsberg.

32. Alvar Aalto: *Paimio* armchair, no. 41, 1931/2. Plywood. Alvar Aalto Museum, Jyväskylä/photo M. Kapanen.

33. Alvar Aalto: Garden Room displayed at Paris International Exhibition, 1937. Artek Archive/Foto Studio H. de Sarian.

34. Marion Dorn: Hand-knotted wool rug, Wilton Royal Carpet Factory Ltd., c.1937. Board of Trustees of the Victoria and Albert Museum, London.

35. Adolf Syszko-Bohusz and Andrej Pronaszko: Boudoir furniture, Presidential Castle, Wisła, 1930. Chromium-plated tubular steel. Muzeum Narodowe, Warsaw (from Architektura ï Budownictwo, 1931).

36. Adolf Syszko-Bohusz and Andrej Pronaszko: Hall and cloakroom furniture, Presidential Castle, Wisła, 1930. Muzeum Narodowe, Warsaw (from Architektura ï Budownictwo, 1931).

37. Marbett's (White Tower) Restaurant, Camden, NJ, 1938. Tombrock Corporation, New Canaan, CT.

38. Raymond Loewy: Cover of *Time* magazine, 31 October 1949. Katz Pictures, London/© 1939 Time Inc., reprinted by permission.

39. Raymond Loewy: Coldspot Refrigerator for Sears Roebuck, 1935. Sears, Roebuck & Co., Hoffman Estates, IL.

40. Carl Breer and associates: De Soto *Airflow* automobile, Chrysler Corporation, 1934. Chrysler Corporation.

41. Staubsauger: *Champion* vacuum cleaner, Type OK, Holland, late 1930s. Chromium-plated. Die Neue Sammlung, Staatliches Museum für Angewandte Kunst, Munich.

42. Battle of the Centuries: Dishwashing contest between Mrs Drudge and Mrs Modern (using a 1940 Westinghouse dishwasher) at the New York World's Fair, 1939/40. Westinghouse Electric Corporation, Pittsburgh, PA.

43. General Motors Exhibit at the New York World's Fair 1939/40, showing envisaged street scene of 1960 with General Motors buses and cars. Lerner-Zim World's Fair Collection, National Museum of American History, Smithsonian Institution, Washington, DC.

44. Jacques-Emil Ruhlmann: Interior of the *Hotel d'un Collectioneur*, Exposition des Arts Décoratifs et Industriels, Paris, 1925. Philippe Garner, London.

45. André Fréchet, Lahalle and Lavard: Reception hall for the Studium-Louvre Pavilion, Exposition des Arts Decoratifs et Industriels, Paris, 1925. Jean-Loup Charmet, Paris.

46. Jaap Gidding: Foyer of the Tuschinki Cinema, Amsterdam, 1918–21. ANP Foto, Amsterdam.

47. Stanislaw Brukalski: Interior of the America Bar, on the ocean liner *MS Bathory*, 1936. Muzeum Architektury, Wroclaw (from Architektura ï Budownictwo, 1936).

48. Cedric Gibbons/Richard Day: Art Deco set for the MGM film *The Kiss*, 1929. Turner Entertainment Co./© 1929 Turner Entertainment Co. All rights reserved.

49. Eric Slater: Vogue shape teaset, Shelley Potteries, Longton, 1930. Geffrye Museum, London.

50. Y. Utida and Y. Matsui: Interior of the Japanese Pavilion at the New York World's Fair, 1939. Lerner-Zim World's Fair Collection, National Museum of American History, Smithsonian Institution, Washington, DC.

51. Józef Czajkowski: Chair for the office in the Polish Pavilion at the Paris Expositions des Arts Décoratifs et Industriels Modernes, 1925. Central Library of the Academy of Fine Arts, Kraków/photo Paivel Grawicz.

52. Józef Czajkowski and Wojciech Jastrzebowski: Office interior in the Polish Pavilion, Paris, 1925. Central Library of the Academy of Fine Arts, Kraków/photo Paivel Grawicz.

53. V. Maslov: *The Tractor*, textile design, USSR, late 1920s. State Russian Museum, St Petersburg/photo Scala, Florence.

54. Central Russian Folk Art, USSR Pavilion, Paris Internationale Exposition, 1937. Roger-Viollet, Paris.

55. The *Henry VIII* Dining-Lounge, Bolsom's Furniture Catalogue, *c.*1935. Geffrye Museum, London.

56. Gentleman's Sporting Equipment from the British Display at Monza, 1930. The Studio.

57. E. Ravilious: *Boat Race*, 1938. Earthenware bowl, transfer-printed and overpainted in enamel colours, manufactured by Josiah Wedgwood & Sons. Trustees of the Wedgwood Museum, Barlaston, Staffordshire.

58. Approved colour scheme for an STL double-decker London bus from a hand-painted specification book prepared at Chiswick works, late 1940s. London Transport Museum.

59. *Kleinempfänger*, Little Radio, Germany, 1938: Die Neue Sammlung, Staatliches Museum für Angewandte Kunst, Munich.

60. Members of the Reichsarbeitsdienst (RAD) listening to a radio broadcast, 1935. Walter Maria Kersting: Volksempfänger VE 301, People's Radio, 1928. Moulded plastic. Ullstein Bilderdienst, Berlin.

61. Illustrated cover of *Kampf der Gefahr* (Fight Against Danger), December 1939. Werkbund-Archiv, Museum der Alltagskultur des 20. Jahrhunderts, Berlin.

62. Traditional German interior, 1935. Ullstein Bilderdienst, Berlin.

63. Canteen crockery, Schönheit der Arbeit (Beauty in Work) model, 1937. Werkbund-Archiv, Museum der Alltagskultur des 20. Jahrhunderts, Berlin.

64. National Socialist Propaganda Exhibition, 'Gebt Mie Vier Jahre Zeit', May, 1937. Ullstein Bilderdienst, Berlin.

65. Grande Salon of the *Normandie*, ocean liner, 1932–5. Philippe Garner, London.

66. 'Radiorurale', built with slight variations by various companies, 1934. RAI (Radiotelevisione Italiana), Turin.

67. A. Libera and M. de Renzi: Façade of the Pavilion for the Exhibition commemorating the 10th anniversary of the Fascist revolution, Rome, 1932. Giancarlo Costa, Milan.

68. Mario Sironi: poster, *Fiat 500, La Vetturetta del Lavoro e del Risparmio*, 1936. Fiat (UK) Ltd., London.

69. Ruth Reeves: *Manhattan*, for W. & J. Sloane, New York City, 1930. Block-printed cotton. Cooper Hewitt National Design Museum, New York.

70. Russell Wright: *American Way* displays at Macy's, New York, 1940. Syracuse University Library (Department of Special Collections), NY.

71. 'Up in the Sky', Coca-Cola advertisement from *The Saturday Evening Post*, USA, 1920s. Advertising Archive Ltd., London (Coca-Cola is a registered trademark of the Coca-Cola Company).

72. Workers preparing ground for seeding, Levittown, USA, *c.*1950. Levittown Public Library, NY.

73. Component parts of a Levitt Home prior to on-site assembly, *c.*1950. National Archives, College Park, MD.

74. Cadillac Fleetwood advertisement, late 1950s. Cadillac/General Motors Corporation.

75. General Motors Show, Los Angeles, 1954. © General Motors Corporation, Detroit.

76. Frigidaire *Kitchen of Tomorrow*, 1956: General Motors Corporation, Detroit.

77. Utility living-room layout as revealed to the public in Board of Trade exhibition in London's West End, October 1942. Hulton Getty Picture Company, Ltd., London.

78. Die-lines as issued to manufacturers participating in the Festival Pattern Group, *c.*1950. © Warner Fabrics PLC., Tilbrook, Milton Keynes.

79. Parlour, designed by Eden and Bianca Minns from the Homes and Gardens Pavilion on the South Bank, London, at the Festival of Britain, 1951. Design History Research Centre, University of Brighton/Design Council.

80. Füred and Lelle furniture sets manufactured in the Metal-Furniture Factory, Hungary, 1950s. Design Center KFT, Budapest.

81. Alec Issigonis: Austin Mini (1959) as seen in the Paramount Picture Corporation's film *The Italian Job*, 1969. © 1996 by Paramount Pictures. All rights reserved.

82. Ignazio Gardella: Apartment for three people, RIMA Exhibition, Milan, 1946. Studio di Architettura Gardella, Milan.

83. Ignazio Gardella: Little Sideboard (Piccola Credenza), RIMA Exhibition, Milan, 1946. Studio di Architettura Gardella, Milan.

84. Corradino d'Ascanio: Workers riding Piaggio *Vespa* motor scooters designed at the Piaggio factory, Pontedera, January 1949. Publifoto, Milan.

85. Gio Ponti: *Zeta* sanitaryware for Ideal Standard, 1954. Ideal Standard SpA, Milan/Centro Servizi Fotografici.

86. Paolo Venini: Bottles in 'incalmo' glass, Venini, 1950. Venini SpA, Murano (Venice).

87. Citroën DS display at the Salon d'Automobile, Paris, 1955. Citroën, Neuilly-sur-Seine.

88. Arne Jacobsen: Cutlery, AJ pattern, produced by A. Michelsen, Copenhagen, 1957. Royal Copenhagen Ltd., Frederiksberg (made by Georg Jensen, Silversmiths).

89. Kartell: Cover page from the company magazine *Qualität*, no. 6, Winter 1957. Kartell SpA, Noviglio (Milan)/Von Wedel srl.

90. Marco Zanuso & Richard Sapper: Television 201 for Brionvega, 1969. Acrylic. Brionvega SpA, Cernusco sul Naviglio (Milan).

91. *Isabella* coupé, Borgward, West Germany, 1956. Ullstein Bilderdienst, Berlin.

92. Käte Gläser: Model no. 1 Living Room furnished by the Deutscher Werkbund, Berlin, 1953. Werkbund-Archiv, Museum der Alltagskultur des 20. Jahrhunderts, Berlin.

93. One of the Bijenkorf department store displays from 'Pioneers of Today' display, Amsterdam, 1961. Premesla Vonk/ Gemeentemuseum, Amsterdam.

94. Stiletto Studios: Consumer's Rest, no. 11 lounge chair prototype, 1986 (prototype developed in 1983). Remodelled and varnished supermarket trolley. Cooper Hewitt National Design Museum, New York/Art Resource.

95. TR 610 Pocket Transistor Radio, Sony, 1958. Advertising Archives Ltd., London/ Sony.

96. 'You Meet the Nicest People on a Honda' advertising campaign in the USA, late 1950s. American Honda Motor Co. Inc./Honda Motor Europe Ltd., Reading.

97. Pre-Pentagram: Lucas Identity Programme: Constituent Companies (before redesign), illustrated in Pentagram, 1970s. Lucas Varity PLC.

98. Pentagram: Lucas Identity Programme: Constituent Companies (after redesign), 1975. Lucas Varity PLC. Pentagram Design Ltd., London.

99. Stanley C. Meeston: McDonald's at Des Plaines, Illinois, 1955. McDonald's Corporation, Oak Brook, IL.

100. Sony Walkman advertisement, 1980s. Advertising Archives Ltd., London/Sony.

101. American Express Credit Card, 1990s. American Express.

102. Cover of *Time* magazine showing Coca-Cola as the 'World's Friend', 15 May 1950. Katz Pictures, London/© 1950 Time Inc.

103. Levi's advertisement, Japan, early 1980s: 'Since 1850 Jeans Have Been Called Levi's in the USA'. Levi Strauss Japan.

104. Eliot Noyes: Selectric typewriter, IBM, 1961. IBM United Kingdom Ltd.

105. Corporate logos: Paul Rand for IBM (1956) and Westinghouse (1960), Henrion

Design for KLM (1964), Wolff Olins for BT (1991). Allan Cooper Design Associates (IBM logotype is a registered trademark of the International Business Machines Corporation); Westinghouse Electric Corporation, Pittsburgh, PA; KLM Royal Dutch Airlines; British Telecom.

106. Knoll International furniture showroom, USA, 1950s. The Knoll Group, New York.

107. Gerd Alfred Muller and Robert Oberheim: Kitchen Machine KM 32, Braun, 1957. Braun AG, Kronberg/Taunus.

108. 'Good Design Show' organized by Edgar Kaufmann Jr. for MOMA, NY, 1951. Chicago Merchandise Mart/Museum of Modern Art, New York.

109. Frank Gehry: Interior of the Vitra Design Museum at Weil am Rhein, 1989. Vitra Design Museum, Weil am Rhein, Freibourg.

110. Publicity for Scenicruiser Greyhound bus, designed by Raymond Loewy Associates, 1954. Greyhound Lines Inc., Dallas, TX.

111. Philippe Starck: Toothbrush for L'Oréal/Goupil Laboratories, France, 1990. L'Oréal/Goupil SA, Cachan.

112. Robert Venturi: *Village*, 4-piece tea and coffee set, Swid Powell, 1986. Swid Powell, New York/ Venturi, Scott Brown & Associates Inc., Philadelphia, PA/photo Matt Wargo.

113. Kazumasa Yamashita: 5-piece tea and coffee set, *Tea and Coffee Piazza* series, Alessi, 1983. Alessi SpA, Crusinello.

114. W. H. Gispen: Poster for the Nederlandsche Bund voor Kunst in Industry (BKI), 1941. Stedlijk Museum, Amsterdam.

115. Toshiba Rice Cooker, 1957. Toshiba Corporation (Europe), London.

116. GK Design: Soy sauce bottle for Kikkoman Corporation, Japan, late 1950s. GK Design Group Inc., Tokyo.

117. Hans Gugelot *et al.*: M125 Furniture system, 1957. Stadt Ulm (HfG-Archiv).

118. King's Fund Mark I Hospital Bed, manufactured by J. Nesbit-Evans & Co., 1960s. J. Nesbit-Evans & Co., Wednesbury.

119. Henry Dreyfuss: Joe and Josephine anthropometrics charts, 1960s. Used with the permission of Henry Dreyfuss Associates, New York.

120. Toshiyuki Kita: *Wink* Chair, Cassina, 1980. Cassina SpA, Meda (Milan).

121. James Dyson: *G-Force Cyclonic Vacuum Cleaner* manufactured by Apex Inc., Tokyo, 1986. Dyson Appliances Ltd., Malmesbury/photo Ian Dobbie.

122. Richard Sapper: Kettle with bronze whistle, Alessi, 1983. Alessi SpA, Crusinello.

123. Alison and Peter Smithson: 'House of

the Future', Ideal Home Exhibition, London, 1956. Ideal Home.

124. John Stephen attending the opening of Carnaby House in Via Margutti, Rome, 1967. Hulton Getty Picture Company Ltd., London.

125. Vivienne Westwood: *Savages* collection, 1981. Rex Features, London.

126. Zanotta stand at the Eurodomus 3, Turin, featuring the *Blow* inflatable chair, designed by Jonathan De Pas, Donato D'Urbino, Paolo Lomazzi, and Carla Scolari, 1967. Zanotta SpA, Nova Milanese.

127. Archizoom Associati, *Naufragio di Rose* dream bed, 1967. Andrea Branzi Architetto, Milan.

128. Ettore Sottsass: *Carlton Bookcase*, Memphis, 1981. Memphis srl, Milan.

129. Hans Hollein: Interior of the Austrian Travel Centre, Vienna, 1976–8. Studio Hollein/photo Jerzy Surwillo.

130. Gary Panter: *Raw* magazine cover, no. 3, 1981. © 1981 RAW Books, New York and Gary Panter.

131. Tom van den Haspel and Henk Elenga: Front cover of *Lecturis*, 1981. Lecturis, Eindhoven.

132. Neville Brody: Brochure cover for *FontFont 5*, Fontshop International, 1992. Neville Brody/Research Studios Ltd., London.

133. Colonial Williamsburg's Ayscough's Cabinet Making Shop, 1937. Colonial Williamsburg Foundation, Williamsburg, VA.

134. Western-styled Sofa-beds, Montgomery Ward, 1950s. Montgomery Ward, Chicago, IL.

135. Customagic Slipcovers advertisement, USA, 1950s. Advertising Archives Ltd., London.

136. Peter Windett: Crabtree & Evelyn shop interior and packaging, 1982. Crabtree & Evelyn, London.

137. *Baroque* service in porcelain, no. 9355, Zsolnay Ceramics Factory Hungary, 1945 onwards. Design Center KFT, Budapest.

138. Harold Holdcroft: *Old Country Roses* bone china tableware, Royal Albert (Royal Doulton), 1962 onwards. Royal Doulton PLC., Stoke-on-Trent.

139. 'Victorian' designs from *Past Times* catalogue, Autumn, 1995. Past Times/ Historical Collections Group PLC., Witney.

140. Cover *Consumer Reports*, Issue no. 1, May 1936, USA. Consumers Union, New York.

141. Cover from *Which?* magazine, no. 1, 1957 (reprinted 1960). Which Ltd./The Consumers' Association, London.

142. Richard Buckminster Fuller: Patent drawing from the *Dymaxion Bathroom*, 1937. © 1960 Allegra Fuller Snyder. Buckminster Fuller Institute, Santa Barbara, CA.

143. Cutlery designed for people with single-hand function, Ergonomi Design Gruppen, Sweden, c.1980. Ergonomi Design Gruppen, Bromma.

144. Peter Opsvik and Hans Christian Menghshoel: *Balans* chair, 1979, Norway. Håg as, Oslo.

145. John Habraken: Early wooden prototypes of WOBO bottle and WOBO House, early 1960s. A. H. Heineken, Amsterdam.

146. Drop City, USA, 1960s. Architectural Association Photo Library, London/photo Charlene Koonce.

147. *Body Shop* product ranges, 1980s. The Body Shop International PLC, Littlehampton/photo Apertures.

148. Neville Brody: Men's Bigi frisbee, 1990. Neville Brody/Research Studios Ltd., London.

The publisher and author apologize for any errors or omissions in the above list. If contacted they will be pleased to rectify these at the earliest opportunity.

Bibliographic Essay

This bibliography should be used in conjunction with the chapter footnotes, a number of which provide evaluative commentary as well as useful textual references. It is intended to point the way for further study and research in many areas of the history of twentieth-century design.

1: Towards the Twentieth Century
General introductory texts on twentieth-century design
Among useful discussions of approaches to the study of design history in the twentieth century are Penny Sparke, *An Introduction to Design and Culture in the Twentieth Century* (Allen & Unwin, London, 1986), Hazel Conway (ed.), *Design History: A Students' Handbook* (Allen & Unwin, London, 1987), Adrian Forty, *Objects of Desire: Design and Society 1750–1980* (Thames & Hudson, London, 1986), and John A. Walker, *Design History and the History of Design* (Pluto, London, 1989). The latter considers the widest range of possible approaches to the subject, embracing theoretical and feminist concerns (on which there is a valuable chapter by Judy Attfield). Also of considerable significance in this respect is the pioneering collection of essays edited by Judy Attfield and Pat Kirkham, *A View from the Interior: Feminism, Women and Design* (Women's Press, London, 1989; rev. edn. 1995).

For a broad overview of a number of more specific areas of design activity reference may be made to John Heskett's concise, thematically-organized text, *Industrial Design* (Thames & Hudson, 1980). Much more weighty in terms of length of text and number of illustrations is Jocelyn de Noblet (ed.), *Industrial Design: Reflections of a Century* (Flammarion/APCI, Paris, 1993), which contains essays by various specialists, many of which provide useful introductions to particular facets of design from the late nineteenth century onwards. For the study of the history of interior design Paula Yates provides a useful overview in her essay on 'Thirty Years of Growth in the Literature of Interior Design', *Journal of Design History*, 4.4 (1991), 241–50, whilst Stephen Calloway, *Twentieth Century Decoration; the Domestic Interior from 1900 to the Present Day* (Weidenfeld & Nicolson, London, 1988), is a well-illustrated account of mainstream 'designer' interiors. More open-ended is my own *Twentieth Century Ornament* (Studio Vista, London, 1990), which covers issues of ornamentation across a wide range of design media, including anonymous as well as attributed designs. Philip Meggs provides a solid and informative, if unexciting, account of graphic and communication design in *A History of Graphic Design* (Allen Lane; London, 1983). However, its emphasis is on the appearance of design rather than its wider social and cultural significance. More challenging and rewarding in terms of historical approach is Christopher Breward's introduction to the history of fashion, *The Culture of Fashion* (Manchester University Press, 1995), although this deals with a larger timescale. Clive D. Edwards, in his *Twentieth Century Furniture: Materials, Manufacture and Markets*, (Manchester University Press, 1994), offers an essentially British-centred study with an emphasis on issues of production and consumption.

There have also been a number of accounts of the use of materials in the twentieth century, such as Ezio Manzini, *The Material of Invention* (Arcadia, Milan, 1986), which provides a theoretical and philosophical approach to the study of new materials. On plastics there are Sylvia Katz, *Plastics Design and Materials* (Studio Vista, London, 1978), Sylvia Katz, *Plastics: Common Objects, Classic Designs* (Abrams, New York, 1984), and Penny Sparke (ed.), *The Plastics Age: From Modernity to Post-Modernity* (Victoria and Albert Museum, London, 1990), all of which are more straightforwardly historical texts than Manzini's. By far the most complete study to date is Jeffrey Meikle, *American Plastic: A Cultural History* (Rutgers University Press, New Brunswick, 1995). His extensive use of archival sources and exhaustive referencing makes it a definitive, yet very readable, volume.

Differing approaches to the study of the history of design
A wide range of debates about possible approaches to the history of design by authors such as Clive Dilnot and Cheryl Buckley were published in *Design Issues* in the 1980s, at that time published by the University of Chicago Press. These have been conveniently gathered together in Section III on 'Writing Design History', in Victor Margolin (ed.), *Design Discourse: History, Theory, Criticism* (University of Chicago Press, 1989). The references, particularly in Dilnot's articles, also provide a useful checklist for those wishing to examine the historiography of the subject prior to the mid-1980s. More recently, in the spring of 1995, *Design Issues* (now published by MIT, Cambridge, Mass.) devoted an entire issue to debates about the nature and relative value of the history of design and its significance within the wider embrace of design studies.

Museological concerns and the history of design
For a range of museological perspectives and concerns relating to the history of design one of the most useful collections of essays is that edited by Peter Vergo, *The New Museology* (Reaktion, London, 1991), which contains a helpful select bibliography. This is an important area for reflection since museum collections and displays, being often based on aesthetic distinctiveness rather than wider social or broad cultural significance, have played a determining role in the ways in which many writers, historians, and the general public have interpreted particular aspects of design. Also published by Reaktion is John Elsner and Roger Cardinal (eds.), *The Culture of Collecting* 1994, which also provides useful insights into collecting and display from a range of psychological, theoretical, historical, and social perspectives.

Material culture, social anthropology, and the history of design
A number of design historians have laid increasing stress on studies in material culture and social anthropology as a means of moving attention away from the traditional design-historical emphasis on named designers and movements towards a focus on the consumption of design. Texts which are often cited in this context include Mary Douglas and Baron Isherwood, *The World of Goods: Towards an Anthropology of Consumption* (Allen Lane, London, 1975), Daniel Miller, *Material Culture and Mass-Consumption* (Blackwell, Oxford, 1987), and Grant McCracken, *New Approaches to the Symbolic Character of Consumer Goods and Activities* (Indiana Press, Bloomington, 1988). A more recent publication offers a number of possible approaches to the use of objects to interpret the past: Steven Lubar and W. David Kingary, *History from Things: Essays on Material Culture* (Smithsonian, Washington, DC, 1993). Perhaps of more immediate practical use to historians wishing to initiate an exploration of design from a consumer perspective are Tim Putnam and C. Newton (eds.), *Household Choices* (Futures Publications, London, 1990).

Encyclopaedias and dictionaries of design
There are also many indexes and encyclopaedias of twentieth-century design, of which one of the most affordable, Guy Julier, *Encyclopaedia of 20th Century Design and Designers* (Thames & Hudson, London, 1993), is one of the best, with a wide range of topics and intelligent definitions. Useful for the study of the history of graphic design is Alan and Isabel Livingstone, *Encyclopaedia of Graphic Design* (Thames & Hudson, London, 1992), which covers a wide variety of designers, countries, movements, periodicals, typefaces, and related concerns. Of larger-scale indexes with an emphasis on design the most useful and comprehensive in relation to recent design-historical writing and criticism is the *Design and Applied Arts Index* (Design Documentation, Bodiam, 1987–), which covers more than 200 periodicals and is available on CD-ROM. A number of design-related developments in the earlier part of the century are listed in the *Art Index* (H. Wilson, New York, 1933–). Although it covers the period from 1929 to the present day its design coverage is limited by the comparatively modest range of dedicated design periodicals embraced by its searches. Also useful for research into twentieth-century designers is the three-volume *Designers International Index* (Bowker-Saur, London, 1991). Edited by Janette Jagger and Roger Towe, it provides references to a wide range of designer-oriented published material throughout the century. In this respect Colin Naylor, *Contemporary Designers* (St James Press, London, 1990), is also a handy resource. However, it should be borne in mind that a number of such design-led publications tend to celebrate the success of

individual designers rather than provide any penetrating analysis of the wider social, cultural, or economic impact of design in everyday life, thus reinforcing many of the tendencies seen as limiting and partial by feminist historians, social anthropologists, and many of those active in the field of academic design historical research. Of considerable importance in the development of design-historical studies is the location of appropriate and useful primary sources. For this a good starting point is Gillian Varley, *Art & Design Documentation in the UK and Ireland: A Directory of Resources* (ARLIS/UK & Ireland, 1993).

Journals
In response to the growing interest of design historians in the consumption of design, studies in material culture, and the historical significance of social, economic, business, cultural, and other considerations, the range of journals carrying design historical material has expanded considerably over the past fifteen years. The *Journal of Design History* (Oxford University Press, 1988–), is the mainstream periodical in the field.

Twentieth-century industrialization, technological and cultural change
There are a number of books relating to the impact of industrialization on everyday life which provide a useful backcloth for the study of twentieth-century design. These include C. Singer (ed.), *A History of Technology*, v. *The Late Nineteenth Century, c. 1850–1900* (Clarendon Press, Oxford, 1958), H. J. Habakkuk, *American and British Technology in the Nineteenth Century* (Cambridge University Press, 1962), and S. B. Saul, *Technological Changes: the United States and Britain in the Nineteenth Century* (Methuen, London, 1970). More recent is Colin Chant (ed.), *Science, Technology and Everyday Life 1870–1950* (Open University/Routledge, London, 1989). Still useful is Siegfried Giedion, *Mechanisation Takes Command: A Contribution to Anonymous History* (Oxford University Press, 1948), which examines the ways in which technology has impinged upon human activities such as eating, sleeping, washing, and bathing. Encompassing broader cultural concerns are Raymond Williams, *Culture and Society 1780–1950* (Penguin, Harmondsworth, 1958), and C. Harvey, G. Martin, and A. Scharf, *Industrialization and Culture 1830–1914*, (Macmillan, London, 1970), which contains a number of key extracts from important original texts. Charles Harvey and Jon Press, *William Morris: Design and Enterprise in Victorian Britain* (Manchester University Press, 1991), provides a number of useful fresh insights into a widely-researched field and D. A. Hounshell's absorbing study, *From the American System to Mass Production 1800–1932* (Johns Hopkins University Press, Baltimore, 1984), is an extremely valuable tool for the study of design, society, and cultural change in the United States.

Later nineteenth- and early twentieth-century design: key texts
Design in the late nineteenth and early twentieth centuries has been widely covered in a number of publications including Gillian Naylor's important text *The Arts and Crafts Movement* (Studio Vista, London, 1971). Its subtitle, 'A Study of Sources, Ideals and Influences on Design Theory' indicated her location of the Arts and Crafts in a broader context, particularly in terms of its legacy for modernist designers. Turn-of-the-century developments are also the focus of Bernard Denvir's compilation of contemporary documents and criticism entitled *The Late Victorians: Art, Design and Society 1852–1910* (Longmans, London, 1988). Nikolaus Pevsner's classic *Pioneers of Modern Design: From William Morris to Walter Gropius* (Penguin, Harmondsworth, 1975), which had undergone a number of revisions since its appearance in 1936 as *Pioneers of Modern Movement*, traces a very particular line of development from mid-nineteenth-century design reform in England to progressive design thinking in Continental Europe, which acknowledged a more central place for the machine in design production. Herwin Schaefer, *The Roots of Modern Design* (Studio Vista, 1970), offers an alternative account of the emergence of a functional tradition in modernism of the early twentieth century, looking to its roots in the long-standing recognition of functionalism in vernacular design rather than the work of leading design reformers of the nineteenth century. Reyner Banham, *Theory and Design in the First Machine Age* (Architectural Press, 1960), another landmark text in the genesis of the history of design, provides a far more through-going analysis of early twentieth-century avant-garde movements, emphasizing the roles of Italian Futurism and Expressionism, which were largely ignored by Pevsner.

Design in Germany before 1918
German design for the years leading up to the

end of the First World War is well-covered in John Heskett, *Design in Germany 1870–1918* (Trefoil, London, 1986), which draws on a significant and fresh range of contemporary evidence. Also significant in scholarship for the period is Tilmann Buddensieg, *Industriekultur: Peter Behrens and the AEG* (MIT, Cambridge, Mass., 1984). Indispensable for an examination of the origins of the Deutscher Werkbund as well as the broader picture of cultural, political, and economic change, is Joan Campbell's scholarly book, *The German Werkbund: The Politics of Reform in the Applied Arts* (Princeton University Press, 1978). Examining the same period from a feminist perspective is Magdalena Droste's essay on 'Women in the Arts and Crafts and in Industrial Design 1890–1933', in *Frauen im Design: Berufsbilder und Lebenswege seit 1900* (Design Center, Stuttgart, 1989), 174–202.

French design before 1914
Although not considered at length in Chapter 1, French design has commanded a considerable literature, particularly at the luxury end of the market, such as C. Arminjon *et al.*, *L'Art de Vivre: Decorative Arts and Design in France 1789–1989* (Thames & Hudson, London, 1989). One of the best scholarly studies is Nancy Troy, *Modernism and the Decorative Arts in France: Art Nouveau to Le Corbusier* (Yale University Press, London, 1991).

Austrian design before the First World War
Many aspects of Austrian design are covered in Werner Schweiger, *Wiener Werkstätte: Design in Vienna 1903–1932* (Thames & Hudson, London, 1985), although the highly-researched and detailed text has received some mild criticism on account of the painstaking emphasis on detail at the possible expense of analysis of the wider social, cultural, and economic significance of design. More approachable in this respect is Jane Kallir, *Viennese Design and the Wiener Werkstätte* (Thames & Hudson, London, 1986).

Design in Italy in the early twentieth century
For Italian developments a general account is given in Penny Sparke, *Italian Design 1870 to the Present* (Thames & Hudson, London, 1988). More detailed in its coverage of industrial design of the period is Vittorio Gregotti, *Il disegno nel prodotto industriale* (Electa, Milan, 1982). For material relating to the late nineteenth and early twentieth centuries the essay by Manfredi Nicoletti on 'Art Nouveau in Italy', in Nikolaus Pevsner and J. M. Richards,

The Anti-Rationalists: Art Nouveau Architecture and Design (Architectural Press, London, 1973), covers much still relatively unfamiliar ground. (*The Anti-Rationalists* is also useful for many other aspects of turn-of-the century design in Spain, Austria, France, former Czechoslovakia, Hungary, Germany, and Britain.) Much of the passionate, violent, often misogynist, spirit of Futurism can be gleaned from a reading of their original proclamations, many of which are reprinted in Umberto Apollonio (ed.), *Futurist Manifestos* (Thames & Hudson, London, 1973). Dennis Doordan's essay on 'Political Things: Design in Fascist Italy', in Wendy Kaplan (ed.), *Designing Modernity: The Arts of Reform and Persuasion 1885–1945* (Wolfsonian/Thames & Hudson, Miami/ London, 1995), examines the politics of Futurism from its beginnings through to the Second World War. Many other facets of Futurism can be found in Pontus Hulten's well-illustrated *Futurism & Futurisms* (Thames & Hudson, London, 1987), which provides much detailed information on the subject, as does Caroline Tisdall and Angelo Bozzola, *Futurism* (Thames & Hudson, London, 1977).

2: Design and Modernism
Modernism has commanded a high profile in terms of design-historical publication for well over fifty years for the reasons outlined in the main body of the text. Related historiographic issues have been considered in the footnotes to the main text. A useful entry to a number of modernist debates may be found in Paul Greenhalgh (ed.), *Modernism in Design* (Manchester University Press; Reaktion, London, 1990), which examines the field from a number of ideological and national perspectives, including Germany, France, the United States, Britain, Sweden, Italy, and Spain. Particularly useful is Tim Benton's essay on 'The Myth of Function' in which the problems of using terms such as 'functionalism' are critically probed.

Modernism in German design
German modernism is addressed in a large number of texts. The activities of the Deutscher Werkbund, an organization keenly advocating modernism, are covered thoroughly in Joan Campbell's authoritative account, *The German Werkbund: The Politics of Reform in the Applied Arts* (Princeton University Press, 1978). Lucius Burckhardt (ed.), *The Werkbund: Studies in the History and Ideology of the Deutscher Werkbund 1907–1933* (Design Council, London, 1980), also examines the role of Werkbund

organizations in other countries in addition to Germany.

German modernism: the Bauhaus
As suggested in the main text, the Bauhaus, and the many publications emanating from it and its staff and students, has played an important role in the dissemination of a modernist ideology. H. M. Wingler, *The Bauhaus— Weimar, Dessau, Berlin, Chicago* (1962; new edn., MIT, Cambridge, Mass., 1977), charts this comprehensively, drawing extensively on archival documentation and photographs. The bibliography is also useful. Gillian Naylor, *The Bauhaus Reassessed: Sources and Design Theory* (Herbert Press, London, 1985), examines the theoretical outlook of Bauhaus teachers in a wider context. Also valuable in opening up debate about the early years of the Bauhaus is M. Franciscono, *Walter Gropius and the Creation of the Bauhaus in Weimar* (University of Illinois, Chicago, 1971). Giving a contemporary 1930s retrospective, and partial, view of the achievements of the Bauhaus is a book originally published to accompany a 1938 exhibition at the Museum of Modern Art, Herbert Bayer, Walter Gropius, and Ise Gropius, *Bauhaus 1919–1928* (1938; Secker & Warburg, London, 1975). Considerably later is the Royal Academy exhibition catalogue, *50 Years Bauhaus* (London, 1968), which provides a useful compendium of quotations, illustrations, and documents. For a rather different perspective reference should be made to S. W. Weltge, *Bauhaus Textiles: Women Artists and the Weaving Workshop* (Thames & Hudson, London, 1993), an area of Bauhaus activity often downplayed because most of the weavers were women. Magdalene Droste, in her essay on 'Women in the Arts and Crafts and Industrial Design' in *Frauen im Design* (above, p. 261), considers such issues as well as Gropius's attitudes to women. Droste has also written *Bauhaus: 1919–1933* (Bauhaus Archiv/Taschen, Cologne, 1990).

The Frankfurt kitchen and domestic organization
For discussion of the Frankfurt Kitchen see the essay in *Frauen im Design* (above, p. 261), 160–9, which also has a useful range of references. Another valuable essay on this theme is Nicholas Bullock, 'First the Kitchen—Then the Facade', in *AA Files* (May 1984, reprinted in the *Journal of Design History*, 1.3–4, 177–92), which also references widely, both with regard to German practice and American precedent and contemporary practice. Sonja Günter, *Lilly Reich 1885–1947:*

Innerarchitektin, Designerin, Ausstellungsgestalterin (Deutsche Verlagsanstalt, Stuttgart, 1988), discusses the work of an important woman designer in the field. Over the past twenty years there has been a growing literature focused on women and domestic technology. Ruth Schwartz Cowan has been an important contributor to such debates, commencing with her 1976 essay on 'The "Industrial Revolution" in the Home: Household Technology and Social Change in the Twentieth Century', which was reprinted in Thomas Schlereth (ed.), *Material Culture Studies in America* (American Association for State and Local History, Nashville, Tenn., 1982), a volume which contains other interesting work in the field of material culture. Cowan's book, *More Work for Mother: The Ironies of Household Technology from Open Hearth to the Microwave* (Pantheon, New York, 1983), is very useful. Periodicals such as *Technology and Culture* and the *Journal of American Culture* also offer a large number of articles on the theme.

Modernist design in France
For links between France and Germany see the weighty exhibition catalogue *Berlin/Paris: Rapports et Contrasts France-Allemagne 1900–1933* (Pompidou Centre, Paris, 1978), which covers a broad sweep of visual and cultural activity, including industrial design, graphic, and architecture, as well as literature, film, music, and theatre. It is well illustrated, and the essays are thoroughly referenced. For a discussion of the place of modernism in France in the interwar years Nancy Troy (above, p. 261) provides a scholarly insight. For Corbusier's own views *The Decorative Art of Today* (1925; trans. J. Dunnett, Architectural Association, London, 1987) provides a clear exposition.

De Stijl and modernism in the Netherlands
Nancy Troy, *The De Stijl Environment* (MIT, Cambridge, Mass., 1983), offers a thorough introduction to the work and theoretical concerns of the group, as does Paul Overy, *De Stijl* (Thames & Hudson, London, 1991). Useful also is C. Blotkamp *et al., De Stijl: The Formative Years* (MIT, Cambridge, Mass., 1982). Although in the main texts the emphasis on design has centred on the avant-garde, the modernist vocabulary was widely adopted in housing, leisure, and industrial development of the interwar years, and there is much useful material in the English language. Many aspects are taken up in the Stedelijk Museum's *Design in Industry in the Netherlands 1850–1950*, which

has useful introductory essays and information on a number of manufacturers and retail outlets. Although there is a strong architectural emphasis there are a number of good publications on modern architecture with useful sections on design. These include the Stedelijk Museum, *Het Nieuwe Bouwen: Amsterdam 1920–1980* (University of Delft, 1982), and Boymans-van Beuningen Museum, *Het Nieuwe Bouwen in Rotterdam 1920–1960* (University of Delft, 1982), both of which have a full English translation.

Scandinavian modernism in the interwar years

For Scandinavian design see D. McFadden (ed.), *Scandinavian Modern Design 1880–1980* (Abrams, New York, 1982), which presents a well-illustrated overview of the field, though never penetrating deeply into the wider social, economic, or political circumstances in which design was produced and consumed. On a more focused plane Jennifer Opie, *Scandinavian Ceramics & Glass in the Twentieth Century* (Victoria and Albert Museum, London, 1989), offers some useful distinctions between designs in the different Scandinavian countries, with a sound discussion of modern movement concerns, as does E. Zahle (ed.), *Scandinavian Domestic Design* (Methuen, London, 1963). Gillian Naylor's essay on 'Swedish Grace . . . or the Acceptable Face of Modernism', in P. Greenhalgh (above, p. 261) is a sound and interesting account of developments in Sweden, with a good range of references. The essays by Penny Sparke and Arthur Hald in Nicola Hamilton (ed.), *Svensk Form: A Conference About Swedish Design* (Design Council, London, 1981), are also good summaries of contemporary Swedish issues. For Swedish furniture design of the period a valuable insight is afforded by Gunilla Frick's essay 'Furniture Art or a Machine to Sit On? Swedish Furniture and Radical Reforms', *Scandinavian Journal of Design History* (Danish Museum Of Decorative Art, Copenhagen), 1 (1991), 77–116. For Finnish design in a number of media, see G. Schildt, *Alvar Aalto: The Complete Catalogue of Architecture, Design and Art* (Academy, London, 1994), a comprehensive and exhaustive study of Aalto's work.

Modern design in Britain between the wars

Still useful in discussions of modernism in Britain is the Hayward Gallery exhibition catalogue, *Thirties—British Art and Design before the War* (Arts Council, London, 1979), with introductory essays, many illustrations, and bibliography. Fiona MacCarthy, *A History*

of British Design 1830–1979 (Allen & Unwin, London, 1979), provides an overview although from a perspective largely sympathetic to the Design and Industries Association, which wavered between the progressive tenets of the avant-garde in Europe and the legacy of the Arts and Crafts. Noel Carrington, *Industrial Design in Britain* (Allen & Unwin, London, 1976), covers similar territory. The earlier sections of my own brief text *The Industrial Designer and the Public* (Pembridge, London, 1983), provide a rather broader perspective. From a very different and highly significant perspective D. L. LeMahieu, *A Culture for Democracy: Mass Communication and the Cultivated Mind between the Wars* (Clarendon Press, Oxford, 1988), offers a thorough analysis of the cultural location of the modernist debate in England.

Italian modernism

The modern movement in Italy is succinctly discussed in Leonardo Benevolo's essay on 'The Beginning of Modern Research 1930–1940', in Emilio Ambasz (ed.), *Italy: the New Domestic Landscape* (Museum of Modern Art, New York, 1972). Ellen Shapiro's article 'The Emergence of Italian Rationalism', in *Architectural Design*, 51. 1/2 (1981), and Bruno Zevi, 'Gruppo 7: the Rise and Fall of Italian Rationalism' in the same issue, both provide good, brief introductions to the national and international aspirations of the group, whilst Silvia Danesi and Luciano Patteta, *Il razionalismo e l'architettura durante il fascismo* (Electa, Milan, 1976), offers a more comprehensive and well-illustrated catalogue of architectural developments. A broader overview of key developments in Italy is provided by Penny Sparke, *Italian Design 1870 to the Present* (Thames & Hudson, London, 1988).

Modernism in Eastern Europe

G. Gibian and H. W. Tjalsma (eds.), *Russian Modernism: Culture and the Avant-Garde, 1900–1930* (Cornell University Press, New York, 1988), introduces many key issues in Russia. D. Elliott, *New Worlds: Russian Art and Society* (Thames & Hudson, London, 1986), and *Art into Production: Soviet Textiles, Fashion and Ceramics 1917–35* (Museum of Modern Art, Oxford, 1984), I. Yasinskaya, *Soviet Textile Design of the Revolutionary Period* (Thames & Hudson, London, 1983), N. Lobanov-Rostovsky, *Revolutionary Ceramics: Soviet Porcelain 1917–1927* (Studio Vista, London, 1990), all provide useful information, written and visual. For packaging and poster design see M. Anikst (ed.), *Soviet Commercial Design of the Twenties* (Thames & Hudson/Alexandra Press, London, 1987), and S. White, *The Bolshevik Poster* (Yale University Press, New Haven, 1988). There are a number of monographs on individual designers of which S. O. Khan-Magomedov, *Alexander Rodchenko: the Complete Work* (MIT, Cambridge, Mass., 1987), is one of the most informative. For other aspects of Eastern European modernism see David Crowley's authoritative, well-written and referenced *National Style and Nation State: Design in Poland from the Vernacular Revival to the International Style* (Manchester University Press, 1992). Exhibition catalogues provide useful introductory studies in the English language to a number of design themes in eastern Europe, though almost always centred on the avant-garde. Useful examples include *Constructivism in Poland 1923–1926* (Kettle's Yard, Cambridge, 1986), *Constructivism in Poland 1923–1926* (Museum Folkwang, Essen, 1973), and *Czech Avant-Garde Art, Architecture and Design of the 1920s and 30s* (Museum of Modern Art, Oxford/Design Museum, London, 1990). Reference may also be made to V. Slapeta, *Czech Functionalism 1918–1938* (Architectural Association, London, 1987).

3: Commerce, Consumerism, and Design
Industrial design in the United States
Jeffrey Meikle, *Twentieth Century Limited—Industrial Design in America* (Temple University Press, Philadelphia, 1979), is one of the most reliable and thorough considerations of American interwar design, locating it within a broad social, economic, and cultural context. Particularly valuable is his discussion of sources, which range from archives, indexes, and periodicals through to contemporary and historical texts. (His survey of literature centred on the history of American design, but within a broader American studies framework, 'American Design History: A Bibliography of Sources and Interpretations', *American Studies International*, 23. 1 (April 1985), 3–40, is another key source for American design-historical study.) Less demanding, but providing a useful overview, is Donald J. Bush, *The Streamlined Decade* (Braziller, New York, 1975), although it inclines towards a style-oriented account. Arthur J. Pulos, *American Design Ethic, A History of American Industrial Design to 1940* (MIT, Cambridge, Mass., 1983), written from the perspective of a designer, provides an informative examination of many significant

developments in the period under discussion. Conceived in relation to a major exhibition at Brooklyn Museum was the comprehensive, well-illustrated text by R. G. Wilson *et al.*, *The Machine Age in America 1918–1941* (Abrams, New York, 1986), which addresses the theme from a variety of cultural perspectives. A thorough analysis of advertising and consumption patterns in the interwar years is provided by Roland Marchand, *Advertising the American Dream: Making Way for Modernity 1920–1940* (University of California Press, Berkeley, 1985).

American exhibitions and the technological imperative
For the large-scale exhibitions of the period see J. E. Findling, *Chicago's Great Worlds Fairs* (Manchester University Press, 1995), Robert W. Rydell, *World of Fairs: the Century of Progress Expositions* (University of Chicago Press, 1993), and chapter 9 of J. Meikle (see above) which focuses on the New York World's Fair of 1939/40 and is well referenced. For visual information reference may be made to Richard Wurts, *The New York World's Fair 1939/40* (Dover, New York, 1977), and Larry Zim *et al.*, *The World of Tomorrow: The New York World's Fair* (Harper & Row, New York, 1988).

Wider concerns in American interwar design: interiors, architecture, and housing
Karen Davies's exhibition catalogue on the theme of *At Home in Manhattan: Modern Decorative Arts, 1925 to the Depression* (Yale University Art Gallery, New Haven, 1983) is well worth examining and contains a number of useful references. Covering American as well as European issues, with a leaning towards the decorative arts, are two important and very readable texts by Martin Battersby, *The Decorative Twenties* (1969) and *The Decorative Thirties* (1971), both republished in revised editions by Herbert, London, in 1989. Alastair Duncan, *American Art Deco* (Thames & Hudson, London, 1986), C. Robinson and R. H. Bletter, *Skyscraper Style: Art Deco New York* (Oxford University Press, New York, 1975), Carol Krinsky, *Rockefeller Center* (Oxford University Press, 1978), and H. Wirz and R. Striner, *Washington Deco: Art Deco in the Nation's Capital* (Smithsonian, Washington, DC, 1984), are among the more useful of the many books devoted to American Deco. The cinema is also an important vehicle for conveying stylistic ideas both modernizing and historicizing, whether in the buildings themselves or on the screen.

Reference may be made to D. Naylor, *American Picture Palaces: the Architecture of Fantasy* (Van Nostrand Rinehold, New York, 1981), Thames Television, *The Art of Hollywood* (London, 1979), D. Atwell, *Cathedrals of the Movies* (Architectural Press, London, 1981), and D. Sharp, *The Picture Palace* (Thames & Hudson, London, 1969).

Design and everyday life in the United States
For many aspects of everyday (as well as designer-conceived) furniture production reference should be made in Sharon Darling's scholarly *Chicago Furniture: Art, Craft, & Industry, 1833–1983* (Norton, New York, 1984). Wider patterns of housing may be examined in Gwendolyn Wright, *Building the Dream: A Social History of Housing* (Pantheon, New York, 1981), whilst something of vernacular roadside culture may be gleaned from collections of photographs with brief texts, such as P. Hirschorn, *White Towers* (MIT, Cambridge, Mass., 1979). From a sociological perspective the contemporary way of life is examined in R. S. and H. M. Lynd, *Middletown: A Study in Contemporary American Culture* and *Middletown in Transition: A Study in Cultural Conflicts*, both published by Harcourt Brace, New York, in 1929 and 1937, respectively.

French design and commerce in the interwar years
Many aspects of French Art Deco may be seen in Yvonne Brunhammer, *The Nineteen Twenties Style* (Paul Hamlyn, London, 1969), the collected essays in *Cinquantenaire de L'Exposition de 1925* (Musée des Arts Décoratifs, Paris, 1977), Patricia Bayer, *Art Deco Interiors: Decorative and Design Classics of the 1920s* (Thames & Hudson, London, 1990), and Nancy Troy (above, p. 262).

British design and commerce in the interwar years
Nikolaus Pevsner, *An Enquiry into Industrial Art in England* (Cambridge University Press, 1937), presents a survey of patterns of taste in Britain of the 1930s, showing many of the best selling lines across a range of products. Several of the chapters, especially 7 and 8, in Paul Oliver *et al., Dunroamin: The Suburban Semi and Its Enemies* (Barrie & Jenkins, London, 1981), look at everyday commercial consumption in aspects of home decoration and furnishing. Looking across the broad spectrum of design activity and consumer goods is the Hayward exhibition catalogue, *The Thirties* (Arts Council, London, 1979). The whole area of shopping and consumerism may be approached through Bill Lancaster,

The Department Store: A Social History (Leicester University Press, London, 1995).

4: Design and National Identity

A useful, succinct introduction to issues of national identity is Jeremy Aynsley's *Nationalism and Internationalism: Design in the 20th Century* (Victoria and Albert Museum, London, 1993). Nicola Gordon Bowe (ed.), *Art and the National Dream: the Search for Turn of the Century Vernacular Design* (Irish Academic Press, Dublin, 1993), provides interesting insights from various national perspectives offered by leading specialists, as does the well-illustrated collection of essays in Wendy Kaplan (ed.), *Designing Modernity: The Arts of Reform and Persuasion 1885–1945* (Wolfsonian/Thames & Hudson, Miami/ London, 1995).

National identities as represented at international exhibitions
International exhibitions, venues where the projection of national identity and cultural values has been an important consideration, are well covered in Paul Greenhalgh, *Ephemeral Vistas: Expositions Universelles, Great Exhibitions and World's Fairs, 1851–1939* (Manchester University Press, 1988), which also contains a useful bibliography of major sources. The large exhibition catalogue, *Art and Power: Europe Under the Dictators 1930–45* (Hayward Gallery, London, 1995), provides an important range of essays. Centred on the Paris International Exhibition of 1937, Rome, Moscow, and Berlin, they provide an excellent flavour of contemporary political and cultural tensions and their visual and material expression. The historian Eric Hobsbawm offers some interesting thoughts in *Nations and Nationalism since 1750 — Programme, Myth, Reality* (Cambridge University Press, 1990).

Design and identity in Germany
B. Taylor and W. van der Will (eds.), *The Nazification of Art: Art, Design, Music, Architecture and Film in the Third Reich* (Winchester Press, Winchester, 1990), contains many useful essays for study of the key issues, particularly that by John Heskett on 'Modernism and Archaism in the Third Reich', reprinted from 1980. Heskett further develops this idea in Wendy Kaplan (see above) in 'Design in Inter-War Germany'. B. Hinz, *Art in the Third Reich* (Blackwell, Oxford, 1980), has something to say of design in his discussion of art and architecture of the period. For a broad insight into the social

and political context see e.g. D. F. Crewe, *Nazism and German Society 1933–45* (Routledge, London, 1994).

British design and national identity
Frederique Huygen, *British Design: Image and Identity* (Thames & Hudson, London, 1989), is interesting as a foreign appraisal of British design by the design curator at the Boymans Van Beuningen Museum, Rotterdam. Also raising some interesting issues is Paul Greenhalgh's essay in Wendy Kaplan (see above) on 'The English Compromise: Modern Design and National Consciousness 1870–1940'. John Taylor, *A Dream of England: Landscape, Photography and the Tourist's Imagination* (Manchester University Press, 1994), provides a compelling insight into a range of concerns from a documentary standpoint and also provides an extremely useful bibliography. A number of essays in Raphael Samuel (ed.), *Patriotism: the Making and Unmaking of British National Identity*, vols. 1, 2, and 3 (Routledge, London, 1989), provide useful historical adjuncts to the discussion. Imperialism was an important ingredient in material culture of the period and many aspects are covered in John Mackenzie (ed.), *Imperialism and Popular Culture* (Manchester University Press, 1986) and *Propaganda and Empire— the Manipulation of British Public Opinion 1880–1960* (Manchester University Press, 1985).

Other useful texts
Commune di Milano, *L'anni trenta, arte e cultura in Italia* (Mazotta, Milan, 1982), is a very comprehensive coverage of almost all aspects of design in the 1930s. David Crowley, *National Style and Nation State: Design in Poland from the Vernacular Revival to the International Style* (Manchester University Press, 1992), provides an engaging account of the tensions between national and international identity.

5: The Second World War: Reconstruction and Affluence
General surveys
K. Hiesinger, *Design Since 1945* (Thames & Hudson/Philadelphia Museum of Art, London, 1983), provides a broad, rather art-historically conceived survey of major developments in design for the home and is subdivided into various design media. There are many other survey volumes such as Peter Dormer, *Design Since 1945* (Thames & Hudson, London, 1993), but they are mainly rather lightweight surveys with the emphasis on style

rather than examination of issues of economics or consumption. A useful overview of more helpful published sources may be found in Victor Margolin, 'Postwar Design Literature: A Preliminary Mapping', in Margolin (ed.), *Design Discourse: History, Theory, Criticism* (University of Chicago, 1989).

Postwar developments in design in the United States
For a broad view of postwar developments in the United States reference may be made to Arthur J. Pulos, *The American Design Adventure 1940–1975* (MIT, Cambridge, Mass., 1988). George Nelson and Henry Wright, *Tomorrow's House: A Complete House for the Home-Builder* (Simon and Schuster, New York, 1946), was widely read in the immediate postwar housing drive. Nelson's outlook as a designer is comprehensively covered in Stanley Abercrombie, *George Nelson: the Design of Modern Design* (MIT, Cambridge, Mass., 1995), which also contains a full bibliography. For a broader picture of American housing styles and aspirations Gwendolyn Wright, *Building the Dream: A Social History of Housing in America* (Pantheon, New York, 1981).

Design and consumption in the United States in the postwar years
Other dimensions of suburban life can be seen in Herbert Gans's dense study, *The Levittowners: Ways of Life and Politics in a New Suburban Community* (Pantheon, New York, 1967). Also revealing is the gender perspective afforded by Betty Friedan's classic *The Feminine Mystique* (1963); Penguin, Harmondsworth, 1965), which examines the pressures on American suburban women to conform to a particular set of social mores.

Indispensable as a catalyst for thought about consumerist aspiration of the 1950s is Thomas Hine, *Populuxe* (Bloomsbury, London, 1987), although its use for further research is limited by a lack of references. Stephen Bayley, *Harley Earl and the Dream Machine* (Weidenfeld & Nicolson, London, 1990), provides a glamorous account of exuberant car styling, with references also to the involvement of women in the design process. Looking at the wider picture of influences on consumption are texts such as Karal Ann Marling, *As Seen on TV: The Visual Culture of Everyday Life in America in the 1950s* (Harvard University Press, Cambridge, Mass., 1994).

Design in Italy after 1945
Surveys of postwar Italian design are provided

in Anty Pansera and Alfonso Grassi, *Atlante del Design Italiano 1940–1980* (Fabbri, Milan, 1980), and their *L'Italia del Design: Trent'Anni del Dibattito* (Marietti, Casale Monferrato, 1986); still handy is V. Gregotti's essay, 'Italian Design 1945–1971', in Emilio Ambasz (ed.), *Italy: The New Domestic Landscape—Achievements and Problems of Italian Design* (MOMA, New York, 1973). Many concerns of the avant-garde are covered in the appropriate chapters in Andrea Branzi, *The Hot House: Italian New Wave Design* (Thames & Hudson, London, 1984). *Il Design Italiano degli Anni '50* (Editoriale Domus, Milan, 1985), usefully covers the work of a number of leading designers and firms in the period. For consideration of a wider range of social, political, cultural, and economic issues Z. Baranski and R. Lumley, *Culture and Conflict in Postwar Italy* (Macmillan, London, 1990), is helpful. Penny Sparke, ' "A Home for Everybody?": Design, Ideology and the Culture of Home in Italy, 1945–1972', in P. Greenhalgh (above, p. 261), examines a wide range of social and cultural issues in her examination of design.

British design 1940–1960
In Britain Utility design is succinctly covered in J. Daniels, *Utility Furniture and Fashion 1941–1951* (Geffrye Museum, London, 1974). Penny Sparke (ed.), *Did Britain Make It? Critical Issues in British Design of the Last 40 Years* (Design Council, London, 1986), contains a number of useful essays about a variety of aspects of British design since 1945. The second half of my own study, *The Industrial Design and the Public* (Pembridge, London 1983), covers the same period and provides a range of references and bibliography. Very useful for following up a number of directions in Anthony Coulson, *A Bibliography of British Design 1851–1970* (Design Council, London, 1979). For the 1950s Lesley Jackson, *The New Look—Design in the Fifties* (Thames & Hudson, London, 1991), straightforwardly charts design of the period with an inclination towards the higher echelons of the marketplace. S. Macdonald and J. Porter, *Putting on the Style: Setting Up Home in the 1950s* (Geffrye Museum, London, 1990), is rather more ambitious in its approach.

Japanese design after the Second World War
For design in Japan see Penny Sparke, *Japanese Design* (Michael Joseph, London, 1987). For a broad consideration of changing Western cultural responses to Japan

Endymion Wilkinson, *Japan versus Europe* (Penguin, Harmondsworth, 1983), provides an interesting perspective. Joseph J. Tobin (ed.), *Re-Made in Japan: Everyday Life and Consumer Taste in a Changing Society* (Yale University Press, New Haven, 1992), examines many aspects of consumerism in Japan, with a useful introductory essay by the editor.

Other European design developments after 1945
Other European developments may be studied in G. Staal and H. Wolters (eds.), *Design in the Netherlands 1945–1987* (Stichting Holland in Vorm, Gravenhage, 1987), a wide-ranging, well-illustrated study, *Les Années 50* (Centre Georges Pompidou, Paris, 1988). For Germany see M. Erlhoff (ed.), *Designed in Germany since 1949* (Prestel, Munich, 1990), which provides a broad picture of German postwar design. An overview may also be found in H. Fuchs and F. Burckhardt, *Product-Design-History: German Design from 1820 down to the Present Era* (Institute of Foreign Cultural Relations, Stuttgart, 1985).

Eastern European design after 1945
Eastern European design developments in the postwar years are not generally well covered. However, for developments in Poland David Crowley, 'Building the World Anew: Design in Stalinist and Post-Stalinist Poland', *Journal of Design History*, 7.3 (1994), 187–203, provides important insights. Containing an interesting range of illustrations and charting a broad picture of Russian design since the First World War is Alexander N. Lavrantiev and Yuri V. Nasarov, *Russian Design: Tradition and Experiment 1920–1991* (Architectural Design, London, 1995). For a comprehensive visual survey and year-by-year chronology of design developments in postwar Hungary see *Örökség: Tárgy— és Környezetkultúra Magyarországon/Heritage: Design and Man-Made Environment in Hungary* (Mücsarn ok Design Center, Budapest, 1985). For very much more recent developments the essays on Hungary and Russia by Hugh Aldersey-Williams in *Nationalism and Globalism in Design* (Rizzoli, New York, 1992) provide a gloss. More substantial is Angela Schönberger (ed.), *The East German Take-Off: Economy and Design in Transition* (Ernst & Sohn, Berlin, 1994), which contains a number of short essays about design since November 1989 and was produced to accompany a travelling exhibition of the same title.

6: Multinational Corporations and Global Products

General trends in the literature of the history of design and multinationals

There has been a considerable growth of literature in this area of design and business activity, although it has tended to be dominated by a journalistic, pro-corporate, outlook. Hugh Aldersley-Williams in *Nationalism and Globalism in Design* (Rizzoli, New York, 1992) covers a wide range of issues in the recent past, examining developments in a range of mainline industrialized nations in Europe, Scandinavia, North America, and the Far East, but also including emerging competitors such as South Korea and Singapore. India and Egypt are also considered. More typical of the general literature in the field is Murray J. Lubliner, *Global Corporate Identity: the Cross-Border Marketing Challenge* (Rockport Publishers, Rockport, Me., 1994), a slickly presented set of case studies of companies with large multinational clients.

The documentation of corporate design: self-promotion and self-appraisal

As indicated in the main text, design consultants and companies have themselves written about the importance of corporate design as an element of business strategy. The problems that this can raise for design historians are carefully appraised in Steve Baker, 'Re-reading *The Corporate Personality*', *Journal of Design History*, 2.4 (1989), 272–95. As the title of the article may indirectly suggest, Wally Olins, *The Corporate Personality: An Enquiry into the Nature of Corporate Identity* (Design Council, London, 1978), is considered to be an important text in this vein; Olins, a leading consultant on corporate design, has also written *Corporate Identity: Making Business Strategy Visible through Design* (Thames & Hudson, London, 1989). Other books written from a design-oriented perspective include F. H. K. Henrion and A. Parker, *Design Co-ordination and Corporate Image* (Studio Vista, London, 1967), John and Avril Blake, *The Practical Idealists: Twenty-Five Years of Designing for Industry* (Lund Humphries, London, 1969), James Pilditch, *Communication by Design: A Study in Corporate Identity* (McGraw-Hill, Maidenhead, 1970), and David Bernstein, *Company Image and Reality: A Critique of Corporate Communications* (Holt, Rinehart & Winston, Eastbourne, 1984).

Design consultancies have also produced their own celebrations of success in the publication of case studies. This genre is typified by Peter Gorb (ed.), *Living by Design: the Pentagram Partnership* (Lund Humphries, London 1978). Corporations also have had numerous supportive studies devoted to their activities, often sponsored and published by themselves, such as the catalogue for the Frederick S. Wight Art Gallery, UCLA, *Design Process Olivetti 1908–1978* (Olivetti, 1979); Stephen Bayley, *Coke! Coca-Cola 1886–1986: Designing a Megabrand* (Conran Foundation, London, 1986), and *Sony Design* (Conran Associates, London, 1982), play a similar promotional role, as does the text by A. Morita, *Made in Japan: Akio Morita and Sony* (HarperCollins, New York, 1994). The German company Braun is the main focus of Francois Burckhardt and Inez Franksen, *Design: Dieter Rams &* (Gerhardt, Berlin, 1981). Other corporate histories may be traced in books such as N. Fry, *The IBM World* (Eyre Methuen, London, 1974). Among the more penetrating analyses of design within a corporate set-up has been John Heskett, *Philips: A Study of the Corporate Management of Design* (Trefoil, London, 1989), which provides an account of the design policy of one company, although it too is tinged with partiality.

Multinational cultural trends: the promotion of 'Good Design'

The literature of a Good Design aesthetic in America emerged positively in the 1930s with the MOMA, New York, 1934 *Machine Art* Exhibition but gained a considerable impetus through the output of the museum in the post-Second World War period. Arthur Drexler and Greta Daniel, *Introduction to the 20th Century Design from the Collection of the Museum of Modern Art* (MOMA, New York, 1959), promoted a very modernist viewpoint whilst Edgar Kaufmann, Jr. in *What is Modern Design?* (MOMA, New York, 1959), moved more emphatically towards a definition of Good Design, a theme taken up in the exhibitions of the same name which ran from 1950 to 1955. For a historical critique of such developments see Terence Riley and Edward Eigen's essay 'Between the Museum and the Marketplace: Selling Good Design', in MOMA, *The Museum of Modern Art at Mid-Century: At Home and Abroad* (MOMA/Abrams, New York, 1994), 150–79, which contains many useful references to MOMA's propagandist outlook of the 1950s, particularly with regard to the large retailing display at the Merchandise Mart, Chicago. This Good Design ethos, rooted in the modernist aesthetic of the interwar years (but divorced from any of its wider social and political involvements), also found expression in the furniture and interiors of many companies, often produced by firms such as Herman Miller and Knoll. For these see Ralph Caplan, *The Design of Herman Miller* (Whitney Library of Design, New York, 1976), and E. Larrabee and M. Vignelli, *Knoll Design* (1981; Abrams, New York, 1989). For designers involved in corporate work see e.g. Paul Rand, *Thought on Design* (1946; rev. edn., Studio Vista, London, 1970), and *A Designer's Art* (Yale University Press, New Haven, 1985), or Pat Kirkham, *Charles & Ray Eames: Designers of the Twentieth Century* (MIT, Cambridge, Mass., 1995).

Broader horizons and critiques of corporate power
Giving a broader cultural perspective of American developments is J. S. Allen, *The Romance of Commerce and Culture* (University of Chicago Press, 1983). For other perspectives, the American economist J. K. Galbraith refers critically to the enormous power wielded by corporations in *The New Industrial State* (Hamish Hamilton, London, 1967), as does G. Bannock in *The Juggernauts: the Age of the Big Corporation* (Penguin, Harmondsworth, 1973). More radical in its criticism is A. Mattelart, *Multinational Corporations and the Control of Culture: the Ideological Apparatuses of Imperialism* (Harvester, Brighton, 1979).

7: Design Promotion, the Design Profession, and Design Management
The design profession
The development of the design profession has been covered in Penny Sparke's brief volume, *Consultant Design: The History and Practice of the Designer in Industry* (Pembridge, London, 1983), which traces the main threads from the nineteenth century through to the 1980s. Much of the shaping of the design profession took place in the United States in the 1920s and 1930s, as discussed in Chapter 3, as well as in the context of multinational corporations and the growth of corporate identity in the post-1945 era examined in Chapter 6. Since the Second World War design management has emerged as an increasingly important preoccupation of the profession, following on from publications such as Herbert Read (ed.), *The Practice of Design* (Lund Humphries, London, 1946), Joshua Gordon Lipincott, *Design for Business* (Paul Theobald, Chicago, 1954) and Dorothy Goslett, *The Professional Practice of Design* (1960; rev. edn., Batsford, London, 1971).

Systematic approaches to design and the design methods movement
The development of a systematic approach to design was an increasingly important consideration for designers seeking wider professional validation, an outlook endorsed in the curriculum of the Hochschule für Gestaltung (HfG) at Ulm, the literature for which has been surveyed by Robin Kinross in a review article in the *Journal of Design History*, 1.3–4 (1988), 249–56. The institution's own journal, *Ulm*, published between 1958 and 1959, and again from 1962 to 1968, with text in German and English, is the most direct way of gaining an insight into the curriculum, as well as the ideology of both staff and students. Worthy of attention also is H. Lindinger (ed.), *Ulm Design: the Mortality of Objects, Hochschule für Gestaltung* (Ernst and Sohn, Berlin, 1990). Following on from developments in Ulm in the late 1950s and 1960s an interest in design methods emerged with key publications such as D. G. Thornley (ed.), *Conference on Design Methods* (Pergamon, Oxford, 1963), which contained a number of landmark essays by Christopher Alexander, J. Christopher Jones, and others. L. Bruce Archer's *Systematic Method for Designers* (Council of Industrial Design, London, 1965), reveals an Ulm-influenced outlook, whilst a more rounded approach can be examined in J. Christopher Jones, *Design Methods: Seeds of Human Futures* (Wiley, London, 1970). Significant also for such thinking has been Nigel Cross who has written extensively in the field, including *Design Methods Manual* (Open University, Milton Keynes, 1975).

Design management
Michael Farr, *Design Management* (Hodder & Stoughton, London, 1966), was a significant landmark in the development of the field, one which assumed particular importance in the 1980s and 1990s. The Society of Industrial Artists and Designers' (SIAD) Design Management Group was founded in London in 1981, publishing *Design Management Seminars* (SIAD, London, 1983). In similar vein the London Business School Design Management Seminars, which dealt with such issues as design identity, corporate strategy, and product innovation, were published through another key figure in the definition and development of the field, Peter Gorb. His edited papers, *London Business School: Design Talks* (Design Council, London, 1988), were followed by another set, also edited by him, entitled *Design Management: Papers*

from the London Business School (Architecture, Design & Technology Press, London, 1990). Other publications include M. Oakley, (ed.), *Design Management: A Handbook of Issues and Methods* (Blackwell, Oxford, 1990), and Liz Lydiate (ed.), *Professional Practice in Design Consultancy: A Design Business Association Guide* (Design Council, London, 1992). Anne Valkonen (ed.), *Qualities of Success* (University of Industrial Arts, Helsinki, 1993), contains eleven essays drawn from the proceedings of the Second International Conference of Design Management at the University, relating to such themes as corporate identity and design management education.

8: Pop to Post-Modernism: The Assault on Modernism

Pop design: its origins and influence
Pop design has been covered in texts such as Nigel Whiteley, *Pop Design: Modernism to Mod* (Design Council, Design Council, 1987), which contains a wide number of references to contemporary articles as well as a large number of illustrations. Useful too, in its focus on the significance of mass-culture in Britain after the war, is Anne Massey, *The Independent Group: Modernism and Mass Culture in Britain, 1945–1959* (Manchester University Press, 1995), which has an excellent bibliography. Of particular value is chapter 8, 'The Myth of the Independent Group: Historiography and Hagiology', which demonstrates the shortcomings of traditional interpretations of the Group's cultural location in British art and design of the period. Something of a contemporary critical outlook on design may be gleaned from one of the key participants, in Richard Hamilton, *Collected Words* (Thames & Hudson, London, 1992). The activities of Archigram are covered in Peter Cook, *Archigram* (Studio Vista, 1972). Certain aspects of the wider influence of Pop in Italy may be seen in chapter VI, 'Pop Realism', of Andrea Branzi (above, p. 267), or in Penny Sparke, *Ettore Sottsas Jr.* (Design Council, London, 1982).

Some key texts relating to Post-Modernism
There has been an extensive literature devoted to Post-Modern design, early considerations emerging in such texts as Gillo Dorfles, *Il Disegno e la sua Estetica* (Capelli Editore, Bologna, 1963), and Robert Venturi's landmark *Complexity and Contradiction in Modern Architecture* (Museum of Modern Art, New York, 1966). Also widely influential has been Robert Venturi, D. Scott Brown,

and S. Izenour, *Learning from Las Vegas* (MIT, Cambridge, Mass., 1972). Other well-known contributions have included Charles Jencks's two books, *The Language of Post-Modern Architecture* (Academy, London, 1973), and *What Is Postmodernism?* (Academy, London, 1986). John Thackera (ed.), *Design After Modernism: Beyond the Object* (Thames & Hudson, 1988), also contains useful material; well-illustrated is Michael Collins and Andreas Papadakis, *Post-Modern Design* (Rizzoli, New York, 1989). Architectural Design, *The Post-modern Object: AD. An Art and Design Profile* (Academy, London, 1987) provides another survey. A more theoretical perspective is embraced in B. C. Brolin, *Flight of Fancy: the Banishment and Return of Ornament* (Academy, London, 1985); also useful in this respect are D. Harvey, *The Condition of Postmodernity: An Enquiry into the Origins of Cultural Change* (Oxford University Press, 1990), and J.-F. Lyotard, *The Post-Modern Condition: A Report on Knowledge*, (1986); translated for Manchester University Press, 1989). John Docker, in *Postmodernism and Popular Culture: A Cultural History* (Cambridge University Press, 1995), considers the problems of analysis of consumption in a stimulating manner, providing a number of potential approaches for the contemporary design historian.

Post–Modern design: the international dimension
The international nature of Post-Modernism is exemplified by Memphis, for which there is an extensive literature. Barbara Radice, *Memphis* (Thames & Hudson, London, 1984), gives an informative, if descriptive, account of the group's aims and achievements, and is ultimately more useful than texts such as Richard Horn, *Memphis: Objects, Furniture and Patterns* (Running Press/Quarto, Philadelphia, 1985). Many wider issues concerning design and decoration across the whole period are considered in Volker Fischer (ed.), *Design Now: Industry or Art?* (Prestel, Munich, 1989). A number of national perspectives may be seen in Hugh Aldersley-Williams, *New American Design: Products and Graphics for a Post Modern Age* (Rizzoli, New York, 1988), Andrea Branzi (above, p. 267), and John Thackera, *New British Design* (Thames & Hudson, London, 1986). For a different cultural perspective there are a number of useful essays in M. Miyoshi and H. Harootunian (eds.), *Postmodernism in Japan* (Duke University Press, Durham, NC, 1989).

9: Nostalgia, Heritage, and Design

There has been a considerable body of writing about tradition, nostalgia, and heritage over the past twenty years, the 1980s being a prolific decade in this respect. Although the literature cited below is mainly centred on British publications, such concerns have emerged elsewhere. Nostalgia and tradition have resonances in design and marketing in many other countries, including Japan, as seen in M. Ivy's essay on 'Critical Texts, Mass Artefacts: the Consumption of Knowledge in Postmodern Japan', in M. Miyoshi and H. Hirootunian (above, p. 270).

Amongst the more noteworthy contributions by British authors have been David Lowenthal, *The Past Is a Foreign Country* (Cambridge University Press, 1985), Robert Hewison, *The Heritage Industry* (Methuen, London, 1987), and Patrick Wright, *On Living In an Old Country* (Verso, London, 1985) all of which were important landmarks. Useful also are the articles on historical representation contained in Robert Lumley (ed.), *The Museum Time-Machine* (Routledge, London, 1988). Eric Hobsbawm and Trevor Ranger (eds.), *The Invention of Tradition* (1983; Cambridge University Press, 1992), also provides an interesting range of differing approaches to the subject. Other useful texts include John Corner and Sylvia Harvey (eds.), *Enterprise and Heritage: Crosscurrents of National Culture* (Routledge, London, 1991), Russell Keat and Nicholas Abercrombie (eds.), *Enterprise Culture* (Routledge, London, 1991), K. Walsh, *The Representation of the Past: Museums and Heritage in the Post-Modern World* (Routledge, London, 1992), and Peter J. Fowler, *The Past in Contemporary Society: Then, Now* (Routledge, London, 1992), which examines the issue of heritage from many standpoints, albeit conditioned by an expertise in archaeology. Nostalgia is helpfully considered in Fred Davis, *Yearning for Yesterday: A Sociology of Nostalgia* (Macmillan, London, 1979). Useful also for consideration of a wide number of debates about heritage and nostalgia, particularly the use of photography as historical evidence, is Raphael Samuel, *Theatres of Memory*, i. *Past and Present in Contemporary Culture* (Verso, London, 1995). However, the text has attracted a certain amount of criticism on account of his attacks on the defenders of a puritanical approach to heritage interpretation.

10: Design and Social Responsibility

Design and consumer protection
Consideration of consumer organizations has been somewhat underplayed in many histories of design history, despite the fact that the implementation of standards, both national and international, has been an important facet of twentieth-century design production. A number of these concerns in relation to Britain have been covered in C. D. Woodward, *The Story of British Standards* (British Standards Institution, London, 1972), which examines major developments from the beginning of the century to the date of its publication. Covering a narrower period is J. Perry's account, *The Story of Standards* (New York, 1955), in which such issues are viewed from an American standpoint. From a wider angle American consumer rights are discussed in a wide range of essays included in D. A. Aaker and G. S. Day (eds.), *Consumerism: Search for the Consumer Interest* (2nd edn., Free Press, New York, 1974). Particularly useful with regard to the history of the American Consumers' Union is chapter 12, an essay on 'Consumer Action Programs of the Consumers' Union', by Colston E. Warne, one-time President of the CU. Covering similar ground is a section on 'The Role of the Consumers' Union' (reprinted from *Business Week*, 23 December, 1967, in G. S. McClellan, *The Consuming Public* (H. W. Wilson, New York, 1968), which also contains other useful information on many aspects of changing American legislation and consumer campaigning: Ralph Nader is featured in a section entitled 'A One Man Crusade' which was reprinted from *Newsweek*.

Moral crusaders and attacks on consumer society
There has been a spate of colourful writing against the manipulation of the consumer, typified by Vance Packard, *The Hidden Persuaders* (1957; Penguin, Harmondsworth, 1960). This was followed by his equally committed *The Waste-Makers: A Startling Revelation of Planned Obsolescence* (Longman, London, 1960). A similar sensational tone was adopted by Ralph Nader in his indictment of the American automobile industry, *Unsafe at Any Speed: the Designed-In Dangers of the American Automobile Industry* (Grossman, New York, 1965).

For a broad sweep of the wider issues in Britain see my brief chapter, 'The Post-war Consumer: Design Propaganda and Awareness, 1945-1964', in Nicola Bailey (ed.), *From Spitfire to Microchip: Studies in the History of Design from 1945* (Design Council, London, 1985). For a thorough examination of the ways in which advertising techniques were seen to be significant in this context, Cynthia White,

The Women's Periodicals Press in Britain 1946–1976 (Royal Commission on the Press, HMSO, London, 1977), is extremely informative.

Indictments of the design profession
A number of those connected with the design world have published indictments of those in their profession, including Richard Neutra, *Survival Through Design* (Oxford University Press, New York, 1954). More notable, perhaps, for their quantity if not consistent quality, are the extensive writings of Buckminster Fuller, to whom reference has been made in the text and footnotes. For an informative overview of his ideas, reference may be made to R. Buckminster Fuller and Robert Marks, *The Dymaxion World of Buckminster Fuller* (1960; rev. edn., Doubleday Anchor, New York, 1973), which also contains a useful range of illustrations as well as a full account of Fuller's design projects and philosophy. For a more recent text on Fuller, Martin Pawley, *Richard Buckminster Fuller* (Trefoil, London, 1990), offers a more detached analysis. In addition to J. Meller (ed.), *The Buckminster Fuller Reader* (Penguin, Harmondsworth, 1972), reference may also be made to R. Buckminster Fuller, *Utopia or Oblivion: the Prospects for Humanity* (Penguin, Harmondsworth, 1970).

Design, the designer, and social responsibility
Victor Papanek's text on *Design for the Real World: Human Ecology and Social Change* (1971; rev. edn., Thames & Hudson, 1991), has been widely read, although the extent of its actual impact upon the workings and attitudes of the design profession is harder to gauge. There have been several attempts to examine the wider moral and social implications taken up by Papanek, as in Nigel Whiteley, *Design for Society* (Reaktion, London, 1993). There is a lot of useful factual information for those concerned with the examination of issues of design and responsibility in the late twentieth century, although ultimately Whiteley provides more of a moral crusade against the excesses of consumer society than any weighty historical analysis. The media attention paid to campaigning individuals such as Anita Roddick, co-founder of the Body Shop, has perhaps underlined the commercial dividends that can accrue from 'ethical consumerism', as seen in her journalistic autobiography, *Anita Roddick: Body and Soul* (Ebury Press, London, 1991).

Design and the disabled
Little design-historical scrutiny has been focused on design for the disabled, although this has been examined in such books as K. Bayes, *Designing for the Handicapped: the Mentally Retarded* (G. Godwin, London, 1971), and Alexander Kira, *The Bathroom Book* (rev. edn., Penguin, Harmondsworth, 1976). This is an area also usefully, albeit briefly, covered by Nigel Whiteley (above), chapter 3, 'Responsible Design and Ethical Consuming'. A wide range of recent initiatives in a number of countries are referenced in the *Design and Applied Arts Index* (above, p. 259). Swedish design consultancies such as Ergonomi Design Gruppen and A & E Design have been particularly significant in the field. A brief survey of their work may be seen in 'Not Visibly Disabled', *Form*, Sweden, 85, no. 663, 70–3, 100, 102, 124–6.

The design profession and responses to wider social and environmental concerns
Design conferences also provided important fora for debate, as seen in Reyner Banham (ed.), *The Aspen Papers: Twenty Years of Design Theory from the Design Conference in Aspen* (Pall Mall Press, London, 1979), a number of which were concerned with broader social, environmental, and philosphical concerns. The ICSID conference on 'The Relevance of Industrial Design' was published as a book of the same title by Edinburgh University Press, Edinburgh, 1973. A number of the wider issues of design and social responsibility were also examined in J. Bicknell and Liz McQuiston (eds.), *Design for Need: the Social Contribution of Design* (Pergamon/ICSID, Oxford, 1977), which included a number of significant contributions from the Royal College of Art conference of the same title of the previous year, many of them morally and emotionally charged.

Design and ecology: the emergence of Green Design
Many of the wider issues relating to the historiography of design and ecology are indicated in Pauline Madge's extensive article 'Design, Ecology, Technology: A Historigraphical Review', *Journal of Design History*, 6.3 (1993), 149–66. There was a steady stream of publications in the 1960s and, more particularly, the 1970s, when Martin Pawley, *Garbage Housing* (Architectural Press, 1975), examined the potential of recycling and secondary-use design. The late 1980s and 1990s have been

marked by a spate of publications on many aspects of 'green design' and 'green consumerism', including Dorothy Mackenzie, *Green Design: Design for the Environment* (Lawrence King, London, 1991), and a number of others to which reference has been made in the chapter footnotes. Victor Papanek has also updated his own position in *The Green Imperative: Ecology and Ethics in Design and Architecture* (Thames & Hudson, London, 1995). Those texts that have emanated from a design consultancy background, such as Mackenzie's, have tended to endorse the consumer process, albeit mediated by wider ethical considerations. A number of wider considerations of the economic implications of environmentally responsible design have been taken up in publications such as D. Pearce *et al., Blueprint for a Green Economy* (Earthscan Publications, London, 1989), and K. Turner (ed.), *Sustainable Environmental Management* (Bellhaven, London, 1988).

Timeline

	1900	1905	1910	1912	1914
Design	● 1901 Société des Artistes Decorateurs established, France ● 1902 Gödöllő Workshops (1902–21), founded, Hungary ● 1903 Wiener Werkstätte (1903–32) founded, Austria ● 1904 Hermann Muthesius' *Das Englische Haus* published, Germany	● 1906 Third German Applied Arts Exhibition, Dresden, Germany ● 1907 Danish Society of Arts and Crafts and Industrial Design founded ● 1908 Adolf Loos's *Ornament and Crime* published ● 1909 Italian Futurist Manifesto launched	● 1911 Czech Cubism begins	● 1913 Cracow Workshops established, Poland	● 1915 Design and Industries Association founded, London
Industry/Design	● 1901 Ford Motor Company founded, USA	● 1907 Deutsche Werkbund founded, Germany ● 1908 Olivetti office equipment company founded, Italy – Alfa Romeo automobile company founded – General Motors founded, USA	● 1910 Black and Decker tool company founded, USA ● 1911 Frederick Winslow Taylor's *Principles of Scientific Management* published, USA – Nissan established, Tokyo, Japan (as Kwaishinsha Co until 1934)	● 1913 Model T Ford production-line system introduced, USA	● 1914 Deutsche Werkbund Exhibition, Cologne – IBM founded in USA (as CTR, becoming IBM in 1924)
Other		● 1909 Louis Blériot flies the Channel			● 1914 Outbreak of First World War ● 1915 Christine Frederick's *Principles of Household Management* published, USA

● 1917 De Stijl founded, Holland
– Svenska Slödföreningen exhibition *The Home*, Stockholm
– Wilhelm Kåge joined Gustavsberg ceramics company, Sweden, as art director
– Standards Commission of German Industry established
– Russian Constructivism established

● 1919 Bauhaus founded, Weimar, Germany, with Walter Gropius as first director

● 1920 Devetsil Group (1920–31) founded, Czechoslovakia
– Vkhutemas art and design school established, Moscow

● 1923 First Triennale exhibition, Monza, Italy
– Bauhaus Exhibition, Weimar
– First Salon des Arts Ménagers, Paris
– Le Corbusier's *Vers Une Architecture* published

● 1924 British Empire Exhibition, Wembley, London
● 1925 Bauhaus moves to Dessau, Germany
– Exposition des Arts Décoratifs et Industriels, Paris
– Cranbrook Academy of Art established, USA

● 1926 Gruppo 7 founded, Italy
– Praesens group established, Poland
– Ład design group established, Poland
● 1927 Weissenhof Siedlung Exhibition, Stuttgart, Germany
– General Motors established its Art and Colour Section

● 1916 BMW motor works founded, Germany
– Gispen metalware company founded, Netherlands

● 1918 Matsushita electronics company founded, Japan

● 1921 Braun domestic appliances company founded, Germany
– Alessi metalware company founded, Italy

● 1923 Herman Miller furniture company founded

● 1925 Chrysler Corporation founded, USA

● 1926 Container Corporation of America founded, USA
● 1927 Cassina furniture company launched

● 1916 First Piggly-Wiggly self-service grocery store, USA
● 1917 October Revolution, Russia

● 1918 End of First World War

● 1922 Mussolini takes power Italy
– Stalin elected General Secretary of Central Committee, USSR

● 1926 Edna Meyer's *Der Neue Haushalt* published
– Fritz Lang's film *Metropolis*
● 1927 Chase and Schlink's *Your Money's Worth: A Study in the Waste of the Consumer's Dollar* published, USA

	1928	1930	1932	1934	1936
Design	● 1928 Bratislava School of Applied Arts established, Czechoslovakia – *Domus* magazine launched, Italy – CIAM (1928–56) initiated – AUDAC founded, USA ● 1929 Museum of Modern Art, New York, founded – Raymond Loewy established his industrial design office, New York – Union des Artistes Modernes (UAM) founded in Paris	● 1930 Stockholm Exhibition, Sweden – Society of Industrial Artists founded, London ● 1931 Den Permanente established, Copenhagen	● 1932 The International Style exhibition, MOMA, New York – Bel Geddes's *Horizons* published, USA – Bauhaus moved to Berlin – *De 8 en Opbouw* periodical established, Netherlands ● 1933 Bauhaus closed – Council for Art and Industry appointed, London	● 1933–4 A Century of Progress International Exhibition, Chicago, USA ● 1934 Machine Art Exhibition, MOMA, New York – Herbert Read's *Art and Industry* published – Schönheit der Arbeit division of the Labour Front established, Germany	● 1936 Nikolaus Pevsner's *Pioneers of the Modern Movement* published, UK ● 1937 Exposition Internationale des Arts et Techniques dans la Vie Moderne, Paris, France – Nikolaus Pevsner's *Enquiry into Industrial Art in England* published
Industry/Design		● 1930 Pininfarina automobile design company established, Italy	● 1933 Boeing 247 and Douglas DC-1 passenger aircraft launched, USA – Istituto per la Ricostruzione Industriale established, Italy	● 1934 Erco lighting company founded, Germany – Pullman Car Corporation, M10,000 locomotive for Union Pacific railway, USA ● 1935 Jaguar motor company established Coventry, Britain	● 1937 Saab founded, Sweden (diversifying from aircraft manufacture to automobiles and other commodities after the Second World War)
Other	● 1928 First Five-Year Plan, USSR ● 1929 Wall Street Crash, USA	● 1930 *Fortune* magazine established	● 1932 Sheldon and Arens's *Consumer Engineering: A New Technique for Prosperity* – Aldous Huxley's *Brave New World* – Adoption of Second Five-Year Plan, USSR ● 1933 New Deal, USA – Hitler comes to power as Chancellor, Germany	● 1934 Socialist Realism presented at first Soviet Writers Congress, USSR	● 1936 Consumers' Union formed, USA – First regular television broadcasts by BBC, Britain – Charles Chaplin's film *Modern Times* – Outbreak of Spanish Civil War – Front Populaire elected, France

● 1939–40 New York World's Fair, USA	● 1940 Harold Van Doren's *Industrial Design: A Practical Guide* published, USA	● 1942 Utility Design programme introduced, Britain ● 1943 Design Research Unit founded, Britain	● 1944 Council of Industrial Design (COID) founded, Britain – Libby-Owens-Ford 'Day After Tomorrow' Kitchen tour, USA	● 1946 Britain Can Make It Exhibition, London – RIMA Exhibition of Popular Furnishing, Milan, Italy ● 1947 Society of Industrial Designers founded, USA – Office for Supervision of Aesthetic Production established, Poland	● 1949 *Design* magazine founded, London
		● 1943 IKEA founded, Sweden	● 1945 Brion Vega radio and television manufacturing company founded, Milan, Italy	● 1946 Arteluce lighting company founded, Italy – Sony electronics company founded (as TTK), Japan – Knoll furniture company founded, USA	● 1948 Honda motor company founded ● 1949 Gavina furniture company founded, Italy – Kartell plastics company founded, Italy – Porsche motor company founded, Germany
● 1939 Outbreak of Second World War	● 1940 Commercial television launched in the USA – Activ Hushalling established, Sweden		● 1944 Hemmens – Forskningsinstitut established, Sweden (becoming National Institute for Consumer Information in 1957) ● 1945 End of Second World War	● 1947–51 First Levittown, Long Island, USA	● 1948 Marshall Plan for European postwar recovery

	1950	**1952**	**1954**	**1956**	**1958**
Design	● 1950 'Italy at Work: Her Renaissance in Design Today' touring exhibition, USA ● 1950–5 Edgar Kaufmann Jr. organized 'Good Design' Exhibitions at MOMA, New York ● 1951 Festival of Britain – Aspen International Design Conferences inaugurated, Colorado, USA	● 1952 Independent Group formed, London ● 1953 Hochschule für Gestaltung, Ulm, offers first courses – Rat für Formgebung founded, Germany	● 1954 *Stile Industria* magazine founded, Italy – *Industrial Design* magazine founded, USA – Compasso d'Oro design awards launched, Italy	● 1956 Design Centre of COID opens, London ● 1957 GK Industrial Design Associates founded, Japan – Design Awards scheme launched by Council of Industrial Design, London – MITI establish G-Mark Design Awards scheme, Japan – ICSID founded	● 1958 Exposition Universelle, Brussels ● 1959 MITI Design Division established, Japan
Industry/Design	● 1951 Konosuke Matsushita visits USA on industrial fact-finding tour	● 1953 First General Motors 'Motorama' exhibition, New York – First Frigidaire 'Kitchen of Tomorrow' event, New York			● 1958 First IKEA shop opened, Sweden
Other	● 1951 Outbreak of Korean War		● 1955 First McDonald's restaurant opens, USA – Disneyland opens, USA	● 1957 Launch of Sputnik satellite – Treaty of Rome and launch of European Common Market – Vance Packard's *Hidden Persuaders* published – Formation of Consumers' Association, Britain	

1960   **1962**   **1964**   **1966**   **1968**   **1970**

● 1960 Reyner Banham's *Theory and Design in the First Machine Age* published, London
– Dieter Rams appointed Design Director at Braun, Germany
– Bauhaus Archive established in Darmstadt, Germany
– Council of Design and Aesthetics of Industrial Production established, Poland

● 1963 ICOGRADA founded
– Archigram group and magazine *Archigram* founded, London

● 1964 Terence Conran's first Habitat shop opened, London
● 1965 Kilkenny Design Workshops founded, Ireland

● 1966 Robert Venturi's *Complexity and Contradiction in Modern Architecture* published, USA
– Superstudio and Archizoom groups founded, Italy
– *Ottagono* design periodical launched, Italy

● 1968 Hochschule für Gestaltung, Ulm, closed
● 1969 Centre de Création Industrielle founded, Paris, France
– JIDPO established, Japan

● 1971 Victor Papanek's *Design for the Real World* published, USA and elsewhere

---

● 1961 First manned spacecraft orbits the earth, USSR
– Construction of Berlin Wall

● 1963 Betty Friedan's *The Feminine Mystique* published

● 1964 Tokyo Olympic Games
● 1965 Ralph Nader's *Unsafe at Any Speed* published

● 1967 Arab-Israeli Six Day War

● 1968 Student unrest, Paris and elsewhere
● 1969 Apollo 11 and 12 (USA) and man's first moon walks
– First flight by Anglo-French supersonic airliner, Concorde
– Woodstock music festival, USA

	1972	**1974**	**1976**	**1978**	**1980**
Design	● 1972 *Italy: the New Domestic Landscape* exhibition, MOMA, New York	● 1975 Conseil Supérieur de la Création Esthetique Industrielle established, France	● 1976 ICSID 'Design for Need' Conference, London – Studio Alchymia founded, Milan, Italy ● 1977 Charles Jencks's *The Language of Post-Modern Architecture* – Centre Georges Pompidou opened, Paris, France – Danish Design Council established – Design History Society founded, Britain	● 1979 Ergonomi Design Gruppen founded, Sweden – Taiwan Design Promotion Centre established	● 1981 Japan Design Foundation established – Giugaro Design consultancy founded, Italy – Memphis Design group formed, Milan, Italy
Industry/Design					
Other	● 1973 American forces withdraw from Vietnam – International oil crisis – Eugene Schumacher's *Small is Beautiful* published	● 1975 Death of Franco, Spain			● 1980 Second oil crisis

● 1982 Domus Academy founded, Milan, Italy
● 1983 Osaka International Design Festival established on biennial basis, Japan

● 1984 *Design Issues* journal founded, USA
– Salón Internacional de Disegno del Equipamiento para el Habitat (SIDI) established, Spain
● 1985 Plan Créatif consultancy founded, France

● 1986 GD 'Good Design' Mark instituted, Korea

● 1988 *Journal of Design History* founded, Britain
● 1989 Design Museum founded, London

● 1992 International Design Centre established, Nagoya, Japan
● 1994 Design Council reorganized, Britain
– Design Centre, London, and regional offices of Design Council closed, Britain

---

● 1982 Swid-Powell tableware company founded, USA
● 1983 Alessi Officina research and experimental division established, Italy

---

● 1982 Falklands War
● 1983 Compact disc is launched

● 1984 Apple Macintosh PCs marketed

● 1989 Demolition of Berlin War and demise of Eastern
– European communist regimes.

● 1990 Reunification of Germany
● 1991 Gulf War
– Start of civil war, Yugoslavia
– Collapse of Communist regime USSR

Index

Note: References to illustrations are in *italic*.
There may also be textual references on the
same page.

Aalto, Aino 50, 56, 59–60
Aalto, Alvar 30, *58–60*, *59*, 156
Abrams, Mark 189
abstract form 31, 34, 37, 40, 45, 62, 79, 131, 154
advertising 145, 184, 210, 221, 227, 238
agencies 15, 150, 169, 227
Agnew, Kenneth *179*
Aicher, Otl 153, 178
Akioka, Yoshio 137
Albeck, Pat 215
Albers, Josef 177
Albini, Franco 125–6, 159
Alix, Charlotte 54
Alloway, Lawrence 184–5
Ambasz, Emilio 193
anthropometrics 180–1
Archer, L. Bruce *179*–80
Arens, Egmont 66
Armani, Giorgio 163
Armitage, Joseph 215
Arndt, Gertrud *44*
Arp, Hans 123
Art Deco 77, 79–81, 84–5
Arts and Crafts movement 11, 14–15, 18, 24–5,
    26, 88, 227
Ashbee, C. R. 24
Asplund, Gunnar 57–8, 159
Atkinson, Ronald 84
Austria 25

Baker, Steve 144
Baldessari, Luciano 55
Baldwin, William 210
Balla, Giacomo 12, *13*, 54
Banham, Peter and Mary 184
Banham, Reyner 120, 183–6
Barassi, Carlo 126
Barlow, Sir Thomas 119
Barry, Gerald 121
Barthes, Roland 183
Barton, Ralph 109
Bauhaus 8, 30, 32, 38–*46*, *44*, *47*, 48, 50, 56, 60,
    63, 100, 132, 149, 151, 177, 179
Baumeister, Willi 131
Bayer, Herbert 41, *46*, 150

Beck, Henry C. *26*
Behrens, Peter 18, 23–5, *24*, *25*, 36, 53, 149
Bel Geddes, Norman 65, 67–8, 70–1, 74, 151,
    170, 175
Bellgioioso, Ludovico 125
Bellini, Mario 150, 159, 191
Benktzon, Maria *232*–3
Bentley, Nicholas 120
Bergsten, Carl 56
Berlage, H. P. 36
Bernard, Oliver 84
Bernège, Paulette 85
Bertoria, Harry *154*
Bertram, Anthony 118
Betjemen, John 120
Bill, Max 123, 177
Black, Misha 169, 171
Blake, John E. 187
Bogler, Theodore *51*
Bojesen, Kay 60
Bonsiepe, Giu 178
Bourgeois, Victor 52
Boyle, Geoffrey 235
Brandt, Edgar 77
Brandt, Marianne 45, *47*
Branzi, Andrea 122, 160, 192, 194
Breer, Carl 70
Breton, Jules-Louis 85
Breuer, Marcel 41, 52, 61, 151–4,
    156–7, 159
Britain:
    commerce and consumerism 83–5
    consumerism 223–5, 229–30
    design profession 168–70
    modernism 41, 60–1
    national identity 89–96
    nostalgia 213–19
    pop culture 189–90
    pre World War One 11–12, 25, 26–7
    utility and beyond 117–21
British Standards Institute 224–5, 230
Brody, Neville 199, *202*, *203*, *238*
Brugola, Renzo 196, 198
Brukalski, Stanislaw *81*
Buckley, Cheryl 235
Buckminster Fuller, Richard 75–6, 156, *231*,
    234–6
Burall, Paul 237
Burck, Gilbert 112

Burke, T. 239
Büscher, Alma 45

Callen, Anthea 8
Campbell, Joan 44–5
Cassandre, Arn 150
Castelli, Giulio 126, *131*
Castelli-Ferrieri, Anna 127
Castiglione, Achille and Pier 127
Celati, Fausto 196
Chareau, Pierre 54
Chase, Stuart 221
Chermayeff, Serge 61
China 31
Cliff, Clarice 84
Clinch, Edwin 118
Coates, Nigel 137
Coates, Wells 51, 61
Colani, Luigi 132
Colombini, Gino 126, 131
Colombo, Joe 127
commerce and consumerism 65–86
Conran, Terence 215
Constructivism, Russia 30, 35, 37, *40*, *43*,
    62–3, 91
consumerism 65–86, 131–2, 144, 147–8, 221–39
Cooper, Susie 84
corporate identity 23–4, 141–63, 179, 212, 239
Council of Industrial Design (COID) 9,
    119–21, 158–9, 171, 173–4, 187, 190, 213, 230
Crabtree and Evelyn 211–14
Crane, Walter 18
Craven, Shirley 189
Curtice, Harlow K. 228
Cutler, H. T. 118
Czajkowski, Józef 87, *89–90*
Czeschka, C. O. *22*, 23

Dalton, Sir Hugh 119
Darley, Gillian 219
Davis, Fred 211
Day, Lucienne 121
Day, Richard 81, *83*
De Pas, Jonathan *192*
De Stijl, Holland 35–8, 40, 44, 62, *80*
del Renzio, Tony 184
Dell, Christian 43
Denby, Elizabeth 118
Depero, Fortunato 54
Deskey, Donald 80, 175
Deutsch, Oscar 84
Deutscher Werkbund 20–7, *22*, 32, 35–7,
    41, 44–9, 51, 56–7, 60, 77, 100, 103, 130, 134,
    165, 167, 169, 226
Devas, Prosper 212
Doblin, Jay 158–9
Dohner, H. Creston 111
Dorfles, Giles 183
Dorfman, Ariel 147
Dorn, Marion *61*
Dreyfuss, Henry 67, 69, 82, 167, 180–1
Droste, Magdalene 45
Dufrène, Maurice 77

Dufy, Raoul 79
Dunand, Jean 78
Dupas, Jean 77
D'Urbino, Donato *192*
Dylan, Bob 196
Dyson, James *185*

Eames, Charles 60, 123, 131, *135*, 151, 153, *157*,
    159
Eames, Ray 60
Earl, Harley J. *115*, 116, 228
Ehmcke, Fritz Hellmut *21*
Eiermann, Egon 131
Eitner, Lorenz 131
Elenga, Henk *201*
Elkington, John 237, 239
English, Michael 202
ergonomics 180–1
Erté 79
Evans, Beresford 170
exhibitions:
    Black Eyes and Lemonade (Whitechapel
        1951) 214
    Britain Can Make It (1946) 119–20, 171
    British Empire (Wembley 1924/5) 90–1
    Century of Progress (Chicago 1933/4) 65,
        72, 205–6
    Cologne (1914) 23, 25, 27, 38, 44
    Dresden (1906) 19–21
    Exposition Internationale (Paris 1925) 53,
        76–8, 80–1, 87–8, 90, 102
    Exposition Internationale (Paris 1937) 88–9,
        92–5
    Festival of Britain (1951) *120–1*
    Form ohne Ornament (1924) 47
    Gebt Mie Vier Jahre Zeit (1937) 100
    Good Design Show (MOMA 1951)
        156, 173
    Graphic Language of Neville Brody
        (V&A 1988) 199
    Green Designer (1986) 237
    Ideal Home 84, 91, 186
    Italy; The New Domestic Landscape
        (MOMA) 193
    Italy at Work (USA 1950) 124–5
    Machine Art (MOMA 1934) 30, *32*, 156
    Monza (1930) *92–4*
    motoramas 116–17, 129
    New York World's Fair (1939/40) 65, 72–4,
        76, 109, 115, 206
    Osaka International Design Festivals 137, 175
    RIMA (Milan 1946) 122
    Sesquicentennial (Philadephia 1926) 205–6
    Stockholm (1930) 56–8
    This is Tomorrow (Whitechapel 1956) 185–6
    Triennali 55–6, 60, 105, 122, 125, 127–8, 172,
        191, 194, 226
    Useful Objects in Wartime (MOMA 1942)
        111
    Weissenhof Siedlungen (Stuttgart 1927) 49,
        51–3, 97
Exner, Virgil 116
Expressionism 23, 38–9, 47

Farr, Michael 181
Fehlbaum, Rolf 157
Festival style 120–1
Figini, Luigi 55
Fischer, Volker 203
folk art 87–9, 92, 210–11, 214
Follot, Paul 77
Ford, Henry 12, 66, 75, 128, 206
Forty, Adrian 8
Foster, Norman 137
France 15, 25–7, 53–4, 76–81, 84–5, 87–9, 172
Frank, Josef 50
Frankl, Paul T. 76, 109
Franko, Lawrence 134–5
Fréchet, André 79
Frederick, Christine 49–50
Friedan, Betty 113
functionalism 35, 47, 49–50, 58–9, 62, 65, 130, 132
Futurism, Italy 12–14, 54–5

Galbraith, J. K. 117, 131, 146, 223, 228
Gans, Herbert 113
Gardella, Ignazio 124–5
Garret, Michael 203
Gate, Simon 167
Gebhardt, Ernst 51
Gehry, Frank 157
geometric form 30–1, 35, 37, 41, 44, 61, 79–80, 83–5
Germany:
    consumerism 226
    design profession 172, 177–80
    modernism 32–3, 35–6, 38–53
    national identity 96–102
    postwar reconstruction 128–32, 136
    pre World War One 11–12, 14, 17, 18–27
Gernsback, Hugo 71
Gibbons, Cedric 81, 83
Gidding, Jaap 80
Giedion, Siegfried 7
Giocosa, Dante 107, 122
Gismondi, Ernesto 196
Gispen, W. H. 39, 167
Gläser, Käte 134
Gloag, John 89–90, 118–19
Godani, Mario and Brunella 196
Gorell, Lord 168
Graves, Michael 137, 160, 162–3
Graves, Robert 90
Gray, Eileen 54
Gray, Milner 169
green design 236–9
Gregotti, Vittorio 163
Greiman, April 199
Gretsch, Hermann 52, 98, 100
Griffin, Rick 202
Groag, Jacques 118
Gropius, Walter 21, 23, 32, 38–41, 43–5, 44, 47, 52, 61, 151, 153, 177
Guerriero, Allessandro and Adriana 194
Gugelot, Hans 153, 178

Guild, Lurelle 67
Guilleré, René and Charlotte Chaucet- 77

Haas, Herman 20
Habraken, John 234
Hailes, J. 239
Hald, Edward 167
Hallet, Roy 215
Hamilton, Richard 178, 184, 185, 187
Hamilton, Terry 184
Harper, Peter 235
Harvey, Cyrus 212
Havinden, Ashley 169
Heal, Ambrose 25–6
Hebdige, Dick 189
Heineken, Alfred 234
Henderson, Nigel 184
Henrion, F. H. K. 141, 143, 153
Herbst, René 54
heritage 159–63, 205–19
Heskett, John 52, 96
Hewison, Robert 217
Heyman, J. D. 22, 23
Hildebrand, Margaret 100
Hine, Thomas 116
hippy movement 234–6
Hitchcock, Henry Russell 34
Hobsbawm, Eric 141, 211
Hochschule für Gestaltung (Ulm) 177–80
Hofmann, Josef 24
Hoggart, Richard 189
Holdaway, Bernard 189
Holdcroft, Harold 96, 217
Holland 34, 36–8, 40, 165
Hollein, Hans 160, 162–3, 199
Hollós, Ruth 45
Honda, Soichiro 136
Hulanicki, Barbara 205
Hungary 122, 165, 216
Hussey, Christopher 93
Huszár, Vilmos 37
Huxley, Aldous 75
Huygen, Frederique 89

Igishaki, Taizo 136
Illich, Ivan 235
Ingram, Tom 213
Inoue, Takeshi 136
International Style 34–5, 52
Ireland 172
Irvine, Sandy 239
Isozaki, Arata 160, 163
Issigonis, Alec 123
Italy 12–14, 34, 54–6, 102–7, 121–8, 191–7
Itten, Johannes 177

Jacobsen, Arne 130
Jacobsen, Egbert 150, 157
Japan 88, 132–7, 173, 176
Jastrzebowski, Wojciech 90
Jeanneret, Pierre 54, 159
Jencks, Charles 162, 191, 235
Jensen, Georg 60

Jensen, Gustav 76
Johnson, Howard 144
Johnson, Philip 30, 32, 34, 156
Johnston, Edward 26
Jones, Barbara 213
Jones, Terry 199
Juhl, Finn 156
Juhlin, Sven-Eric 232–3

Kåge, Wilhelm 57–8, 167
Kamman, J. 39
Kandinsky, Wassily 38, 40, 167
Kaufmann Jr, Edgar 31, 151, 154, 156,
    187
Kawakubo, Rei 135
Keck, G. F. 72
Kepes, Gyorgy 150
Kersting, Walter Maria 97
Kimura, Kazuo 175
Kinross, Robin 179
Kira, Alexander 181
Kita, Toshiyuki 184
Klein, Calvin 163
Klint, Kaare 60
Knight, Clayton 109
Knoll, Hans and Florence 153–4
Kohlmann, Étienne 77
Koike, Prof. Iwataro 135
Korea 175
Kosugi, Jiro 137
Kramer, Ferdinand 43
Kuramata, Shiro 135, 160

Lacroix, Christian 163
Lambert, Margaret 213
Landmann, Ludwig 48
Landor, Walter 169
Lang, Fritz 75
Laura Ashley 96, 205, 215–16
Lazlo, Paul 76
Le Corbusier 33, 52–4, 53, 56, 77, 156–7,
    159
Léger, Fernand 54, 150
Leowald, Georg 131
Lescaze, William 76
Leslie, S. C. 119
Levitt, William J. 112–13, 205
Libera, Adalberto 105
Lissitsky, El 38, 40, 46, 50
Loewy, Raymond 67–70, 68, 73, 76, 82, 136,
    158–9, 167, 170, 175
Löffelhardt, Heinz 100
Lomazzi, Paolo 192
Loos, Adolf 32, 118
Loti, Pierre 132
Lucchi, Michele de 160, 194, 196
Luce, Henry 67
Lynes, Russell 111

McConnell, John 239
MacEwan, Malcolm 214
McGrath, Raymond 61
McHale, John 184–5

Mackenzie, Dorothy 237
Mackintosh, Charles Rennie 18, 24, 159
McMein, Neyea 109
Madge, Pauline 232, 239
Magistretti, Vico 159, 191
Maldonado, Tomás 177–8
Mallet-Stevens, Robert 54
Marchetti, Alessandro 105
Marinetti, Filippo Tommaso 12, 54
Mariscal, Xavier 160, 199
marketing 15, 143, 147, 215–17, 227
Marriott, Charles 213
Marx, Enid 118, 213
Masera, Paolo 105
Maslov, V. 91
mass-production:
    commerce and consumerism 65, 75, 77,
        83
    modernism 30, 37–8, 40, 44, 48, 51, 54,
        58–9, 62
    pre World War One 11–12, 14, 18, 25, 27
Massey, Anne 185
Matet, Maurice 77
Mathsson, Bruno 59
Matsui, Y. 88
Matsushita, Konosuke 136–7
Mattelart, Armand 148
Matter, Herbert 150
May, Ernst 43, 49
Meeston, Stanley C. 144
Meier, Richard 163
Melnikov, Konstantin 56
Memphis 14, 135, 160–1, 163, 194–9
Mendini, Alessandro 162, 194, 196
Menghi, Roberto 126
Menghshoel, Hans Christian 233
Meyer, Adolf 40
Meyer, Edna 49
Meyer, Hannes 39
Mies van der Rohe, Ludwig 52, 56, 153–4, 156,
    159, 177
Miller, Daniel 8, 69–70
Miller, Herman 153, 159
Minns, Eden and Bianca 121
Minoletti, Giulio 123
Miyake, Issey 135
modernism 23, 29–63, 77, 89, 96–7, 100, 117,
    118, 124, 130, 155–9
    affluence and 117–18, 124
    corporate identity and 150–9
Mögelin, Else 44
Moholy-Nagy, Lázló 40–1, 46, 61, 150
Mollino, Carlo 125–6
Mondrian, Piet 36
Moore, Henry 123
Morris, William 9, 11, 14, 198, 227
Moscoso, Victor 202
Moser, Koloman 24
Muche, Georg 40
Müller, Gerd Alfred 153, 155
Muller-Munk, Peter 76
multinationals and global products 141–63
Munari, Bruno 160

Museum Of Modern Art (MOMA) (New York) 30–4, *32*, 111, 125, 151, 155–9, 190–1, 193–4, 206
museums 29–33, 154–9
Muthesius, Hermann 18–19, 21, 25, 35, 37, 77, 167

Nader, Ralph 117, 226, 228–9
national identity 87–110, 205, 209
Naumann, Friedrich 20
Navone, Paola 194
Nelson, George 82, 151, 153, 194
Neutra, Richard 117, 232
New International Style 137, 160–3, 196, 203
Nichols, J. C. 114
Nizzoli, Marcello 55, 123, 149, 159–60, 167
nostalgia and heritage 205–19
Noyes, Eliot 151–3, *152*, 156

Oberheim, Robert 155
Ohga, Norio 137
Olins, Wally 141, 143–4, 239
Olivetti *55*, 149–52, 157, 159–60, 194
Olivetti, Adriano *55*, 149
Opsvik, Peter *233*
organic form 123–4, 130, 132
Orwell, George 90, 187
Otte, Benita Koche- 41, *51*
Otto, Carl 170
Oud, J. J. P. 38, 49, 52

Packard, Vance 117, 226–7, 229, 233
Paepke, Walter P. 150
Pagani, Carlo 124
Pagano, Giuseppe 105
Pallavicino, Cesare 122
Panter, Gary *201*
Paolozzi, Eduardo 184
Papanek, Victor 232–3
Parisi, Ico 125
Parker, Sanford 112
Paul, Bruno 18, *22*, 23
Paulsson, Gregor *56*–8
Peach, Henry 25–6
Peel, Sir Robert 12
Perressutti, Enrico 125
Perriand, Charlotte 54, *157*, 159
Persico, Edoardo 55
Pevsner, Nikolaus 7, 8, 29, 33, 44, 83, 117, 168, 183–4
Piacentini, Marcello 103
Pick, Frank *26*, 149
Pininfarina, Sergio 123, 126
Pintori, Giovanni 149
Pioneers of Modern Design: from William Morris to Walter Gropius (Pevsner) 7, 29, 44
Poelzig, Hans 18
Poland 51, 62, 81, 87, 89, 165, 171–2
Polglase, Van Nest 81
Pollini, Gino 55
Pollock, Griselda 8
Ponti, Gio 55, 105, 123, 125–7, 159, 167, 191

pop to post modernism 183–203
Popova, Liubov *41*
Portoghesi, Paolo 162–3
Post-modernism 183–203
Powell, Addie 162
Prampolini, Enrico 54
Pritchard, Molly and Jack 61
profession, design 165–81, 230–4
Pronaszko, Andrej *62–3*
Propst, Nelson and Robert 153
psychadelic art 201–2
Pugin, A. W. N. 227
punk 199, 203

Qian Jun-tao *31*
Quant, Mary 189

Race, Ernest 120
Radical design 192–4
Radice, Barbara 196–7
Ragghianti, Carlo Ludovico 160
Rams, Dieter 153, 155
Rand, Paul 151–3
Ranger, Terence 141, 211
Rat für Formgebung 130, 136, 158, 172–3
Rationalism, Italy 55–6, 102, 104, 124
Ravilious, E. *95*
Read, Herbert 32, 61, 168
reconstruction and postwar affluence 111–39
Reeves, Ruth *106*, 109, 206
Reid, Jamie 203
Reilly, Paul 120, 190
Renzi, Mario de *105*
Reynolds, Joshua 198
Rhead, Charlotte 84
Rhoads, William 209
Richards, Charles 79
Rideout, John Gordon 109
Rietveld, Gerrit *37*–8, *44*, 159
Rockefeller Jr, John D. 206
Rodchenko, Alexander 38, *40*, 167
Roddick, Anita 237
Rogers, Ernesto 122, 137
Rohde, Gilbert 153
Romano, Giuseppe 107
Roorda, Frank J. 73
Roselli, Alberto 176
Ruhlmann, Jacques-Emil 77–9, *78*
Russell, Gordon 118–20
Russell, R. D. 118
Russia, modernism in 30, 37–8, 40–1, 43, 50, 62–3

Saarinen, Eero 123, 152–4
Sakashita, Kiyoshi 137
Sakier, George 76
Samuelson, Alexander *109*
Sanders, Harland 144
Sanderson, Arthur 9, 216
Sapper, Richard *132*, 139, *186*
Sato, Shozo 137
Saville, Peter 203

Scandinavia 34, 50, 56–60, 165, 173, 225
Schaefer, Herwin 8
Scharoun, Hans 131
Schawinsky, Alexander 149
Schlink, Frederick J. 221
Schmidt, Joost 40
Schmidt, Karl 20
Schnaidt, Claude 178
Scholl, Inge 177
Schultze-Naumburg, Paul 98
Schumacher, Eugene 226, 235
Schütte-Lihotsky, Grete 49–50
Scolari, Carla *192*
Scott, Douglas 170
Sears Roebuck *16–17, 69*
Segalen, Martine 84
Sert, Josep Lluis 88
Sharp, Martin 202
Sheldon, Roy 66
Shire, Peter 160
Silver, Nathan 235
Singapore 175
Sironi, Mario *105*, 107
Slater, Eric *85*
Sloan, Alfred P. 137
Smith, Sir Hubert Llewellyn 26
Smithson, Alison and Peter 186–7
Soavi, Giorgio 160
social responsibility and design 221–39
Sognot, Louis 54
Soloviev, Yuri 172
Sottsass Jr, Ettore 150, 160, 163, *194*, 196,
    198–9
Sowden, George 163
Sparke, Penny 177
Speer, Albert *100*
Stabler, Harold 25
Stam, Mart 38, 52
standardization 21, 25, 35, 37, 38, 50–1, 53–4, 59,
    65, 75, 97
Starck, Philippe *161*, 205
Steichen, Edward 109
Stepanova, Varvara 38, *40*, 167
Stephen, John 189
Stötzl, Gunta 43, *45*
Studio Alchymia 194–8
Stukenbrok, August 17
Swedish Society of Industrial Design 32, 37–8,
    56–8, 165, 225
Swid, Nan 162
Syszko-Bohusz, Adolf *62–3*

Taiwan 175
Tallents, Stephen 95
Tanaka, Ikko 135
Tatlin, Vladimir 38, 167
Taut, Bruno 23
Taylor, Frederick Winslow 12, 66, 128
Taylor, John 94
Teague, Walter Dorwin 67–8, 70, 72–4, 149,
    167, 175
Teige, Karol *30*
Telakowska, Wanda 172

Terragni, Giuseppe 55–6
Tessenow, Heinrich 49
Thackera, John 198
Thomas, Mark Hartland *120*
Thun, Matheo 160
Troost, Paul Ludwig 23
Tusquets, Oscar 162

Uga, Yoko 137
Ulman, Doris 75
Umeda, Masanori 135
United States:
    colonial revival 205–13
    commerce and consumerism 65–76
    consumerism 221–5, 227–9
    France and 79–81
    national identity 107–9
    postwar Italy and 124–8
    postwar reconstruction 111–17
    pre World War One 11–12, 15–17
Urban, Joseph 76
Utida, Y. *88*
utility design 25, 111, 117–21, 125, 223

Vale, Brenda and Robert 237
van Alen, William 80
van de Velde, Henry 21, 23, 35, 167
van den Haspel, Tom *201*
van der Leck, Bart 37–8
van Doesburg, Theo 36–7, 40, 46
van Doren, Harold 67, 70, 109, 175
Vanderlans, Rudy 199
Velarde, Giles 218
Venini, Paolo *128*
Venturi, Robert 115, *162*–3, 183, 191,
    205
Voelker, John 185
Vydra, Josef 63

Wagenfeld, Wilhelm *48*, 52, 100
Walker, George 116
Walsh, Kevin 219
Wasson-Tucker, Susan 151
Watson, Thomas 152
Weingart, Wolfgang 199
Weissler, Sabine 99
Werkstätten movement 19–20, 27, 43
Westwood, Vivienne *190*
Weymouth, Nigel 202
Wilson, Wes 202
Windett, Peter *212*, 214
Wright, Frank Lloyd 9, 36, 159
Wright, Henry 82, 151
Wright, Joseph 226
Wright, Patrick 214, 238
Wright, Russel 67, *107*, 175

Yamashita, Kazumasa *163*
Yokoo, Tadanori 135

Zanini, Marco 160
Zanuso, Marco 125, *132*
Zevi, Bruno 124

Oxford History of Art

Titles in the Oxford History of Art series are up-to-date, fully-illustrated introductions to a wide variety of subjects written by leading experts in their field. They will appear regularly, building into an interlocking and comprehensive series.

Western Art

Archaic and Classical Greek Art
Robin Osborne
Hellenistic and Early Roman Art
John Henderson & Mary Beard
The Art of The Roman Empire
J. R. Elsner
Early Medieval Art
Lawrence Nees
Late Medieval Art
Veronica Sekules
Art and Society in Italy 1350–1500
Evelyn Welch
Art and Society in Early Modern Europe 1500–1750
Nigel Llewellyn
Art in Europe 1700–1830
Matthew Craske
Nineteenth-Century Art
Modern Art: Capitalism and Representation 1851–1929
Richard Brettell
Western Art 1920-1945
Modernism and its Discontents: Art in Western Europe & the USA since 1945
David Hopkins

Western Architecture

Greek Architecture
David Small
Roman Architecture
Janet Delaine
Early Medieval Architecture
Roger Stalley
Late Medieval Architecture
Francis Woodman
European Architecture 1400–1600
Christy Anderson
European Architecture 1600–1750
Hilary Ballon
European Architecture 1750–1890
Barry Bergdoll
Modern Architecture 1890–1965
Alan Colquhoun
Contemporary Architecture
Anthony Vidler
Architecture in the USA
Dell Upton

World Art

Ancient Aegean Art
Donald Preziosi & Louise Hitchcock
Classical African Art
Contemporary African Art
African-American Art
Sharon Patton
Nineteenth-Century American Art
Barbara Groseclose

Twentieth-Century American Art

Erica Doss
Australian Art
Andrew Sayers
Byzantine Art
Robin Cormack
Art in China
Craig Clunas
Ancient Egyptian Art
Marianne Eaton-Krauss
East European Art
Jeremy Howard
Indian Art
Partha Mitter
Islamic Art
Irene Bierman
The Arts in Japanese Society
Karen Brock
Melanesian Art
Michael O'Hanlon
Latin American Art
Mesoamerican Art
Cecelia Klein
Native North American Art
Janet Berlo & Ruth Phillips
Polynesian and Micronesian Art
Adrienne Kaeppler
South-East Asian Art
John Guy

Western Design

Twentieth-Century Design
Jonathan M. Woodham
Design in the USA
Jeffrey Meikle

Western Sculpture

Sculpture 1900–1945
Penelope Curtis
Sculpture Since 1945
Andrew Causey

Photography

The Photograph
Graham Clarke

Special Volumes

Art and Film
Art and Landscape
Malcolm Andrews
Art and the New Technology
Art and Science
Art and Sexuality
Art Critical Theory: A Reader
Donald Preziosi
Portraiture
Women in Art